THE MEASUREMENT OF MEANING

CHARLES E. OSGOOD   GEORGE J. SUCI   PERCY H. TANNENBAUM

THE MEASUREMENT OF MEANING

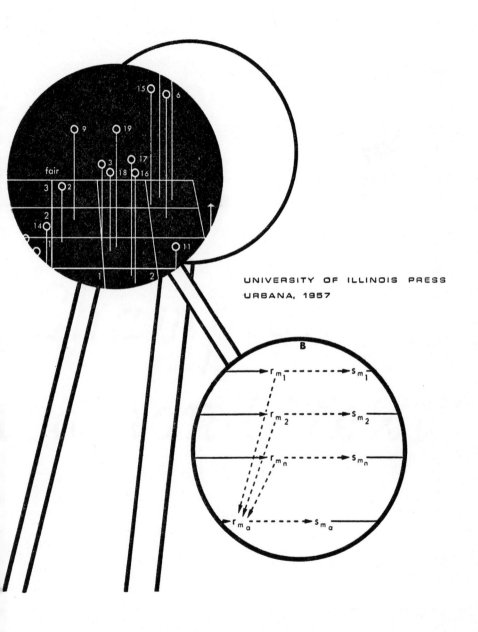

UNIVERSITY OF ILLINOIS PRESS
URBANA, 1957

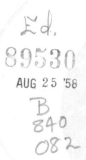

The scientific study of language has been developing with particular rapidity during the past decade or so. One thinks immediately of the basic work of Zipf and Skinner, of the developments in information theory, in concept formation, in second language learning, in word association research, and generally of the increasing integration of the psychological and linguistic approaches as reflected in the activities of the Social Science Research Council Committee on Linguistics and Psychology. Almost every new issue of a social science journal brings additional evidence of this heightened activity. A significant aspect of much of this development has been the devising and application of new quantitative measurement techniques. During the past six or seven years, a group of us at the University of Illinois has been concentrating on the development of an objective measure of *meaning*, and this book is largely a progress report of that research.

As such, this book is truly a collaborative effort — not only by the three authors whose names appear on the title page, but also by some thirty or more colleagues and graduate students whose theses, research assistance, and contributions in seminars have given much in the way of substance and criticism to this work. Throughout we try to give credit where it is due. There have also been many undergraduate clerical assistants who, though they must go nameless, have spent long hours working and reworking over — quite literally — pounds of numbers and figures. It will also become increasingly apparent as the course of our work unfolds that much of this activity would have been quite impossible — at least in this relatively short period if not in a full lifetime — without the availability of the ILLIAC, the University of Illinois electronic digital computer. We wish to give our sincere thanks to Professor J. P. Nash, of the computer laboratory, for his indulgence in scheduling our huge problems on the ILLIAC. It also has been our good fortune to interest investigators elsewhere than on our own campus.

It should be underlined that this book is more a progress report of our work on the measurement of meaning and of some notions about the nature of meaning than it is a finished product. Perhaps this can be said of almost any ongoing research program, but we feel this to be particularly true in our case. Although the results of some fifty or so studies are reported in this book, they represent work covering a period of only six years, and there are still many gaps and insufficiencies. This should be pointed out in the beginning because in writing the body of the book, we probably display a tone of assurance not actually felt. This, however, is a stylistic matter — there is nothing as dreary as a continually tentative and hedging style.

One of the major insufficiencies in our work so far lies in the coordination of a theoretical conception of the nature of meaning with our empirical techniques of measurement. Many readers may feel that we would have been wiser to have entirely deleted the theoretical considerations, and they may be quite correct. But having at hand a theoretical model worked out in some detail, the urge to attempt some correlation with the operations of measurement was almost irresistible — and for this we beg your indulgence.

Beyond the intellectual debt to our colleagues and students, we must acknowledge support of a more material kind that has facilitated this research activity. The Institute of Communications Research and the Department of Psychology at the University of Illinois have provided both the spiritual encouragement and the tangible assistance of money, time, and space. The University Graduate Research Board has repeatedly made funds available to carry out various portions of the program. The senior author owes a special vote of thanks to the officers and council of the Social Science Research Council for the support extended in the form of a three-year faculty fellowship. He also must express his gratitude to the John Simon Guggenheim Foundation for a fellowship in 1955-56, part of which was spent in the writing of this book.

Our thanks too to Mrs. Barbara Mitchell for handling the typing chores with speed and accuracy, and to the editors of the University of Illinois Press for their aid in the preparation of the manuscript. And we owe a special debt to our wives — Patty, Nancy, and Brocha — for bearing with us throughout.

Charles E. Osgood, George J. Suci, Percy H. Tannenbaum
Institute of Communications Research   University of Illinois

CONTENTS

1

Apart from the studies to be reported here, there have been few, if any, systematic attempts to subject meaning to quantitative measurement. There are probably several reasons for this, even in a period of intense objectivity in psychology: For one thing, the term "meaning" seems to connote, for most psychologists at least, something inherently nonmaterial, more akin to "idea" and "soul" than to observable stimulus and response, and therefore to be treated like the other "ghosts" that J. B. Watson dispelled from psychology. For another thing, it certainly refers to some implicit process or state which must be inferred from observables, and therefore it is the sort of variable that contemporary psychologists would avoid dealing with as long as possible. And there is also, undoubtedly, the matter of complexity — there is an implication in the philosophical tradition that meanings are uniquely and infinitely variable, and phenomena of this kind do not submit readily to measurement. Whatever the reasons, psychologists have generally been quite willing to let the philosopher tussle with the problem.

This does not imply, however, that psychologists and other social scientists have denied the significance, both practical and theoretical, of this variable. Most social scientists would agree — talking freely on common-sense grounds — that how a person behaves in a situation depends upon what that situation means or signifies to him. And most would also agree that one of the most important factors in social activity is meaning and change in meaning — whether it be termed "attitude," or "value," or something else again. Even at the core of psychological theorizing, in the field of perception as well as in the field of learning (see Osgood, 1953), one encounters the problem of representational or symbolic processes. The problem of meaning in behavior is probably no more difficult and certainly not greatly different from the problems of dealing with other intervening variables, like emotion and intelligence. Any variable of this sort is useful to the extent that it can be integrated, conceptually and empirically, with existing theory and indexed quantitatively. Although our chief concern in this book will be with measurement, it will be useful at the outset to sketch at least the theoretical conception of meaning to which our type of measurement is relevant.

MEANINGS OF "MEANING"

There are at least as many meanings of "meaning" as there are disciplines which deal with language, and of course, many more than this because exponents within disciplines do not always agree with one another. Nevertheless, definitions do tend to correspond more or less with the purposes and techniques of the individual doing the defining, focusing on that aspect of the phenomenon which his discipline equips him to handle. Thus, the sociologist or anthropologist typically defines the meaning of a sign in terms of the common features of the situations in which it is used and of the activities which it produces. A careful correlation of occurrences of the term STICK, for example, with external situations and behaviors will gradually isolate its "meaning" from BRANCH, from PIPE, from STRING, and so on. This clearly applies better to denotative meanings than to connotative meanings, and it says nothing about the behavioral principles operating within human organisms which bring about such correlations.

Linguistic Meaning

American linguists have a split tradition with respect to the meaning of "meaning." On the one side, following Bloomfield (1933), they are prone to dismiss the problem from their own sphere of legitimate interest in messages per se by adopting the sociological type of definition. Bloomfield defined the meaning of a linguistic form as "the situation in which the speaker utters it and the response which it calls forth in the hearer," and expressed discouragement as to the linguist's ability to handle it, rather relegating the task to other sciences. The only judgment about meaning the linguist was required to make in applying his own methods was that of "same or different." On the other side, some linguists (see Joos, 1950; Harris, 1951) have sought a definition of meaning within their own methodology, defining it in terms of the total linguistic context within which a given sign appears. "Now the linguist's 'meaning' of a morpheme . . . is by definition the set of conditional probabilities of its occurrence in context with all other morphemes (Joos, 1950)." Needless to say, such a procedure involves immense practical difficulties. There is yet another sense in which linguists use the term "meaning"; this is in connection with the concept of "structure" of a language code, the "meaning" of a linguistic unit (phoneme, morpheme, etc.) being its function or position in the code system as a whole. Thus the "linguistic meaning" of *the happy boy* in the utterance *the happy boy is playing in the pond* is "nominative substantive form class" (see Bloch and Trager, 1942). It is clear that these meanings of "meaning" serve to define the relationship of signs to other signs in the message matrix, but are independent operationally of both the sociological situation-behavior matrix and the psychological organismic-process matrix.

Psychological Meaning

Following the classification scheme used by Charles Morris (1946), we may call the relation of signs to situations and behaviors (sociological) *pragmatical meaning*, and the relation of signs to other signs (linguistic) *syntactical meaning*. Both philosophers and psychologists have tended to be more interested in what Morris calls *semantical meaning* — the relation of signs to their significates. The philosopher is typically interested in stating the logically necessary and sufficient conditions for signification, which may or may not involve the behavior of the sign-using organism as a component; the psychologist is typically interested in the role of the organism's behavior system in mediating the relation between signs and significates. Or, to put it another way, the psychologist is typically interested in defining that distinctive mediational process or state which occurs in the organism whenever a sign is received (decoded) or produced (encoded). However, psychological theories of meaning differ among themselves as to the nature of this distinctive process or state.

We may start a logical analysis of the psychological problem here with a self-evident fact: *The pattern of stimulation which is a sign is never identical with the pattern of stimulation which is the significate*. The word "hammer" is not the same stimulus as the object it signifies. The former is a pattern of sound waves; the latter, depending on its mode of contact with the organism, is some complex of visual, tactual, proprioceptive, and other stimulations. Nevertheless, the *sign* ("hammer") does come to elicit behaviors which are in some manner relevant to the *significate* (HAMMER), a capacity not shared by an infinite number of other stimulus patterns that are not signs of this object. In simplest terms, therefore, the problem for the psychologist interested in meaning is this: *Under what conditions does a stimulus which is not the significate become a sign of that significate?* In other words, we are seeking criteria for defining a sub-set of the class "stimulus," this sub-set to be called "sign." On the basis of the criteria proferred we can identify a number of different psychological theories of meaning.

Mentalistic View. The classic interpretation takes for granted the dualistic philosophy of lay Western culture and seeks a correlation between material and nonmaterial events. Since meanings are obviously "mental" events and the stimuli representing both signs and significates are obviously "physical" events, any satisfactory theory must specify the interrelation between these levels of discourse. At the core of all mentalistic views, therefore, we find an association between signs and "ideas" (or their equivalents, "expectations," "thoughts," "engrams"), the latter term usually being unanalyzed. In other words, *something which is not the significate becomes a sign of that significate if it gives rise to the idea or thought of that significate.* There are, of course, many ways in which the essential dualism may be disguised, but it always is present as long as the term referring to the organismic mediation process remains undefined with respect to materialistic observables. Probably the most sophisticated expression of the mentalistic view is to be found in Ogden and Richards, *The Meaning of Meaning* (1923). These writers clearly isolate the essential representational character of signs, the learning or experiential criterion, and the lack of any direct connection between signs and the things they signify (the point made again and again by the General Semanticists in more recent years), but the process which mediates the relation of signs to their significates is a "mental" one. Of course, if a dualistic view is harmonious with the truth, then the Ogden and Richards theory is the most tenable one available.

Substitution View. Naïve application of Pavlovian conditioning principles by early behaviorists like Watson led to the theory that signs achieve their meaning simply by being conditioned to the same reactions originally made to significates. The significate is the unconditioned stimulus and the sign is the conditioned stimulus, the latter merely being substituted for the former and thus acquiring its meaning. The resulting definition of the sign-process thus becomes: *Whenever something which is not the significate evokes in an organism the same reactions evoked by the significate, it is a sign of that significate.* The very simplicity of this theory highlights its inadequacy. Signs almost never evoke the same overt responses as the things they represent. Nevertheless, this formulation is objective and includes the learning criterion; it represents a first step toward a behavioral interpretation of the sign-process.

Dispositional View. Although Charles Morris was trained as a philosopher in the tradition of Peirce and other American pragmatists, it has been clear in his recent writings, particularly his *Signs, Language and Behavior* (1946), that he feels it necessary to anchor a theory of meaning to the behavior of sign-using organisms. To further this end, he worked with two prominent behavior theorists, Tolman and Hull, and the effects of this immersion in learning theory are evident in his book, which is a pioneering attempt to reduce semeiotics to an objective basis. The essence of his definition may be phrased as follows: *Any pattern of stimulation which is not the significate becomes a sign of the significate if it produces in the organism a "disposition" to make any of the responses previously elicited by the significate.* This definition avoids the substitution fallacy, but it involves the danger that "disposition" may serve as a mere surrogate for "idea" without further explication. This and certain other difficulties with Morris' view are discussed in an earlier article (Osgood, 1952) and will not be detailed here. The following conception of the sign-process can, in fact, be viewed as an attempt to make more explicit the behavioral nature of what Morris has termed "dispositions."

Meaning as a Representational Mediation Process

Certain stimulus patterns have a "wired-in" connection with certain behavior patterns (unconditional reflexes) and additional stimuli have acquired this capacity (conditional reflexes). Food-powder in the mouth regularly and reliably elicits a complex pattern of food-taking reactions in the hungry animal (including salivating, swallowing, and the like); a shock to the foot-pads regularly and reliably elicits a complex pattern of escape reactions (leaping, running, urinating, autonomic "fear" reactions, and the like). We may define a *significate*, then, as any stimulus which, in a given situation, regularly and reliably produces a predictable pattern of behavior. For the naïve organism, there are multitudes of stimuli which do not have this capacity — a buzzer sound does not reliably produce escape behavior like the shock does; the sound of a metronome does not reliably produce food-taking reactions, initially; the auditory effects of hearing "hammer" do not produce behavior in any way relevant to HAMMER object in the pre-verbal child. How can such initially meaningless stimuli become meaningful signs for the organisms affected by them?

We have seen that ordinary single-stage conditioning does not provide a satisfactory answer — reactions made to signs are seldom identical with those made to the objects signified. But if we look into the conditioning situation more carefully, a possible solution to the problem may be seen. Many experiments on the details of the conditioning process combine to support the following conclusion: Components of the total unconditioned reaction vary in their dependence on the unconditioned stimulus and hence in the ease with which they may become conditioned to another stimulus. Typically, the less energy-expending a reaction component (e.g., "light-weight" components like glandular changes and minimal postural adjustments) and the less interfering a reaction component with ongoing overt behavior (e.g., components which do not hinder overt approaches, avoidances, manipulations, and the like), the more promptly it appears in the conditioned reaction and hence the more readily available it is for the meditation function. The argument thus far may be summarized as follows: *Whenever some stimulus other than the significate is contiguous with the significate, it will acquire an increment of association with some portion of the total behavior elicited by the significate as a representational mediation process.* As diagramed in Figure 1 (A), this stimulus-producing process ($r_m \rightarrow s_m$) is *representational* because it is part of the same behavior (R_T) produced by the significate itself ($\dot{s}$) — thus the buzzer becomes a sign ($\boxed{s}$) of shock ($\dot{s}$) rather than a sign of any of a multitude of other things. It is *mediational* because the self-stimulation (s_m) produced by making this short-circuited reaction can now become associated with a variety of instrumental acts (R_X) which "take account of" the significate — the anxiety state generated by the buzzer may serve as a cue for leaping, running, turning a rachet, or some other response sequence which eliminates the signified shock.

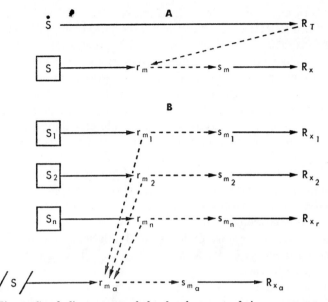

Fig. 1. Symbolic account of the development of sign processes.
A. Development of a sign; B. Development of an assign.

Whereas Morris linked sign and significate through partial identity of significate-produced and "disposition"-produced behaviors, we have linked sign and significate through partial identity of the "disposition" itself (r_m) with the behavior produced by the significate. Thus, according to this view, words represent things because they produce in human organisms some replica of the actual behavior toward these things, as a mediation process. This is the crucial identification, the mechanism that ties particular signs to particular significates rather than others. Stating the proposition formally: *A pattern of stimulation which is not the significate is a sign of that significate if it evokes in the organism a mediating process, this process (a) being some fractional part of the total behavior elicited by the significate and (b) producing responses which would not occur without the previous contiguity of non-significate and significate patterns of stimulation.* It will be noted that in this statement we have chosen the term "mediating process" rather than "mediating reaction"; this is to leave explicitly open the question of the underlying nature of such representational mediators — they may well be purely neural events rather than actual muscular contractions or glandular secretions in the traditional sense of "reaction." In any case, in the formal statement of the theory they are presumed to have all the functional properties of stimulus-producing reactions. The above definition of a sign-process may be somewhat cumbersome, but all the limiting conditions seem necessary. The mediational process must include some part of the same behavior produced by the significate if the sign is to have its particularistic representing property; the presence of this property must depend upon the prior contiguity of non-significate and significate patterns of stimulation in the experience of the organism if the definition is to include the criterion that sign-processes are learned.

What this conception does in effect is to divide the usual $S \rightarrow R$ paradigm into two stages. The first stage, which we may call *decoding*, is the association of signs with representational mediators, i.e., "interpretation." The second stage, which we may call *encoding*, is the association of mediated self-stimulation with overt instrumental sequences, i.e., "expression of ideas." One advantage of this is that, since each stage is itself an S-R process, we are able to transfer all of the conceptual machinery of single-stage S-R psychology into this two-stage model without new postulation. Returning for a moment to Morris' trichotomy, it can be seen that this view encompasses two of his aspects of meaning, *semantical meaning* (sign is related to significate via the common properties of r_m and R_T) and pragmatical meaning (signs are related to overt behavior via the mediation function). To take account of *syntactics*, including the transitional relations between signs in messages, it is necessary to go beyond this model, but this need not concern us here.

The vast majority of signs used in ordinary communication are what we may term *assigns* — their meanings are literally "assigned" to them via association with other signs rather than via direct association with the objects signified. The word *zebra* is understood by most six-year-olds, yet few of them have encountered ZEBRA objects themselves. They have seen pictures of them, been told that they have stripes, run like horses, and are usually found wild. As indicated in Figure 1 (B), this new stimulus pattern, *zebra*, /s/, acquires portions of the mediating reactions already associated with the primary signs. In learning to read, for example, the "little black bugs" on the printed page are definitely assigns; these visual patterns are seldom associated directly with the objects signified, but rather with auditory signs (created by the child and teacher as they verbalize). Most of the signs with which we shall deal in this book are assigns in this sense.

It is apparent that, according to this view, the meanings which different individuals have for the same signs will vary to the extent that their behaviors toward the things signified have varied. This is because the composition of the representational process — which is the meaning of the sign — is entirely dependent upon the nature of the total behavior occurring while the sign is being established. Given the essential sameness of human organisms and the stability of physical laws, of course, the meanings of most primary perceptual signs should be quite constant across individuals (e.g., the significance of the visual cues arising from APPLE object). Given stability of learning experiences within a particular culture, also, meanings of most common verbal signs will be highly similar (e.g., the adjective *sweet* will be heard and used in much the same types of total situations regardless of the individual in our culture). On the other hand, the meanings of many signs will reflect the idiosyncrasies of individual experience, as, for example, the meanings of FATHER, MOTHER, and ME for individuals growing up in "healthy" vs. "unhealthy" home environments. Variation in meaning should be particularly characteristic of *assigns* since their representational processes depend entirely upon the samples of other signs with which they occur.

Meaning as a Relational Concept

The meaning of "meaning" for which we wish to establish an index is a psychological one — that process or state in the behavior of a sign-using organism which is assumed to be a necessary consequence of the reception of sign-stimuli and a necessary antecedent for the production of sign-responses. Within the general framework of learning theory, we have identified this cognitive state, *meaning*, with a representational mediation process and have tried to specify the objective stimulus and response conditions under which such a process develops. At a later point we shall try to show how a particular kind of measurement operation, *the semantic differential*, relates to the functioning of representational processes in language behavior and hence may serve as an index of these processes.

But it must be emphasized that merely because we choose for our purposes to study this psychological aspect of "meaning" does not imply that other meanings of "meaning" are incorrect. "Meaning," like "emotion," is a relational or process concept. It is because language signs have certain meanings in the psychological sense (i.e., are associated with certain representational processes) that they are used consistently in certain situations and consistently produce certain behaviors (sociological meaning), and this is also the reason, in part at least, that they occur in predictable association with other signs in messages (linguistic meaning). But, on the other hand, as we have seen, it is the very consistencies among situations and behaviors in human experience, including the experience of hearing and seeing message sequences, that determines the nature of representational processes and hence psychological meaning.

Serious questions will undoubtedly be raised — by the philosopher, by the linguist, and by others whose traditions in this field differ from those of the psychologist — as to whether it is really "meaning" that we are measuring. The issue here is both subtle and difficult to discuss. It is also necessary that the reader be reasonably familiar with our logic and our methods of measurement before it can be handled in any fundamental way. Therefore, at this point we merely promise to return to the question — in what sense is the semantic differential a measure of meaning? — in the final, summary chapter of this book.

THE PROBLEM OF MEASUREMENT

Of all the imps that inhabit the nervous system — that "little black box" in psychological theorizing — the one we call "meaning" is held by common consent to be the most elusive. Yet, again by common consent among social scientists, this variable is one of the most important determinants of human behavior. It therefore behooves us to try, at least, to find some kind of objective index.

To measure anything that goes on within "the little black box" it is necessary to use some observable output from it as an index. Looking back at the theoretical paradigm for the representational mediation process (Figure 1, A) — a hunch about how "the little black box" is wired, if you will — we can see that the process $(r_m \rightarrow s_m)$, which we have identified with meaning, is assumed to be an antecedent, initiating condition for overt behavior (R_X). It is clear that we need to "tap" this line somehow, need to use some aspect, characteristic, or sampling of R_X as a means of inferring what is happening at r_m. To put the problem yet another way, we wish to find a kind of measurable activity or behavior of sign-using organisms which is maximally dependent upon and sensitive to meaningful states, and minimally dependent upon other variables.

The search for such indices of meaning, while never very extensive and often inadvertent, has followed a number of different directions. These may be classified as physiological methods, learning methods, perceptual methods, association methods, and scaling methods. They may be evaluated against the usual criteria for measuring instruments: (1) *Objectivity.* The method should yield verifiable, reproducible data which are independent of the idiosyncrasies of the investigator. (2) *Reliability.* It should yield the same values within acceptable margins of error when the same conditions are duplicated. (3) *Validity.* The data obtained should be demonstrably covariant with those obtained with some other, independent index of meaning. (4) *Sensitivity.* The method should yield differentiations commensurate with the natural units of the material being studied, i.e., should be able to reflect as fine distinctions in meaning as are typically made in communicating. (5) *Comparability.* The method should be applicable to a wide range of phenomena in the field, making possible comparisons among different individuals and groups, among different concepts, and so on. (6) *Utility.* It should yield information relevant to contemporary theoretical and practical issues in an efficient manner, i.e., it should not be so cumbersome and laborious as to prohibit collection of data at a reasonable rate. This is not an exhaustive list of criteria of measurement, but it is sufficient for our purposes. What follows is a digest of an earlier review of measurement problems in this area (Osgood, 1952).

Physiological Methods

It has proven convenient in theorizing about meaning to define the representational mediation process as an implicit *response* which produces its own distinctive *self-stimulation.* As said earlier, this makes it possible to import the standard conceptual machinery of S-R psychology. However, if we accept the peripheral theory of consciousness or cognition, a literal mediating reaction with its self-stimulation becomes a necessary condition for meaning, and hence the investigator is encouraged to discover direct physiological correlates.

Action Potentials in Striate Musculature. Introspective psychologists of another generation generally agreed in finding kinaesthetic sensations present as a residue when everything but "meaningful thought" was excluded from consciousness. But the method of introspection did not allow them to determine whether these vague muscular and organic sensations were actually meanings or merely a background of bodily tonus. Experimentalists picked up the problem at this point. Following J. B. Watson's dictum that thought was nothing but implicit speech, a small host of gadgeteers (see Thorson, 1925) filled subjects' mouths with an astounding variety of mechanical devices while they both thought and mumbled unusual items like "psychology." Little or no correspondence between thought-movements and speech-movements was found. Electrical amplification and recording methods later provided apparatus of sufficient sensitivity for the problem, and both Jacobson (1932) and Max (1935, 1937) made detailed records of muscle potentials during periods of directed "thought." Although a consistent and localized correlation was found — while imagining lifting one's arm muscle potentials are picked up from the appropriate muscles, deaf-mutes show greater potential in finger muscles than normals solving the same mental problems, etc. — this provides at best a very cumbersome and crude index of meaning. There is no way of "reading" the meaning of a sign to a subject from the recorded activity, no satisfactory demonstration of the necessity of the motor component has ever been offered, and the apparatus required is extremely complicated and expensive.

Salivary Reaction. Another pioneer exploration into the organic correlates of meaning was that of Razran (1935-36), using himself as subject, words for "saliva" in several languages with which he was differentially familiar as stimuli, and amount of salivation as the dependent response. Salivation was greatest in his childhood language (Russian), next in his most proficient one (English), and less in three slightly known languages (French, Spanish, and Polish). We have here a demonstration of a relation between the magnitude of secretion of a gland and the meaningfulness of a set of signs, but this method would provide a most restricted index of meaning in general.

The Galvanic Skin Response. GSR is one of several indices of autonomic activity, and to the extent that meanings include emotional components this measure should be useful. It is readily elicited by warning or preparatory signals, has been used to index the intensity of emotional reactions to words and other stimuli, and thus may be said to reflect at least some aspects of the mediational process. Unfortunately, the two most directly relevant experiments using this measure — one by Mason (1941) relating "discovery" and "loss" of meaningfulness of a sign to GSR and another by Bingham (1943) relating degree of "meaningfulness, significance and importance" of signs to GSR — leave much to be desired in the way of methodological finesse.

All of these physiological methods are of somewhat dubious validity, since there has been no demonstration of the necessity of these peripheral components, and they are not sensitive measures in that we are unable to interpret details of the records in our present ignorance. Their chief drawback, however, is cumbersomeness — the subject has to be "rigged up" in elaborate gadgetry to make such measurements. For this reason, even should validity and sensitivity problems be solved, it seems likely that physiological indices will be mainly useful as criteria against which to evaluate more practicable techniques.

Learning Methods

There are many learning studies employing meaningful materials, but only rarely is meaning itself the experimental variable. And even where meaning has been deliberately varied, interest has generally centered on the effect upon learning rather than upon the use of learning as an index of meaning.

Semantic Generalization. When a reaction conditioned to one stimulus transfers to another, and the amount of transfer varies directly with the similarity between the two stimuli, we speak of stimulus generalization. In semantic generalization the necessary similarities lie in the *meanings* of the stimuli rather than their physical characteristics. Many experiments have demonstrated semantic generalization from significate to sign: Here some reaction is first conditioned to the significate (say, a flash of blue light), and then it is shown that this new reaction appears without training to the sign (say, when the word "blue" is spoken). Traugott and Fadeyeva (1934), for example, associated excitatory CR's to certain significates and inhibitory CR's to others, demonstrating that subsequent free associations to the signs (words) for these stimuli were faster for excitatory than inhibitory significates. Many other experiments have demonstrated semantic generalization *from sign to sign*: here some reaction is first conditioned to one sign (say, the word "tree") and then tested for transfer to another sign (say, the word "bush"). Razran (1939), for example, has shown that generalization is greater between semantically related words (e.g., STYLE and FASHION) than between phonetically related words (e.g., STYLE and STILE), and Riess (1940) has obtained similar results. The latter investigator has also demonstrated (1946) that the importance of meaningful or semantic similarity increases with age while that of physical (phonetic) similarity decreases.

Transfer and Interference Studies. If there is generalization among meanings as shown above, then it would be anticipated that practice on learning one list of words should facilitate subsequent learning of another list, to the extent that there are meaningful similarities involved. Just such facilitative transfer has been shown by Cofer and Foley (1942) and their various associates (see Cofer, *et al.*, 1943). On the interference side, Osgood (1946) has shown that there is less interference among similar meaningful responses than among unrelated meaningful responses in the successive learning of lists of paired associates; furthermore, it was also shown (see Osgood, 1948) that there is a special kind of reciprocal inhibition operating between meaningfully opposed responses in such lists, the learning of one verbal response tending to block or decrease the speed of responding with the opposite verbal response to the same stimulus.

These findings suggest a general law in this area — *that when a sign or assign is conditioned to a mediator, it will also tend to elicit other mediators in proportion to their similarity to the original reaction and will tend to inhibit other mediators in proportion to the directness of their antagonism, or oppositeness, to the original reaction* — but they offer very little in the way of measurement of meaning. Beyond considerable cumbersomeness procedurally, these learning measures lack comparability as indices of meaning. This is because any measure of generalization or interference is necessarily made relative to the original learning of some standard, which, of course, varies from case to case. We can tell that HAPPY is more similar in meaning to JOYFUL than is SMOOTH, but this cannot be compared in any way with other such relations. The chief value of these learning methods, therefore, lies in the testing of specific hypotheses about meaningful processes deriving from learning theory.

Perceptual Methods

That there is an intimate relation between perceptual and meaningful phenomena is borne out by the confusion which psychologists display in using these terms. The voluminous literature on memory for forms, for example, has been interpreted both as demonstrating perceptual dynamics (see Koffka, 1935) and semantic dynamics (see Bartlett, 1932) — witness particularly the experiment by Carmichael, Hogan, and Walter (1932) in which the deliberate introduction of different meaningful words in association with the same abstract forms markedly influenced the way they were reproduced. But, as was the case with learning studies, there are few experiments in which meaning has been deliberately introduced as a variable and none in which anything resembling a measuring technique for meaning is offered. The effects of *motives* upon the perception (or meaning) of ambiguous stimuli has been amply demonstrated (see McClelland and Atkinson, 1948; Postman and Bruner, 1948), and there is some evidence that personal values can influence both perceptual significance (Bruner and Goodman, 1947) and the tachistoscopic availability of printed words (see Postman, Bruner and McGinnies, 1948). Skinner (1936) has devised a "verbal summator" technique for studying language behavior which resembles these perceptual methods. Samples of meaningless speech sounds are repeated until the subject perceives some meaningful form — a kind of verbal inkblot. Like the tachistoscopic method, this gets at the relative availability of meaningful forms but does not distinguish among them semantically.

The chief drawback with perceptual methods in general, then, is that they serve to index the comparative availability or habit strength of alternative meaningful forms, but not the meaning itself. The fact that a religious person perceives VESPERS with a shorter presentation time than a theoretically oriented person says nothing about how the meanings of this term differ for them; the fact that the religious person perceives VESPERS more quickly than THEORY says nothing about the difference in meaning of these two words to this individual. The same statements apply to Skinner's "verbal summator" technique.

Association Methods

Freud would have been the first to agree that the associations produced when a patient "allows one idea to lead to another" are in no sense free, but rather are semantically determined. Inspection of the Kent and Rosanoff (1910) lists of associates obtained from 1,000 subjects also makes it clear that the vast majority of responses depend upon the meaning of the stimulus word. Similarly, from the fact that two subjects differ in their associations to a given stimulus word we can probably infer at least momentary differences in their meanings of the stimulus word. The association method is sensitive to differences in the *mode* of the stimulus sign: Dorcus (1932) showed that associations to color words (linguistic signs) and colored papers (perceptual signs) differed, and Karwoski, Gramlich and Arnott (1944) have found that associations to the verbal labels of objects differ from those to either pictures or direct perception of these objects. Other studies demonstrate that the association method is also sensitive to the *context* in which the stimulus word appears, whether it be the situational context of the subject (see Bousfield, 1950; Foley and MacMillan, 1943) or the linguistic context of the sign itself (Howes and Osgood, 1954).

But does the association method provide us with an adequate index of the meanings of the signs used as stimuli? The answer is "no," and for several reasons. For one thing, this measure lacks comparability; the responses of two individuals to the same stimulus, or of the same individual to two stimulus words, are essentially unique as bits of data. For another thing, word associations depend upon more than the meaning of the stimulus word, specifically upon the strengths of transitional habits based upon contingencies in experience. Thus, for example, MARY is often encountered in company with her sister SALLY and therefore, given MARY as a stimulus, our subject is likely to respond by saying "Sally" — but does the response "Sally" in any way index the *meaning* of MARY to our subject, his affection for her, for example? A basic distinction must be drawn between the meaning of a sign and its associations.

This point needs to be labored because one recent writer (Noble, 1952), at least, has seriously proposed that the meaning of a sign is nothing more than the number of different associations between it as a stimulus and other signs as responses. According to Noble, "The index of meaning (m) of a particular stimulus was defined . . . as the grand mean number of (acceptable) written responses given by all Ss within a 60 sec. period." This solution to the troublesome problems of the nature and measurement of meaning is as simple as it is ludicrous. Looking into his data we find, for example, that JELLY, JEWEL, and HEAVEN have approximately the same *m*-scores and hence, presumably, nearly the same meaning. It is his basic notion — that meaning and association can be equated — which is wrong. Does BLACK mean *white* because this is the most common associate? Does NEEDLE mean *sew*, BREAD mean *butter*, MAN mean *woman?* Noble's *m* might be identified as meaningfulness rather than meaning, or better, simply the association value of the stimulus, since this is actually what he is measuring.

Scaling Methods

Considering the number of traits, attitudes, and abilities that psychologists have scaled, it is perhaps surprising that there has been little effort to measure meaning in this way. What has been done along somewhat relevant lines has been motivated by the need to provide learning experimenters with standardized materials with respect to certain dimensions of variation. Thus Glaze (1928), Hull (1933), and others have scaled the "associative value" of nonsense materials on the basis of the relative frequency with which they evoke meaningful words as associates; Noble's (1952) *m*-measure, discussed above, essentially extends this method to meaningful as well as nonsense verbal stimuli. Working from a similar orientation, Haagen (1949) scaled 400 pairs of common adjectives in terms of their synonymity, vividness, familiarity, and association value; although useful for standardization in learning experiments, these scales do not provide us with measures of meaning — the judgments required of the subjects were always relative to some particular standard word, which varied from one set of test words to another (i.e., the measure does not meet the criterion of comparability). The most relevant scaling study was one by Mosier (1941) in which subjects rated adjectives on an 11-point scale in terms of their favorableness — unfavorableness. Mosier was able to demonstrate a reasonable ordering of evaluative words in terms of their mean locations (e.g., *excellent, good, common, fair, poor,* etc.), including such bits of information as the fact that *better* is connotatively less favorable than *good* (grammarians to the contrary). The limitation in Mosier's technique, however, is that he tapped only one dimension of meaning, the admittedly important evaluative dimension, whereas we may assume at the outset that meanings vary multidimensionally.

THE SEMANTIC DIFFERENTIAL

Let us glance back at the theoretical paradigm shown in Figure 1 again. What we shall call *encoding* is the selective evocation of overt instrumental acts (R_X) by the representational mediation process, ($r_m \rightarrow s_m$), presumably on the basis of differential reinforcement. These R_X's are responses to the *sign*, which are assumed to depend upon the prior association of sign and significate and which are therefore, presumably appropriate to the meaning of the sign. What types of overt responses may constitute R_X and hence serve as an index of r_m? Many intentionally encoded responses are *non-linguistic*. We often infer (rightly or wrongly) the meaning of a sign to an individual from his facial expressions, gestures, gross bodily movements, etc. — he smiles and stretches out his arms in welcome, he draws back his head and wrinkles up his nose in disgust, or he flees or strikes with his fists. But not only is such behavior difficult to quantify and cumbersome to record, it also does not yield comparable units and is probably insensitive to subtler meanings, at least in most of us.

Language as an Index of Meaning

What about *linguistic encoding*, ordinary intentional language? After all, the basic function of language is supposed to be the communication of meaning — it is often defined as "the expression of ideas." Ordinarily, if we want to find out what something *means* to a person, we ask him to tell us. What does a POLITICIAN mean to you? "Well, it is someone who campaigns and does or does not get elected. It's usually a hearty, husky, good-natured guy who's always on the 'go' — but also a 'glad-hander' and liable to be untrustworthy, a double-talker. Not as good as a statesman, of course. . . ." What does SOPHISTICATED mean? "Well . . . I know what it means, all right, but it's hard to put into words. It's being clever and wise about people and things — knowing the ropes, so to speak. It's sort of smooth and polished, graceful but not awkward . . . poised, 'savvy,' you know. . . ." It might be noted in passing that the responses one gets when he asks what something *means* are usually quite different from those he gets when he asks for associations (e.g., what *other things* X makes him think of). POLITICIAN: Washington, smoke-filled room, insincere, laws, investigations, etc. SOPHISTICATED: lady, cocktails, music, educated, clever, smart, etc. There is some overlap, of course, because a common mediation process (elicited by the stimulus sign) is operating in both cases.

Unrestricted linguistic output of this sort has high presumptive validity, unless we question the honesty of the subject — and there is no more reason to expect malingering here than in other psychological test situations (a poorly instructed or motivated subject in a psychophysical experiment may say "heavier" when it actually feels lighter; he may take a wrong alternative in a finger-maze when he knows it is wrong). At least we can say it has as much validity as any other technique based upon requested introspection. For highly intelligent and verbally fluent subjects this method would be sufficiently sensitive, since it seems likely that a language will tend to include those discriminations which its users find necessary to communicate. Less fluent subjects, however, find it very difficult to encode meanings spontaneously (in a taste test on brands of ice cream, one of the authors found that most subjects could produce "creamy," "tasty," and a few other terms, but little more, yet given a form of the semantic differential these same individuals quickly and confidently indicated a large number of judgments). But what spontaneous linguistic output may gain in validity and sensitivity, it certainly loses on other grounds — casual introspections are hardly comparable and do not lend themselves to quantification. What sort of quantitative index of meaning could be applied to the two sample outputs above? How could we compare the outputs of two different subjects discussing their meanings of the same term and indicate the degree of similarity or difference in meaning?

It is apparent that if we are to use linguistic encoding as an index of meaning we need (a) a carefully devised *sample of alternative verbal responses* which can be standardized across subjects, (b) these alternatives to be *elicited from* subjects rather than emitted so that encoding fluency is eliminated as a variable, and (c) these alternatives to be *representative* of the major ways in which meanings vary. In other words, rather than relying on the spontaneous emission of words relating to a particular stimulating sign, we need to play a game of "Twenty Questions" with our subject: SOPHISTICATED — is it *hard* or *soft*? Is it *pleasant* or *unpleasant*? Is it *fast* or *slow*? Just as in "Twenty Questions" the selection of successive alternatives gradually eliminates uncertainty as to the object being thought about, so selection among successive pairs of common verbal opposites should gradually isolate the "meaning" of the stimulus sign. To increase the sensitivity of our instrument, we may insert a scale between each pair of terms, so that the subject can indicate both the *direction* and the *intensity* of each judgment.

The semantic differential is essentially a combination of controlled association and scaling procedures. We provide the subject with a concept to be differentiated and a set of bipolar adjectival scales against which to do it, his only task being to indicate, for each item (pairing of a concept with a scale), the direction of his association and its intensity on a seven-step scale. The crux of the method, of course, lies in selecting the sample of descriptive polar terms. Ideally, the sample should be as representative as possible of all the ways in which meaningful judgments can vary, and yet be small enough in size to be efficient in practice. In other words, from the myriad linguistic and non-linguistic behaviors mediated by symbolic processes, we select a small but carefully devised sample, a sample which we shall try to demonstrate is chiefly indicative of the ways that meanings vary, and largely insensitive to other sources of variation.

Research Background of the Semantic Differential

The semantic differential as a technique for measuring meaning was not developed directly out of the reasoning described above. As is so often the case, the actual measurement procedures developed more or less "Topsy-like" in the course of experimental research along other, though related, lines, and the reasonings leading to the measurement of meaning in general grew out of interpretations of the findings in this earlier research.

The notion of using polar adjectives to define the termini of semantic dimensions grew out of research on synesthesia with Theodore Karwoski and Henry Odbert at Dartmouth College. Synesthesia is defined by Warren in his *Dictionary of Psychology* (1934) as "a phenomenon characterizing the experiences of certain individuals, in which certain sensations belonging to one sense or mode attach to certain sensations of another group and appear regularly whenever a stimulus of the latter type occurs." This implies a sort of "neural cross-circuiting" that occurs in only a few freak individuals, and it is true that many of the classic case histories gave credence to this view. The series of researches by

Karwoski, Odbert, and their associates, however, related synesthesia to thinking and language in general. Rather than being a freak phenomenon, color-music synesthesia was reported by Karwoski and Odbert (1938) as being regularly indulged in by as many as 13 per cent of Dartmouth College students, often as a means of enriching their enjoyment of music. A much larger number reported that they had such experiences occasionally.

The regular photistic visualizers varied among themselves as to the modes of translation between sound and vision and as to the vividness of their experiences, and their difference from the general population seemed to be one of degree rather than kind. Whereas fast, exciting music might be pictured by the synesthete as sharply etched, bright red forms, his less imaginative brethren would merely agree that *words* like "red-hot," "bright," and "fiery," as verbal metaphors, adequately described the music; a slow, melancholic selection might be visualized as heavy, slow-moving "blobs" of somber hue and be described verbally as "heavy," "blue," and "dark." The relation of this phenomenon to ordinary metaphor is evident: A happy man is said to feel "high," a sad man "low"; the pianist travels "up" and "down" the scale from treble to bass; souls travel "up" to the good place and "down" to the bad place; hope is "white" and despair is "black."

Interrelationships among color, mood, and musical experiences were studied more analytically by Odbert, Karwoski, and Eckerson (1942). Subjects first listened to ten short excerpts from classical selections and indicated their dominant moods by checking sets of adjectives arranged in a mood circle (see Hevner, 1936); on a second hearing they gave the names of colors that seemed appropriate to the music. The colors were found to follow the moods created by the music. Delius' *On Hearing the First Cuckoo in Spring* was judged leisurely in mood and predominantly green in color; a portion of Wagner's *Rienzi Overture* was judged exciting or vigorous in mood and predominantly red in color. When another group of subjects was merely shown the mood adjectives (with no musical stimulation) and asked to select appropriate colors, even more consistent relations appeared. There is a great deal of supporting evidence, of course, for consistent relations between colors and moods.

These results indicate that stimuli from several modalities, visual, auditory, emotional and verbal, may have shared significances or meanings — cross-modality stimulus equivalence. Further experiments with even simpler stimuli by Karwoski, Odbert, and Osgood

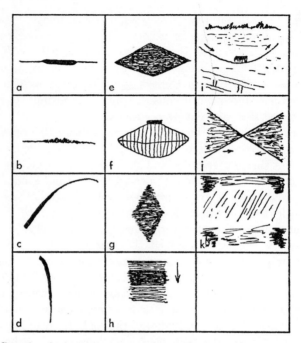

Fig. 2. Sample of photisms drawn by complex synesthetes to represent a simple tone which grows louder and then softer.

(1942) indicated that such equivalence across modalities shows continuity along dimensions of experience. In one study complex synesthetes drew pictures to represent what they visualized when simple melodic sequences were played by a single instrument. Figure 2 shows a sample of reactions to a tone which simply gets louder and then softer (*crescendo-diminuendo*). Subject *e*, for example, drew a solid form which grows continuously *thicker* and then thinner; subject *h* made a color continuously more and then less *saturated;* subject *i* (who always created meaningful rather than abstract forms) reported a little car that came continuously *nearer* and then farther away. These are functionally or meaningfully equivalent responses to the same auditory stimulus, and they display continuous translation between modalities. That these practiced synesthetes were not exercising a "rare" capacity was shown in two subsequent experiments: In one, subjects who had never even thought of "seeing things" when they heard music were played the same stimulus selections and told that they *had* to draw something to represent each one — exactly the same types of productions

were obtained. In another experiment, 100 unselected college sophomores were given a purely verbal metaphor test in which the
auditory-mood and visual-spatial characteristics, observed in synesthetes, translated into adjectives and presented as pairs (e.g.,
LOUD-soft; SMALL-LARGE), were combined in all possible ways and
judged (by circling that member of the second pair which seemed
to go best with the first, capitalized member of the first pair). Here
again the relations utilized by complex synesthetes were regularly
chosen by unselected subjects — 96 per cent, for example, linking
LOUD with LARGE in the example above.

Are such relations entirely dependent upon culture or is it possible that they represent even more fundamental determinants
operating in the human species? In an early attempt to get at this
question, the senior author[1] studied anthropological field reports on
five widely separated primitive cultures — Aztec and Pueblo Indian,
Australian Bushman, Siberian Aborigine, Negro (Uganda Protec-
torate), and Malayan — with the purpose of obtaining evidence on
semantic parallelism. The generality of certain relationships was
quite striking: for example, *good* gods, places, social positions, etc.,
were almost always *up* and *light (white)*, whereas *bad* things were
down and *dark (black)*. A prevalent myth tells how the gods
helped the original man to struggle from the *dark, cold, wet, sad*
world below the ground *up* to the *light, warm, dry, happy* world on
the surface. Among certain Siberian Aborigines, members of a
privileged clan call themselves the *white* bones in contrast to all
others who are referred to as the *black* bones. Recently he has
studied a small number of Southwest Indian subjects, playing
simple tape-recorded melodic lines of the same type used earlier
with synesthetes in our own culture and having the Indian subjects
draw their visualizations. Although it was often difficult to secure
cooperation, in those cases where it was obtained essentially the
same types of translations again appeared.

It seems clear from these studies that the imagery found in synesthesia is intimately tied up with language metaphor, and that both
represent *semantic* relations. Karwoski, Odbert, and Osgood summarized this work with the statement that the process of metaphor
in language as well as in color-music synesthesia can be described
as the parallel alignment of two or more dimensions of experience,
definable verbally by pairs of polar adjectives, with translations
occurring between equivalent portions of the continua. This is

---

[1] C. E. Osgood, undergraduate thesis in psychology, Dartmouth College.

translatable into our learning theory model as an instance — complex, to be sure — of *mediated generalization*. Take the case of parallelism between auditory pitch and visual size (synesthetes typically represent high tones as small and low tones as large): it is characteristic of the physical world that large-sized resonators produce low frequency tones and small-sized resonators, high frequency tones (think of a series of organ pipes, bells, or even hollow logs and sticks, and of the voices of men vs. boys, large dogs vs. little dogs, or lions vs. mice). This means that repeatedly the visual stimulus of large objects will be paired with the auditory stimulus of low-pitched tones, and so on consistently throughout the continuum. Any representational processes associated with one (e.g., danger significance of threatening big dog vs. play significance of little dog) will tend to be associated with the other as well (e.g., sounds produced). Thus will a hierarchy of equivalent signs come to be associated with a common mediation process. Any encoding responses associated with this mediator, such as "large" drawing movements and saying the word "large," will tend to transfer to any sign which elicits this mediator — thus "synesthesia" when a deep tone produces "large" drawing movements and "metaphor" when the word "deep" is associated with the word "large." Much learning of this type is carried in the culture, of course, as when the storyteller speaks of the BIG DADDY BEAR (bass), The Mother Bear (normal voice), and the little baby bear (soprano voice).

Stagner and Osgood (1946) adapted this method for measuring social stereotypes and also made explicit the notion of a continuum between the polar terms, by using such terms to define the ends of seven-step scales. Rather than studying the relations between continua, a set of scales was used to determine the "profiles" of various social stereotypes, such as PACIFIST, RUSSIAN, DICTATOR, and NEUTRALITY. Successive samples of subjects were tested throughout the period of the United States' gradual involvement in World War II. The feasibility of using this method to record the changing structures of social stereotypes (i.e., the changing meanings of a set of social signs) was demonstrated. More important from the point of view of methodology, it was found that, as used by our subjects in making their judgments, the semantic scales fell into highly intercorrelated clusters. For example, *fair-unfair, high-low, kind-cruel, valuable-worthless, Christian-antiChristian,* and *honest-dishonest* were all found to correlate together .90 or better. Such a cluster represents the operation of a single, general factor in social judgments, obviously here an *evaluative* factor. Scales like *strong-weak*, *realistic-unrealistic*, and *happy-sad* were independent of this evaluative group and pointed to the existence of other dimensions of the semantic framework.

Logic of Semantic Differentiation

Most of our work to date has been concentrated on developing the measuring instrument and applying it to a variety of practical problems. Little has been done in testing the various learning theory implications that may arise from the method; what evidence and experimental proposals we do have will be summarized in a later chapter. But this has been a major gap in our work so far: There has been no explicit statement of the relation between the theoretical conception of meaning as a representational mediation process, and the operations of measurement which constitute the semantic differential technique. The account to be given here is admittedly a highly speculative one — a sort of preliminary architect's sketch of what a bridge between these two levels of discourse might eventually resemble. To accomplish the building of such a bridge, it is necessary to analyze and express our operations of measurement in terms of the constructs of the theoretical model.

We begin by postulating a *semantic space*, a region of some unknown dimensionality and Euclidian in character. Each semantic scale, defined by a pair of polar (opposite-in-meaning) adjectives, is assumed to represent a straight line function that passes through the origin of this space, and a sample of such scales then represents a multidimensional space. The larger or more representative the sample, the better defined is the space as a whole. Now, as we have seen in both the synesthesia studies and in the measurement of social stereotypes, many of the "directions" established by particular scales are essentially the same (e.g., the evaluative cluster in the Stagner and Osgood study) and hence their replication adds little to the definition of the space. To define the semantic space with maximum efficiency, we would need to determine that minimum number of *orthogonal dimensions* or axes (again, assuming the space to be Euclidian) which exhausts the dimensionality of the space — in practice, we shall be satisfied with as many such independent dimensions as we can identify and measure reliably. The logical tool to uncover these dimensions is factor analysis, and in the following chapter we shall describe a number of such investigations.

What is meant by "differentiating" the meaning of a concept? When a subject judges a concept against a series of scales, e.g.,

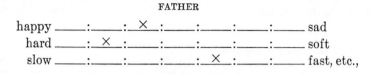

FATHER

happy ____:____:__×__:____:____:____:____ sad
hard ____:__×__:____:____:____:____:____ soft
slow ____:____:____:____:__×__:____:____ fast, etc.,

each judgment represents a selection among a set of given alternatives and serves to localize the concept as a point in the semantic space. The larger the number of scales and the more representative the selection of these scales, the more validly does this point in the space represent the operational meaning of the concept. And conversely, of course: Given the location of such a point in the space, the original judgments are reproducible in that each point has an orthogonal projection onto any line that passes through the origin of the space, i.e., onto any scale. By semantic differentiation, then, we mean the successive allocation of a concept to a point in the multidimensional semantic space by selection from among a set of given scaled semantic alternatives. Difference in the meaning between two concepts is then merely a function of the differences in their respective allocations within the same space, i.e., it is a function of the multidimensional distance between the two points. It is apparent that some index of this generalized distance is a desideratum of the system, and such a measure is introduced in Chapter 3.

We now have two definitions of meaning. In learning-theory terms, the meaning of a sign in a particular context and to a particular person has been defined as the representational mediation process which it elicits; in terms of our measurement operations the meaning of a sign has been defined as that point in the semantic space specified by a series of differentiating judgments. We can draw a rough correspondence between these two levels as follows: The point in space which serves us as an operational definition of meaning has two essential properties — *direction* from the origin, and *distance* from the origin. We may identify these properties with the *quality* and *intensity* of meaning, respectively. The direction from the origin depends on the alternative polar terms selected, and the distance depends on the extremeness of the scale positions checked.

What properties of learned associations — here, associations of signs with mediating reactions — correspond to these two attributes of direction and intensity? At this point we must make a rather tenuous assumption, but a necessary one. Let us assume that there is some finite number of representational mediation reactions available to the organism and let us further assume that the number of these alternative reactions (excitatory or inhibitory) corresponds to the number of dimensions or factors in the semantic space. Direction of a point in the semantic space will then correspond to what reactions are elicited by the sign, and distance from the origin will correspond to the *intensity* of the reactions.

Let us try to clarify this assumed isomorphism somewhat. Corresponding to each major dimension of the semantic space, defined by a pair of polar terms, is a pair of reciprocally antagonistic mediating reactions, which we may symbolize as r_{mI} and $\bar{r}_{mI}$ for the first dimension, r_{mII} and $\bar{r}_{mII}$ for the second dimension, and so forth. Each successive act of judgment by the subject using the semantic differential, in which a sign is allocated to one or the other direction of a scale, corresponds to the acquired capacity of that sign to elicit either r_m or $\bar{r}_m$, and the extremeness of the subject's judgment corresponds to the intensity of reaction associating the sign with either r_m or $\bar{r}_m$. There is actually evidence that words of opposed meaning are mediated by such reciprocally antagonistic reactions. Osgood (1948) demonstrated that the successive pairing of words of opposed meaning with the same stimulus produced significant amounts of blocking (failure of response) and decreased speed of responding, as compared with words of similar meaning, both phenomena predictable from the reciprocal inhibition hypothesis. Evidence for a direct relation between extremeness of graphic judgment on the semantic differential and speed of associative judgment (an index of reaction intensity) will be offered later in this book.

Figure 3 represents an attempt to coordinate these models graphically. The sign is represented as a point in an *n*-dimensional space (here, three dimensions). As a point in space, the sign has projections onto each of the dimensions. The magnitude and direction of the coordinate on each dimension is, on the one hand, estimated from the direction and extremeness of the subject's judgment against those scales of the differential representing this dimension and, on the other hand, is assumed to be proportional to the intensity with which the sign elicits the r_m or $\bar{r}_m$ corresponding to this dimension. The lower portion of Figure 3 represents the meaning of this sign as a simultaneous hierarchy of representational reactions,

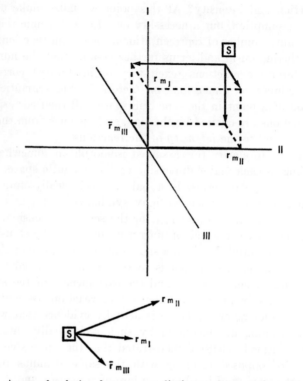

Fig. 3. Assumed relation between mediation and semantic space models.

the intensity of evocation varying for $r_{mII} > r_{mI} > \bar{r}_{mIII}$. It should be noted that whereas the reciprocal reactions *within* each dimension are assumed to be incompatible, those corresponding to independent dimensions are assumed to be compatible and hence capable of simultaneous excitation. What we have done, in other words, is to divide the total representational mediation process into a set of bipolar components, the meaning of a sign corresponding to the pattern and intensity with which these components are elicited.

It remains to express the actual behavior of subjects taking the semantic differential in terms of the learning theory model. Each item (pairing of a specific concept with a specific scale) presents the following situation:

(CONCEPT)

polar term X ____:____:____:____:____:____:____ polar term Y
(1)   (2)   (3)   (4)   (5)   (6)   (7)

in which the scale positions have already been defined for the subject in the instructions (see Chapter 3) as:

(1) *extremely* X   (7) *extremely* Y
(2) *quite* X   (6) *quite* Y
(3) *slightly* X   (5) *slightly* Y
(4) *neither* X nor Y; *equally* X and Y

We shall assume that, on the basis of a great deal of prior experience in encoding, the terms "extremely," "quite," and "slightly" as linguistic quantifiers have been associated with more or less equal *degrees* of intensity of whatever representational process (X or Y) happens to be elicited, and therefore, that the sign combinations "extremely X," "quite X," and so forth will elicit an r_m of the quality X and of the intensity given by the quantifier. In a subsequent chapter, data will be offered to substantiate this scaling assumption. We shall also assume that, even though the instructions relating scale positions to quantifying terms are only given once at the beginning of the "test," they persist throughout.

Now, following our general analysis, any concept being judged is a sign eliciting a distinctive set of component r_m's and $\bar{r}_m$'s with differing intensities. Similarly, the polar terms defining the scales are signs eliciting their own characteristic patterns of r_m's and $\bar{r}_m$'s, and, when combined with quantifiers associated with scale positions, each scale position elicits an r_m pattern whose selection depends upon the polar term and whose intensity depends upon the quantifier. Two additional comments about the representational processes associated with the scales should be made: First, since the polar terms X and Y are meaningful opposites, we assume that the r_m pattern characteristic of X will be reciprocally antagonistic to that characteristic of Y (i.e., wherever a component of X is r_m, the same component of Y will be $\bar{r}_m$, and conversely). Second, since, as will be seen in subsequent chapters, scales are chosen which maximize one factor or component and minimize all others, the r_m pattern elicited by any X-Y set will tend to have one dominant component.

To summarize our theoretical analysis, it can be seen that what is operationally quite simple (the procedure of the subject in responding to the semantic differential) proves to be quite complex behaviorally. The location of a concept in the semantic space defined by a set of factors is equated with the evocation by the concept of a set of component mediating reactions, direction in space

being equated to *what* mediators are evoked (from among reciprocally antagonistic pairs) and distance from the origin being
equated to *how intensely* (with what habit strength) these are
evoked. Each position on one of our semantic scales is also assumed
to be associated with a complex mediating reaction, the dominant
component depending on the polar terms, X and Y, and its intensity
depending upon the qualifiers, "extremely," "quite," etc. These different mediators are associated, in encoding, with checking the
various scale positions. Through the functioning of a generalization
principle, the concept will elicit checking of that scale position
whose dominant mediator component most closely matches in intensity the corresponding component in the process associated with the
concept itself. Since the positions checked on the scales constitute
the coordinates of the concept's location in semantic space, we assume that the coordinates in the measurement space are functionally equivalent with the components of the representational
mediation process associated with this concept.

This, then, is one rationale by which the semantic differential,
as a technique of measurement, can be considered as an index of
meaning. One may well ask whether such an elaborate and speculative analysis — which perhaps impresses the reader as a *tour de
force* — is necessary? It is true that many of the practical uses of
the semantic differential, indeed its own empirical validity, depend
little, if at all, on such a tie-in with learning theory. On the other
hand, if we are to use the semantic differential as an hypothesis-
testing instrument, and if the hypotheses regarding meanings and
changes in meaning are to be drawn from learning-theory analyses,
some such rationale as has been developed here is highly desirable.
Further, from the writers' point of view, it is an awkward and somewhat embarrassing state of affairs to entertain simultaneously a
theoretical conception of the nature of meaning and a procedure
for measuring it which have no relation to one another. Whether
this attempt at resolving this state of affairs has reduced this awk-
wardness is another matter.

2

THE DIMENSIONALITY OF THE SEMANTIC SPACE

The meaning of a sign has been defined as a representational mediation process, a complex reaction divisible into some unknown but finite number of components. This learning theory construct has been tentatively coordinated with our measuring operations by identifying this complex mediation reaction with a point in a multidimensional space. The projections of this point onto the various dimensions of the semantic space are assumed to correspond to what component mediating reactions are associated with the sign and with what degrees of intensity. The essential operation of measurement is the successive allocation of a concept to a series of descriptive scales defined by polar adjectives, these scales selected so as to be representative of the major dimensions along which meaningful processes vary. In order to select a set of scales having these properties, it is necessary to determine what the major dimensions of the semantic space are. Some form of factor analysis seems the logical tool for such a multidimensional exploratory task. In this chapter we describe a series of factor analytic studies designed to isolate and identify the major factors operating in meaningful judgments.

Before describing particular factor studies, it will be useful to discuss a few of the general requirements of this approach. One of the most important requirements is, of course, *representative sampling*. Our problem is different from most factor studies in that we are dealing with three sources of variability — subjects, scales, and concepts judged. Since the purpose of our factoring work is to discover the "natural" dimensionality of the semantic space, the system of factors which together account for the variance in meaningful judgments, it is important that our sample be as free from bias as possible. The nature and number of factors obtainable in any analysis is limited by the sources of variability in the original data — in a real sense, you only can get out what you put in — and we wished to avoid both the production of artificial factors by deliberately inserting scales or concepts according to a priori hypotheses and the omission of significant factors through insufficient sampling.

Our sampling has not been entirely satisfactory. Perhaps the greatest inadequacy has been in subject variance. Ideally, our subject sample should be a representative cross-section of the general population. As the reader will realize, it is difficult and expensive to obtain such a sample; it is also hard to use subjects of this sort in a prolonged study (subject-time in the three major factor analyses to be described here averaged about three hours) and get across instructions for what seems superficially to be a rather trivial and repetitive task. For the major factorial studies, then, we have employed college undergraduates. There are some advantages in this choice, of course — such subjects are probaby more representative of the sorts of populations that will be used in most applications of the final instruments; having a higher average intelligence they probably yield a clearer picture of the most finely differentiated semantic space. Finally, we have available subsidiary factor data from the general population to serve as a check on the college population.

Our greatest care has been taken with the *sampling of descriptive scales,* since it is dimensionality of the scale system in which we are mainly interested. And the chief danger was that some a priori conceptions of what the semantic space should look like would influence our sampling. To avoid such bias, we have sampled scales in terms of an external criterion (with respect to the experimenters). In the first case this criterion was sheer frequency-of-usage in the college population of descriptive terms as qualifiers. Since it became apparent that this criterion resulted in a relative overloading of scales representing the dominant factor, and did not permit identification of many minor factors at all, in a subsequent factorization we used Roget's *Thesaurus* as a source of scales, logically a more exhaustive sampling criterion. In several other factor studies to be reported, scales have been sampled on still other grounds.

The results of any factor analysis, including the somewhat intuitive identification and labeling of factors, at best merely provides an hypothesis to be tested in further factor analyses. One's confidence in the validity of a particular factor structure grows as this structure persistently reappears in replications of the analysis. However, there is a danger of forcing the same structure to appear again by using the factors obtained in the first study as a criterion for selecting the scales to be used in the subsequent studies. In other words, it is no trick to get the same factors in a second study if one deliberately selects groups of variables to go with, and duplicate, the variables already isolated as factors. But this tests neither the validity nor the generality of the factor structure originally obtained — it merely reaffirms whatever biases were present in the first analysis. Therefore, whenever we have varied the sample of scales, we have made the sampling independent of previous factor results (except for the inclusion of a small number of reference scales). To test the generality of the factor structure obtained, we have in our several studies (a) varied the subject populations, (b) varied the concepts judged (and in one case eliminated specific concepts entirely), (c) varied the type of judgmental situation used in collecting data, and (d) varied the factoring method used in treating the data. Since the same primary factors keep reappearing despite these modifications, we conclude that the factor structure operating in meaningful judgments is not dependent upon these variables, at least.

ANALYSIS I: CENTROID FACTORIZATION, GRAPHIC METHOD

Sampling

In obtaining a sample of scales of semantic judgment, a frequency-of-usage or availability criterion was used. Forty nouns were taken from the Kent-Rosanoff list of stimulus words for free association and these were read in fairly rapid succession to a group of approximately 200 undergraduate students. These subjects were instructed to write down after each stimulus noun the first descriptive adjective that occurred to them (e.g., TREE — *green*; HOUSE — *big*; PRIEST — *good*). These subjects were asked not to search for exotic qualifiers, simply to give whatever occurred to them immediately, and the rapid rate of presentation further restricted the likelihood of getting rare associates. These data were then analyzed for frequency of occurrence of all adjectives, regardless of the stimulus words with which they had appeared. As might be expected, the adjectives *good* and *bad* occurred with frequencies more than double those of any other adjectives. Perhaps less expected was the fact that nearly half of the 50 most frequently appearing adjectives were also clearly evaluative in nature. Also among the frequently given adjectives were most of the common sensory discriminations, such as *heavy-light, sweet-sour,* and *hot-cold.* These frequently used adjectives were made into sets of polar opposites and served as the sample of descriptive scales used in this study. For theoretical reasons, a few additional sensory continua were inserted in this set of 50; these scales were *pungent-bland, fragrant-foul,* and *bright-dark.* The kind of bias that this method of sampling has probably introduced will be considered later. The entire set of scales is given in Table 1.

The sampling of concepts presented a less critical problem, since our purpose was a factor analysis of scales of judgment rather than of concepts. It was important, however, that these concepts be others than those on which the adjective sample had been based (the 40 original stimulus words from the Kent-Rosanoff lists), that they be as diversified in meaning as possible so as to augment the total variability in judgments, and that they be familiar to the subjects we intended to use. On these bases the experimenters simply selected the following 20 concepts: LADY, BOULDER, SIN, FATHER, LAKE, SYMPHONY, RUSSIAN, FEATHER, ME, FIRE, BABY, FRAUD, GOD, PATRIOT, TORNADO, SWORD, MOTHER, STATUE, COP, AMERICA. The availability and test-sophistication of the college student population dictated our sampling of *subjects.* A group of 100 students in introductory psychology served; they were well paid for their work, and internal evidence testifies to the care with which they did a long and not very exciting task.

Procedure

The pairing of 50 descriptive scales with 20 concepts in all possible combinations generates a 1000-item test form. For checking reliability, 40 of these 1000 items, chosen at random, but with the restriction that no concept should be used more than twice and no scale more than once, were repeated as a final page of the mimeographed test booklet (see Chapter 4). The ordering of concept-scale pairings was deliberately rotated rather than random; it was felt that this procedure would better guarantee independence of judgments, since the maximum number of items (19), would intervene between successive judgments of the same concept and the maximum number of items (49) would intervene between successive judgments on the same scale. Each item appeared as follows:

LADY rough ____:____:____:____:____:____:____ smooth,

with the subject instructed to place a check-mark in that position indicating both the direction and intensity of his judgment. The instructions given may be found in Chapter 3 (pp. 82-84).

Treatment of Data

The combination of scales, concepts, and subjects used in this study generates a $50 \times 20 \times 100$ cube of data. Each scale position was assigned a number, from 1 to 7 arbitrarily from left to right, and hence each cell in this cube contains a number representing the judgment of a particular concept, on a particular scale, by a particular subject.

Matrix of Intercorrelations. Each subject provides a complete set of 50 judgments on each of 20 concepts — one judgment on each scale. Since both subjects and concepts are replicated, it would be possible to obtain separate matrices of scale intercorrelations for individual subjects (summing over concepts) as well as for individual concepts (summing over subjects). However, since our long-run purpose was to set up a semantic measuring instrument which would be applicable to people and concepts in general, we wished to obtain that matrix of intercorrelations among scales which would be most representative or typical. We therefore summed over both subjects and concepts, generating a single 50×50 intercorrelational matrix of every scale with every other scale to which the total data contribute. Another reason for summing over concepts was to avoid spuriously low correlations resulting from low variability of judgments on single concepts. If nearly all subjects call TORNADO extremely *cruel* and also agree in calling it extremely *unpleasant,* the correlation between *kind-cruel* and *pleasant-unpleasant* would approach indeterminacy, despite the fact that over concepts in general there is a high positive correlation between these scales.

Each of the 50 scales was responded to 2000 times, each of the 100 subjects responding once to each of 20 concepts. Thus, every scale can be paired with every other scale 2000 times, each subject contributing 20 pairs to the total and each concept contributing 100 pairs. In computing each correlation — the summations for cross-products — means and variances were taken across both subjects and concepts. If X_{ijv} is the score on the ith scale, for the jth concept, and vth subject, and $\bar{X}_i$ .. is the mean for the ith scale found by summing over concepts and subjects and dividing by 20×100, then the cross-products between scales i and k in deviations from the means were found from:

$$\sum_j \sum_v (X_{ijv} - \bar{X}_{i\,.\,.}) (X_{kjv} - \bar{X}_{k\,.\,.}).$$

The expression for the variance on scale i is then:

$$\frac{\sum_j \sum_v (X_{ijv} - \bar{X}_{i\,.\,.})^2}{N}.$$

These intercorrelations were calculated with IBM equipment. The variance due to differences between concept means (the difference between $\bar{X}_{ij}$'s) is necessarily included in the correlation values. The possible effect of this on our results will be considered at a later point.

Factor Analysis. Thurstone's Centroid Factor Method (1947) was applied to this matrix of correlations. Four factors were extracted and rotated into simple structure, maintaining orthogonality. The rotated factor matrix for this first analysis appears as Table 1. Since orthogonal relations were maintained in rotation, the matrix in this table represents uncorrelated factors. We stopped extracting factors after the fourth; this factor accounted for less than 2 per cent of the variance and appeared by inspection to be a residual. The pattern of scales having noticeable loadings on it (between .20 and .27) made no sense semantically. It is to be expected that a larger sampling of scales, with less emphasis on the evaluative factor, would allow some number of additional factors to appear.

The problem of labeling factors is somewhat simpler here than in the usual case. In a sense, our polar scales label themselves as to content. The first factor is clearly identifiable as *evaluative* by listing the scales which have high loadings on it: *good-bad, beautiful-ugly, sweet-sour, clean-dirty, tasty-distasteful, valuable-worthless, kind-cruel, pleasant-unpleasant, sweet-bitter, happy-sad, sacred-profane, nice-awful, fragrant-foul, honest-dishonest,* and *fair-unfair.* All of these loadings are .75 or better, and it will also be noted by referring to Table 1 that these scales are "purely" evaluative in the sense that the extracted variance is almost entirely on this first factor. Several other scales, *rich-poor, clear-hazy, fresh-stale,* and *healthy-sick,* while not as highly loaded as the first set on the evaluative factor, nevertheless restrict their loadings chiefly to this factor.

The second factor identifies itself fairly well as a *potency* variable (or, as one of our undergraduate statistical assistants puts it, a "football player" factor): *large-small, strong-weak, heavy-light,* and *thick-thin* serve to identify its general nature, these scales hav-

Table 1

ROTATED FACTOR LOADINGS — ANALYSIS I

	I	II	III	IV	h²
1. good-bad	.88	.05	.09	.09	.79
2. large-small	.06	.62	.34	.04	.51
3. beautiful-ugly	.86	.09	.01	.26	.82
4. yellow-blue	−.33	−.14	.12	.17	.17
5. hard-soft	−.48	.55	.16	.21	.60
6. sweet-sour	.83	−.14	−.09	.02	.72
7. strong-weak	.19	.62	.20	−.03	.46
8. clean-dirty	.82	−.05	.03	.02	.68
9. high-low	.59	.21	.08	.04	.40
10. calm-agitated	.61	.00	−.36	−.05	.50
11. tasty-distasteful	.77	.05	−.11	.00	.61
12. valuable-worthless	.79	.04	.13	.00	.64
13. red-green	−.33	−.08	.35	.22	.28
14. young-old	.31	−.30	.32	.01	.29
15. kind-cruel	.82	−.10	−.18	.13	.73
16. loud-soft	−.39	.44	.23	.22	.45
17. deep-shallow	.27	.46	.14	−.25	.37
18. pleasant-unpleasant	.82	−.05	.28	−.12	.77
19. black-white	−.64	.31	.01	−.03	.51
20. bitter-sweet	−.80	.11	.20	.03	.69
21. happy-sad	.76	−.11	.00	.03	.59
22. sharp-dull	.23	.07	.52	−.10	.34
23. empty-full	−.57	−.26	−.03	.18	.43
24. ferocious-peaceful	−.69	.17	.41	.02	.67
25. heavy-light	−.36	.62	−.11	.06	.53
26. wet-dry	.08	.07	−.03	−.14	.03
27. sacred-profane	.81	.02	−.10	.01	.67
28. relaxed-tense	.55	.12	−.37	−.11	.47
29. brave-cowardly	.66	.44	.12	.03	.64
30. long-short	.20	.34	.13	−.23	.23
31. rich-poor	.60	.10	.00	−.18	.40
32. clear-hazy	.59	.03	.10	−.16	.38
33. hot-cold	−.04	−.06	.46	.07	.22
34. thick-thin	−.06	.44	−.06	−.11	.21
35. nice-awful	.87	−.08	.19	.15	.82
36. bright-dark	.69	−.13	.26	.00	.56
37. bass-treble	−.33	.47	−.06	.02	.33
38. angular-rounded	−.17	.08	.43	.12	.23
39. fragrant-foul	.84	−.04	−.11	.05	.72
40. honest-dishonest	.85	.07	−.02	.16	.75
41. active-passive	.14	.04	.59	−.02	.37
42. rough-smooth	−.46	.36	.29	.10	.44
43. fresh-stale	.68	.01	.22	−.11	.52
44. fast-slow	.01	.00	.70	−.12	.50
45. fair-unfair	.83	.08	−.07	.11	.71
46. rugged-delicate	−.42	.60	.26	.27	.68
47. near-far	.41	.13	.11	−.05	.20
48. pungent-bland	−.30	.12	.26	.05	.17
49. healthy-sick	.69	.17	.09	.02	.59
50. wide-narrow	.26	.41	−.07	−.11	.25
Per Cent of Total Variance	33.78	7.62	6.24	1.52	.4916
Per Cent of Common Variance	68.55	15.46	12.66	3.08	.9975

ing the highest and most restricted loadings. The tendency for scales representing this factor to be contaminated, as it were, with the evaluative factor is apparent in Table 1. The following scales are mainly potency continua, but reflect considerable evaluative meaning as well: *hard-soft, loud-soft, deep-shallow, brave-cowardly, bass-treble, rough-smooth, rugged-delicate,* and *wide-narrow.* It also should be noted from inspection of this table that in general loadings on the evaluative factor are higher than those on potency, even where "pure" scales are involved.

The third factor appears to be mainly an *activity* variable in judgments, with some relation to physical sharpness or abruptness as well. The most distinctively loaded scales are *fast-slow* (.70), *active-passive* (.59), and *hot-cold* (.46); somewhat different in apparent meaning, but displaying similar factor loadings, are *sharp-dull* (.52) and *angular-rounded* (.43). The following scales have considerable loading on this activity factor, but also as much or more loading on evaluation: *red-green, young-old* (the subjects were college undergraduates), *ferocious-peaceful,* and *tense-relaxed.* The noticeable tendency for both activity and power to be associated with positive evaluation (e.g., *good, strong,* and *active* tend to go together rather than *good, weak,* and *passive*) may represent a cultural semantic bias. We can say that there appear to be independent *factors* operating, even though it is difficult to find many specific *scales* which are orthogonal with respect to evaluation.

The percentages of total variance and common variance accounted for by the three factors isolated are given at the bottom of Table 1. These values suggest that the evaluative factor plays a dominant role in meaningful judgments, here accounting for almost 70 per cent of the common (extracted) variance, and this impression will be confirmed in subsequent studies to be reported. It is also somewhat startling to note that, even with college students of considerable sophistication and intelligence as subjects, almost half of the total variance in meaningful judgments of 20 varied concepts against 50 varied scales can be accounted for in terms of only these three factors, *evaluation, potency,* and *activity.* Is it possible that the apparently rich and complex domain of meaning has such a simple structure as this? Although we shall want to delay any answer to this question until the results of more factor studies are reported, it nevertheless should be noted that 50 per cent of the total variance does remain unexplained. Even though some part of this remainder can be attributed to sheer unreliability (error variance), part of it does represent the presence of some unknown number of additional factors, here appearing as specific to particular scales, but potentially extractable in more extensive analyses.

ANALYSIS II: D-FACTORIZATION, FORCED-CHOICE METHOD

The first factor analysis of meaningful judgments raises a number of methodological questions. For one thing, the method used to obtain correlations — summing over both concepts and subjects — necessarily includes the variance attributable to the mean differences between both subjects and concepts. In a small-scale analysis, using only 10 subjects, 10 concepts, and 10 scales drawn from the original data, in which the variance attributable to first subjects and then concepts was held constant statistically, it was found that although there was no change in factor structure attributable to subjects, there was some change due to concepts. To the extent that there are differences in factor structure as between concepts, and to the extent that our sampling of only 20 concepts was nonrepresentative, the factorial results of the first analysis could be biased. For another thing, there was the question of whether our factor results were somehow a function of the graphic method and would not appear when only the polar terms themselves were associated by another technique. The second factor analysis was an attempt to eliminate these possibilities.

Sampling

Since this second analysis was designed as a direct check on the first, it was decided to use exactly the same sample of descriptive continua, e.g., the same 50 sets of polar terms. The subjects were different individuals, but drawn from the same undergraduate college population. There were 40 subjects used in this analysis. A method of collecting data was employed which eliminates concept differences entirely as a variable; since no specific concepts were given for judgment, the factorial structure of the scales obtained cannot be attributed to the particular sample of concepts used.

Procedure

The method used involves a forced choice between pairs of polar terms as to the direction of their relationship. Given the following item, for example:

SHARP-dull; relaxed-tense

the subject is asked to simply encircle that one of the second pair which seems closest in meaning to the capitalized member of the first pair. There is no restriction here on the concept (if any) that may be used. Some subjects might think of "people" concepts, others of "object" concepts, and yet others of "aesthetic" concepts. Introspectively (and as judged from the comments of subjects), there is usually no particular concept involved. If 100 per cent of the subjects select *tense*, as might happen in this case, it would indicate that *sharp*-with-*tense* vs. *dull*-with-*relaxed* is an appropriate parallelism or association over concepts in general; if subjects divide randomly (e.g., half one way, half the other) on an item such as

FRESH-stale; long-short

it would appear that either the multitude of conceptual contexts in which these qualities might be related are random with respect to direction or that subjects differ randomly in their judgments of the relation — in either case, no particular concept or set of concepts is forcing the direction of relation. The exact instructions were as follows:

We want to find out what dimensions of meaning are related and what the basic factors in the system seem to be. This is a very important problem for building any measuring instrument and we ask your complete co-operation in carrying out the following instructions.

Procedure to follow:

(a) Each item you see will be composed of two pairs of words. Your job is to encircle the word in the second pair which goes best with the capitalized word in the first pair.

STRAIGHT-crooked   noble bestial

(b) Don't look back over the judgments you have already completed. Judge each item by itself.

(c) Be sure to look at *both* words in each pair, so as to be judging the relation of the scales as wholes.

(d) Check back after you have made each judgment to be sure you answered the way you wanted to. Correct any judgment that you feel was not what you meant.

(e) Try not to base your judgments on your "likes" or "dislikes" of particular individual words. It is the relation among scales as wholes that you are judging.

Treatment of Data

The pairing of each of 50 pairs of polar terms with every other pair generates a test comprising 1225 items. Again, a rotational procedure was used to maximize the separation of identical pairs. The measure of relation used in this analysis was simply the percentage of agreement in direction of alignment, e.g., the percentage of subjects circling *noble* as going with STRAIGHT is entered into a 50 × 50 matrix of such percentages for all pairings. Since the number of subjects circling one of the terms entirely determines the number circling the other, calculations are necessary for only one term (the left-hand term was used consistently, since this corresponded to the original direction taken as positive in the first factor study). A perfect relation is inferred from 100 per cent (with left-hand term) or from 0 per cent (with right-hand term); 50 per cent indicates no relation, since equal numbers of subjects choose both terms. The resulting 50 × 50 matrix of percentages was factored by a technique described below and the results compared with those obtained in the original centroid analysis.

Factor Analysis. The method of factoring used in this analysis is based on a slightly different logic than are the conventional factoring techniques. Therefore, a brief description of the method itself will be given before reporting its application to the present problem. We begin with a symmetric matrix of percentages — analogous to a matrix of intercorrelations — of order 50 × 50. The logic is simply this: If two scales are equivalent, i.e., mean the same thing, their percentages of agreement with all the other scales will be equivalent. In other words, we may think of each column of percentages of agreement as sets of scores wherein the higher any single score, the greater the relation between two given scales. If two columns contain perfectly co-varying scores, they are considered equivalent. One can now find the sum of the cross-products between each column of percentages of agreement and every other column and factor the resulting matrix. The factoring may be done by the diagonal method as given by Thurstone (1947), selecting any one of the scales as a pivot to begin with and continuing the factoring until the residuals are zero.

The method has been shown to yield results corresponding closely with those obtained with the centroid method when both are applied to correlation matrices. This technique has been applied to raw score matrices. When this is done the distances (D) between variables can be reproduced. For this reason, the method has been called the D-method of factoring. The technique is described in detail in the Appendix.

The method results in a matrix of coordinates (loadings) for each variable on a set of dimensions (factors) which are orthogonal to each other. Each dimension coincides with a variable chosen as a pivot. The higher the coordinate of a variable on a dimension, the more closely related is that variable with the dimension. The scales which appeared as the successive pivotal dimensions are *good-bad*, *rugged-delicate, sharp-dull, heavy-light*, and *empty-full*, in this order. After this fifth dimension had been extracted by the present method, it became clear that only dimensions with a single high coordinate (the pivotal variable, a "specific") would continue to emerge, and therefore the analysis was discontinued. Unlike factor loadings, the coordinates of variables against the pivotal dimensions may have absolute values greater than 1.00.

Comparison of Factor Analyses I and II

The five dimensions extracted in the D^2 factor analysis were rotated graphically, maintaining orthogonality among the dimensions. This was not done "blindly," but rather we deliberately tried to maximize the similarity between this structure and that obtained with the centroid method. The question was how close a correspondence between the structures obtained in these two studies could be demonstrated, despite the differences in subjects, methods of collecting data, and methods of factoring. Table 2 gives the coordinates of each variable on the five rotated dimensions.

In comparing these two analyses we refer to "loadings" of variables on "factors" in speaking of results of the centroid method, and to "coordinates" on "dimensions" in speaking of results of the D^2 method. Similarity between the results of the two methods was estimated in three ways: (1) qualitatively, by the extent to which variables heavily loaded on factors also had high coordinates on dimensions; quantatively, (2) by the magnitude of correlations between factor loadings and dimension coordinates across variables and (3) by the magnitude of indices of factorial similarity, the *coefficient of proportionality, e,* between loadings and coordinates across the variables.[1]

---

[1] We thank Dr. C. F. Wrigley for bringing this measure to our attention. References to the use of this index are found in Burt (1948) and Tucker (1951).

Table 2

ROTATED DIMENSION COORDINATES — ANALYSIS II

	I	II	III	IV	V
1. good-bad	2.29	.84	.07	1.54	.00
2. large-small	.12	1.76	−.02	1.00	−.34
3. beautiful-ugly	2.40	.41	.38	1.48	−.01
4. yellow-blue	−.31	−.27	−.15	.73	−.44
5. hard-soft	−1.39	1.06	.68	.45	.39
6. sweet-sour	2.29	.71	.14	.98	−.26
7. strong-weak	.38	1.81	.67	1.36	−.53
8. clean-dirty	2.38	.46	.60	1.26	−.06
9. high-low	1.35	1.21	1.00	1.00	−.26
10. calm-agitated	2.25	.36	−.62	.48	−.14
11. tasty-distasteful	2.11	1.05	.21	1.21	−.33
12. valuable-worthless	1.87	1.12	.25	1.53	−.46
13. red-green	−.59	1.03	.78	.58	−.19
14. young-old	1.22	.83	1.26	.87	−.33
15. kind-cruel	2.40	.49	−.18	1.23	−.23
16. loud-soft	−1.71	1.03	.61	.69	.06
17. deep-shallow	.30	1.46	−.65	.72	.97
18. pleasant-unpleasant	2.38	.56	.24	1.38	−.29
19. black-white	−2.11	.18	−.64	−.53	.13
20. bitter-sweet	−2.22	−.30	.16	−.82	.43
21. happy-sad	2.09	.97	.61	1.50	−.22
22. sharp-dull	.51	1.31	1.88	.53	.00
23. empty-full	−.62	−1.22	−.05	−.72	1.47
24. ferocious-peaceful	−2.25	.25	.44	.16	−.09
25. heavy-light	−1.60	1.68	−.92	.06	.00
26. wet-dry	−.62	.35	−.46	.00	−.34
27. sacred-profane	2.29	.58	−.25	1.04	−.24
28. relaxed-tense	2.17	.24	−.63	.62	−.30
29. brave-cowardly	1.45	1.56	.40	1.66	−.50
30. long-short	.59	1.01	.02	.72	−.38
31. rich-poor	1.31	1.33	.22	1.19	−.36
32. clear-hazy	1.92	.69	.98	.93	−.09
33. hot-cold	.42	.83	.65	.57	−.50
34. thick-thin	−.35	1.48	−.37	.60	−.61
35. nice-awful	2.39	1.07	−.02	1.15	−.07
36. bright-dark	1.71	.78	1.32	1.07	−.21
37. bass-treble	−1.15	.18	−1.42	−.06	.01
38. angular-rounded	−1.31	.30	.77	−.08	.42
39. fragrant-foul	2.32	.62	.23	1.12	−.31
40. honest-dishonest	1.99	.89	.10	1.50	−.37
41. active-passive	.30	1.64	1.39	.79	−.40
42. rough-smooth	−2.32	.28	.17	−.07	.31
43. fresh-stale	2.05	.82	.68	1.27	−.32
44. fast-slow	.42	1.10	1.50	.63	−.02
45. fair-unfair	2.22	.89	.37	1.33	−.29
46. rugged-delicate	−2.41	.60	.05	1.10	.00
47. near-far	.85	1.09	.67	.74	−.17
48. pungent-bland	−1.41	.66	.48	.06	−.39
49. healthy-sick	1.79	1.38	.63	1.81	−.54
50. wide-narrow	.60	1.24	−.14	.99	−.60

The latter measure is obtained from the formula

$$e_{ij} = \frac{\sum_k f_{ki}g_{kj}}{\sqrt{\sum_k f_{ki}^2 g_{kj}^2}} \tag{1}$$

where f_{ki} and g_{kj} represent the loading and coordinate respectively of the kth variable on the ith factor and the jth dimension obtained from the two analyses (see Burt, 1948; Tucker, 1951). In the qualitative comparison, "heavily loaded" and "highly coordinate" were defined by arbitrarily selected criterion values: The criteria for "heavily loaded" were that variables have loadings $>.80$, $>.50$, and $>.50$ for factors I, II, and III respectively; the criteria for "highly coordinate" were that variables have coordinates >2.25, >1.30, and >1.30 for dimensions I, II, and III respectively.

Table 3 provides a comparison between factor loadings and dimension coordinates for the two analyses. The variables are placed in one of the following categories: Variables having both heavy loadings and high coordinates; variables having heavy loadings but low coordinates; and variables having light loadings but high coordinates. The values for r and e between factors and dimensions are given at the top of each column.

I. Evaluation. The near identity of dimension I with factor I is apparent from both quantitative indices, e (.967) and r (.966), and the qualitative agreement between them is also very high. Even the variables that only meet the criterion on one method are actually close to the criterion on the other — *honest-dishonest* and *fair-unfair* on the factor only, *delicate-rugged* and *smooth-rough* on the dimension only. There is thus no question about identification of the first dimension of the semantic space — an *evaluative factor* is first in magnitude and order of appearance in both analyses.

II. Potency. The potency determinant in semantic judgments displays the poorest correspondence between factor and dimension, but even here the evidence is fairly satisfactory. The correlation over all 50 variables is .445 and the index of factorial similarity is .634. The three variables most heavily loaded on factor II are also exactly the same variables having the highest coordinates on dimension II, *strong-weak, large-small,* and *heavy-light.* However, of the two variables meeting the factor criterion only, only *hard-soft* has a sizable coordinate on the dimension. *Rugged-delicate* appears chiefly as an evaluative variable in the forced-choice method. Of the five variables meeting the dimension criterion only, three do have siz-

Table 3

RELATIONS BETWEEN FACTORS (METHOD I) AND DIMENSIONS (METHOD II)

	Factor I (Criterion,.80)	Dimension I (Criterion,2.25)		Factor II (Criterion,.50)	Dimension II (Criterion,1.30)		Factor III (Criterion,.50)	Dimension III (Criterion,1.30)
	r = .966	e = .967		r = .445	e = .634		r = .682	e = .741
	Both			*Both*			*Both*	
good-bad	.88	2.29	strong-weak	.62	1.81	fast-slow	.70	1.50
nice-awful	.87	2.39	large-small	.62	1.76	active-passive	.59	1.39
beautiful-ugly	.86	2.40	heavy-light	.62	1.68	sharp-dull	.52	1.88
fragrant-foul	.84	2.32						
sweet-sour	.83	2.29						
clean-dirty	.82	2.38						
pleasant-unpleasant	.82	2.38						
sacred-profane	.81	2.29						
	Factor Only			*Factor Only*			*Factor Only*	
honest-dishonest	.85	1.99	rugged-delicate	.60	.60	(none)		
fair-unfair	.83	2.22	hard-soft	.55	1.06			
	Dimension Only			*Dimension Only*			*Dimension Only*	
rugged-delicate	−.42	−2.41	active-passive	.04	1.64	bass-treble	−.06	−1.42
rough-smooth	−.46	−2.32	brave-cowardly	.44	1.56	bright-dark	.26	1.32
			thick-thin	.44	1.48			
			deep-shallow	.46	1.46			
			healthy-sick	.17	1.38			

able loadings on the corresponding factor — *brave-cowardly, thick-thin*, and *deep-shallow*. *Healthy-sick*, however, has nearly as high a coordinate on the evaluative dimension, where it belongs according to the first analysis, and *active-passive* has nearly as high a coordinate on the activity dimension (1.39), where it belongs according to the first analysis.

III. Activity. Dimension III and factor III correlate .682 and have an index of factorial similarity of .741. It is also clearly interpretable as an activity determinant on a qualitative basis. The three most highly loaded variables, *sharp-dull, active-passive,* and *fast-slow,* are among the five variables having the highest coordinates on dimension III. Of the two variables meeting the coordinate criterion only, *bright-dark* is actually higher on the evaluative dimension, where it belongs according to the first analysis. *Treble-bass* does not correspond to the results of the first analysis, but its high coordinate on the activity dimension does correspond to the findings of earlier studies on synesthesia in which high notes were typically associated with greater movement.

The two factor analytic studies just described yield highly similar structures among the relations of 50 bipolar descriptive scales. The first determinant operating in meaningful judgments is clearly *evaluative* in nature and it accounts for more than half of the extractable variance. The second and third factors to appear in both studies seem to represent what may be called *potency* and *activity* determinants in meaningful judgments, and again there is considerable agreement between the two analyses. Since entirely different subjects and entirely different methods of collecting the data (concepts rated on scales in the first analysis and forced-choice among the scales themselves in the second) were employed, this over-all correspondence increases our confidence that we are dealing with something consistent in the structuring of human thinking. The fact that different factoring methods were used would, if anything, be expected to *reduce* the correspondence, i.e., the correspondence appears *despite* this difference in methodology. The reader may ask if we did not force this correspondence by the manner of rotating in the second analysis; in one sense this is true, but on the other hand, had the variables been randomly related, not clustered in similar ways, no placement of the axes could have produced such correspondence.

ANALYSIS III: THESAURUS SAMPLING[2]

Do the three factors so far isolated, *evaluation, potency,* and *activity,* represent an exhaustive description of the semantic space, the remaining 50 per cent or so of the variance being simply attributable to error? Or is there some number of additional factors, probably more restricted in application and appearing as "specifics" in the first two analyses, which a more refined exploration could reveal? In the first place, there are quite a few scales (presumably meaningful) for which very little of the variance is accounted on these general factors: Looking at the h^2 values in Table 1 (proportion of total scale variance extracted), we find that less than one-third of the variance in judgments on *yellow-blue, red-green, young-old, wet-dry, long-short, hot-cold, thick-thin, bass-treble, angular-rounded, near-far, pungent-bland,* and *wide-narrow* is accounted for. It is obvious from inspection that these scales are largely *denotative* in character — they refer to the properties of objects experienced through the senses (with the possible exception of *young-old*) and not dependent upon inference and implication. In the second place, it is apparent also that our original method of sampling scales — depending upon frequency of usage as qualifiers — resulted in an overwhelming proportion of evaluative terms. While this probably reflects a real tendency in human thinking to place high priority on the evaluative significance of things, it also made it difficult for us to obtain a sufficient number of other scales to permit additional factors to appear clearly. For these reasons a third factor analysis was designed, with a sampling procedure that was both more extensive in size and more logically exhaustive with respect to possible dimensions.

Sampling

To obtain a logically exhaustive sampling of *semantic dimensions* which would also be independent of our own theoretical biases and our previous factorial results, we decided to use Roget's *Thesaurus* (1941 edition) as a source. The task set by Roget and his subsequent editors was precisely to provide a logically exhaustive classification of word meanings, and this source had the added ad-

---

[2] The authors wish to thank Mrs. Mary Snowden, who collaborated on this study as research assistant and herded the data through the ILLIAC. They also thank Mr. Ray Twery for his help on this and other problems.

vantage that most categories were already arranged in terms of polar opposition. The senior author and a co-worker, independently, went through Roget, extracting from each paired category, one pair of polar terms from the adjective listings and trying to select the most familiar yet most representative terms. These two listings were then combined, the judges eliminating in discussion one alternative where their independent selections had disagreed. This procedure resulted in a sample of 289 adjective-pairs.

However, we were also faced with a limitation, imposed by the intended use of the ILLIAC (the Illinois digital computer), that its "memory" could only handle 76 variables in the centroid method of factoring. Therefore, it was decided to employ a preliminary sorting procedure with a small number of subjects to reduce these 289 variables to 76. From an advanced class in advertising copy writing, 18 people who would presumably be sensitive to subtleties in word meanings were individually given a deck of cards containing the 289 polar terms and asked to sort them into 17 piles in terms of similarity of meaning. These subjects were free to define these 17 categories as they pleased, and there was no requirement that the piles be equal in size. Our reasoning was that if a set of variables kept appearing together in the same piles across various sorters, then they would presumably be highly correlated in a subsequent factor analysis, would not contribute to our exploration of the total semantic space, and therefore, all but one of them could be discarded. Since computations on the basis of 18 subjects sorting into 17 categories shows that co-occurrence of variables in the same category in five or more subjects is significant at the 1 per cent level, this criterion of significant clustering or association was used.

Using this clustering criterion, the original sample of 289 variables was reduced to 105. In selecting the alternatives to discard, we tried to eliminate more unfamiliar terms and ones difficult to treat as scales. An additional 29 pairs were finally discarded by the experimenters themselves, using the same criteria, to bring the sample down to 76. The scales finally used in the factor analysis appear in Table 5, to the left; other discarded scales which had been clustered with these by the preliminary sorters are also listed in Table 5, to the extreme right — we assume that in general these scales would have clustered closely about the one selected, in the factor space, had they been used.

The 100 *subjects* used in the factor analysis of the retained 76 scales were college undergraduates, again for the same reasons given

Table 4

CONCEPTS JUDGED IN THESAURUS ANALYSIS

(Parenthetical numbers refer to order of appearance)

Person Concepts	*Physical Objects*	*Abstract Concepts*
FOREIGNER (3)	KNIFE (2)	MODERN ART (1)
MY MOTHER (8)	BOULDER (7)	SIN (6)
ME (13)	SNOW (12)	TIME (11)
ADLAI STEVENSON (18)	ENGINE (17)	LEADERSHIP (16)

Event Concepts	*Institutions*
DEBATE (5)	HOSPITAL (4)
BIRTH (10)	AMERICA (9)
DAWN (14)	UNITED NATIONS (15)
SYMPHONY (20)	FAMILY LIFE (19)

---

earlier. They were well paid for their less than three hours' work. In sampling the *concepts* to be judged, we tried to draw from a variety of categories so as to increase representativeness; in order to provide a direct tie-in with Factor Analysis I, we included one of the concepts used there in each of the present categories (i.e., five repeat concepts altogether). The 20 concepts used in the present analysis, listed according to the categories they represent and with the repeat concepts underlined, are given in Table 4.

Procedure

Rather than rotating the concepts against the scales as had been done in Analysis I, in this case the subject judged the same concept against a series of scales before shifting to another concept. Research had been done between the time of these two factor analyses (see Chapter 3, p. 82) which indicated that no differences in results were occasioned by these two methods of presentation, and the method used here, in which a single concept is kept in mind while making a series of judgments, is much more satisfying to the subjects. Four-page booklets were made up with 76 scales (seven-step graphic method) appearing in a constant order but random with respect to semantic content; the concept being judged was stamped at the top of each page in these booklets. Each subject thus received 20 booklets, one for each concept. But rather than going through an entire booklet at a time, the subjects were instructed to do all the first pages (through all 20 booklets), then all the second pages, and so on; in this way an increased degree of shifting from concept to concept was obtained, which it was hoped would decrease the boredom inherent to some degree in this task.

The general instructions about the use of the semantic differential — the meanings of the scale positions, the stress on giving immediate impressions and not struggling over individual items, etc., as had been used in the first analysis, were repeated here. The subjects gathered in groups of about 20 and were given considerable freedom to take cigarette breaks and the like. The experimenters monitored these sessions and answered in standard fashion occasional questions about the meanings of polar terms (particularly concerning *heterogeneous-homogeneous, tangible-intangible, altruistic-egotistic, inherent-extraneous,* and *heretical-orthodox*).

Treatment of Data

The raw data were first transferred to IBM cards, one card for each subject-concept pairing, with the scores (1-7) for the 76 scales arranged in constant order. There were thus 100×20 or 2000 cards, and this was the number of pairs entering into each correlation since means, variances and cross-products were taken across both subjects and concepts as had been done in the first analysis (and for the same reasons). These ordered data were transferred directly to punched tape by an automatic machine method, and Pearson product-moment correlations of each scale with every other scale were obtained on the ILLIAC, yielding a 76×76 matrix.

Factor Analysis

Centroid Factor Analysis. This correlation matrix was first factored by Thurstone's centroid method, the method used in the first analysis. The analysis was stopped after eight factors had been extracted, since the eighth factor accounted for only about 1 per cent of the variance. The first three factors in this unrotated centroid matrix were clearly interpretable; the remainder were not.

The first factor was again the *evaluative factor* (the scales most heavily loaded on this factor were: *good-bad, kind-cruel, grateful-ungrateful, harmonious-dissonant, beautiful-ugly, successful-*

unsuccessful, true-false, positive-negative, reputable-disreputable, wise-foolish). The second was identifiable as the *potency factor* (the scales most heavily loaded being *hard-soft, masculine-feminine, severe-lenient, strong-weak, tenacious-yielding, heavy-light,* and *mature-youthful* in that order). And the third was identifiable as an *activity factor* (the most heavily loaded scales being *fast-slow, active-passive, excitable-calm, rash-cautious,* and *heretical-orthodox* in that order). Factor IV in this unrotated analysis, characterized chiefly by *awkard-graceful, hot-cold, constricted-spacious, private-public* and *excitable-calm,* might possibly be interpreted as some kind of anxiety variable; factor V, characterized by such scales as *masculine-feminine, heavy-light, healthy-sick, unusual-usual, passive-active, blunt-sharp, unimportant-important, public-private,* and *large-small,* defies consistent interpretation; factor VI (*weak-strong, cautious-rash, incomplete-complete, straight-curved, transparent-opaque, rational-intuitive,* and *complex-simple*), factor VII (*light-dark, clean-dirty, small-large*), and factor VIII (*hot-cold, healthy-sick, dry-wet, humorous-serious, straight-curved, stable-changeable*) also yield no obvious interpretation. The relative magnitudes of these factors correspond to what was found in the first analysis — the first factor accounts for about double as much variance in judgments as the next two and these in turn account for about double as much as any of the remaining factors. We conclude (1) that the three dominant factors isolated in the two previous factor analyses are also dominant in the present Thesaurus analysis and (2) that if any clearly identifiable subsidiary factors are to be revealed, this structure must be rotated.

Quartimax Rotation of the Centroid. The ILLIAC was used to rotate this centroid structure by what is known as the Quartimax method (see Neuhaus and Wrigley, 1954). This is a "blind" procedure; the experimenters do not observe any plots of one variable against another and do not determine in any way the location of the rotated axes. The procedure essentially uses a fourth power criterion instead of a least squares criterion; i.e., the distances from the variables to the factors are minimized for the fourth power instead of the second power. In the present case, this kind of rotation seemed to provide only a little increased clarity of interpretation.

Upon rotation, the original factors were still evident in the structure, although they no longer appeared in the same order. Factor I was still the dominant *evaluative factor,* but factor II appeared as the *activity factor,* with some additional implications (*active-*

passive, important-unimportant, meaningful-meaningless, pungent-bland, hot-cold, interesting-boring, sharp-blunt, savory-tasteless, and *fast-slow* in that order.) The analogue of the *potency factor* was now factor V (*hard-soft, heavy-light, masculine-feminine, strong-weak, tenacious-yielding, severe-lenient,* and *dark-light*), but it was second again in terms of magnitude of loadings. Factor IV might be dubbed a *"chaos" factor,* judging from the pattern of scales having relatively high loadings on it (*excitable-calm, unusual-usual, erratic-periodic, incomplete-complete, changeable-stable,* and *heterogeneous-homogeneous*). Factor III in the Quartimax rotation seemed to be a subsidiary or residual kind of evaluation, a sort of *"personal-social misery factor"* (*constricted-spacious, constrained-free, colorless-colorful, painful-pleasurable, plain-ornate, weary-refreshed, awkward-graceful,* and *ugly-beautiful*). Factor VI resembled what in our final analysis of these data will be termed a *"tautness" factor* (*straight-curved, angular-rounded, sharp-dull, intentional-unintentional, proud-humble, competitive-cooperative,* and *severe-lenient* in that order). Factor VII was difficult to interpret — perhaps a kind of *inept insecurity* (*private-public, simple-complex, near-far, youthful-mature, tangible-intangible, rash-cautious,* and *untimely-timely*).

Square Root Factorization of the Same Data. There are some questions as to the value of rotation by the Quartimax method, and in the present case the factors yielded are somewhat dubious as to interpretation. With the correlational matrix and an ILLIAC program available, it was a simple matter to apply the Square Root method of factoring (see Wrigley and McQuitty, 1953). In this method, as in Thurstone's Diagonal method (see Thurstone, 1947), scales are selected as pivots through which a given factor is placed, and all variance of other scales in this dimension is exhausted before selecting another scale as a second pivot. Since we already had ample evidence for the presence of three dominant factors, evaluation, potency, and activity, in the unrotated centroid analysis of the present as well as in both previous studies, we decided to select arbitrarily the first three pivotal scales, allowing the ILLIAC to proceed mechanically beyond this point. In other words, in an attempt to clarify the finer factorial composition of our data, we first extracted the three known sources of variance without allowing residual scales to influence the choice of the pivotal scales.

The ILLIAC was instructed to select *good-bad, hard-soft,* and *active-passive* as the first, second, and third pivots respectively. The

Table 5

UNROTATED SQUARE ROOT FACTOR ANALYSIS — THESAURUS STUDY

Scales (Evaluation)		I	II	III	IV	V	VI	VII	VIII	h²	Scales Related to Those in Analysis
1. good	bad	1.00	.00	.00	.00	.00	.00	.00	.00	1.00	beneficial-harmful; safe-dangerous; superior-inferior
2. optimistic	pessimistic	.37	−.05	.07	.05	−.05	.06	.09	.05	.16	hopeful-hopeless; happy-sad; jubilant-plaintive
3. complete	incomplete	.32	.05	.05	.05	−.08	−.06	.01	−.01	.12	whole-partial; sufficient-insufficient; perfect-imperfect
4. timely	untimely	.37	.04	.04	.05	.05	.01	.05	.01	.15	contemporary-noncontemporary
5. altruistic	egotistic	.31	−.13	−.08	.08	−.02	.01	.02	−.05	.13	selfish-unselfish
6. sociable	unsociable	.42	−.19	.18	.13	−.12	−.02	.15	.04	.30	affectionate-hateful; friendly-unfriendly
7. kind	cruel	.52	−.28	.00	.16	−.07	.02	.12	−.07	.41	merciful-merciless
8. grateful	ungrateful	.49	−.14	.08	.19	−.08	.04	.13	−.05	.34	repentant-unrepentant
9. harmonious	dissonant	.49	−.12	−.01	.11	−.08	−.04	.02	.06	.28	congenial-quarrelsome; approving-disapproving; assenting-dissenting; willing-unwilling; voluntary-compulsory

Table 5. Continued.

UNROTATED SQUARE ROOT FACTOR ANALYSIS — THESAURUS STUDY

Evaluation Scales	I	II	III	IV	V	VI	VII	VIII	h²	*Scales Related to Those in Analysis*
10. clean / dirty	.45	−.26	.02	.18	−.02	.06	.09	.02	.32	pure-impure
11. light / dark	.38	−.30	.01	.11	−.02	.11	.01	.02	.26	radiant-shaded; white-black
12. graceful / awkward	.38	−.23	.05	.07	.02	.03	.08	.12	.23	refined-vulgar; artful-artless; skillful-bungling
13. pleasurable / painful	.37	−.25	.07	.00	−.09	−.04	.16	.08	.25	comfortable-uncomfortable; soothing-aggravating
14. beautiful / ugly	.52	−.29	−.02	.03	−.06	.06	.14	.02	.38	sweet-sour; tasty-distasteful; fragrant-fetid
15. successful / unsuccessful	.51	.08	.29	.06	.00	.06	.09	.12	.38	fortunate-unfortunate
16. high / low	.45	.07	.17	.10	−.04	.03	.08	.03	.26	top-bottom; elevated-depressed; rising-falling; upright-inverted
17. meaningful / meaningless	.41	.04	.25	.04	−.04	−.08	.16	.07	.27	educational-mystifying; interpreted-unexplained; intelligible-unintelligible; lucid-obscure
18. important / unimportant	.38	.04	.31	.04	.00	−.02	.09	.02	.25	famous-obscure; useful-useless; influential-uninfluential

19. progressive	regressive	.43	.08	.24	.06	.06	.14	.02	.15	.30	increasing-decreasing; approaching-receding; progressive-degenerate; restoring-relapsing; attracting-repelling; pursuing-avoiding
20. true	false	.50	−.03	.01	.29	−.06	−.01	.00	.05	.34	authentic-facsimile; honest-dishonest; virtuous-sinful; right-wrong; legal-illegal; innocent-guilty; warranted-unwarranted
21. positive	negative	.48	.00	.07	.12	−.04	.03	.04	.06	.26	
22. reputable	disreputable	.68	−.02	.05	.13	−.01	.03	.07	.01	.49	candid-deceitful; pious-profane; heavenly-hellish; angelic-diabolic
23. believing	skeptical	.38	−.06	.02	.18	−.10	−.02	.03	.05	.20	indiscriminate-critical; gullible-incredulous
24. wise	foolish	.57	.06	.11	.22	−.03	−.02	.10	.05	.40	educated-ignorant; thoughtful-vacuous; intelligent-unintelligent
25. healthy	sick	.33	−.03	.04	.14	−.11	.00	.10	.14	.17	therapeutic-toxic; wholesome-morbid

Potency

26. hard	soft	−.24	*.97*	.00	.00	.00	.00	.00	.00	1.00	tough-fragile
27. strong	weak	.30	.40	.10	.12	.00	−.03	.04	.11	.28	potent-impotent; vigorous-feeble; prolific-sterile

Table 5. *Continued.*

UNROTATED SQUARE ROOT FACTOR ANALYSIS — THESAURUS STUDY

Scales		I	II	III	IV	V	VI	VII	VIII	h^2	Scales Related to Those in Analysis
Potency. Continued.											
28. severe	lenient	−.25	.43	.04	−.04	.11	−.02	−.09	.14	.28	domineering-lax
29. tenacious	yielding	−.06	.34	.06	.11	.04	−.03	.01	.04	.14	brave-cowardly; inelastic-elastic
30. constrained	free	−.16	.21	−.04	.04	.07	−.09	−.11	−.07	.10	prohibitive-permissive
31. constricted	spacious	−.16	.26	.04	.10	.03	−.08	−.10	−.07	.12	urban-rural; convergent-divergent; contracted-expanded; central-peripheral; concise-diffuse
32. heavy	light	−.20	.48	−.02	.00	−.04	−.12	−.03	.01	.29	thick-thin; deep-shallow; wide-narrow
33. serious	humorous	.01	.23	.09	.07	.05	−.03	−.03	.01	.07	
34. opaque	transparent	−.05	.24	−.08	.02	.01	−.01	−.07	.04	.07	
35. large	small	.09	.21	−.05	−.05	.03	.04	.02	.00	.06	long-short
36. masculine	feminine	−.14	.47	.03	−.01	.16	−.05	−.01	.06	.27	

Oriented Activity

37. active	passive	.17	.12	.98	.00	.00	.00	.00	.00	1.00	alive-dead; energetic-inert; moving-still
38. excitable	calm	−.15	.03	.26	−.13	.00	.05	.13	−.04	.13	violent-moderate; impulsive-deliberate; intemperate-temperate; emotional-unemotional
39. hot	cold	.12	.09	.26	.02	−.08	.01	.13	.04	.12	
40. intentional	unintentional	.29	.09	.23	.06	.01	−.01	.01	.07	.15	determinate-fortuitous; motivated-aimless
41. fast	slow	.01	.26	.35	−.05	.15	−.01	.05	.15	.24	
42. complex	simple	.17	.05	.25	−.02	.06	.12	.06	.00	.12	difficult-easy; laborious-effortless; multiple-single

Stability

43. sober	drunk	.40	.02	.01	.92	.00	.00	.00	.00	1.00	temperate-intemperate
44. stable	changeable	.16	.14	−.08	.19	−.04	−.11	−.04	−.02	.10	obstinate-vacillating; resolute-irresolute; lasting-transient; eternal-momentary
45. rational	intuitive	.11	.10	.04	.14	.06	.02	−.06	−.06	.06	

Table 5. Continued.

UNROTATED SQUARE ROOT FACTOR ANALYSIS — THESAURUS STUDY

Stability. Continued.

Scales		I	II	III	IV	V	VI	VII	VIII	h²	*Scales Related to Those in Analysis*
46. sane	insane	.48	−.07	.09	.32	−.08	−.05	.10	.03	.36	
47. cautious	rash	.33	−.02	−.05	.24	−.02	−.01	.01	−.18	.20	leisurely-hasty; careful-careless
48. orthodox	heretical	.26	.02	−.12	.17	−.06	−.12	−.06	−.03	.13	obedient-disobedient; respectful-disrespectful; loyal-disloyal; courteous-discourteous

Tautness

		I	II	III	IV	V	VI	VII	VIII	h²	
49. angular	rounded	−.12	.26	.16	−.06	*.95*	.00	.00	.00	1.00	
50. straight	curved	.08	.12	.14	.06	.27	.05	−.03	−.02	.12	direct-circuitous; parallel-oblique
51. sharp	blunt	−.06	.17	.29	.03	.18	.09	.10	.05	.17	tingling-numb

Novelty

		I	II	III	IV	V	VI	VII	VIII	h²	
52. new	old	.20	−.09	.09	.00	.05	*.97*	.00	.00	1.00	initial-final; early-late; unused-used; prior-subsequent

Item												Descriptors
53. unusual	usual	−.04	.02	.03	.00	.03	.25	.12	.03	.08		eccentric-conventional; impossible-possible; improbable-probable; uncertain-certain; absurd-axiomatic; infrequent-frequent
54. youthful	mature	−.10	−.23	.03	−.12	−.04	.22	.01	−.05	.13		young-old; filial-paternal

Receptivity

Item												Descriptors
55. savory	tasteless	.23	−.12	.18	.04	−.05	.06	.95	.00	1.00		
56. refreshed	weary	.28	−.17	.07	−.01	.01	.10	.16	.10	.16		contented-discontented
57. colorful	colorless	.20	−.20	.09	−.04	−.10	.09	.27	.08	.18		
58. interesting	boring	.40	−.09	.22	.01	−.07	.00	.20	.05	.26		witty-dull; eager-indifferent; curious-indifferent; attentive-inattentive; retentive-forgetful
59. pungent	bland	−.05	.09	.25	−.01	.03	.06	.16	.04	.10		resonant-muted; loud-soft; rough-smooth; abrasive-oily
60. sensitive	insensitive	.25	−.25	.18	.10	−.05	.10	.23	−.02	.24		vigilant-heedless

Aggressiveness

Item												Descriptors
61. aggressive	defensive	.02	.13	.16	.01	.05	.03	.03	.98	1.00		impelling-resisting; propelled-drawn; leading-following

Table 5. Concluded.

UNROTATED SQUARE ROOT FACTOR ANALYSIS — THESAURUS STUDY

Unassigned	Scales	I	II	III	IV	V	VI	VII	VIII	h²	Scales Related to Those in Analysis
62. ornate	plain	.01	−.19	.09	−.13	−.02	.02	.12	.05	.08	
63. near	far	.13	−.10	.15	.09	−.04	−.03	.11	−.04	.07	
64. heterogeneous	homogeneous	−.02	.04	.09	−.09	.02	.06	.09	−.05	.03	unrelated-related
65. tangible	intangible	.11	.08	.06	.08	−.03	−.02	−.04	−.11	.04	substantial-insubstantial; material-immaterial; visible-invisible; recorded-erased; existent-nonexistent; apparent-unapparent; identified-anonymous; revealed-concealed
66. inherent	extraneous	.24	−.09	.09	.05	−.07	−.02	.05	.00	.08	interior-exterior; intrinsic-extrinsic
67. wet	dry	.08	−.24	.06	−.07	−.06	.10	.04	.03	.08	
68. symmetrical	asymmetrical	.18	−.02	−.03	.05	−.08	−.02	.06	.01	.05	

	1	2	3	4	5	6	7	8	9	
69. competitive	−.30	.14	.02	−.05	.09	.06	−.01	.10	.13	belligerent-peaceful; contrary-agreeable; vindictive-conciliatory; obstructive-helpful; destructive-productive
70. formed	.26	.13	.10	.10	−.03	.01	−.01	−.05	.11	orderly-disorderly; consistent-inconsistent; arranged-disarranged; organized-unorganized
71. periodic	.19	−.04	−.08	.09	−.03	−.01	−.03	.02	.06	regular-irregular
72. sophisticated	.24	.03	.19	.11	.05	.04	.09	−.09	.13	blasé-astonished
73. public	.08	−.02	−.11	−.02	.08	.06	−.06	.02	.03	open-closed; overt-covert
74. humble	−.04	−.12	−.09	.01	−.03	−.06	−.06	−.07	.04	subservient-masterful; servile-haughty; modest-vain; common-noble
75. objective	.09	.14	.01	.02	.05	−.03	−.03	.11	.04	explicit-implicit
76. thrifty	−.15	.16	−.03	.06	.02	−.08	−.08	−.06	.07	stingy-lavish; cheap-expensive; abstinent-gluttonous
Per Cent Common Variance	38.00	16.54	11.22	8.20	6.20	6.20	7.37	6.24		

computer then continued to select *sober-drunk, angular-rounded, new-old, savory-tasteless,* and *aggressive-defensive* in that order; the variance taken out with the last pivot was only half of 1 per cent of the total variance and the factorization was stopped. Table 5 gives the results of this analysis. The scales in Table 5 are ordered in terms of absolute size as well as in terms of the pattern of factor loadings (thus *sane-insane* has somewhat higher loading on the pervasive evaluative factor than on the subordinate stability factor, but is located in the latter category). The increased interpretive clarity of the factors obtained in this manner will be evident in a review of the scales contributing to each.

I. Evaluative Factor. The scales having the *purest* loading on this factor, regardless of size of loading, are *good-bad* (pivot), *optimistic-pessimistic, positive-negative, complete-incomplete,* and *timely-untimely.* Inspection of the loading patterns of the scales that are chiefly evaluative in nature indicates what may be called "modes" of evaluation — clusters of scales which are dominantly evaluative, but also share sizable loading on some subsidiary factor. We may classify these as follows: *"meek goodness,"* having subsidiary negative loading on the potency factor (II), includes *altruistic, sociable, kind, grateful, clean, light* (dark), *graceful, pleasurable,* and *beautiful*; what might be called *"dynamic goodness,"* having subsidiary positive loading on the activity factor (III), includes *successful, high, meaningful, important,* and *progressive*; what might be called *"dependable goodness,"* having subsidiary loading on factor IV, includes *true, reputable, believing, wise, healthy,* and *clean* — and it should be noted that the scales assigned to factor IV are also positive on factor I; finally, what might be called *"hedonistic goodness,"* having subsidiary loading on factor VII, includes *pleasurable, beautiful, sociable,* and *meaningful* — and again the scales assigned to factor VII generally have positive loadings on factor I. These findings suggest that the general evaluative factor is itself further analyzable into a set of secondary factors — various "modes" of evaluation which are appropriate to different frames of reference or objects of judgment. Preliminary analysis in this direction has been done and will be reported briefly at a later point in this chapter.

II. Potency. The scales which have high loadings on factor II, as shown in Table 5, are *hard-soft* (pivot), *heavy-light, masculine-feminine, severe-lenient, strong-weak,* and *tenacious-yielding.* Other scales dominantly representative of the potency factor, but with less loading, are *constrained-free, constricted-spacious, serious-*

humorous, opaque-transparent, and *large-small.* Scales assigned elsewhere in terms of their loading patterns, but including considerable loading on this factor, are *cruel-kind, dirty-clean, dark-light, awkward-graceful, painful-pleasurable, ugly-beautiful, fast-slow, angular-rounded, mature-youthful, insensitive-sensitive,* and *dry-wet.* The common character of potency or "toughness" is apparent in the first terms of these pairs.

III. Oriented Activity. The collection of scales loading on the third factor seem to justify the modified label, "oriented activity," rather than plain "activity." Scales having relatively "pure" loading on this factor are *active-passive* (pivot), *excitable-calm,* and *hot-cold.* Scales having positive loading on evaluation as well as activity loading, and justifying the "oriented" characterization, are *intentional-unintentional,* *complex-simple, successful-unsuccessful, meaningful - meaningless, important - unimportant, progressive - regressive,* and *interesting-boring. Fast-slow* has subsidiary loading on the potency factor and is thus related to *sharp-blunt.* It is also to be noted that in general the scales representing this factor are not as independent of other factors as would be desirable, all tending to be somewhat positive in evaluation and potency.

IV. Stability. We turn now to the factors which appeared in the automatic operation of the square root method, after extraction of the evaluation, potency, and activity sources of variance. The fourth factor suggests another dimension of the semantic space which we have called "stability," although all of the particular scales characterizing this dimension are also biased toward good evaluation; *sober-drunk* (pivot), *stable-changeable, rational-intuitive, sane-insane, cautious-rash,* and *orthodox-heretical.* Scales assigned elsewhere in terms of loading pattern, but contributing to this stability factor, are *true-false* and *wise-foolish,* also mainly evaluative scales.

V. Tautness. This factor is labeled with considerable tentativeness. The scales assigned to this factor in the present analysis are *angular-rounded* (pivot), *straight-curved,* and *sharp-blunt.* Other scales having some loading on this factor are *masculine-feminine* and *fast-slow.* It will be recalled that the Quartimax rotation of the centroid analysis gave even a clearer factor through these same three scales (factor VI); other scales loading on the same factor in that analysis were *egocentric, light* (dark), *progressive, severe, active, intentional, fast, aggressive, competitive, sophisticated,* and *proud* which, along with *angular, straight,* and *sharp,* do seem to have a kind of tautness, alertness, and tension as a central tendency.

VI. Novelty. Evidence for this type of factor is provided by a small number of scales having quite consistent meaning. Assigned to this factor were *new-old* (pivot), *unusual-usual*, and *youthful-mature*. The only other scales having noticeable loading on this factor were *progressive-regressive* and *complex-simple*. What was referred to in the centroid rotation as a "chaos" factor seems to be broken up here into the "stability" and "novelty" factors.

VII. Receptivity. The seventh factor isolated in this analysis, which we have dubbed "receptivity," seems quite clearly identified as to nature by a large number of scales having relatively low loading, i.e., as compared with factor VI above, this is a rather diffuse factor. Scales assigned in this category are *savory-tasteless* (pivot), *colorful-colorless*, *sensitive-insensitive*, *interesting-boring*, *refreshed-weary*, and *pungent-bland*. All of these scales, with the exception of *pungent-bland*, are also positive in evaluation, suggesting that even though there may be an independent *factor* of meaning identified here, these particular scales also constitute a "mode" of evaluating. Other scales having some loading here are *sociable, pleasurable, beautiful, meaningful*, and *excitable*, which are consistent with the same interpretation.

VIII. Aggressiveness. Only one scale, the pivot item *aggressive-defensive*, has sizable loading on this factor. Slight loadings appear for *progressive, healthy, severe, fast*, and *rash*. It is probably best treated as a "specific" source of variance until further analyses strengthen the evidence for its status.

Variance Accounted For by This Factor Analysis

The proportion of total variance accounted for by the first three factors in the Thesaurus analysis — indeed, by all eight factors — is much less than in the first analysis. This is a direct result of the method of sampling employed in the Thesaurus study, in which tight clusters of scales were deliberately broken up to increase the diversity of the sampling. A moment's consideration of the factorization model will clarify this: Imagine an *n*-dimensional pincushion, with large pins representing the placement of the factors. The more closely aligned a particular scale with a factor, the greater the proportion of its reliable variance extracted, or accounted for, by that factor. Now, if the pins fall in closely related bundles through which the factor-pins are made to run, a relatively large portion of their variance will be accounted for; if, on the other hand, the pins are widely dispersed about the cushion and the same number of factor-pins are run through the space, a smaller amount of their variance will be accounted for. In the Thesaurus study we purposely "pruned" our pincushion before making the quantitative analysis, plucking out and discarding whole clumps of neighboring pins. Of course, this coin has another side too — the fact that this "pruning" procedure did reduce markedly the proportion of the total variance accounted for necessarily means that there are a large number of dimensions (factors) within which meanings can vary.

Since the same dominant factors appeared in all factor analyses, one would expect the same types of scales to show the greatest amounts of explained variance, and this is the case. Scales assigned to evaluative, potency, and activity factors show the largest reductions in original variance. Two types of scales, narrowly denotative and highly abstract (perhaps unfamiliar to many subjects), show the least reduction in original variance: In the former category, scales like *opaque-transparent, large-small, ornate-plain, near-far, wet-dry,* and *periodic-erratic* have less than 10 per cent of their variance extracted; in the latter category, scales like *rational-intuitive, heterogeneous-homogeneous, tangible-intangible, inherent-extraneous, symmetrical-asymmetrical,* and *objective-subjective* have less than 10 per cent extracted.

This leads us directly into a consideration of the scales which were not actually used in the quantitative factor analysis but which were closely related in clusters according to the judgments of a preliminary group of sorters. It is at least possible that had such clusters of similar scales been included they would have defined an independent factor. Take for example the unassigned scale *tangible-intangible* — almost none of its variance is accounted for by any of the factors extracted in this analysis, yet had the entire cluster from which it was selected (*substantial-insubstantial, material-immaterial, visible-invisible, recorded-erased, existent-nonexistent, apparent-unapparent, identified-anonymous,* and *revealed-concealed*) been included in the factor analysis, an additional factor might have been clearly specified. This assumes both that such clusters of scales would in fact "hang together" (be highly correlated) in the quantitative analysis and that they would also be independent of (uncorrelated with) other factors. A cluster like that associated with *complete-incomplete (whole-partial, sufficient-insufficient,* and *perfect-imperfect*), for example, might well fail to be highly correlated in the judgment of concepts; a cluster like that associated with *competitive-cooperative* (*belligerent-peaceful, contrary-agreeable, vindictive-conciliatory, obstructive-helpful,* and *destructive-productive*) might well describe itself as a combination of other factors, like negative evaluation and positive potency. In most cases, however, the clusters associated with scales clearly assigned to existing factors would probably represent the same factors, and hence can be used in constructing semantic measuring instruments.

ADDITIONAL FACTORIAL STUDIES

In the course of the past few years, a number of theses and other experiments have been carried out which involved factor analyses of semantic scale data. The availability of ILLIAC programs for computing correlations and doing both factor analyses and rotations has also led researchers to submit their data to factorization even where the major purposes of the investigations lay in other directions. In this section we report briefly on studies aimed directly at the factorial structure inherent in a group of adjectival scales.

Judgments of Sonar Signals by Sonar Operators

In his thesis research, Solomon (1954) had trained Navy sonar men judge the "meanings" of a varied set of passive sonar signals against a set of 50 bipolar seven-step scales. The scales were selected from the descriptive terms most frequently given spontaneously by naïve subjects listening to sonar signals, from adjectives being used in another study on aesthetic judgments (see Tucker thesis, below), from lists of recognition cues used by sonar operators, from our previous factor analyses, and from rational analysis of sensory processes in human organisms. The final list of 50 scales is shown in Table 6. Thurstone's centroid method of factoring was applied to the 50×50 matrix of correlations obtained by correlating each scale with every other scale, summations being taken over both subjects and stimuli. Table 6 presents the unrotated factor matrix. According to Solomon (p. 54), "a striking thing to note in the results . . . is that even with such a limited and unusual set of concepts such as sonar sounds, the first three factors evident in the unrotated matrix may be identified as evaluation, potency, and

Table 6

UNROTATED CENTROID FACTOR LOADINGS AND COMMUNALITIES (SOLOMON STUDY)

	I	II	III	IV	V	VI	VII	VIII	h²
1. pleasant-unpleasant	.55	.35	−.06	.13	−.07	−.24	.13	−.10	.53
2. repeated-varied	.24	.16	.24	.02	.20	.15	.04	.08	.21
3. smooth-rough	.22	.58	.02	.15	.08	−.24	−.06	−.07	.48
4. active-passive	.07	−.05	.29	.27	−.05	.23	.10	.13	.25
5. beautiful-ugly	.38	.56	.05	.12	−.16	−.18	.15	−.16	.58
6. definite-uncertain	.32	.14	.36	.26	.13	.29	.14	.02	.44
7. low-high	.52	−.45	−.28	.07	.09	−.15	.07	−.06	.60
8. powerful-weak	.43	−.49	.32	−.03	−.08	.18	.03	−.10	.58
9. steady-fluttering	.29	.03	.28	.21	.15	.16	.02	−.24	.31
10. soft-loud	.10	.41	−.37	.23	.07	−.29	.05	.11	.47
11. full-empty	.51	−.28	.29	−.06	−.13	−.06	.07	.04	.45
12. good-bad	.50	.39	.16	−.10	−.16	−.12	.10	−.10	.50
13. rumbling-whining	.60	−.48	−.19	.09	.06	−.07	.05	.05	.65
14. solid-hollow	.39	−.08	.22	.14	−.09	−.03	.12	−.08	.26
15. clear-hazy	.32	.17	.46	−.10	.03	.15	−.12	−.07	.40
16. calming-exciting	.28	.13	−.32	−.26	.21	−.10	.13	−.02	.34
17. pleasing-annoying	.61	.35	−.06	.13	−.17	−.07	.01	−.16	.57
18. large-small	.51	−.61	.05	−.09	−.08	.07	.05	−.14	.68
19. clean-dirty	.13	.51	.21	−.10	−.20	−.02	.03	.02	.37
20. resting-busy	.09	.21	−.42	−.02	.12	.02	−.04	−.15	.27
21. dull-sharp	.42	−.47	−.39	−.11	.08	−.08	−.02	.04	.58
22. deep-shallow	.54	−.45	−.01	−.13	−.08	−.03	−.06	−.04	.52
23. gliding-scraping	.30	.29	−.07	.28	.03	.02	−.25	−.08	.33
24. familiar-strange	.45	.16	.15	.21	.08	.16	.10	.09	.34
25. soft-hard	.21	.35	−.36	.02	−.07	−.07	−.13	.15	.35
26. heavy-light	.48	−.69	−.01	−.11	−.03	.04	.10	−.12	.75
27. wet-dry	.24	−.13	−.12	.33	−.11	.09	−.07	.14	.24
28. safe-dangerous	.26	.42	−.18	−.32	−.07	.08	.17	.12	.43
29. concentrated-diffuse	.21	.01	.42	−.10	.20	−.04	−.10	−.04	.28
30. pushing-pulling	.10	−.01	−.06	−.15	.08	−.09	.10	.12	.08
31. labored-easy	.09	−.58	.09	−.21	.15	−.12	.14	−.07	.46
32. dark-bright	.15	−.66	−.15	.14	.14	−.02	−.07	−.10	.54
33. even-uneven	.29	.31	.35	.09	.23	.08	−.06	.10	.38
34. loose-tight	.27	.04	−.40	.10	−.27	.20	−.18	−.15	.41
35. relaxed-tense	.38	.24	−.43	−.09	−.25	.19	−.20	−.08	.54
36. colorful-colorless	.29	.16	.22	.05	−.25	−.16	−.15	.17	.30
37. hot-cold	.04	.17	.30	−.22	−.05	−.17	−.17	−.02	.23
38. rich-thin	.49	−.17	.06	−.09	−.15	−.10	−.26	.17	.41
39. obvious-subtle	.22	.06	.34	−.24	.17	.03	−.02	.11	.27
40. wide-narrow	.54	−.50	−.08	−.09	−.03	.06	−.12	−.01	.58
41. deliberate-careless	.36	−.07	.42	−.06	.13	−.10	−.08	.21	.39
42. happy-sad	.13	.50	.14	−.11	−.19	−.03	.09	.17	.37
43. gentle-violent	.25	.50	−.40	.08	−.02	.09	.14	.14	.53
44. mild-intense	.28	.39	−.43	−.19	.04	.03	.05	.10	.47
45. rounded-angular	.41	−.13	−.17	.19	.02	.04	−.18	−.03	.29
46. slow-fast	.37	−.41	−.31	−.19	.10	.11	.11	−.14	.49
47. rugged-delicate	.36	−.56	.19	−.12	−.02	−.05	−.07	−.12	.52
48. simple-complex	.14	.25	−.17	−.28	.20	.16	.11	.12	.28
49. green-red	.07	−.03	−.28	.11	−.07	.12	.10	.18	.16
50. masculine-feminine	.46	−.56	.11	.07	.08	−.09	−.10	−.10	.58

activity." Scales loading high on factor I were *pleasant-unpleasant*, *low-high* (note the effect of sonar experience on rotation of this scale), *full-empty*, *good-bad*, *rumbling-whining*, *pleasing-annoying*, *large-small*, *deep-shallow*, and *wide-narrow*. The influence of sonar culture upon what is good is evident in the presence of scales like *wide*, *deep*, *rumbling*, and *large* among the favorably evaluative. Scales loading highest on factor II were *rough-smooth*, *large-small*, *heavy-light*, *labored-easy*, *dark-light*, *rugged-delicate*, and *masculine-feminine*. The correspondence with the potency factor is obvious. The case for the activity factor is nearly as clear; scales loading on factor III are *clear-hazy*, *busy-resting*, *sharp-dull*, *concentrated-diffuse*, *tight-loose*, *tense-relaxed*, *deliberate-careless*, *violent-gentle*, and *intense-mild*. As a matter of fact, there seems to be here the same character of "organized activity" as was noted in our own Thesaurus analysis. The results of a graphic, orthogonal rotation were, Solomon says, to bring out more clearly the special effects of the "sonar culture" of the subjects, factors like "clarity," "security," and "detection" appearing, along with "aesthetic evaluation" and "potency" as the first in magnitude.

Judgments of Representational Paintings by Non-Artists

In the course of his thesis research, Tucker (1955) had groups of artists and non-artists judge both representational and abstract paintings against 40 adjectival scales. These scales were derived from the free associations of both artists and non-artists observing color slides of paintings, from terms used spontaneously by visitors at the 1952 Contemporary Arts Festival at the University of Illinois, and from the previous factor work of the authors, to be sure that reference scales for the three major factors were also included. Since the judgments by artists and the judgments of abstract paintings involve rather special problems (see description of this work in Chapter 7), we report here the factorial results obtained when non-artists judged representational paintings. Factoring was accomplished by the D method (described in the Appendix) applied to the original ratings, i.e., to the raw scores. The obtained co-ordinates were squared and divided by the original vector lengths squared; therefore, the loadings in Table 7 are analogous to the proportion of variance of each variable explained by each of the first three factors. These three factors in aesthetic judgments by non-artists are readily identifiable as *activity*, *evaluation*, and

Table 7

FACTOR LOADINGS FOR NON-ARTISTS ON SEVEN REPRESENTATIONAL PAINTINGS (TUCKER STUDY)

Scale	Factor I (Activity)	Factor II (Evaluation)	Factor III (Potency)
hot-cold	.64	−.08	.00
pleasant-unpleasant	−.02	.59	−.60
lush-austere	.64	−.16	−.23
vibrant-still	.91	−.08	.29
repetitive-varied	−.81	−.48	.29
happy-sad	.34	.38	−.71
chaotic-ordered	.55	−.84	.00
smooth-rough	−.57	.83	.00
superficial-profound	.18	−.72	−.58
passive-active	−1.00	.00	.00
blatant-muted	.80	−.26	.11
meaningless-meaningful	−.33	−.79	.28
simple-complex	−.66	.55	−.48
relaxed-tense	−.57	.39	−.54
obvious-subtle	−.23	.80	.01
serious-humorous	−.22	−.05	.97
violent-gentle	.41	−.37	.69
sweet-bitter	−.32	.23	−.67
static-dynamic	−.78	.19	−.53
clear-hazy	−.04	.85	.38
unique-commonplace	.50	.22	.72
emotional-rational	.67	.09	.40
ugly-beautiful	.12	−.51	.42
dull-sharp	−.53	−.34	−.74
sincere-insincere	.18	.80	.34
rich-thin	.56	.35	.46
bad-good	−.33	−.77	−.27
intimate-remote	.09	.45	−.46
masculine-feminine	.31	.13	.76
vague-precise	−.04	−.84	−.43
ferocious-peaceful	.39	−.46	.58
soft-hard	−.39	.09	−.84
usual-unusual	−.52	−.16	−.70
controlled-accidental	.00	.80	.34
wet-dry	−.37	−.89	.35
strong-weak	.37	.46	.81
stale-fresh	−.45	−.54	−.51
formal-informal	−.58	−.40	.24
calming-exciting	−.54	.26	−.55
full-empty	.60	.31	.52

potency, even though the particular scales contributing certainly vary from those obtained previously. Scales having highest loading on the activity factor are *active-passive, vibrant-still, varied-repetitive, blatant-muted,* and *dynamic-static;* scales having highest loading on the evaluative factor here are *dry-wet* ("all wet"?), *clear-hazy, precise-vague, ordered-chaotic, smooth-rough, controlled-accidental, sincere-insincere, obvious-subtle, meaningful-meaningless,* and *good-bad;* scales loading highest on the potency factor are *serious-humorous, hard-soft, strong-weak, masculine-feminine,* and *sharp-dull.* It is evident that "goodness" in representational paintings is identified with "orderliness" and "clarity" rather than with the more abstractly moral attributes with which we are familiar from our previous more general analyses.

ANALYSIS OF THE GENERAL EVALUATIVE FACTOR

As early in our work as our inspection of the correlational matrix leading to factor analysis I, it was apparent to us that the evaluative dimension of the semantic space was a very general one — a sort of sheath with leaves unfolding toward various other directions of the total space. In fact, at that time (1951) two of the authors made up a table of evaluative clusters on the basis of the correlations of evaluative scales with a set of reference scales (*good-bad, strong-weak, sharp-dull, heavy-light, hot-cold, angular-rounded,* and *active-passive*) which seemed relatively independent of each other. One cluster which we called "morally evaluative" (*clean, tasty, sacred, fair, clear, valuable*) had sizable negative correlations with *heavy;* another which we called "aesthetically evaluative" (*pleasant, sweet* (sour), *sweet* (bitter), *nice,* and *fragrant*) had sizable negative correlations with both *heavy* and *angular;* one which we called "socially evaluative" (*honest, beautiful, white, healthy, brave, full, rich,* and *high*) had sizable positive correlations with *strong;* and another which we called "emotionally evaluative" (*soft* (loud), *calm, peaceful, relaxed, smooth,* and *bland*) had negative correlations with *hot* and *active.* Additional evidence for such a breakdown of the "general" evaluative factor into more "specific" evaluative factors was found in the Thesaurus analysis, where we were able to classify most evaluative scales into categories like "meek goodness," "dynamic goodness," "dependable goodness," and "hedonistic goodness" in terms of their loading patterns.

In another study, the intercorrelations among the 34 scales with the highest loadings on the evaluative factor of the Thesaurus study were factored. By using only evaluative scales, it was hoped to minimize the effect of other factors (like "potency" and "activity") and permit more purely evaluative clusters to emerge as factors. Factoring was accomplished with the principal axes technique.

The first factor was, as would be expected, a general evaluative factor on which all scales were highly and positively loaded. Loadings ranged from .78 for *good-bad* down to .36 for *intentional-unintentional* on this factor. Scales with loadings of .30 or greater on other factors were: *important-unimportant, meaningful-meaningless, interesting-boring, successful-unsuccessful, dark-light, cruel-kind,* and *dirty-clean,* all on factor II; on factor III, *grateful-ungrateful, sober-drunk, sane-insane, awkward-graceful, weary-refreshed, ugly-beautiful;* factor IV, *savory-tasteless, sensitive-insensitive, interesting-boring, meaningful-meaningless;* and factor V, *complete-incomplete, altruistic-egotistic, naïve-sophisticated, sick-healthy, regressive-progressive.*

Apparently scales defined as evaluative do produce factors beyond the general evaluative factor. An interesting possibility presents itself in this last analysis: the tapping of ambivalent judgments, i.e., of making simultaneous judgment of good and bad. Factor II, for example, presents *successful* and *meaningful,* judgments regarded as favorable, as positively related to *cruel* and *dirty,* judgments which are unfavorable. The actions of an infantryman, for example, in saving his own life, may be successful and quite meaningful, however cruel and dirty the means by which this success is achieved. This seeming ambivalence is apparent in another study of attitudes toward political concepts which will be discussed in more detail in the next chapter.

THE SEMANTIC SPACE

What have we learned about the dimensionality of the semantic space from this series of factor analyses? For one thing, it is clear that it is a multidimensional space. In every analysis more than three factors have been contributing to the meaningful judgments by subjects. It is also clear that these N factors or dimensions are not equally important in mediating judgments, or perhaps better, are not equally used by subjects in differentiating among the things judged. Three factors appear to be dominant, appearing in most of the analyses made and in roughly the same orders of magnitude — *evaluation, potency,* and *activity.* However, it is also evident the functional semantic space is to some degree modifiable in terms of what kinds of concepts are being judged, i.e., the relative importance and relationship among factors may vary with the frame of reference of judgments. Certainly, specific scales may change their meaning, in the factorial composition sense, as a function of the concept being judged. And finally, it is clear that what we have called the three dominant factors do not exhaust the dimensions along which meaningful judgments are differentiated. Let us look into some of these conclusions more carefully.

1 *Meanings Vary Multidimensionally.* Many of the phenomena for which psychologists and others have devised measuring instruments seem to be handled satisfactorily on a unidimensional basis — intelligence, manifest anxiety, attitude, and so on are examples. Some attempts to treat meaning in the same manner were noted in the first chapter (e.g., Mosier, 1941; Noble, 1952). Our own research has demonstrated repeatedly that, when subjects differentiate the meanings of concepts, variance along certain scales (e.g., activity scales) may be quite independent of variation along other scales (e.g., evaluation). To put the matter yet another way, some of the things judged "good" may also be judged "strong" (e.g., HERO) but other things judged equally "good" may also be judged "weak" (e.g., PACIFIST). If meanings vary multidimensionally, then any adequate measuring instrument must encompass this fact.

2 *Stability of the Evaluative, Potency, and Activity Factors.* In every instance in which a widely varied sample of concepts has been used, or the concept variable eliminated as in forced-choice among the scales, the same three factors have emerged in roughly the same order of magnitude. A pervasive *evaluative factor* in human judgment regularly appears first and accounts for approximately half to three-quarters of the extractable variance. Thus the *attitudinal* variable in human thinking (see Chapter 5), based as it is on the bedrock of rewards and punishments both achieved and anticipated, appears to be primary — when asked if she'd like to see the *Dinosaur* in the museum, the young lady from Brooklyn first wanted to know, "Is it good or is it bad?" The second dimension of the semantic space to appear is usually the *potency factor,* and this typically accounts for approximately half as much variance as the first factor — this is concerned with power and the things

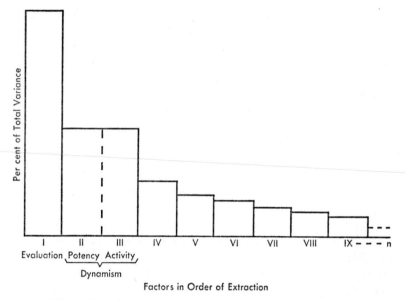

Fig. 4. Relative importance of semantic space dimensions.

associated with it, size, weight, toughness, and the like. The third dimension, usually about equal to or a little smaller in magnitude than the second, is the *activity factor* — concerned with quickness, excitement, warmth, agitation and the like. And when other factors can be extracted and identified they typically, again, account for no more than half the amount of variance attributable to the second and third factors.

The relative importance of various dimensions of the semantic space, described in Figure 4, seems to represent our findings. In other words, the differentiation among concepts in terms of their evaluation is about twice as fine as differentiation in terms of their potency or activity, which in turn are about twice as fine as differentiations on the basis of subsequent factors. As noted earlier, one may express the same fact about human thinking in terms of the relative use made of these dimensions of meaningful discrimination. Considering the variety of scales, concepts, subjects, and methods of collecting data that have been employed in this series of analyses, the regularity with which this factorial picture repeats itself is impressive.

3 *Modifiability of the Semantic Space.* When the sample of things being judged is restricted in some fashion, the nature and order of

magnitude of the factors may change. For example, when judgments are limited to sociopolitical concepts (people and policies), there seems to be a coalescence of the second and third factors into what might be called a "dynamism factor"; this was apparent in a study of the 1952 presidential election, in a study of ethnic stereotypes, and in a cross-cultural (and cross-language) study of political concepts relating to the Far East. It is as if things in this frame of reference that are "strong" are also necessarily "active" while things that are "weak" are also necessarily "passive." We also noted in factorization of the judgments of a mental patient (case of triple personality) that there was nearly a restriction of the semantic space to a single dimension, combining "good," "strong," and "active." An hypothesis to be explored here is this: The greater the emotional or attitudinal loading of the set of concepts being judged, the greater the tendency of the semantic framework to collapse into a single, combined dimension. Other types of interaction probably operate as well: When, for example, the sample of concepts is limited to aesthetic objects (paintings, in this case), a type of activity factor becomes relatively more prominent. This problem of concept-scale interaction will be considered more fully, in connection with factor analyses done on single concepts, in terms of the comparability of the measuring instrument across concepts (Chapter 4).

That the factorial composition of particular scales can change with the concept being judged against it has already been amply demonstrated. While *high-low* is parallel with *good-bad* in judging social concepts (and in our general analyses), it switches direction when sonar signals are the objects of judgment — presumably it comes to mean *high-pitch* vs. *low-pitch* in this context, the latter being more pleasant.

4 *Dimensionality of the Semantic Space.* It was made particularly clear in the Thesaurus analysis that the three major factors, evaluation, potency, and activity, do not exhaust the ways in which meanings may vary. Here a broad sample was guaranteed both by discarding highly similar scales and by increasing the total number of scales entering into the analysis. Several additional factors could be tentatively identified: a *stability factor*, a *tautness factor*, a *novelty factor*, and a *receptivity factor*. These subsidiary factors are much less clearly defined, have not been checked for reliability, and hence should be held as hypotheses for further testing. However, their appearance along with the large proportion of total

variance remaining unaccounted for indicates that the semantic space for concepts-in-general has a large number of dimensions. We believe that from this point onward the best way to more rigorously identify additional factors will be to deliberately test for them, i.e., by inserting presumptive clusters in a matrix of reference scales for known factors and seeing if, in the judgment process, they both correlate highly with each other and lowly with other factors. The existence of a large number of dimensions in the total semantic space is not disastrous as far as measurement is concerned; this is because these added dimensions account for relatively little of the total variance.

3

**THE SEMANTIC DIFFERENTIAL
AS A MEASURING INSTRUMENT**

The factor analysis of meaningful judgments, although of considerable theoretical interest, is a means to an end rather than an end in itself. It is a necessary step in the development of efficient instruments for measuring the meaning variable in human behavior. In this chapter we discuss the mechanics of constructing and applying the semantic differential as a measuring device. We also will describe the kinds of information yielded by this instrument and consider various ways and means of analyzing and interpreting this information. Finally, as an illustration of the application of this method to a practical social problem, we will report a study made of the 1952 presidential election and some ideas about human thinking that it generated.

CONSTRUCTION AND ADMINISTRATION OF A SEMANTIC DIFFERENTIAL

Although we often refer to *the* semantic differential as if it were some kind of "test," having some definite set of items and a specific score, this is not the case. To the contrary, it is a very general way of getting at a certain type of information, a highly *generalizable technique of measurement* which must be adapted to the requirement of each research problem to which it is applied. There are no standard concepts and no standard scales; rather, the concepts and scales used in a particular study depend upon the purposes of the research. Standardization, and hence comparability, lies in the allocation of concepts to a common semantic space defined by a common set of general factors, despite variability in the particular concepts and scales employed. It is true, of course, that in some areas of measurement, e.g., psychotherapy or attitude, a particular form of the differential, with standardized concepts and scales, may be developed, but there is no general "semantic differential test" as such.

Content of a Semantic Differential

Selection of Concepts. We use the term "concept" in a very general sense to refer to the "stimulus" to which the subject's checking operation is a terminal "response." What may function as a concept in this broad sense is practically infinite, and in our own work to be described throughout this book the reader will encounter a considerable variety. Concepts are often verbal; they are more often printed than spoken, because of convenience in presentation, but we have also used spoken terms. Because of the structure of English, the concepts are more likely to be nouns like FIRE and BABY than other parts of speech, but we have also used adjectives and plan to study verbs as concepts in some future research. Although single "words" most often serve, a unitary semantic concept may require a noun phrase, e.g., MY IDEAL SELF. But nonverbal concepts can also be differentiated; the investigator may be interested in the meanings of TAT pictures (see pp. 237-38); or Rorschach cards (see pp. 238-39) as stimuli; he may be interested in the meanings of aesthetic stimuli, such as representational and abstract paintings (see pp. 291-95) or solid sculptured abstracts (see pp. 301-2); or he may wish to investigate the connotative meanings of sonar signals (see pp. 66-68). It is evident that the concepts judged against a semantic differential may be as varied in nature as may be the modes of signs, and the type selected depends chiefly upon the interests of the investigator.

It is the nature of the problem, then, that chiefly defines the class and form of concept to be selected. Interest in identification (see pp. 251-54) dictates one sampling area; interest in ethnocentrism dictates another (see pp. 222-23). Usually, however, time and subject limitations do not permit complete coverage of all the relevant concepts in a given area, so the investigator must sample. The problems here are no different than elsewhere — the objects of judgment should, ideally, be both relevant to and representative of the area of research interest. Sometimes the investigator may actually make a sampling analysis, but more often (in our experience, at least) he simply uses "good judgment" with respect to his problem. In exercising "good judgment" here, the investigator will usually (a) try to select concepts for the meanings of which he

can expect considerable *individual differences,* since this is likely to
augment the amount of information gained from a limited number
of concepts, (b) try to select concepts having a single, *unitary
meaning* for the individual (e.g., MY IDEAL SELF, but not CASE or
BUTTERFLIES AND MOTHS), since otherwise the subject may vacillate
in what is being judged, and (c) try to select concepts which can
be expected to be *familiar* to all of his subjects, since unfamiliar
concepts for some subjects will produce a "spurious" regression
toward the middle of the scales.

Selection of Scales. Since the purpose of the factorial work described in Chapter 2 was to reduce the great variety of potentially
usable scales of judgment to some limited but representative number, the process of choosing scales is necessarily more structured
than that of choosing concepts. Ideally we should like to use one
specific scale to represent each of the factors or dimensions of the
semantic space, this scale being both perfectly aligned with or
loaded on its factor and perfectly reliable. In practice, however, since
specific scales are neither perfectly aligned with factors nor perfectly reliable, we use a small sample of closely related scales to
represent each factor, deriving a score from their average which is
assumed to be both more representative and more reliable than
scores on individual scales. These average scores we call *factor
scores.*

The first criterion for selecting scales is thus their *factorial
composition* — we usually select about three scales to represent each
factor, these being maximally loaded on that factor and minimally
on others. The question probably arises as to why — when we
know that the various factors have unequal weight in meaningful
judgments — do we not represent these factors in proportion to
their weight? What we do is to provide the subject with a balanced
space which he may actually use as he sees fit; if he makes more
discriminative use of the evaluative factor relative to others this
will show up in his data (in an elongation of his space along this
dimension), but he is not forced by the sample of scales to do this.

Another criterion in scale selection is *relevance* to the concepts
being judged. For example, in judging a concept like ADLAI STEVEN-
SON, one evaluative scale like *beautiful-ugly* may be comparatively
irrelevant while another like *fair-unfair* may be highly relevant;
on the other hand, just the reverse would be true for judging paintings. Since irrelevant concept-scale pairings usually yield neutral
or "4" judgments, their inclusion reduces the amount of informa-

tion gained with a given number of scales. There is here, however, the question of subtlety or masking of the purposes of the experiment: in certain clinical uses, for example, one may deliberately use scales which are only relevant via metaphor, e.g., judging the significant persons in the patient's life against scales like *hot-cold*, *hard-soft*, and *tasty-distasteful* rather than against scales like *passionate-frigid*, *aggressive-timid*, and *pleasant-unpleasant* in order to get more valid data. Again, the purpose of the investigator dictates the choice.

Yet another criterion governing the selection of scales is their *semantic stability* for the concepts and subjects in a particular study. Whereas *high-low* can be expected to be stable across a set of sonar signals, it would not across a set of concepts which included both auditory and social concepts. Similarly, a scale like *large-small* is liable to strict denotative usage in judging physical objects like BOULDER and ANT, but is likely to be used connotatively in judging concepts like SIN and TRUMAN. Yet another criterion — and one for which we do not as yet have adequate data — is that scales should be linear between polar opposites and pass through the origin. One example of nonlinearity we have discovered is that the scale *rugged-delicate* is not linear with respect to evaluation — both terms, when used separately, tend to be favorable in meaning, and hence this scale cannot both pass through the origin and be linear. At present we merely assume that the scales defined by familiar and common opposites have these properties, but research on the problem needs to be done.

One final comment on the use of scales in forms of the semantic differential is in order. Often scales of unknown factorial composition are highly relevant to a particular problem, e.g., the scale *liberal-conservative* in a study of political concepts. Such scales may, of course, be used and their factorial composition determined directly from the data of the experiment (either through factor analysis of the results or less rigorously from inspection of its correlations with other scales) — but in this case it is necessary to include standard reference scales in the total set. It is also true, of course, that the three dominant factors we have isolated do not exhaust the semantic space, and therefore dimensions highly significant for differentiating the concepts in a particular study might be lost entirely if one stuck to only evaluative, potency, and activity scales. Furthermore, one of the purposes of a specific study may be to determine how different subjects use certain scales of variable semantic significance: for example, the investigator may want to know whether high ethnocentrics feel that *conservatism* is *good* and *liberalism* is *bad*, and *vice-versa* for low ethnocentrics; *liberal-conservative* may then be included among the scales and its relation with other scales of known evaluative composition determined for both high and low ethnocentrics. In other words, the ways in which subjects structure scales of judgment may itself be the focus of research interest. In conclusion then, although there are, we believe, standard *factors* of judgment, the particular scales which may, in any given research problem, best represent these factors, are variable and must be carefully selected by the experimenter to suit his purposes.

Administration of a Semantic Differential

Amount of Material. Experimenters are usually limited in the amount of time they can demand of their subjects, the funds available for handling data once it is collected, and so on. It is therefore useful to know in advance about how much time it takes subjects to complete differentials of varying size and how much data is accumulated. What we call an *item* is the pairing of a particular concept with a particular scale, and each subject's judgment of such an item provides one bit of information — in the ordinary sense, not the Information Theory sense, of course. The number of items on any form of the semantic differential is simply the number of scales times the number of concepts, and the number of bits of information which must be handled statistically will therefore be equal to the number of scales times the number of concepts times the number of subjects. Based on our own experience over the past several years, even the slowest college student subjects can be expected to make judgments at the rate of at least 10 items per minute, and most come closer to 20 items per minute once they get under way. This means that one should allow about 10 to 15 minutes for a 100-item test (e.g., 10 concepts times 10 scales), about an hour for a 400-item test (40 concepts times 10 scales, or the equivalent). These time estimates are only rough approximations, of course, and will vary somewhat with the types of concepts, scales, and subjects being used. Nevertheless, this means that a very large amount of information is being collected per unit time from the individual subject — rather than a single measure being obtained (e.g., as in taking an intelligence test), several factor scores are

being obtained on each of N concepts. The experimenter will therefore adjust the amount of material in the differential to the limitations in his own situation.

Form of Differential. We have used two types of graphic (scale)
differentials and one latency procedure. In the latter, the scale to be
used is projected on a screen as a pair of polar terms, then the
concept with the scale, and the time required for the subject to
react by moving a lever toward one or the other of the polar terms
is automatically recorded. Since this method is applicable only to
one subject at a time, and since the film-recorded data first needs to
be transformed, we have only used this for special research problems on the nature of the method itself. The two graphic-scale
methods, which we may call Form I and Form II and which are
both applicable to groups of any size, differ chiefly in the way in
which concepts are paired with scales. Form I presents items as
follows:

LADY rough ____:____:____:____:____:____:____ smooth
  ME   fair ____:____:____:____:____:____:____ unfair, etc.

Each capitalized concept appears on the same line as the scale
against which it is being judged, and the items are ordered in such
a way that a maximum number of different concepts and scales
occur between the repetitions of each concept and scale (i.e., concepts and scales are rotated against each other). This was the form
we used in our original factor analytic work. It has the advantage
of minimizing the possibility of any "halo" effect, since the subject
is kept shifting from concept to concept and since he cannot easily
compare his judgments on one scale with those on another. But it
has the disadvantage that what is actually being judged (the meaning of the concept) may change from time to time. Form II uses
one sheet of paper for each concept, with all of its judgments elicited successively, e.g.,

LADY

rough ____:____:____:____:____:____:____ smooth
  fair ____:____:____:____:____:____:____ unfair
active ____:____:____:____:____:____:____ passive, etc.

Here the ordering of concepts for different subjects may be varied,
but the form of the differential itself is constant (i.e., the same
ordering of scales and a constant polarity direction for each scale).
This form has the advantage that it is both easy to mimeograph
(one standard sheet, with various concepts simply rubber-stamped
or hand-printed at the top) and easy to score (with cut-out card-

board forms for each factor). It also has the distinct advantages of greater constancy of meaning in the thing being judged and of being much more satisfying to the subjects of the experiment. In both forms, it should be added, the scales representing the same factor are alternated in polarity direction (e.g., *fair-unfair* but *worthless-valuable*) to prevent the formation of position preferences and the order of factors represented is rotated (as illustrated above).

Are there any differences in results to be expected from use of one or the other of these two graphic forms? Does a "halo" effect operate in one but not the other? Some aspects of this problem were studied[1] experimentally as part of another piece of research. The two alternate forms, with eight concepts (RADIO COMMERCIALS, MARILYN MONROE, IDEAL HAND LOTION, SOFT TOUCH HAND LOTION, ROMANCE, HAND LOTION I BUY, SCIENTIFIC DISCOVERIES, and TONI PRODUCTS) being judged against ten scales (*good-bad, tasty-distasteful, serious-humorous, expensive-cheap, pleasing-annoying, high class-low class, interesting-boring, believable-unbelievable, important-trivial,* and *active-passive*), were given in different orders to the same subjects at the same sitting. For each of the 80 items, differences between the mean scale positions on the two forms taken across the 50 subjects were tested for significance by the *t*-test for correlated data. Only three of the 80 tests were significant at the 5 per cent level, which is about what would be expected by chance on the null hypothesis. There is no evidence here for differences between these two graphic forms.

Instructions to Subjects. With no evidence to favor one form over the other, Form II has most frequently been used because of its greater convenience to the investigator and satisfaction to the subject. The sample instruction form given below assumes this form of differential. In essence, instructions to the subject include (1) orientation to the general nature of the task, (2) the significance of the scale positions and how to mark them, and (3) the attitude to be taken toward the task (speed, first impressions, but true impressions). Certain details of instruction — e.g., that he will see color advertisements on the screen before him to judge — vary from experiment to experiment, of course.

Typical Instructions

The purpose of this study is to measure the *meanings* of certain things

---

[1] By Dr. Jean S. Kerrick at the University of Illinois in 1954.

to various people by having them judge them against a series of descriptive scales. In taking this test, please make your judgments on the basis of what these things mean *to you*. On each page of this booklet you will find a different concept to be judged and beneath it a set of scales. You are to rate the concept on each of these scales in order.

Here is how you are to use these scales:

If you feel that the concept at the top of the page is *very closely related* to one end of the scale, you should place your check-mark as follows:

fair __×__:_____:_____:_____:_____:_____:_____ unfair

OR

fair _____:_____:_____:_____:_____:_____:__×__ unfair

If you feel that the concept is *quite closely related* to one or the other end of the scale (but not extremely), you should place your check-mark as follows:

strong _____:__×__:_____:_____:_____:_____:_____ weak

OR

strong _____:_____:_____:_____:_____:__×__:_____ weak

If the concept seems *only slightly related* to one side as opposed to the other side (but is not really neutral), then you should check as follows:

active _____:_____:__×__:_____:_____:_____:_____ passive

OR

active _____:_____:_____:_____:__×__:_____:_____ passive

The direction toward which you check, of course, depends upon which of the two ends of the scale seem most characteristic of the thing you're judging.

If you consider the concept to be *neutral* on the scale, both sides of the scale *equally associated* with the concept, or if the scale is *completely irrelevant*, unrelated to the concept, then you should place your check-mark in the middle space:

safe _____:_____:_____:__×__:_____:_____:_____ dangerous

IMPORTANT: (1) Place your check-marks *in the middle of spaces*, not on the boundaries:

THIS   NOT THIS

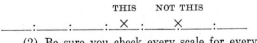

        (2) Be sure you check every scale for every concept — *do not omit any*.

        (3) Never put more than one check-mark on a single scale.

Sometimes you may feel as though you've had the same item before on the test. This will not be the case, so *do not look back and forth* through the items. Do not try to remember how you checked similar items earlier in the test. *Make each item a separate and independent judgment.* Work at fairly high speed through this test. Do not worry or puzzle over individual items. It is your first impressions, the immediate "feelings" about the items, that we want. On the other hand, please do not be careless, because we want your true impressions.

Problem of Contextual Contamination. "Central tendency" effects and "anchoring" effects are familiar phenomena in psychophysical experiments. When a subject has been judging a set of relatively light weights, the judgments of "neutral" tends to shift toward the middle range of the set, and if a relatively heavy weight is inserted, it is now judged "heavy" where it would ordinarily not be. Will such an effect operate in our judgmental situation, or will the subject's long past history of meaningful comparisons and use of quantifiers like "extremely," "quite," and "slightly" maintain stability despite the presence of other concepts in the set being judged? In either Form I or Form II, the subject judges a set of different concepts — does the meaning attributed to a particular concept depend upon the meanings of the other concepts with which it appears on the test form? The assumption of independence between the concepts judged on the same form of a differential is a basic one, for otherwise the "meaning" as measured would vary with every sample of concepts in which a given concept was imbedded.

One study[2] tested the validity of the independence assumption in the following way: A set of "test" concepts (FOREIGNER, PLANS, MASCULINITY, and MY ACTUAL SELF) was imbedded in three different conceptual contexts and judged by three different groups of 15 subjects each. In one of these contexts all of the other concepts were extremely positive on the evaluative dimension (BEAUTY, CLEANLINESS, KINDNESS, HONESTY, FRAGRANCE, and FAIRNESS); in another, all of the other concepts were extremely potent (STEEL, ARMED FORCES, OAK TREE, BEAR, FORTRESS, and THE SEA); in the third context, all of the other concepts were extremely active (ELECTRICITY, MOTION, SPEED, BIRD, BREEZE, FISH). The three scales used in this study were *valuable-worthless* (evaluative), *strong-weak* (potency), and *active-passive* (activity). To the extent that the subjects' frames of reference are not stable and independent of the immediate context, one would expect the meanings of the neutral concepts to be "pushed" away from the direction of the loading, e.g., MY ACTUAL SELF should be less good in the first context, less potent in the second, and less active in the third. In each case, the other two conditions served as control, since the bias was exerted on only one

---

[2] Conducted by Dr. E. Aiken at the University of Illinois in 1953.

factor in each context. The results of this study showed no significant differences in the scalar locations of the test concepts as a function of the context in which they were imbedded. Although this experiment was not extensive, it was a case of extreme bias — ordinarily in making up a sample of concepts for a differential we try to balance off good concepts with bad, strong with weak, and so forth — and the fact that no effects were produced strengthens our assumption that judgments of the semantic differential are relatively independent of the immediate conceptual context.

The Use of Seven Alternatives. The question may well have arisen in the reader's mind as to why we happened to choose seven-step scales rather than five or nine or eleven and so on. Over a large number of different subjects in many different experiments it has been found that with seven alternatives all of them tend to be used and with roughly, if not exactly, equal frequencies. As part of some early research (see Stagner and Osgood, 1946), scales having various intervals were tried out on college students: when more than seven steps were used (e.g., nine steps, where "quite" is broken into "considerably" and "somewhat" on both sides of the neutral position), it was found that all three discriminative positions on each side had much lower frequencies; on the other hand, when only five steps were allowed (e.g., "extremely," "somewhat," and "neutral"), college students, at least, expressed irritation at being unable to indicate "slightly" as different from "quite a bit." This does not mean that there are no individual differences here — in fact, this is one of the interesting empirical problems with which we've done very little. In the study with Stagner, for example, samples of American Legion members were obtained, and it was noted that they had a definite tendency to use only three positions — all, or nothing, or neither (1, 4, 7, on the seven-step scales). Grade-school children seem to work better with a five-step scale, and there is probably some relation here to intelligence differences. Bopp's study (1955) with schizophrenics showed that these patients used the finely discriminative positions of seven-step scales (2, 3, 5, and 6) significantly less frequently than their controls.

ANALYSIS OF SEMANTIC DIFFERENTIAL DATA

The raw data obtained with the semantic differential are a collection of check-marks against bipolar scales. To each of the seven

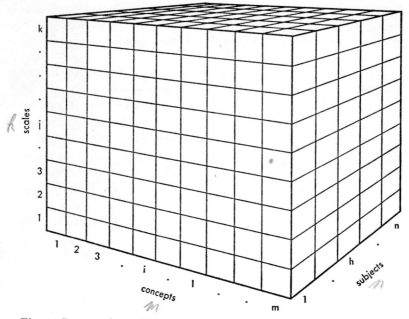

Fig. 5. Rectangular solid of data generated by the semantic differential.

positions on these scales we arbitrarily assign a digit. These digits may be either 1, 2, 3, 4, 5, 6, and 7 or $+3$, $+2$, $+1$, 0, -1, -2, -3. For most of the mathematical treatments to be described, the choice here makes no difference; the set from $+3$ to -3 has the heuristic advantage of fixing an origin in the center of the semantic space, which corresponds to the neutral "4" position on the scales, as well as reflecting the bipolar nature of the scales we use. A person's score on an item is the digit corresponding to the scale position he checks. If there are k scales and m concepts, each subject generates a $k \times m$ score matrix. If there is a group of n such subjects, a $k \times m \times n$ matrix of scores is generated. This entire set of raw scores may be represented as a rectangular solid as shown in Figure 5. Each cell in this matrix of data represents the judgment of a particular concept against a particular scale by a particular subject; each of the n slices represents the complete judgments of a single subject; each of the m columns represents the judgments by all subjects against all scales for a single concept; and each row represents the complete data for each of the k scales, all subjects' ratings of all concepts against this scale. Another source of variation not shown is *time:*

the entire test may be replicated on the same subjects t times, generating a four dimensional data matrix, each three dimensional matrix as shown here representing a testing at a given t and comparisons being possible across these times. These digit scores are the basic data from which all operations and analyses follow.

In many operations we deal with means or averages. Conceptually, this involves *summations* over our four dimensional matrix of scores, i.e., collapsing the matrix along one axis or another. Since the purpose of the instrument is differentiation in terms of scales, we never sum completely over the k scales; we do sum partially over this dimension, however, to obtain *factor scores*. It will be recalled that usually the k scales are organized into several factorial categories, evaluative, potency, etc., the scales within which are highly similar as to semantic content; we may sum and average over the scales within each category, yielding k' factors scores for each concept judged by each subject. When we are interested in groups, or cultural data rather than individual data, we sum and average over the n subjects, yielding a $k' \times m$ matrix of averaged factor scores. Although we have usually employed the *mean* to represent such group measures, there are some reasons for favoring the median or even the mode in dealing with semantic data. Except for factor analytic work where we are interested in the relations among the scales (see Chapter 2), we seldom sum over the m concepts—in most research problems it is the differences and similarities among and between the concepts in which we are interested. If a series of tests have been made, we may wish to sum and average over the t times.

Descriptive Measures

The Meaning of a Concept. Although what follows applies to any number of scales, we shall assume for simplicity of presentation that only three factors are represented in the set of k scales (e.g., evaluation, potency, and activity) and that the scores on these scales have been summed and averaged to $k' = 3$ factor scores. A single subject, then, produces a matrix of the order $3 \times m$, representing his judgments of each of m concepts in terms of three semantic factors. This would be the data in one slice of the solid facing the reader. *The meaning of a concept to an individual subject is defined operationally as the set of factor scores in the column representing that concept.* If we collapse our rectangular data solid

Table 8

FACTOR SCORES OF RATINGS OF 10 CONCEPTS BY ONE SUBJECT

		Evaluation	Potency	Activity
A	QUICKSAND	−3	3	−3
B	WHITE ROSE BUDS	3	−3	−3
C	DEATH	−3	1	−3
D	HERO	3	3	3
E	METHODOLOGY	3	0	2
F	FATE	−1	0	−2
G	VIRILITY	2	3	2
H	GENTLENESS	2	−2	−3
I	SUCCESS	2	3	2
J	SLEEP	2	0	−2

along the subject dimension by summing and averaging over subjects, another matrix of the order $3 \times m$ is generated in which each
column contains the mean (or median, or modal) factor scores for
each of m concepts as judged by the group. *The meaning of a concept in the culture is defined operationally as the set of averaged
factor scores in the column representing that concept.* The average
factor scores for a group are associated with some measure of dispersion or variability (e.g., the standard deviation); this measure
is presumably an index of the consistency of the meaning of that
concept in the culture.

In Table 8 we give for illustration a 3×10 matrix of factor
scores representing the actual judgments of ten concepts by a single
individual. Each factor was represented by three scales, and the
score in each cell is here the median judgment taken over the three
scales in each factor. For this subject we can say that WHITE ROSE
BUDS are *good, impotent,* and *passive* (+3, −3, −3), that HERO
is *good, potent,* and *active* (+3, +3, +3), that FATE is *somewhat
bad, indifferently potent,* and *quite passive* (−1, 0, −2), and so
on. If the numbers in the matrix had been averaged over a group
of subjects, these descriptions would have characterized the cultural
meanings of these concepts (assuming, of course, that the group
was representative of the culture as a whole). Such descriptions may
seem rather gross — and in a sense, because of the limited number
of factors sampled, they are — but it should be kept in mind that
even a $k' = 3$ system with seven alternatives for each k' yields a
total space of 343 regions.

This definition of meaning as a set or profile of factor scores, while accurate in terms of measurement procedures, is conceptually clumsy and inefficient. One may compare concepts in terms of their positions on single factors at a time and compare subjects' judgments of the same concept similarly, but this is about all. Let us return to our spatial model. The meaning of a concept for a subject or a group can be also defined, and more efficiently and usefully, as that point in the semantic space identified by its coordinates on several factors. In this representation we can "see" the similarity between various concepts on all factors simultaneously in terms of their closeness in the space. In this model, the consistency of the cultural meaning of a concept would be represented by the dispersion of individual subject points about their central tendency, i.e., a "cloud" of varying concentration in the space.

Similarity and Difference in Meaning. Being able to "see" the relative distances between concept-points in the semantic space is not the same thing as being able to express these similarities and differences in meaning quantitatively. The most common question asked in science concerns similarity and difference, i.e., comparison. In our own case, we wish to be able to say quantatively that concept A is more or less similar in meaning to concept C than is concept B. We wish to be able to measure a change in meaning over time, to be able to say that one group of subjects differentiates more between the meanings of two concepts than another group, and so on. Such relations among concepts are describable in a very efficient way in terms of our geometrical model, which we shall now treat in some detail.

1 *The Semantic Space.* Each column in a $k \times m$ matrix can be considered a set of k coordinates fixing each of the m concepts as a point in a space. Each coordinate gives the distance of a concept from the origin in one direction or the other along an axis which represents one of the k scales or factors. These axes are placed in a mutually orthogonal relation to each other and are made to intersect at the origin, this origin being defined as the neutral positions on the scales (0, 0, 0 in the $+3$ to -3 numbering system). The 3×10 matrix of Table 8, for example, generates three such axes, one for each of the factors. The coordinates of QUICKSAND are -3, $+3$, -3 (*bad, strong,* and *passive*). This indicates that a point representing QUICKSAND is situated in the three dimensional space defined by the three axes such that it is -3 units from the origin along an axis representing evaluation, $+3$ units from the origin

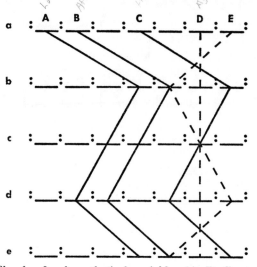

Fig. 6. Profiles for five hypothetical variables (A, B, C, etc.) judged on five scales (a, b, c, etc.). Variables A, B, and C constructed so as to have identical profiles; variables C, D, and E constructed so as to have nearly identical mean differences from A.

on the potency axis, and −3 units from the origin on the activity axis. Since in this case there are only three rows in the matrix, all concept points can be represented in a three (or fewer) dimensional space. As we shall see, under certain circumstances fewer dimensions than the number of rows in the data matrix may be adequate to represent the data in a $k \times m$ matrix. We have come to call the space defined by the k orthogonal axes the *semantic space*, and we assume it to be Euclidean as the simplest starting hypothesis.

2 *The Distance Notion.* How are two columns of coordinates, or two profiles of scores, to be compared so that quantitative statements regarding similarity of meaning can be made? One immediately thinks of the correlation coefficient as an index of the similarity between two profiles. It can easily be shown, however, that r fails to give a valid representation of semantic relations. In Figure 6 we reproduce a hypothetical system of five concepts (A, B, C, D, E) rated against five scales (a, b, c, d, e). Suppose that A represents the concept LOVE, B the concept AFFECTION, and C the concept HATE. These concepts are shown to covary perfectly and hence, despite the gross absolute discrepancies, intercorrelations among them would be all 1.00, leading to the inference that LOVE is just as similar to HATE in meaning as it is to AFFECTION. The correlation of

any other concept with D (AGGRESSION) would be indeterminate, since the variance of D across the scales is zero — yet concept C (HATE) is obviously closer to D than either A or B. Thus it can be seen that the product-moment correlation not only distorts the information, but may be completely inapplicable in some cases. What is required to express semantic similarity is some measure of relation that takes into account both the profile covariation and the discrepancies between the means of the profiles, thereby reflecting more fully the information available in the data.

Such a measure is provided by the *generalized distance formula* of solid geometry:

$$D_{il} = \sqrt{\sum_j d_{il}^2} \tag{1}$$

where D_{il} is the linear distance between the points in the semantic space representing concepts i and l and d_{il} is the algebraic difference between the coordinates of i and l on the same dimension or factor, j. Summation is over the k dimensions. As an example, consider the D between QUICKSAND and WHITE ROSE BUDS found from their coordinates in Table 8. This D is found by taking the difference between the scores of the two concepts on each factor, squaring this difference, summing these squares, and taking the square root of the sum — a set of operations handled very easily on a desk calculator. In this particular case, $(-3 - +3)^2 + (+3 - -3)^2 + (-3 - -3)^2 = 72$, the desired D^2, and the square root of this value is 8.49, the desired D or distance.

The D given by equation (1) is not unrelated to r. If the scores in the matrix of ratings are standardized down the columns (across the scales), the D between concepts taken over the standardized scores using equation (1) is related to the product-moment correlation coefficient by the formula $D_{il} = \sqrt{2k(1 - r_{il})}$, where k is the number of scales, or rows of the matrix, and r_{il} is the correlation coefficient between the two concepts, i and l. Cronbach and Gleser (1953) have discussed this and other characteristics of D at length, and Webster (1952) has pointed out that D is a special case of the Mahalanobis D (see Rao, 1948). However, it should be emphasized that standardizing down columns involves the same loss of information as in computing r.

Similarly, as Webster (1952) has also indicated, D bears a relationship to *intraclass* r (see Fisher, 1941). Suci and Tannenbaum (1955) have explored this relationship somewhat further, and have arrived at an expression for *intraclass* r (r') in terms of D^2 measures,

$$r' = 1 - \frac{D_{XY}^2}{D_{X\bar{Z}}^2 + D_{Y\bar{Z}}^2}$$

where X and Y represent two given arrays of paired data, and $\bar{Z}$ is the mean of the X- and Y-scores combined. However, for this relationship to hold, the data must satisfy certain conditions allowing for the application of the r' statistic, and the relationship is not a general one.

3 *Uses of* D. Although D is most often used to index the distance between (and hence similarity among) concepts as judged by an individual or a group, it is not limited to this use. It can also be applied in the comparison of two subjects, or two groups of subjects, on how similarly they perceive the same concept — for example, how similar are the meanings of MY MOTHER for male and female patients as compared with their meanings of MY FATHER? In this case we operate on a $k \times 2$ matrix taken from the rectangular solid in Figure 6; in other words, we have two subjects or groups of subjects (means) rating one concept (e.g., MY FATHER) on k scales. Formula (1) is applied by taking the sum of the squared differences between the ratings of the concept by the two groups and summing over the k scales. We are still dealing with the distance between two points in the semantic space, one point representing the placement in the semantic space of MY FATHER by one group of subjects, and the other point the placement of this concept by the second group of subjects. D may also be taken between the profiles produced by the same individual or group judging the same concept but at different times, t. The formula for D is here applied to the corresponding columns of the two data matrices obtained at two times.

All of the above uses of D take differences (between subjects, concepts, or times) across a set of scales; this is the normal operation with the semantic differential since, as its name implies, it is a way of differentiating meanings against a set of scales. However, it would also be possible to treat the *concepts* as a set of variables and determine distance relations between pairs of subjects or scales. Thus a D between two subjects across the set of concepts in Table 8 would indicate their "conceptual congruence," i.e., the degree to which they agree in the allocation of this set of concepts in terms of a single factor or, if summations are continued over all factors, in the total semantic space. Clusters of individuals obtained in such a way would specify subgroups who "think alike" with respect to these concepts. D's between *scales,* across concepts or subjects or both simultaneously, would yield data analogous to that on which our factor analytic work was based. These and other possible applications of D to our four dimensional semantic data matrix we have explored only casually so far.

4 *Assumptions Involved in the Use of* D. When we score the semantic differential by assigning digits from $+3$ to -3 to the seven categories and proceed to treat these scores statistically, there are a number of assumptions made. (a) For one thing, it is assumed that the intervals both within a single scale and between different scales are equal. If these units are not in fact equal, the distance in semantic space between A and B is not strictly comparable with that between C and D, say, and the D formula is inappropriate. This is a scaling problem, and in the next chapter empirical evidence will be presented to support our assumption of equal scale intervals. (b) A second assumption that must be made when D is used is that the variables (scales or factors) across which the differences are taken are independent. This is apparent in the geometric model in which the factors are represented by orthogonal axes. If the scales are not essentially independent, the investigator may conclude that a large D between two variables represents a large psychological discrimination between them in the total semantic space, when in reality the discrimination is mainly in one dimension which happens to be magnified by summing over correlated variables. This, incidentally, is also the reason why we must use an equal number of scales to represent each factor in constructing any form of the differential. In part, at least, we satisfy this assumption by choosing scales shown to be essentially independent by our factor analytic work. However, to the extent that the relations among scales (and factors) vary with the classes of concepts being judged (see section in Chapter 4 on comparability across concepts), some error in the interpretation of D is being introduced for certain concepts.

Conceptual Structures. Instead of limiting one's attention to separate pairs of concepts (or subjects) as above, all $m(m-1)/2$ pairs can be studied simultaneously. Using formula (1), the distances between each concept and every other concept can be calculated and entered into an $m \times m$ matrix. This matrix represents the semantic structure of the set of m concepts, giving the distances or similarity relations among all concepts. The set of distances representing the semantic structure are "plotable" in a space having the same (or

Table 9

DISTANCE MEASURES (D_{ij}) RELATING THE 10 CONCEPTS IN TABLE 8★

	A	B	C	D	E	F	G	H	I	J
A										
B	16.70									
C	9.32	19.10								
D	17.75	14.90	20.27							
E	15.30	11.45	16.13	10.25						
F	9.45	15.33	5.29	17.52	13.12					
G	17.70	16.73	20.40	4.36	9.90	17.83				
H	13.60	6.86	16.61	15.40	12.33	13.68	16.43			
I	17.40	14.56	20.22	3.74	9.95	17.64	3.87	14.80		
J	12.10	7.21	15.72	15.30	12.21	12.61	16.22	4.58	14.56	

★ The D's in this matrix are taken over all scales rather than the factor scores given in Table 8.

fewer) dimensions as the number of dimensions represented in the measuring instrument. Such plotability has definite advantages in the case of three dimensions.

Table 9 gives the $m \times m$ matrix of distances generated by applying D to the ratings by one subject of the 10 concepts described in Table 8. These D's were found by summing over all 20 scales, not over the factor scores. Mere inspection of the numbers in such a table, of course, does not immediately create any picture of the conceptual structure, although all of the necessary information is given. If most of the variance in the subject's judgments is restricted to no more than three factors, then the values in this D matrix can readily be plotted in a solid, three dimensional space as a concrete model of the subject's conceptual structure. Such a model, for the data in Table 9, is shown as Figure 7. These models are constructed in the following way:

One first selects a convenient metric, i.e., a unit on a linear scale, such as one inch equals a D of 1.00, which will produce a model whose size fits the construction materials at hand. Each D value in the table is conceived as the radius of a sphere. Using the data from Table 9, variable B may be placed anywhere on a sphere 16.70 units from variable A; variable C must fall somewhere on the circle defined by the intersection of two spheres, one 9.32 units from A and the other 19.10 units from B; variable D must fall at one of the two points of intersection of three spheres with radii 17.75, 14.90, and 20.27 from A, B, and C respectively; the position

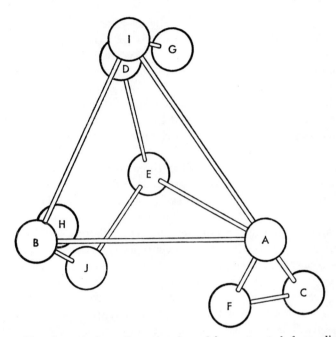

Fig. 7. Drawing of three-dimensional model constructed from distance measures. Variables D, G, I (HERO, VIRILITY, SUCCESS), B, H, J (WHITE ROSE BUDS, GENTLENESS, SLEEP), A, C, F (QUICKSAND, DEATH, FATE), and E (METHODOLOGY).

of variable E is completely determinate within three dimensions, as are the positions of all remaining variables.

The reader may ask what happens if the spheres do not span, e.g., if variable C is only 1.30 units from A and only 1.50 from B, yet A and B are separated by a distance of 10.00 units — the answer is simply that this situation is impossible from the operations of the D measure, and if such a situation appears it indicates an error in computations. The opposite situation — in which, with variables A, B, C, and D fixed, variable E cannot be placed accurately without being too near one of the other variables — can occur, and this indicates that more than three factors were operating in the original data, i.e., the model requires more than three dimensions for accurate plotting. In such cases we make compromises and plot as best we can in the three dimensions we have available. To estimate the plotting error, we measure the distances between each variable and every other variable in the final model, enter these values in a new $m \times m$ matrix, and compute the average error of measurement between the D's in the original matrix and the corresponding D's in the model. In our own work we have used small rubber balls (obtainable from the Barr Rubber Company, St. Louis, Missouri) to represent the concepts and thin wooden dowels (obtainable from any lumber company) to maintain the distances accurately; the sharpened dowels can be pressed into the resilient rubber balls to get accurate distances and the structure as a whole is surprisingly sturdy.

The model in Figure 7 specifies three clearly isolated clusters of variables: A, C, and F (QUICKSAND, DEATH, and FATE), B, H, and J (WHITE ROSE BUDS, GENTLENESS, and SLEEP), and D, G, and I (HERO, VIRILITY, and SUCCESS). The remaining variable, E (METH-ODOLOGY), is separated from these clusters. The face validity of this empirical categorization of these concepts is obvious. The fact that these concepts plotted with almost perfect accuracy within three dimensions despite taking the D's over 20 scales is testimony to the operation of only three major factors in the judgment process. Such a conceptual structure is a kind of map, a bit of "semantic geography," if you will, which provides an objective picture of subjective meaning states within the subject. In many research problems the production and interpretation of such "cognitive maps" may be the major objective, e.g., in a blind analysis made of a case of triple personality, to be reported in a later chapter (see Figures 23, 24, and 25). The model has the advantage over the D matrix from which it is constructed, of being immediately apprehensible — clusters of concepts, their relative distances and arrangements, can be viewed directly and simultaneously and hence interpreted more easily. It is an excellent device for generating hypotheses. These models are necessarily restricted to three dimensions, however; the D matrix is valid for any number of dimensions.

It is often desirable to plot the origin of the semantic space into these models, i.e., that point in the space which signifies "meaninglessness." If a "real" concept were checked at the mid-points of all scales, it would fall precisely at this origin of our space. Therefore, to locate the origin in a model, we manufacture a "hypothetical" concept having this property; we add to the score-matrix a column in which each cell is "4" if the scoring is 1, 2, 3, 4, 5, 6, 7, or "0" if the scoring is +3, +2, +1, 0, −1, −2, −3, and the distances (D's) from this "variable" to every other variable are computed from formula (1) as before. This origin is then plotted in the same space and in the same manner as described above. The insertion of the origin is an aid to interpretation: one can then immediately perceive which variables or clusters of variables tend to be opposite in meaning to the subject, which variables or clusters tend to be independent in meaning, i.e., at 90 degree angles to each other through the space. One can also estimate the *meaningfulness* of concepts to the subject, those variables falling near the origin being relatively meaningless (within the aspects of meaning sampled) and those falling far out toward the edges of the space being relatively "saturated" in meaning.

Finally, knowing the locations of all concepts on each factor, one can estimate the location of each factor in this space by placing a linear indicator through the origin in such a way that the right-angle projections of the concepts onto this indicator match their values on the factor, e.g., so that the most favorable concept projects to the top of the indicator, the next most favorable concept below it, and so on. It must be kept in mind, of course, that the construction and use of these models is purely an aid to understanding and interpretation; nothing is added conceptually that is not available in the D matrix.

Significance Estimates

The investigator is usually not satisfied with the intuitive conclusions which inspection of descriptive data provides. He wishes to know how much confidence he can place in his findings — can this result be said to be different from that result with a certain degree of confidence, can we reject this hypothesis with such and such a degree of confidence? These are questions of statistical inference. But before going into the problems and methods here, let us see what typical questions are asked about data derived from the semantic differential. One question concerns the individual scales or factor scores: for example, Is this advertisement "better" (evaluative factor) than that one? Does this concept, as predicted, have a more polarized potency score than activity score? Does this group perceive X as more *happy* than does that group? Probably the questions most often asked concern differences in meanings as wholes, i.e., significance of D's and of differences between D's (since D takes into account relations on all factors simultaneously) — is the subject's meaning of FATHER significantly different from his meaning of MOTHER? Is his meaning of ME significantly different at the end of therapy from what it was at the beginning? Does this group have a significantly different sterotype of FRENCHMEN than that group? Concerning conceptual structures we have questions like these: Can concept X be said confidently to fall within this cluster or that? Is the total conceptual structure of this individual significantly different now than it was then? Is the political conceptual structure of a Democratic group significantly different from that of a Republican group? There are also some rather special statistical significance problems that arise with particular research problems which will be taken up in context later in this book.

Individual vs. Group Data. As we have seen, all of the descriptive measures obtainable with the semantic differential — factor scores, distances (D's), and conceptual structures — can be had for either individual subjects or for groups of subjects. The interest of the researcher, and hence the point of application of his significance tests, may be in either the individual (e.g., the case of triple personality) or the group (e.g., the election study to be reported later in this chapter). However, the problems of statistical inference are entirely different in the two cases. In the group case we have replication over different individuals and many of the usual statistical tests can be applied directly. In the individual case, however, we run into the problem of statistical independence (N in the usual sense equals one). This does not necessarily eliminate all tests of significance, however.

Actually, as mathematical statisticians assure us, the question of statistical independence of measurements comes down to independence of the *errors of measurement* of the two things being compared. Now, within the individual case we have replication of scales (when comparing concepts), replication of concepts (when comparing scales), and replication of both (when comparing across time). If it can be shown (see Chapter 4, p. 135) that the errors of measurement for the same individual judging different concepts on correlated scales (representing same factor) are uncorrelated, then certain significance tests at least become feasible. In other words, rather than dealing with a sample of individuals from a certain group, we may deal with a sample of judgments from a certain individual — the nature of the population within which sampling is made is different, but not necessarily the statistical character of the problem. In any case, we shall have to distinguish between the individual and group situations in discussing statistical tests of significance.

Difference in Scale Position or Factor Score. In the *group situation* this problem is no different than elsewhere when we wish to determine whether the central tendency of one group is different from that of another on some measure. If the distributions of judgments of a concept on a particular scale (*strong-weak*, say) or a particular factor (*potency*, say) are demonstrably normal, then the usual *t-test* can be applied. If, as will often be the case with semantic differential data, the judgments do not approximate normality of distribution, then some non-parametric test must be applied. From the results of such a test we are able to conclude that Democrats, say, perceive OUR POLICY IN CHINA as significantly *stronger* (or more *potent* in general) than do Republicans at some level of significance.

In the *individual situation* this question is not answered so easily. A given subject ordinarily provides us with just one datum relating OUR FOREIGN POLICY, say, to the scale *strong-weak* (a digit from +3 to −3), and he only provides us with three bits of data relating this concept to the potency factor (e.g., −1 on *strong-weak*, −2 on *hard-soft*, and −1 on *deep-shallow*), which is a very small N even if we can assume independence of the judgments. The only way of handling this problem we can discover goes back to the basic notion of *reliability of an instrument* used in all sciences: If we determine the error of measurement of our instrument, here for single scales or factor scores, under test-retest conditions, we can estimate the probability with which a difference of a given magnitude could have occurred by chance simply on the basis of measurement error. Knowing that a subject drawn at random judging an item drawn at random can be expected to deviate as much as two scale units from one test to another only 5 per cent of the time, we can say that a difference for an individual subject between OUR FOREIGN POLICY and TRUMAN on *strong-weak* of the two units or more is significant at the 5 per cent level. The test-retest data for making such estimates on the basis of reliability of measurement is given in detail in Chapter 4. The difficulty with this approach is that such levels of significance apply to particular individuals, particular concepts, and particular scales or factors only by inference from the average performance of the instrument — and can be extended to individuals atypical of the standardizing group only with great insecurity. To obtain such reliability data for each particular research problem would be laborious indeed.

Difference in Meaning. The meaning of a concept to an individual is a point in semantic space; the meaning of a concept to a group is the central tendency of a "cloud" of such individual points in the semantic space. There are two types of questions here: difference in the meanings of two concepts for the same individual or group (which statistically includes difference for the same concept over time); difference in the meaning of the same concept for two different individuals or two different groups. In all these cases we are faced with a *multivariate* problem — differences exist simultaneously along n-dimensions or n-variables for the things being compared. This means that the usual univariate tests of significance (e.g., the t-test) are not applicable. We may consider each type of situation separately.

a *Difference between two different groups in the meaning of the same concept.* This is perhaps the simplest situation conceptually. Here we have two uncorrelated "clouds" of points in our space — let us say, a "red cloud" and a "black cloud" — and we wish to know if they have significantly different locations. If the semantic space had only *one* dimension, and the data were not distributed normally, it is obvious that we could apply the Chi-square test to determine if the distributions could have been drawn from the same population. Now, if we can assume that the n dimensions of the space are independent of each other — and the purpose of our factor analytic work is to approach this condition — then the Chi-squares computed for the separate dimensions (using factor scores) can be summed into an over-all test of significance. If there is a significant difference on any one dimension, the over-all test will be significant — as it should be in our multivariate problem — and separately insignificant differences may sum to a significant difference (e.g., where the direction of displacement between the "clouds" in the total space is not along one factor, but along a diagonal between them). In applying this test it should be kept in mind that a significant Chi-square does not necessarily imply a difference in the central tendencies of the "clouds"; significance may also be obtained when it is the dispersions or shape of distributions which differ.

b *Difference between the meanings of two concepts for the same group.* Here we deal with two "clouds" in our space in which the individual points correspond, i.e., are correlated — each "red point" and each "black point" has a number or tag referring to the particular subject and the numbers correspond perfectly. Such correspondence or lack of independence rules out Chi-square as an appropriate measure. Now, between each pair of corresponding points (meanings of concepts A and B for the n subjects) there is a distance which we measure by D. If these D's were all zero, obviously there would be no difference in the meanings of the concepts for this group (although there could be differences in meanings, as between individuals). Unfortunately, we cannot say there is a difference between the group meanings if the average D is significantly greater than zero; this is because the *directions* of these distances in the space may be random and cancel each other out.

c *Difference between two individuals in the meaning of a concept*, and

d *Difference between the meanings of two concepts for the same individual.* In both of these cases we are comparing only two points in the multidimensional semantic space. Although each of the two concepts (for the same individual or for different individuals) is associated with a series of scores on k scales or k' factors, these are not mere replicates and cannot be treated as a sample over which the usual univariate tests of significance can be taken. Here we have fallen back on the reliability of the instrument as a means of estimating significance. If a distance (D) between the points representing the meanings of the same concept on test and retest, of, say, 1.00 unit will occur only 5 per cent of the time for subjects and materials drawn at random, a difference larger than this between two different concepts should indicate significance at that level. Similarly, if the difference in meaning of a concept for two individuals is no greater than for the same individual on a retest at some level of significance, we conclude that their meanings are not different.

Differences Between Distances. When can one D be considered larger than another to a statistically significant degree? Is this patient's meaning of ME closer to his meaning of FATHER than it is to his meaning of MOTHER? Do Republicans perceive EISENHOWER closer in meaning to MACARTHUR than Democrats do? Here we need to show that a D of 2.53, say, is significantly smaller than a D of 4.22 units. The distribution of D is not known. It is probably not normal in shape, and if not, normal curve statistics are not applicable. In the *group situation* a number of non-parametric tests can be applied. If, for example, the hypothesis states that the distance between concepts A and B will be greater than that between concepts A and C for a particular group, the "sign test" or "Wilcoxon's matched pairs signed ranks test" may be used — i.e., we simply treat each subject's D_{AB} and D_{AC} as ordinary scores and see if the AB and AC values could have been samples from the same population. If the hypothesis concerns two different groups of subjects, so that pairing is not possible, the "median test" or the "Mann-Whitney 'U' test" may be applied (and the "Wilcoxon 'T' test" may be substituted if the sizes of the two groups are not equal). Of course, there are numerous other statistical procedures which can be employed with such data.

Certain statistical questions may lead to pairing distances not by individuals but by the concepts judged. For example, a hypothesis may state that all possible distances between m concepts produced by Group I are larger than all possible distances between the same m concepts produced by Group II. In this case we would take the D's between concepts using the mean responses for each group as the original scores; then D_{AB} for Group I would be paired with D_{AB} for Group II, D_{AC} for I with D_{AC} for II, and so on until all possible $m(m-1)/2$ distances have been paired for the two groups. The above mentioned tests are then applied. This by no means exhausts the possible uses of non-parametric tests with semantic data; other uses will be found in a later chapter dealing with applications. Again, in dealing with the *individual situation*, we must depend on reliability estimates.

Differences Within a Conceptual Structure. One of the questions we often ask of a conceptual structure is the existence of identifiable clusters of concepts having similar meaning. By clustering is meant the existence of sets of variables, each set containing more than one variable, such that all distances between variables within the sets are smaller than distances with variables not in the set. Simple visual inspection of a three dimensional plot is the easiest way to intuit the existence of clusters — when the dimensionality is restricted mainly to this number of dimensions — but it does not provide any quantitative index. It would be much more satisfactory to have some method for deriving clusters directly from the D matrix; we have been working on this problem, but no complete method has been developed as yet. Neither have statistical tests for clustering been developed, tests which would tell us whether a particular set of clusters is beyond what would be expected by chance. However, when data for the concepts shown in Table 9 were produced by throwing dice, the distribution of D's in a D matrix computed from these scores was found not to differ from a normal distribution significantly, using the Chi-square test; on the other hand, the distribution of D's produced by an actual subject (Table 9) differs markedly from chance according to the same test, the

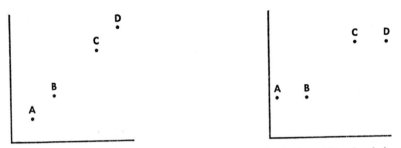

Fig. 8. Two sets of distances which correlate perfectly but differ in their dimensional characteristics.

clustering evident in Figure 7 leading to many more small D's (within clusters) and many more large D's (between clusters) than would be anticipated from chance. This demonstration suggests the possibility of using Chi-square as a test for non-chanceness in the structure of a D matrix.

Differences Between Conceptual Structures. When we ask how similar two conceptual structures are with respect to the way the concepts are clustered, the absolute sizes of the distances are usually ignored and only the relative sizes considered, i.e., it is usually the pattern or "gestalt" in which we are interested. In this case, the correlation coefficient can be used as an index of similarity. The two matrices of D (e.g., for Democrats and Republicans judging the same concepts) are correlated by pairing corresponding cells, D_{AB} with D_{AB}', D_{AC} with D_{AC}', and so on through the $m(m-1)/2$ pairs. The higher the r, the more similar the two structures. If a hypothesis states that structures I and II are more similar in their clustering than structures III and IV, the two correlation coefficients, $r_{I,II}$ and $r_{III,IV}$, may be compared statistically in the usual fashion; however, the result must be interpreted with caution since the cells in the D matrix are not independent from each other.

At first glance it may seem that the comparison of two structures by correlating corresponding cells of the D matrices would reflect directly on how similar are their dimensional characteristics. This is not the case. As shown by the examples in Figure 8, the relative distances between concepts may be similar, yet the dimensional characteristics of the matrices may be quite different — the r between these plots would be 1.00, yet one can be represented by a single dimension and the other requires two dimensions. If one wished to take account of the absolute magnitudes of the differences in distances between two matrices, rather than simply their pattern, one could take a D rather than an r across the pairs of corresponding cells, but there is no simple way to interpret a D obtained in this fashion. Finally, if it is desired to know whether or not the concepts in the two structures are similarly distributed on one of the dimensions (e.g., evaluation), a measure similar but not identical to r may be used. This is the coefficient of proportionality given on page 44, Chapter 2.

The Discriminant Function. Before concluding this section on statistical tools, a word should be said about the possible use of the discriminant function. If it is desired to compare two groups of subjects with respect to the total semantic space generated by a given group of concepts and scales, the discriminant function is the logical technique to apply, at least when the assumption of normally distributed data is met. Each item (concept-scale pairing) would be considered a variable which potentially differentiates the groups. The discriminant function would then tell us whether or not the two groups differ significantly with respect to all items and, in addition, which items contribute to this differentiation independently of the contributions of other items. However, with the number of items normally involved in a form of the semantic differential (e.g., 100 or more), this technique becomes prohibitively laborious. Furthermore, the assumption of normal distribution of data will probably not be met in most cases, especially when groups are chosen to emphasize the differences between them.

A SEMANTIC ANALYSIS OF VOTERS IN THE 1952 PRESIDENTIAL ELECTION[3]

As a means of illustrating many of the descriptive and significance testing measures described in this chapter — as well as introducing a new method for determining the frame of reference within which judgments are made — we present a study made of the 1952 presidential election. The main purposes of this study were to describe with the semantic differential the meanings of political concepts to three groups of subjects expected to have different political biases with respect to the election and, in a preliminary fashion, to inves-

---

[3] Dr. Joseph Bachelder collaborated on the sampling and earlier stages of this study; Dr. Joan Dodge assisted on the statistical analysis; Dr. Suci was generally responsible for the analysis and interpretation of these data.

tigate the natures of the frames of reference used by these subjects in judging political concepts.

Subjects and Procedure

A panel of 150 paid subjects, selected by block sampling to represent a midwestern community of 70,000 persons, was tested on four different occasions: the first week in July, 1952, prior to the nominating conventions; the first week in August, after the conventions; in the middle of September, about two months before the election; and finally, one week prior to election day. After voting, the subjects were asked to return a post card indicating their vote. A total of 107 subjects completed all stages of the study; of these 107, 103 also returned post cards and were classified into three different groups according to their political preferences.

Classification of Subjects. The first breakdown was based on the subjects' reported vote: those who voted for Stevenson were placed in the "Stevenson voter" group; those who voted for Eisenhower were further subdivided into two groups according to how they had ranked the candidates prior to the conventions in order of preference, the possible candidates being Eisenhower, Taft, Stevenson, Harriman, Kefauver, Kerr, MacArthur, Russell, Stassen, and Warren. If an Eisenhower voter had ranked Eisenhower over Taft, he was classified into an "Eisenhower Republican voter" group, and if he had ranked Taft over Eisenhower, he became a "Taft Republican voter." There were 30 Stevenson voters, 36 Eisenhower Republican voters, and 37 Taft Republican voters in the final sample.

It was assumed that these three groups would represent quite different political biases — specifically, that the Taft Republicans would be more pro-Republican than the Eisenhower Republicans, who in turn, of course, would be more pro-Republican than the Stevenson voters. These assumptions were checked in two ways: by

Table 10

PERCENTAGE OF SUBJECTS IN EACH CATEGORY AFFILIATING WITH THE POLITICAL PARTIES

	Republican	Neither	Democratic	Other
Stevenson Voters	17	27	50	7
Eisenhower Republicans	58	25	17	
Taft Republicans	81	8	11	

Table 11

MEAN RESPONSES OF SUBJECTS IN EACH CATEGORY TO NINE OPINION ITEMS*

	Tafts	Eisenhowers	Stevensons
1. The Republicans would cut down waste and bureaucracy in government.	1.03	.78	−.49
5. The Democrats have been too easy on Communists in the United States.	1.16	.61	−.19
8. All in all the Democratic administration of the last four years has been a bad thing for the country.	.97	.94	−.62
9. There would be fewer scandals in government under the Republicans than under the Democrats.	.62	.08	−.92
2. We need strict price controls immediately.	−.43	−.36	.12
3. Defense and war problems can best be handled by the Democrats.	−1.54	−1.09	−.15
4. The Republicans would make more bad mistakes in foreign affairs than the Democrats.	−1.19	−1.00	−.12
6. The Taft-Hartley labor law is unfair to working people.	−1.08	−.64	.32
7. We should go even farther with government welfare programs such as housing, medical care, and social security.	−.97	−.70	.22

* Positive numbers indicate agreement, negative numbers disagreement; the larger the number, the more intense the reaction.

the percentages of each group affiliating themselves with the Republican or Democratic parties, and by the intensity of pro-Republican or pro-Democratic response to nine opinion items (which were used in parallel with the semantic differential). The percentages in each of our groups expressing political affiliation are shown in Table 10. It is clear from these percentages that affiliations correspond to our groupings. The nine public opinion items selected to detect party bias (independently of our subsequent categorization) are given in Table 11, along with the mean responses on a five point agree-disagree scale. Agreement with items 1, 5, 8, and 9 was considered pro-Republican, and agreement with items **2, 3, 4, 6,** and **7** was considered pro-Democratic. In every case the expected order of means materializes for the three groups; the Tafts are most positive on pro-Republican items and most negative on pro-Democratic items, Stevensons fall at the other extreme, and Eisenhowers are consistently between the other two groups.

The Semantic Differential Employed. To represent as adequately as possible the people and issues which, some six months before the election, could be anticipated to be critical, the following set of 10 "person" concepts and 10 "issue" concepts was selected:

Person Concepts	*Issue Concepts*
ROBERT TAFT	UNIVERSAL MILITARY TRAINING
ADLAI STEVENSON	U.S. POLICY IN CHINA
WINSTON CHURCHILL	FEDERAL SPENDING
GENERAL MACARTHUR	SOCIALISM
ESTES KEFAUVER	GOVERNMENT EMPLOYEES
JOSEF STALIN	GOVERNMENT PRICE CONTROLS
HARRY S. TRUMAN	EUROPEAN AID
GENERAL EISENHOWER	LABOR UNIONISM
FRANKLIN D. ROOSEVELT	USE OF ATOMIC BOMB
SENATOR MCCARTHY	UNITED NATIONS

These concepts were judged against a 10-scale differential consisting of the following: *wise-foolish, dirty-clean, fair-unfair, safe-dangerous, strong-weak, deep-shallow, active-passive, cool-warm, relaxed-tense,* and *idealistic-realistic.* The polarities of the scales were as given here and the factor representatives were placed on the form in random order. Form II (single page for each concept) was used. Since preliminary correlation analysis showed that the relationships among the concepts based on only three of these scales, *fair-unfair* (evaluation), *strong-weak* (potency), and *active-passive* (activity), were nearly identical with those obtained with all 10 scales, the data from only these scales was used for the subsequent analyses.

Meanings of Persons and Issues to Voters

Scale ratings were scored by attributing integer values $+3$ to -3 to the seven positions, plus values being assigned to the *fair, strong,* and *active* poles of these scales. The integer "0" denotes neutrality of judgment. The scores for the subjects in each group were summed, yielding three 3×20 $(k \times m)$ matrices which give the average rating of each concept on each of the three scales. We have also summed and averaged over the four samplings through time for most of the data given here (except where indicated).

The mean ratings generated by each of the three groups of voters are given in Table 12. These are equivalent to what have been described earlier as factor scores. We may note first that each group gives the highest positive evaluation to its preferred candidate (TAFT for the Taft Republicans, EISENHOWER for the Eisenhower Republicans, and STEVENSON for the Stevenson voters), which is a kind of validation indicator. It can also be seen that the preferred candidates tend to be judged strongest and most active of all concepts. Looking just at *evaluation,* we find that TAFT, MACARTHUR, USE OF ATOMIC BOMB, and MCCARTHY are most positively evaluated by Taft Republicans, less positively evaluated by Eisenhower Republicans, and least positively, or negatively, evaluated by the Stevenson voters. On the other hand, POLICY IN CHINA, SOCIALISM, GOVERNMENT EMPLOYEES, STALIN, PRICE CONTROLS, TRUMAN, EUROPEAN AID, LABOR UNIONISM, and UNITED NATIONS are most positively evaluated by the Stevenson group and least by the Tafts. Again, these observations jibe with our general expectations in the political area. When we compare *potency* scores with those for *evaluation,* it can be seen that there is considerable correlation between them; in general, the group giving the lowest evaluation of a concept attributes the least potency to it and vice versa — it is evident that for these political, attitudinal concepts, evaluative and potency judgments are not independent.

The non-parametric tests of significance described earlier in this chapter can be applied to both the differences between voting groups judging the same concept and the differences between concepts judged by the same group — on a single scale at a time. For example, we find that SOCIALISM is rated significantly more fair on scale *fair-unfair* by the Stevenson voters than by the Taft Republicans. The "median test" was applied yielding a Chi-square of 6.59, significant at a $p = .02$.

And we find that of the 36 Eisenhower Republicans, only eight rated TAFT more fair than EISENHOWER; i.e., as would be expected, Eisenhower Republicans evaluate EISENHOWER more favorably than TAFT. This result is significant at $p = .01$, using the "sign test."

Table 12

MEAN RATINGS OF CONCEPTS BY THREE POLITICAL GROUPS

	Taft Republicans			Eisenhower Republicans			Stevenson Voters		
	fair	strong	active	fair	strong	active	fair	strong	active
TAFT	2.28	2.25	2.37	1.17	1.26	1.67	.09	1.13	2.18
UMT	.79	.33	1.05	1.31	1.33	1.31	.75	.71	1.33
STEVENSON	.84	1.00	1.34	.95	.68	1.22	2.27	2.22	2.24
POLICY IN CHINA	-1.07	-1.87	-1.15	-.40	-1.42	-1.02	-.23	-.95	-.31
CHURCHILL	1.48	2.32	2.27	1.49	1.96	1.93	1.50	2.29	2.27
FEDERAL SPENDING	-.40	-1.34	1.35	-1.43	-1.06	.78	-.05	.53	1.76
MACARTHUR	2.17	2.51	2.16	1.23	1.40	1.53	.56	1.56	1.50
SOCIALISM	-1.76	-1.50	.36	-1.16	-.86	.62	-.40	-.39	.97
KEFAUVER	1.49	.54	1.66	1.18	.52	1.10	1.44	1.00	1.82
GOV'T. EMPLOYEES	-.30	-.33	.44	-.12	-.18	.16	.63	.35	.76
STALIN	-2.29	2.15	1.97	-2.25	1.54	1.68	-2.13	1.77	2.27
PRICE CONTROLS	-.82	-.66	.42	-.66	-.46	.67	.89	-.10	.93
TRUMAN	-1.30	-1.40	.76	-1.14	-1.22	.80	.95	.75	1.93
EUROPEAN AID	-.28	-.09	.93	.35	.66	.88	1.50	.74	1.24
EISENHOWER	2.02	2.01	2.01	2.05	2.17	2.13	1.16	1.41	2.02
LABOR UNIONISM	-.59	1.59	2.04	-.38	1.35	1.64	.74	1.92	2.19
ROOSEVELT	-.24	1.59	2.15	-.24	1.44	1.60	1.75	2.38	2.42
ATOM BOMB	.50	1.19	1.48	.34	.87	1.24	-.26	1.46	1.47
MCCARTHY	.61	1.32	2.15	-.59	.42	1.70	-1.47	.07	2.04
UNITED NATIONS	.83	-.59	.07	1.35	.11	.69	1.43	.17	1.16

Similarities and Differences in Meaning

The three scores for each concept for each group in Table 12 serve to fix the meaning of each concept as a point in space and the distance between each pair of points can be computed by the D formula. In Table 13 are given the D matrices for each of the three groups of voters. In Figure 9 we present the models representing the data in these D matrices, and also representing the relationships among concepts for each group in terms of their projections on the original three scales. The scales are plotted into the models so that the original ratings are available in the model itself. Each of the concepts, numbered circles, has a projection extending downward to the plane defined by scales *fair-unfair* and *strong-weak*. The base of the projection gives the ratings of the concepts on *fair-unfair* and *strong-weak*. For example, in the model for the Stevenson Voters concept 15, EISENHOWER, has a projection which intersects the plane at coordinates 1.41 and 1.16, indicating average ratings of EISENHOWER of 1.41 toward *strong* and 1.16 toward *fair*. The length of the projection from the concept to the plane indicates the rating of the concept on *active-passive*. If the projection is a broken line, the projection extends below the plane toward the *passive* side; a solid line indicates a rating toward the *active* side. For EISENHOWER, by the Stevenson Voters, the rating extends upward toward *active* 2.02 units.

Finding the D's between concepts for individual subjects, and treating the D value as scores, the non-parametric tests may be applied as above to find (a) whether two concepts are differentiated more than two other concepts by the same group or (b) whether one group of subjects differentiates more between a given pair of concepts than another group of subjects.

As an example, the D between SOCIALISM and GOVERNMENT PRICE CONTROLS was found for each subject in the Eisenhower and Taft groups. The question is: Do the two groups differ significantly in their differentiation between the two concepts? Applying the "median test," the Taft group is found to discriminate more, that is, have greater D's (p = .05) between the concepts than the Eisenhower group. Any other comparisons of the same sort, of interest to the investigator, could be evaluated in the same way.

Conceptual Structures of Voting Groups

The models shown in Figure 9 are bits of the "semantic geog-

Table 13

DISTANCES BETWEEN CONCEPTS FOR THREE POLITICAL GROUPS

Taft Republicans

	1	2	3	4	5	6	7	8	9	10	11	12	13	14	15	16	17	18	19	20
1. TAFT	.00	2.77	2.17	6.37	.81	4.60	.35	5.87	2.01	4.13	4.59	4.68	5.36	3.76	.51	2.96	2.61	2.26	1.92	3.93
2. UMT		.00	.73	3.63	2.43	2.07	2.81	3.21	.95	1.41	3.69	1.99	2.73	1.16	2.29	2.12	1.96	1.00	1.49	1.35
3. STEVENSON			.00	4.25	1.74	2.65	2.17	3.74	.86	1.97	3.39	2.52	3.27	1.62	1.69	1.70	1.47	.41	.90	2.04
4. POLICY IN CHINA				.00	5.98	2.64	6.38	1.70	4.50	2.34	5.23	2.00	1.98	2.85	5.88	4.73	4.85	4.33	4.89	2.60
5. CHURCHILL					.00	4.22	.72	5.36	1.88	3.68	3.79	4.19	4.88	3.27	.68	2.21	1.87	1.69	1.33	3.71
6. FEDERAL SPENDING						.00	4.70	1.69	2.68	1.36	4.02	1.23	1.08	1.32	4.19	3.02	3.04	2.69	2.96	1.93
7. MACARTHUR							.00	5.90	2.14	4.14	4.48	4.69	5.41	3.78	.54	2.91	2.58	2.24	1.96	3.97
8. SOCIALISM								.00	4.05	1.87	4.02	1.26	.62	2.12	5.42	3.71	3.88	3.69	4.10	2.76
9. KEFAUVER									.00	2.33	4.12	2.88	3.52	2.01	1.60	2.36	2.08	1.20	1.27	2.60
10. GOVERNMENT EMPLOYEES										.00	3.53	.62	1.50	.55	3.65	2.52	2.57	2.01	2.54	1.22
11. STALIN											.00	3.53	3.88	3.18	4.31	1.79	2.13	2.99	3.02	4.57
12. PRICE CONTROLS												.00	.95	.94	4.21	2.78	2.90	2.51	2.99	1.69
13. TRUMAN													.00	1.67	4.92	3.33	3.46	3.26	3.60	2.38
14. EUROPEAN AID														.00	3.30	2.04	2.08	1.60	2.07	1.50
15. EISENHOWER															.00	2.64	2.30	1.81	1.58	3.46
16. LABOR UNIONISM																.00	.37	1.29	1.24	3.26
17. ROOSEVELT																	.00	1.08	.89	3.20
18. ATOM BOMB																		.00	.69	2.30
19. MCCARTHY																			.00	2.83
20. UNITED NATIONS																				.00

Table 13. Continued.

DISTANCES BETWEEN CONCEPTS FOR THREE POLITICAL GROUPS

Eisenhower Republicans

	1	2	3	4	5	6	7	8	9	10	11	12	13	14	15	16	17	18	19	20
1. TAFT	.00	.39	.77	4.11	.81	3.60	.21	3.32	.93	2.45	3.43	2.70	3.50	1.29	1.35	1.55	1.42	1.01	1.95	1.52
2. UMT		.00	.75	3.99	.90	3.67	.24	3.37	.85	2.38	3.59	2.74	3.57	1.25	1.39	1.72	1.58	1.08	2.14	1.37
3. STEVENSON			.00	3.35	1.56	2.98	.83	2.68	.31	1.73	3.35	2.05	2.86	.69	2.06	1.55	1.46	.64	1.63	.88
4. POLICY IN CHINA				.00	4.87	2.11	4.14	1.89	3.28	1.73	4.41	1.96	1.98	2.92	5.37	3.84	3.88	3.30	3.29	2.87
5. CHURCHILL					.00	4.36	.74	4.09	1.69	3.21	3.77	3.47	4.28	2.02	.63	1.99	1.84	1.73	2.60	2.23
6. FEDERAL SPENDING						.00	3.70	.37	3.07	1.70	2.87	.98	.33	2.48	4.94	2.77	2.89	2.66	1.93	3.02
7. MACARTHUR							.00	3.41	.98	2.49	3.49	2.79	3.61	1.32	1.28	1.61	1.47	1.08	2.07	1.54
8. SOCIALISM								.00	2.76	1.33	2.84	.64	.40	2.16	4.67	2.56	2.66	2.37	1.77	2.69
9. KEFAUVER									.00	1.75	3.63	2.13	2.92	.87	2.13	1.85	1.76	.92	1.87	.60
10. GOVERNMENT EMPLOYEES										.00	3.13	.79	1.59	1.20	3.76	2.14	2.17	1.58	1.72	1.59
11. STALIN											.00	2.75	3.10	2.86	4.37	1.88	2.01	2.71	2.00	4.00
12. PRICE CONTROLS												.00	.91	1.52	4.05	2.07	2.16	1.76	1.36	2.09
13. TRUMAN													.00	2.40	4.84	2.81	2.92	2.60	1.95	2.83
14. EUROPEAN AID														.00	3.60	1.26	1.21	.42	1.27	1.16
15. EISENHOWER															.00	2.61	2.46	2.33	3.20	2.61
16. LABOR UNIONISM																.00	.17	.95	.96	2.33
17. ROOSEVELT																	.00	.89	1.08	2.26
18. ATOM BOMB																		.00	1.13	1.38
19. MC CARTHY																			.00	2.21
20. UNITED NATIONS																				.00

Table 18. Concluded.

DISTANCES BETWEEN CONCEPTS FOR THREE POLITICAL GROUPS

Stevenson Voters

	1	2	3	4	5	6	7	8	9	10	11	12	13	14	15	16	17	18	19	20
1. TAFT	.00	1.16	2.44	3.26	1.83	.75	.93	2.00	1.40	1.71	2.31	1.93	.97	1.74	1.12	1.02	2.09	.86	1.89	1.94
2. UMT		.00	2.33	2.53	1.98	.93	.89	1.63	.89	.68	3.21	.91	.63	.76	1.06	1.48	2.23	1.27	2.42	.88
3. STEVENSON			.00	4.78	.77	2.91	1.98	3.94	1.53	2.89	4.42	3.00	2.00	1.94	1.39	1.56	.57	2.75	4.32	2.46
4. POLICY IN CHINA				.00	4.49	2.55	3.19	1.41	3.34	1.89	4.20	1.88	3.05	2.87	3.60	3.93	4.74	3.00	2.85	2.48
5. CHURCHILL					.00	2.40	1.42	3.53	1.37	2.61	3.67	2.81	1.67	1.86	.98	.85	.30	2.10	3.72	2.39
6. FEDERAL SPENDING						.00	1.22	1.26	1.56	1.22	2.48	1.40	1.04	1.65	1.52	1.66	2.66	1.00	1.52	1.64
7. MACARTHUR							.00	2.24	1.09	1.42	2.81	1.79	1.00	1.27	.81	.80	1.71	.83	2.58	1.68
8. SOCIALISM								.00	2.46	1.28	3.06	1.32	2.01	2.23	2.60	2.85	3.79	1.92	2.58	1.92
9. KEFAUVER									.00	1.48	3.68	1.52	.56	.64	.54	1.21	1.54	1.80	3.06	1.06
10. GOVERNMENT EMPLOYEES										.00	3.45	.55	1.28	1.07	1.73	2.13	2.85	1.59	2.48	.91
11. STALIN											.00	3.80	3.26	3.91	3.32	2.88	3.93	2.06	1.84	4.06
12. PRICE CONTROLS												.00	1.31	1.08	1.88	2.38	3.02	2.01	2.61	.65
13. TRUMAN													.00	.88	.70	1.22	1.88	1.48	2.52	1.08
14. EUROPEAN AID														.00	1.08	1.70	2.04	1.92	3.15	.58
15. EISENHOWER															.00	.68	1.20	1.52	2.95	1.53
16. LABOR UNIONISM																.00	1.13	1.32	2.89	2.14
17. ROOSEVELT																	.00	2.41	3.98	2.56
18. ATOM BOMB																		.00	1.93	2.15
19. MCCARTHY																			.00	3.03
20. UNITED NATIONS																				.00

Fig. 9a

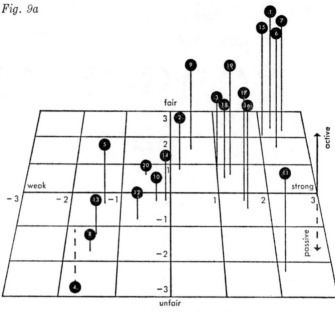

TAFT REPUBLICANS

Fig. 9. Models of the semantic spaces for three voting groups. Each of 20 concepts is numbered according to key. The base of projection from concept gives the ratings on scales fair-unfair and strong-weak. The length of projection from concept to base gives the ratings on scale active-passive, a solid projection indicating a rating toward the active end and a broken projection indicating a rating toward the passive end of the scale.

Key

1. TAFT	8. SOCIALISM	15. EISENHOWER
2. UMT	9. KEFAUVER	16. LABOR UNIONISM
3. STEVENSON	10. GOVT. EMPLOYEES	17. ROOSEVELT
4. POLICY IN CHINA	11. STALIN	18. ATOM BOMB
5. CHURCHILL	12. PRICE CONTROLS	19. MC CARTHY
6. FEDERAL SPENDING	13. TRUMAN	20. UNITED NATIONS
7. MAC ARTHUR	14. EUROPEAN AID	

raphy" of samples from three subcultures of American voters in 1952 — Taft Republicans, Eisenhower Republicans, and Stevenson Democrats. What is particularly striking about these models is the fact that, despite the obvious differences in the locations of particular concepts and in the nature of the clusters, the over-all structures are highly similar. Political concepts, whether judged by Stevenson Democrats or Taft Republicans, tend to distribute them-

Fig. 9b

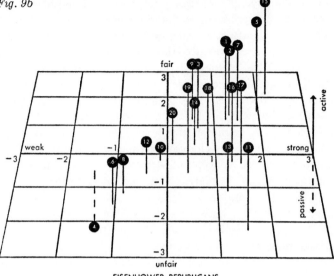

EISENHOWER REPUBLICANS

Fig. 9c

STEVENSON VOTERS

selves from one pole at *fair-strong-active* toward another at *unfair-weak-passive* along a single major dimension. There is more than a single factor operating, but one dominant dimension accounts for most of the variance. Since this dominant dimension does not coincide with any of the factors derived from factorization of concepts-in-general, we are led to consider the possibility of the formation of "characteristic attributes" that function within certain frames of reference (see below). But before undertaking this analysis, let us inspect some of the results at this level.

As noted earlier in this chapter, one measure of the over-all correspondence between conceptual structures is the r across corresponding cells of the D matrices. In the present study, we would expect a closer general correspondence between Taft and Eisenhower structures than between either of these and the Stevenson group. This expectation is borne out in the data. The correlations between the Stevenson and Eisenhower, and Stevenson and Taft matrices are .43 and .41, respectively; whereas the correlation between the Eisenhower and Taft matrices is .79.

Theoretical Analysis of the Characteristic Attributes of a Frame of Reference

It is easily shown that the distances between concepts in semantic space are invariant with respect to any set of orthogonal dimensions which intersect at the origin. The general model used in our semantic measurement work adopts as dimensions the scales (or factors) on which the concepts are rated. The question arises, however, as to whether another set of dimensions might have more discriminatory capacity in a specific measurement situation. And since any other set of dimensions through the same space would obviously differ in semantic composition from the original factors, just what would be their significance? This section presents some preliminary aspects of a theoretical model of the judgment process which is based on the geometry of a semantic space. The model will offer a rationale for using dimensions other than the original factors in certain cases. The following assumptions represent this model:

1 *Semantic judgments can be completely represented in a space defined by a set of elemental semantic factors.* Thus far, three such elemental types have been identified with some confidence (evaluation, potency, and activity) and have been found to account for a large number and variety of discriminations; later these may be modified and certainly must be extended.

2 *Any axis or dimension placed through the origin of the semantic space represents a potential semantic scale or attribute of judgment.* This dimension may or may not have discrete and unitary verbal labels available in the language code.

3 *The semantic nature of any such attribute is given by its relations with the elemental factors.* These relations are determined from the projections of a unit portion of the attribute on the elementary factors, i.e., the relation is given by the cosines of the angles the attribute makes with the original dimensions.

4 *Every concept in semantic space may be said to be "contained" by its characteristic attribute.* The characteristic attribute of a concept is represented by the axis passing through the concept and the origin. All concepts located on this same axis share the same characteristic attribute. The characteristic attribute serves to differentiate a concept from the other concepts in two ways:

a. Another concept is different from this concept by having a characteristic attribute which is independent of (not co-linear with) the characteristic attribute of this concept;

b. another concept is different by virtue of having more or less of the same characteristic attribute.

5 *Two concepts may interact to the extent that they are contained by the same attributes.* This is assumed to include all conceivable kinds of interaction among concepts whereby the meaning of one is influenced by the meaning of the other. For example, when two concepts share the same characteristic attribute, they may be directly *compared;* if their characteristic attributes are orthogonal to each other, they are simply not comparable. Also, as we shall see in a later chapter (see Chapter 7, pp. 282-83), a principle of congruity governing attitude change and the semantic effects of word mixture predicts most accurately when the interacting concepts share the same characteristic attribute and least accurately when characteristic attributes are unrelated. We assume that the ease of making judgments of similarity and difference between concepts varies directly with the cosines of the angles between their characteristic attributes.

Figure 10 provides some illustrations. The points represent concepts, the solid axes A and B are two elementary scale types or factors against which the concepts were originally rated, and the dashed lines represent characteristic attributes. In case (a) the concepts all fall on a single axis and hence are contained by the same characteristic attribute — concepts differ only in degree of

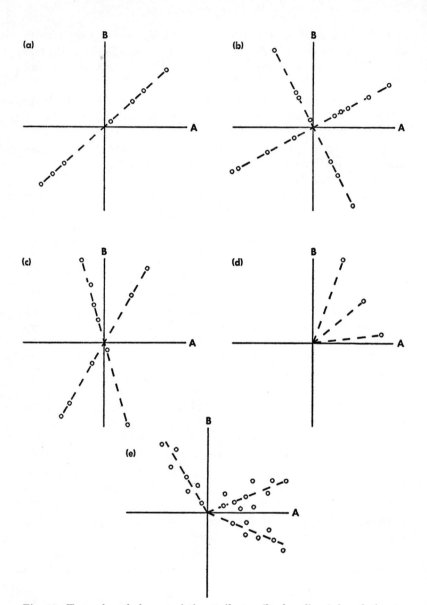

Fig. 10. Examples of characteristic attributes (broken lines) in relation to elemental scale types (axes A and B).

this attribute and comparisons can be made with maximal efficiency. Case (b) shows a conceptual structure wherein there are two sets of concepts, each with a different and orthogonal characteristic attribute. Our inference is that the concepts in one set are not readily comparable with those in the other. However, it is to be noted that some other attribute, not characteristic to either set, but partially containing both (here either original dimensions A or B), may serve as a basis for comparison. In case (c) the characteristic attributes are not orthogonal and the two sets of concepts are comparable with respect to either of the characteristic attributes, or in terms of a compromise attribute which falls in the space between them.

With actual data it is rare that all concepts of a given set lie on the same line. A more likely situation is that the concepts will scatter about a single line much like a set of points in a scatter diagram of a linear correlation coefficient. With such structures, a *dominant characteristic attribute* is defined as that line through the origin which is as close as possible in the least-square sense to all the concepts in the scatter. The dominant characteristic attributes of a structure are analogous to the factors in a simple structure (see Thurstone, 1947).

In Figure 10, plots (b) and (c) both indicate simple structures. Since there is no dispersion of points around the best fitting line, the dominant characteristic attributes in both cases are also the characteristic attributes of each of the points on the lines. In Figure 10, (d), dispersion exists, and the best fitting lines are the three dominant characteristic attributes. It is apparent that unlike the simple structure, the number of dominant characteristic attributes can exceed the rank of the matrix. Thus, in Figure 10, (e), three attributes emerge with a two dimensional structure.

The relation between each characteristic attribute and each of the original factors is given by the cosines of the angles between the attributes and the elemental scale types. The cosines may be found graphically as they are in the process of rotating factors into simple structure positions in factor analysis. The larger a cosine the greater the contribution of the original dimension of meaning to the make-up of the attribute. Two sets of cosines thus obtained — one for a characteristic attribute in each of two structures — may then be compared by inspection (there is no significance test for this comparison). If the characteristic attributes of two conceptual structures have essentially the same meaning in terms of the pro-

Table 14

COSINES OF ANGLES BETWEEN DOMINANT CHARACTERISTIC ATTRIBUTES (I, II, III) AND ELEMENTAL SCALE TYPE REPRESENTATIVE (FAIR, STRONG, ACTIVE) FOR THREE POLITICAL GROUPS

		Stevenson Voters	Taft Republicans	Eisenhower Republicans
fair	I	.58	.55	.55
	II	−.31	−.40	−.33
	III	−.05	−.05	−.10
strong	I	.56	.56	.56
	II	.85	.84	.84
	III	.80	.71	.73
active	I	.57	.60	.57
	II	.45	.38	.47
	III	−.65	−.69	−.66

portional contributions of the several elemental scale types, we interpret the structures as being the same.

The Characteristic Attributes of the Political Frame of Reference

We now may return to the data of the election study. A set of dominant characteristic attributes was found for each of the voting groups described in the three models in Figure 9, by rotating the original scale-factors into simple structure positions. The rotated dimensions were maintained orthogonal to each other. As already indicated, it is rare with real data that the concepts line up perfectly on only one dimension, and in the present case there is considerable scatter about the main axis. This means that there is some reliance on personal judgment in placing the dimensions. To check this, two persons rotated the three structures independently; for no dimension in any structure did the cosines of the angles of rotation differ by more than .05 between the two judges.

Are the characteristic attributes of the political frame of reference the same or different for different types of voters? Table 14 gives the cosines of the angles each set of dominant characteristic attributes makes with each set of original factor-scales (*fair-unfair, strong-weak,* and *active-passive*). It is clear that the three types of voters, Stevenson Democrats, Eisenhower Republicans, and Taft Republicans, generate almost identical characteristic attributes.

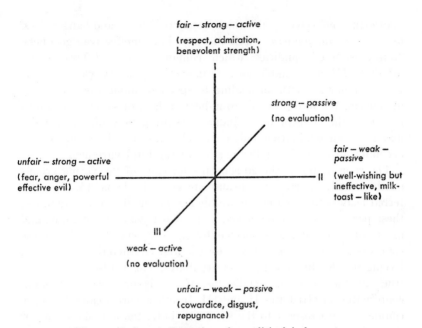

Fig. 11. Inferred dimensions for political judgments.

This indicates, according to our interpretation, that despite their different political outlooks, despite their gross differences in the meanings of particular concepts like TRUMAN, OUR POLICY IN CHINA, and SENATOR MCCARTHY, these groups of voters employ essentially the same frame of reference in making political judgments. They have the same sets of "values," the same relevant discriminations with respect to political persons and issues.

What is the semantic nature of these relevant discriminations? Figure 11 depicts the characteristic attributes of the political frame of reference. The polarities for the dominant dimension, *characteristic attribute I*, are defined by about equal portions of *fair, strong,* and *active* on one end and *unfair, weak,* and *passive* on the other. We interpret this dominant attribute as mediating judgments about the degree of *benevolent dynamism* vs. *malevolent insipidness* assumed to characterize political persons and policies. The positive pole of this factor seems to connote respect and admiration while the negative pole connotes dishonor and coward-like weakness. For *characteristic attribute II* the polarities are identifiable as *unfair-strong-active* vs. *fair-weak-passive*. We interpret this attribute as mediating judgments as to the degree of *malevolent dynamism* (powerful, effective evil which connotes fear and anger) vs. *benevolent insipidness* (well-wishing but ineffective goodness, "milktoast-like" qualities which connote scorn). *Characteristic attribute III* is definable as a *weak-active* polarity vs. a *strong-passive* polarity, with no loading to speak of along the evaluative dimension. We interpret this to indicate a lack of salience or prominence in the concept being judged, resulting in a diminished demand for an evaluative judgment. This last attribute, of course, accounts for a much smaller portion of the total variance.

The coordinates of the 20 concepts for each of the voting groups on these new, inferred dimensions are given in Table 15. The preferred leaders for each group are highest on the first dimension, i.e., these personalities are perceived as most benevolently dynamic and are most admired and respected by the subjects. Note that these concepts are contained entirely by the first characteristic attribute, having zero loading on the other attributes. This is also more or less true for the opposing candidates, if we ignore the very small coordinates on attributes II and III. In other words, candidates are compared with respect to the same attribute, the dominant one for the political frame of reference; in this case all candidates are perceived positively on this dimension, but this may be a special characteristic of the 1952 election. It would be possible for one candidate to be positive with respect to one "kind" of evaluation (benevolent dynamism) and the opposed candidate to be perceived as positive on the other "kind" of evaluation (benevolent but insipid).

With this model it also is possible to infer that a concept is perceived *ambivalently*. Thus Roosevelt, highly and unambivalently respected by the Stevenson voters, is perceived with both respect and fear by the Republicans. On the other hand, Stevenson voters perceive TAFT with ambivalence, in contrast to the Republican groups. Two other interesting examples of ambivalence are MC-CARTHY and STALIN. Whereas MCCARTHY is unambiguously *bad* to the Stevenson voters and tends to be unambiguously *good* to the Taft Republicans, Eisenhower Republicans are more ambivalent toward him — which seems somewhat prognostic of events which were to follow. Although STALIN is highest on the second dimension for all groups (connoting malevolent power), he also enjoys some respect and admiration (the first attribute), at least for Taft Republicans and Stevenson Democrats.

Actually, the only personality who is negative on the first attri-

Table 16

COORDINATES OF CONCEPTS ON INFERRED DIMENSIONS

	Taft Republicans			Eisenhower Republicans			Stevenson Voters		
	I	II	III	I	II	III	I	II	III
TAFT	3.98	.00	.00	2.37	.20	.30	1.95	1.36	.01
UMT	1.26	-.11	.50	2.28	.04	.00	1.61	.28	.41
STEVENSON	1.84	.25	.23	1.64	.02	.40	3.89	.00	.00
POLICY IN CHINA	-2.35	-.36	.57	-1.66	-.62	.27	-.85	-.23	.53
CHURCHILL	3.49	.65	.36	3.11	.35	.01	3.49	.66	.17
FEDERAL SPENDING	-.18	.14	1.93	-1.02	1.16	1.19	1.29	1.07	.75
MACARTHUR	3.94	.12	.36	2.40	.17	.13	2.08	.80	.17
SOCIALISM	-1.64	.93	1.38	-.80	.90	1.01	.10	.66	.90
KEFAUVER	2.15	-.37	.72	1.59	-.33	.48	2.46	.05	.58
GOV'T. EMPLOYEES	-.09	.27	.57	.08	.07	.24	1.01	.03	.28
STALIN	1.08	3.55	.00	.63	3.14	.00	1.08	3.41	.14
PRICE CONTROLS	-.59	.54	.80	-.25	.61	.82	1.00	-.30	.76
TRUMAN	-1.08	.74	1.58	-.89	.82	1.40	2.09	.42	.80
EUROPEAN AID	.34	.54	.73	1.10	.33	.18	2.01	-.40	.37
EISENHOWER	3.48	-.03	.23	3.67	.00	.00	2.65	.23	.58
LABOR UNIONISM	1.77	1.94	.36	1.54	1.50	.20	2.79	1.11	.14
ROOSEVELT	2.04	1.69	.42	1.65	1.25	.64	2.77	.56	.16
ATOM BOMB	1.84	.66	.23	1.43	.56	.24	1.53	1.41	.20
MCCARTHY	2.37	.88	.59	.90	1.36	.87	.36	2.20	1.17
UNITED NATIONS	.18	-.91	.42	1.22	-.79	.44	1.60	-.56	.74

bute for any group is HARRY S. TRUMAN — both Republican groups see him as *bad* in the sense of this attribute, i.e., malevolently insipid, dishonorable, and cowardly. Stevenson Democrats, on the other hand, and as might be expected, place TRUMAN high on the positive side of this first dimension. Of all concepts, OUR POLICY IN CHINA is most like TRUMAN in location within these characteristic attributes. This makes sense when we consider that during the campaign, and afterward as well, the Republicans frequently associated the term "appeasement" (dishonorable and cowardly) with the Truman administration's foreign policy in China. However, the high coordinate of TRUMAN on the third attribute seems to indicate that this concept was not very salient attitudinally. Another concept sharing this high loading on the third attribute is SOCIALISM. It is often assumed that because — when they are asked about it — Americans show unfavorable attitudes toward this concept, they are afraid of it. Our data show SOCIALISM to be *weak*, not strong, in meaning and for the most part nonsignificant to the average voter. The reader can inspect Table 15 himself and make similar observations.

It is apparent that the supposedly unidimensional evaluative factor becomes multidimensional with the characteristic attribute approach, at least when applied to these political judgments. At present, research is being planned to further differentiate "attitude" into several components, using this method. There are other psychological problems that can be approached with this judgmental model. For example, when the characteristic attributes for two groups judging the same concepts can be shown to differ (e.g., for high and low ethnocentrics), do the members of these groups have difficulty communicating with one another? If two concepts are contained by two different and relatively independent characteristic attributes in one person's thinking, is it more difficult for him to deal with them combinatively (e.g., "logic-tight" compartments), will a change in his attitude toward one have less effect on his attitude toward the other than if they shared the same attribute? These are all questions leading to further research. Finally, it should be said that although interpretations based on characteristic attributes of a semantic structure seem to have considerable face validity — at least in our study of the 1952 election — no adequate validation of the model has yet been attempted. We need to show that differential behaviors, voting and otherwise, can be better predicted knowing the characteristic attributes of a subject's reference frame than without this information.

4

EVALUATION OF THE SEMANTIC DIFFERENTIAL

In the first chapter a number of approaches to the measurement of meaning were described and evaluated against the standard criteria for measuring instruments. These criteria included *objectivity, reliability, validity, sensitivity, comparability,* and *utility.* In this chapter we shall submit the semantic differential to evaluation by the same criteria. Our main concerns will be with the reliability, validity, and comparability of the instrument, and as much evidence as we have been able to accumulate over the past five years or so will be summarized.

OBJECTIVITY

A method is objective to the extent that the operations of measurement and means of arriving at conclusions can be made explicit and hence reproducible. The procedures of measurement with the semantic differential are explicit and can be replicated. The means of arriving at results, from the collection of check-marks on scales to the location of concept-points in semantic space and the production of conceptual structures, are completely objective — two investigators given the same collection of check-marks and following the rules must end up with the same meanings of concepts and patterns of conceptual structures. It is true that how one *interprets* these results is a subjective matter, but so is the engineer's interpretation of objective data on the stress which a bridge will stand. It may be argued that the data with which we deal in semantic measurement are essentially subjective — introspections about meanings on the part of subjects — and that all we have done is to objectify expressions of these subjective states. This is entirely true, but it is not a criticism of the method. Objectivity concerns the role of the observer, not the observed. Our procedures completely eliminate the idiosyncrasies of the investigator in arriving at the final index of meaning, and this is the essence of objectivity.

RELIABILITY

The reliability of an instrument is usually said to be the degree to which the same scores can be reproduced when the same objects are measured repeatedly. The basic "score" obtained from the semantic differential is the digit value (1 through 7, or +3 through −3) corresponding to a subject's check-mark with which he indicates his judgment of a particular concept against a particular scale. We shall use the term *item reliability* to refer to the reproducibility of these basic scores. These item scores are typically averaged within factors, e.g., the three evaluative judgments for a single concept, the three potency judgments, and so on; we use the term *factor-score reliability* to refer to the reproducibility of these values under retest conditions. The several factor-scores for a single concept serve to allocate this concept to a point in the semantic space which defines the meaning of this concept; we shall refer to *concept-meaning reliability* when dealing with the reproducibility of points in the semantic space with repetition of the measurement operation.

Item Reliability

The conventional notion of reliability in psychological and educational measurement focuses on how consistently individuals are ranked in successive applications of the instrument, i.e., upon the magnitude of the correlation between test and retest scores. A more general notion of reliability as it is used in science focuses, as we have indicated above, upon the reproducibility of scores under conditions of repeated measurement. In this section we start with the conventional psychological approach through correlation, show why it is of dubious value for semantic differential data, and then turn to evidence on score reproducibility.

Test-Retest Correlation Data (Reliability Coefficients). As part of our first factor analytic study (see Chapter 2, pp. 33-39), 40 items sampled from the total 1000 items were repeated on a single page at the end of the form; this sample included 40 different scales (of

50 used in the experiment) and all 20 concepts, each appearing twice. None of the 100 subjects gave any indication of having noticed that certain items were repeated (presumably because they had been judging so many similar items). Test and retest were correlated across the 100 subjects and the 40 items, producing an N of 4000. The resulting coefficient was .85.

The question immediately arises as to why the reliability coefficients for individual items were not computed, rather than summing over items and thus including the variance attributable to item means. The answer is simply that semantic differential scores are too consistent! On many individual items, e.g., FEATHER on *light-heavy*, LADY on *smooth-rough*, MOTHER on *kind-cruel*, subjects show such close agreement on scale position that the variance approaches zero and computed reliability coefficients become meaningless. Obviously, if all subjects agree in checking "1" for a particular item on both test and retest, reliability is perfect even though a coefficient cannot be computed. This highlights the main difficulty with using r as a measure of reliability with data of the sort we have here: the correlation coefficient does not take into account the absolute differences between the means of the two tests; perfect reliability, r of 1.00, can occur when an absolute difference of several units exists between test and retest measurements such that not a single score is reproduced and, on the other hand, reliability can be indeterminate, as we have seen, when every subject gives exactly the same score on retest as he did on test.

Reproducibility of Item Scores. We therefore shifted our basic notion of reliability to that usually held for physical measurements, the score reproducibility criterion. Perfect reliability exists only when the scores on a second testing are identical with those obtained on the first testing, and any deviation from this criterion represents some degree of unreliability. The difficulty here, however, is to devise some variable and communicable index of the *degree* of reliability (analogous to the reliability coefficient). The following series of reliability studies were attempts to satisfy these requirements.

1 *Joint distributions of test and retest scores.* The responses to the same item on test and retest can be plotted in the form of a scattergram, with the rows defined by the seven alternatives on the first test and the columns defined by the corresponding alternatives on the second test. Such a plot indicates the deviations in scale units from test 1 to test 2: if there is perfect reliability, all

of the points for individual subjects will fall on the main diagonal of this matrix, i.e., zero deviations between the two tests; the greater the dispersion about this main diagonal, the lower the reliability. Both Solomon (1954), as part of his thesis research, and Kellogg Wilson, using the 40-item test-retest data collected in connection with our first factor analysis, have approached the problem of reliability this way.

The crudest estimate of reliability is to determine whether or not the joint distribution differs significantly from that which would be obtained if subjects assigned check-marks purely at random on the two testings. In this case, entries would be equally likely for all of the 7×7 cells in the matrix for each item. Solomon applied this test to the 50 scales used in his experiment (sonar signals as stimuli) and found that all scales deviated from this chance estimate at better than the 1 per cent level. This result tells us that test-retest data are related on something other than a chance basis, but it does not tell us how reliable the items are. And further, it makes the dubious assumption that all scale positions are equally likely to be checked on every item.

Wilson asked the following question: Taking into account the actual distributions of both test and retest check-marks, are the joint distributions of responses such that complete independence is shown between the two testings? Complete independence would mean that a response on the second test could not be predicted with any confidence from a response on the first test. The expected frequency of response in each cell of the joint distribution matrix was calculated by taking the product of the appropriate marginal entries. The sum of the expected frequencies in cells on the main diagonal of the matrix gives the total expected frequency of zero deviation from first to second measurement, the sum of the frequencies in the cells adjoining the main diagonal gives the total expected frequency of deviations of one unit, and so on through the maximal deviation of six units. The actual observed frequencies of deviations of each magnitude were then compared with the expected frequencies and tested for significance. A significant difference rejects the hypothesis that the second response is independent of the first. Wilson found all 40 test-retest items from the original factor analysis data to yield a difference significant at the 1 per cent level or better. Solomon tested the least reliable of his 50 scales, as determined from his original method described above, by this more sensitive method and found it to be significant beyond the 1 per

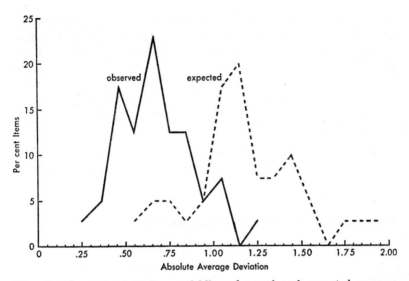

Fig. 12. Per cent of 40 items yielding observed and expected average absolute deviations between test and retest scores.

cent level. In using the present test, it would be possible, of course, to have significant dependence with an extreme lack of correspondence between first and second responses; this would be the case with a high negative correlation in the joint distribution matrix, but inspection easily shows this not to be the case.

Merely knowing that there is a significant degree of dependence between first and second ratings of items does not tell us *how* reliable these ratings are — a very considerable degree of variation can exist even though the dependence is significant at the 1 per cent level, just as a very low *r* may be significantly greater than zero. We turn, therefore, to a consideration of the error of measurement of the instrument, as estimated from the same test-retest data.

2 *Error of measurement.* When an instrument is applied repeatedly (a thermometer, a micrometer, or a semantic differential), we expect to observe some variation in the measurements recorded. The finer or smaller the average magnitude of this error of measurement, the more reliable the instrument. Figure 12 shows the average errors of measurement (e.g., average absolute deviation between first and second testings for the 40 items used above) actually obtained as compared with the deviations expected from the marginal values of the test-retest matrices. The mean of the observed average deviations for items is .67 scale units, whereas the

mean of the expected average deviations for items is 1.20 scale units. Only one of the 40 items has an obtained average deviation as large as the mean of the expected average deviations. Table 16 (A) gives a breakdown of such data into the factor-types. Scales with loadings of .80 or higher on the evaluative factor were placed in one group; scales with loadings of .50 or higher on potency or activity factors were placed in second and third groups respectively. The table presents the average deviations between first and second testings, found by summing and averaging over both persons and items within these groups. Although the number of scales meeting

Table 16

AVERAGE ABSOLUTE DEVIATIONS BETWEEN TEST AND RETEST RATINGS

(A) *40 Items from Original Factorial Study (*N *subjects, 100)*

Factor	N Scales	Average Absolute Deviation in Scale Units
Evaluation	11	.48
Potency	5	.71
Activity	2	.70

(B) *Luria Psychotherapy Study*

	Average Absolute Deviations in Scale Units			
	CONTROL GROUP			THERAPY GROUP
Factor	Immediate (N, 62)	6-8 Weeks (N, 52)	12-15 Weeks (N, 45)	Immediate (N, 38)
Evaluation	.53	.66	.65	.58
Potency	.77	.93	.96	.82
Activity	.86	.97	1.05	.81
All Scales	.74	.85	.90	.74

(C) *Bopp Study, Schizophrenics vs. Normals*

	Average Absolute Deviations in Scale Units			
	CONTROL GROUP (N, 40)		SCHIZOPHRENICS (N, 40)	
Factor	Immediate	2 Weeks	Immediate	2 Weeks
Evaluation	.24	.37	.47	.74
Potency and Activity	.36	.71	.68	.92

these criteria were small, it is clear that evaluative scales yield much smaller errors of measurement than other scales.

These findings for the 40 items drawn from the original factorial study are supported by other data. In a study in the psychotherapy area,[1] the reliabilities of 150 items (15 concepts $\times$ 10 scales) were assessed over test-retest intervals of a few minutes (immediately), 6-8 weeks, and 12-15 weeks for non-therapy controls, and over only the few minute (immediate) interval for therapy patients. The average absolute deviations in response from test to retest, for the three categories of scales and all scales, are shown as Table 16 (B). Summations were over both scales representing the same factors and subjects. Again, evaluative scales produce the smallest average errors of measurement; we also note that there are no apparent differences in reliability between normal controls and (neurotic) patients here and that the magnitude of the average error increases somewhat with the time interval.

A study by Bopp (1955) compared immediate test-retest reliabilities and delayed (two week interval) test-retest reliabilities for normal controls vs. schizophrenics, using a 104-item differential (8 concepts on 13 scales). Average absolute errors of the type already described were obtained for the 40 normals and 40 schizophrenics. The results are shown as Table 16 (C). The evaluative scales show consistently smaller deviations for both retest intervals and for both groups than do the potency and activity scales (in this study treated together). But in contrast to Luria's patients undergoing psychotherapy, Bopp's schizophrenic patients showed significantly poorer reliability than the controls ($p = .001$ by Mann-Whitney U test). Whether this result actually means less reliability of the instrument when applied to schizophrenics, or perhaps less stability in their meanings of concepts (i.e., change in what is being measured), is difficult to ascertain.

Let us reflect a moment about these results. The average errors of measurement of the semantic differential scales are always less than a single scale unit (approximately three-quarters of a scale unit) and for evaluative scales average about a half of a scale unit. This means that we can expect subjects, on the average, to be accurate within a single unit of the scale, which for practical purposes is satisfactory. We also can compare different scales and factors in terms of this type of reliability index. But this still does not pro-

---

[1] This study was conducted by Dr. Zella Luria at the University of Illinois in 1953.

Table 17

PROBABILITY OF OBTAINING GIVEN DEVIATIONS FROM TEST TO RETEST
(Data from Factor Analysis I, 40 Items)

Absolute Deviation	Per Cent of Responses	Probability of Obtaining a Deviation Equal to or Greater than Given Deviation
0	54.0	1.000
1	32.6	.460
2	8.6	.134
3	3.1	.048
4	1.1	.018
5	.4	.006
6	.2	.002

vide us with a set of *confidence limits* beyond which we could say that a deviation is significant.

3 *Probability limits.* Perhaps the most useful way of treating our test-retest data is in terms of the number of responses which yield absolute deviations of each given magnitude. If a subject-item matrix is formed and the cells of this matrix are filled with the obtained absolute deviations of each subject on each item, the number of instances of each size deviation may be counted. If subjects and items are considered to be representative, then statements regarding the *probability* of obtaining deviations of certain size can be made. Such statements have implications for assessing the significance of changes in meaning, as will be seen. The data for the same 40 items from factor analysis I were analyzed in this way and the results are presented in Table 17. The last column gives the proportion of time that a deviation equal to or greater than each size deviation can be expected if subjects and items are chosen at random. The values in this column correspond to confidence levels; they are a gauge of the degree of confidence with which an investigator can conclude that a given change on an item is significant. Thus, a change of greater than two units on the average scale by the average subject would be expected to occur less than 5 per cent of the time by chance (or as a result of random errors of measurement).

An Experiment on the Reliability of Semantic Judgments

In none of the experiments described so far has the problem of reliability been central, and the conditions for testing it were, therefore, considerably less than ideal. It had also been observed (in both the Luria and Bopp studies) that the reliability of the instrument, *as measured*, seemed to decrease as the time interval between test and retest increased. This could be interpreted as due to either increasing unreliability through time or increasing unstability of the thing being measured (meaning of concepts) through time. The reliability experiment to be reported here was designed to check these possibilities, by measuring the relation between absolute deviation and time over a sufficiently long period. The two alternative interpretations of an increasing deviation-time curve are these: (1) Assuming the worst, i.e., that we have stable meanings over time but an increasingly unreliable instrument, we could at least hope that the increasing deviations would approach some asymptote in time which would represent the most conservative estimate of reliability; (2) Assuming the best, i.e., that meanings of concepts do change with time and the instrument reliably and sensitively reflects these changes, one could extrapolate the deviation-time curve to "zero time" on the scale as an index of the "true" reliability. It may be noted in passing that this is a very basic problem in estimating the reliability of any psychological instrument — to what extent is the *measured* unreliability of an instrument really an index of its sensitivity in recording real changes in the thing being measured?

Eight groups of subjects with approximately 25 in each were given a 100-item semantic differential at two times. The intervals between testings were varied for different groups as follows: 3 minutes, 6, 12, 20, and 30 minutes, 1 day, 1 week, and 3 weeks. Although Form I was used (different concepts appearing with different scales on each line), a systematic rather than a random presentation of the materials was used to obtain approximately equal time intervals between test and retest for various items. The maximum of nine concepts intervened between repetitions of each concept and scales were similarly treated. An attempt was made to include concepts which it was thought would differ markedly in what might be called "inherent semantic stability" — thus, MY MOOD TODAY was considered inherently more variable in time than PAPER CLIP. The other eight concepts were: EISENHOWER, MC CARTHY, COMMUNISM, FRENCH GOVERNMENT, MOTHER, ME, SEX, and RABBIT. Ten scales were chosen to represent the three factors: evaluative, *good-bad, beautiful-ugly, clean-dirty,* and *pleasant-unpleasant;*

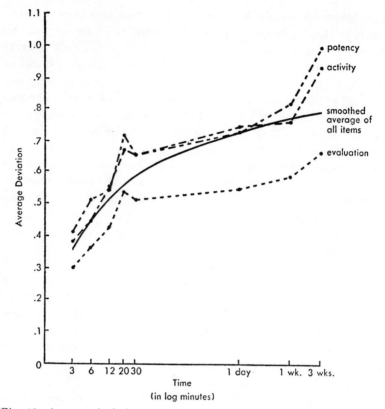

Fig. 13. Average deviation as a function of increasing time between test and retest.

potency, *strong-weak, large-small,* and *heavy-light;* and activity, *fast-slow, active-passive,* and *sharp-dull.*

The first analysis consisted simply in computing the average absolute deviations across the subjects in each time-interval group. This was done for all items separately and for the average of all items involving the same factor. Figure 13 represents the results in the form of a deviation-time curve. Separate curves for the three factors are shown, along with a smoothed all-item curve. To take into account the typical psychological retention function, we have plotted this curve in terms of log time in minutes. Except for the longest time interval (three weeks), this curve has a generally negatively accelerated shape, tending toward an asymptote at about .9 scale units. In other words, from the most conservative viewpoint, the average error of measurement with the semantic differential is no more than one scale unit. Since psychological functions seldom have abrupt changes in direction, it is probably safe to assume that the deviation of the three-week group from the trend is due to sampling errors or some special but unknown circumstance in the testing. We also observe that the greater reliability of evaluative as compared with other scales reappears in these data.

But is this most conservative estimate of reliability the best estimate? It certainly seems likely that the meanings of concepts to people can change from time to time and that changes are more likely over long intervals than short — e.g., one's meaning of MY MOOD TODAY is likely to vary with today's experiences, and experiences are likely to vary more between one day and another than between one minute and the next. The most liberal estimate of reliability of our instrument would be obtained by constructing a best fitting negatively accelerated function for these data and extrapolating it "forward" until it crosses the ordinate at zero time. If we distrust such an extrapolation (as well we may), we can still take the average error for the group having the shortest time interval — the least time for the meanings of concepts to shift — as our best liberal estimate. This value is approximately one-third of a scale unit.

As was pointed out in an earlier chapter, the question of statistical independence of data obtained *within* the individual case comes down to whether or not the *errors of measurement* are correlated. For example, it may be desired to know whether, in the individual case, the concept FATHER is perceived as significantly higher in *potency* than in *evaluation;* the mean judgment on a sample of potency scales could be compared with the mean judgment on a sample of evaluative scales, and degrees of freedom made commensurate with the number of scales, *if* the errors of measurement on scales of the same type are independent. From the data of this reliability study four concepts were selected at random (ME, MY MOOD TODAY, PAPER CLIP, and EISENHOWER). For each of these concepts the correlations between the test-retest deviations on scales representing the same factor were found, e.g., errors on *good-bad* correlated with errors on *clean-dirty*, etc., taking account of the sign of the deviation. The obtained correlations appear in Table 18 (A). To estimate an average r, these correlations were converted to z's and tested for homogeneity (see Snedecor, 1946). The r's could be considered homogeneous by this test; the average r was found to be .09. In other words, the errors of measurement, even on scales representing the same factor, are essentially independent.

It should be noted that, appropriately, the above test was made only for groups having a short retest interval (within 30 minutes). With longer retest intervals, in which the meaning of the concept could be expected to change, one would expect correlations in deviations for related scales to increase in size. The correlations for the

Table 18

A

CORRELATIONS OF TEST-RETEST DEVIATIONS FOR RELATED SCALES AND SAME CONCEPT — 3 TO 30 MINUTE INTERVALS

	ME	MY MOOD TODAY	PAPER CLIP	EISENHOWER
good-bad/clean-dirty	−.23	.21	−.05	.18
good-bad/beautiful-ugly	.04	.16	.04	.05
strong-weak/large-small	(*)	.19	.25	.15
quick-slow/active-passive	.07	.18	.01	.07

B

CORRELATIONS OF TEST-RETEST DEVIATIONS FOR RELATED SCALES AND SAME CONCEPT — 1 DAY TO 3 WEEK INTERVALS

	ME	MY MOOD TODAY	PAPER CLIP	EISENHOWER
good-bad/clean-dirty	.24	.48	−.01	−.04
good-bad/beautiful-ugly	.34	.70	.16	.16
strong-weak/large-small	(*)	.33	−.20	.06
quick-slow/active-passive	.13	.52	.18	.22

C

CORRELATIONS OF TEST-RETEST DEVIATIONS FOR PAIRS OF CONCEPTS JUDGED AGAINST SAME SCALES — 3 TO 30 MINUTE INTERVALS

	good-bad	strong-weak	quick-slow
ME/MY MOOD TODAY	.34	.02	.22
ME/PAPER CLIP	.23	−.06	.12
ME/EISENHOWER	−.02	.14	−.21
MY MOOD TODAY/PAPER CLIP	.14	−.08	.01
MY MOOD TODAY/EISENHOWER	.09	−.06	.10
PAPER CLIP/EISENHOWER	−.02	.09	.04

* Scale mistyped on form given subjects.

Table 19

PROBABILITY OF OBTAINING GIVEN DEVIATION FROM TEST TO RETEST ON INDIVIDUAL ITEMS FOR INDIVIDUAL SUBJECTS

(112 Subjects, Reliability Experiment Data)

Absolute Deviation	Evaluative Items		Potency Items		Activity Items		All Items	
	Per Cent	p	Per Cent	p	Per Cent	p	Per Cent	p
0	67.1	1.000	61.4	1.000	61.4	1.000	63.7	1.000
1	25.0	.329	27.2	.386	27.9	.386	26.5	.363
2	5.3	.079	6.9	.114	6.2	.107	6.1	.098
3	2.0	.026	2.8	.045	3.5	.045	2.7	.037
4	0.4	.006	1.1	.017	0.6	.010	0.7	.010
5	0.1	.002	0.3	.006	0.2	.004	0.2	.003
6	0.0	.001	0.2	.003	0.1	.002	0.1	.001

one day, one week, and the three-week groups combined, for the same concepts, are shown in Table 18 (B) and, as predicted, they tend to be of greater magnitude. Also, as might be expected, the largest correlations are consistently for the concept MY MOOD TODAY. The correlations in Table 18 (B) were not homogeneous and could not, justifiably, be averaged. It should also be noted that in running the above test for independence of errors of measurement on related scales for the same concept we are making the most stringent test, i.e., under conditions where one would expect lack of independence to show up if it exists.

Another test one might wish to make of data for the individual case would be the comparison of two different concepts on the same factor or scale. Taking one scale for each factor and the same four concepts, we may correlate the errors of measurement over short time intervals for each pair of concepts on the same scales. These correlations are shown in Table 18 (C). Again, their average is approximately zero (.06). We conclude that over short time intervals (within 30 minutes), the errors of measurement within the single case are independent, at least for these concepts.

What evidence does this experiment provide us on *probability limits* for individual items? Here we combine the first five groups of subjects whose test-retest intervals were all within 30 minutes, a total of 112 subjects. Table 19 gives the percentages of subjects having absolute deviations of each magnitude (in per cent) and, derived from these data, the empirical probabilities of getting devia-

Table 20

PROBABILITY OF OBTAINING GIVEN DEVIATIONS FROM TEST TO RETEST ON FACTOR SCORED ITEMS FOR INDIVIDUAL SUBJECTS

(112 Subjects, Reliability Experiment Data)

Absolute Deviation	Evaluative Items		Potency Items		Activity Items		All Items	
	Per Cent	p	Per Cent	p	Per Cent	p	Per Cent	p
0	35.5	1.000	34.9	1.000	37.7	1.000	36.1	1.000
.25	31.2	.645	0.0	.651	0.0	.623	10.4	.639
.33	0.9	.333	30.4	.651	27.7	.623	19.7	.535
.50	17.6	.324	2.6	.347	3.8	.346	8.0	.338
.67	0.2	.148	14.7	.321	15.9	.308	10.3	.258
.75	8.4	.146	0.0	.174	0.0	.149	2.8	.155
1.00	3.3	.062	9.3	.174	7.7	.149	6.8	.127
1.25	1.6	.029	0.0	.081	0.0	.072	0.5	.059
1.33	0.1	.013	3.0	.081	3.2	.072	2.1	.054
1.50	0.5	.012	0.5	.051	0.5	.040	0.5	.033
>1.50	0.7	.007	4.6	.046	3.5	.035	2.8	.028

tions equal to or greater than each magnitude on test-retest of the same item (p). These results agree well with those previously reported (in Table 17). For all types of items (evaluative, potency, and activity), a difference of more than *two scale units* can be considered significant at about the 5 per cent level, on the grounds that deviations this large occur only this proportion of the time when randomly selected subjects repeat their judgments of randomly selected items.

Factor-Score Reliability

The data from this same experiment can be analyzed to yield analogous probability limits for deviations in factor scores. Again we use the five groups ($N = 112$) whose retests occurred within 30 minutes. In averaging deviations over the scales representing each factor, the direction as well as the magnitude of deviation from test to retest is taken into account, the signs being consistent with the factor interpretation (e.g., deviations toward *good, beautiful, clean,* and *pleasant* being recorded as plus). Since random errors tend to cancel out in this averaging process, it would be expected that average errors of measurement for factor scores would be smaller than for individual items, and this is the case.

Table 21

PROBABILITY OF OBTAINING GIVEN DEVIATION FROM TEST TO RETEST ON FACTOR SCORED ITEMS FOR GROUPS OF SUBJECTS

(8 Groups of 25 Subjects Each)

Average Deviation in Scale Units	Factors					
	I		II		III	
	Per Cent	p	Per Cent	p	Per Cent	p
.00–.09	.375	1.000	.368	1.000	.398	1.000
.10–.19	.320	.625	.304	.632	.350	.602
.20–.29	.203	.305	.210	.328	.134	.252
.30–.39	.062	.102	.086	.118	.078	.118
.40–.49	.016	.040	.023	.032	.023	.040
>.50	.023	.024	.008	.009	.016	.017

Each subject contributes a separate deviation factor score for each factor on each concept, and as before, we compute the empirical probability of deviations of each size. In Table 20 the percentage of responses giving each deviation (in per cent) and associated probability limits (p) are given. We find that a change in factor score of more than 1.00 for the evaluative factor, more than 1.50 for the potency factor, and more than 1.33 for the activity factor is significant at about the 5 per cent level.

These data apply to what may be expected from the individual subject on test-retest deviations for judgments of the same concept. What about the stability of concept meanings for groups of subjects, the reliability of cultural meanings of concepts? In an experiment to be described later (Chapter 7) on the effects of word mixture, eight groups of about 25 subjects each differentiated the meanings of the same 16 words, eight adjectives and eight nouns. Here we are interested in the deviations in factor scores for the same concepts as judged by different groups drawn from the same general population (college sophomores). Since these are not test-retest data in the strict sense (each group performing only once), we take the mean factor scores for all groups combined as the best estimate of the "true meaning" and record the deviations of each group from these values. We have eight (groups) times 16 (concepts) deviation scores for each factor; the distribution of deviations of varying size for each factor are given in Table 21 along with the probability limits. Here we do not find any appreciable difference between factors in terms of reliability. Cultural meanings of concepts prove to be very stable — for any factor, a shift of only about four-tenths of a scale unit is significant at the 5 per cent level. This degree of stability holds despite the small sizes of the groups, only about 25 in each.

Since the *reliability of concept meaning* conceived as a point in the semantic space is completely dependent upon the reliabilities of the factor scores of which it is composed, no separate estimates need to be given here. The same holds for the *reliability of semantic distances* between concepts in the space, where the D formula is applied to paired arrays of factor scores. In both cases, the variables which determine the point in space of a single concept and over which the D is computed are assumed to be independent, and hence there can be no cancellation of errors in their combination. Therefore, concept meanings and distances between them will be just as reliably determined as the factor scores on which they are based.

VALIDITY

An instrument is said to be valid when it measures what it is supposed to measure. A more refined and quantitative statement is that an instrument is valid to the extent that scores on it correlate with scores on some criterion of that which is supposed to be measured. The semantic differential is proposed as an instrument for measuring *meaning;* ideally, therefore, we should correlate semantic differential scores with some independent criterion of meaning — but there is no commonly accepted quantitative criterion of meaning. In lieu of such a criterion, we have fallen back on what is usually called "face validity." In a few instances we have rather specific external criteria, e.g., how people actually voted in an election. Beyond this general question, there are certain specific validity questions that arise in connection with this method: Do the dimensions we obtain through factor analysis correspond to those ordinarily used by people in making meaningful judgments? Are the assumptions we make in using the differential — about the sizes of scale units, about scale linearity, and so on — demonstrably valid? Is the selective behavior of a subject using the differential indicative of the representational mediation process theoretically set in motion by the sign being judged? These are questions which will concern us in this section.

Face Validity

An instrument may be said to have "face validity" to the extent that the distinctions it provides correspond with those which would be made by most observers without the aid of the instrument. Do the similarities and differences in meaning provided by the semantic differential correspond to those which most of us make about meanings? The only procedure here is to present samples of the discriminations made with the instrument and ask the reader if they correspond with his own judgments. The data presented earlier in Table 9 and Figure 7 offer one example: the results obtained with the semantic differential arrange the ten concepts into three clusters and one exclusion — WHITE ROSE BUDS, GENTLENESS, and SLEEP form one cluster having similar meaning; HERO, VIRILITY, and SUCCESS form another, and QUICKSAND, FATE, and DEATH form the third, with the concept METHODOLOGY by itself. When we say that these results have high "face validity" we mean that most people would have clustered these concepts in much the same way without using the differential.

In most of the applications to be reported in the subsequent chapters of this book, similar illustrations of the "face validity" of the instrument will be provided. For example, in a study on the effect of mixing or combining words, a set of eight adjectives — ARTISTIC, HAIRY, LISTLESS, AVERAGE, SINCERE, SHY, TREACHEROUS, and BREEZY — were differentiated by some 200 subjects, and mean factor scores were computed. On the *evaluative factor,* SINCERE and ARTISTIC were the most favorable and LISTLESS and TREACHEROUS the most unfavorable; on the *potency factor,* TREACHEROUS and HAIRY were the most potent and LISTLESS and SHY the weakest; on the *activity factor,* BREEZY and TREACHEROUS were most active and LISTLESS and SHY most passive. These are "reasonable" characterizations of these adjectives, and the reader will note many other such examples. Throughout our work with the semantic differential we have found no reasons to question the validity of the instrument on the basis of its correspondence with the results to be expected from common sense.

Correlation with Certain External Criteria

There are many instances in the applications to be described in the remaining chapters where validity criteria of specific sorts were available. Unfortunately, they are almost exclusively concerned with the evaluative factor. In Chapter 5, for example, high correlations between the location of concepts on the evaluative factor and scores on standard attitude scales will be described. In Chapter 6, relations between semantic differential results and judgments about psychotherapy cases will be described which also reflect on the validity of the instrument. In a thesis by Reeves (1954), for example, the evaluative locations of TAT pictures judged by subjects against the differential are found to correlate significantly with the clinical judgments of stories told about the pictures by the same subjects. If we consider the assignment of voters to political groups according to their expressed preferences (Taft Republicans, Eisenhower Republicans, and Stevenson Voters) to be a satisfactory criterion of political attitude, then the data given in Table 12 of Chapter 3 contribute to our validity assessment; as our general political knowledge leads us to expect, Taft Republicans are most favorable to concepts like MCCARTHY and GENERAL MACARTHUR and least favorable to concepts like POLICY IN CHINA, PRICE CONTROLS, and LABOR UNIONISM — and vice versa for Stevenson Democrats.

This 1952 election study provides us with another check on the validity of semantic measurement, with actual voting behavior as a criterion. At each sampling period the subjects in this study indicated how they planned to vote — for Eisenhower, for Stevenson, or "don't know." Particular interest attaches to the "don't know" voters, since it is this category that plays a disproportionate role in deciding elections as well as in confounding the pollsters. Three and a half months before Election Day, 18 subjects placed themselves in this category. At the same time, 12 subjects expressed themselves as "very certain" they would vote for Stevenson and 25 subjects as "very certain" they would vote for Eisenhower. If voting behavior depends upon one's attitudes and meanings, then the vote of each "don't know" should be predictable from the correspondence of his concept-meanings to the typical Stevenson voter vs. the typical Eisenhower voter. Each "don't know" subject's ratings of the 20 concepts on the *fair-unfair* (evaluative) scale were compared with the mean responses of the two "certain" groups. This correspondence was determined by the distance measure, D. If a given subject's D from the Stevenson "certain" mean profile was smaller than from the Eisenhower "certain" profile, it was predicted that he would vote for Stevenson "when the chips were down," and so on for the 18 "don't know" subjects. Of the 18 "don't knows," 14 voted as predicted according to this criterion, which is significant at the 5 per cent level by the Dixon-Mood "sign test." When the results of the *strong-weak* scale were combined with evaluation, prediction rose to 17 out of 18 and a significance level of 1 per cent by the same test. Addition of the *active-passive* scale (which failed to predict better than chance by itself), however, lowered the total prediction. To a limited extent, then, these results support the behavioral validity of semantic measurement; they also have interesting implications for polling work.

Validity of Semantic Factors

When the intercorrelations among many scales are factor analyzed and certain basic factors, such as evaluation, potency, and activity, repeatedly appear, we assume that these factors correspond to the major dimensions which people "naturally" and "spontaneously" use in making meaningful judgments. We also assume that the D's computed between concepts validly represent the psychological similarities and dissimilarities in meaning among these concepts — which necessarily implies that the space within which our factors lie is Euclidean in character. Are these valid assumptions? If subjects were asked to make judgments of similarity and difference among concepts *without* use of the semantic differential, would approximately the same distances among the concepts appear, in a space having the same number of dimensions?

Rowan (1954) made a direct comparison between the semantic differential and the method of triads: "The semantic relations among a group of concepts were determined both with and without the use of the semantic differential scales, and the results of these two analyses were compared. . . . If this comparison reveals essentially comparable semantic structures one can conclude that the representation of concepts by means of the semantic differential is a 'natural' one, in the sense that the scales are representative of the semantic dimensions people actually use in judging the meaning of concepts." Rowan presented 160 subjects with 10 concepts, (a) to be rated on 20 differential scales and (b) to be compared on the basis of meaningful similarity without the use of scales. The concepts were the 10 given in the model in Figure 7 — GENTLENESS, SLEEP, HERO, SUCCESS, FATE, etc. — and the total 20 scales originally used there were also used by Rowan (cf. Osgood and Suci, 1952). In the comparison experiment, the same subjects were presented with all 120 possible triadic combinations of the 10 concepts and in each instance asked to choose the two most similar concepts of the three given.

The similiarity judgments obtained in the triad method generated a "similarity space" (to differentiate it from the "semantic space" generated by the differential) wherein the distance between any two concepts i and j is given by $1 - p_{ij}$, where p_{ij} is the percentage of times i and j are chosen as most similar out of the total number of times they appeared together in the triads. This distance function was found by Rowan to be nearly identical to Torgerson's (1952) measure of distance derived for triadic judgments of this type. The distances in "semantic space" were found by summing over the squared differences between the means of concepts on each of the 20 scales and taking the square root of the sum, i.e., the usual formula for D. As a check on the reliability of the spatial relations among the concepts, Rowan divided his total group of subjects into two halves by random selection and compared both the "similarity" and "semantic" spaces — the two "similarity" matrices of distances correlated .983 and the two "semantic" D matrices .975, indicating equivalently high degrees of reliability.

Rowan's first task was to test the adequacy of the Euclidean representation of the "similarity" space. This space was dimensionalized by factoring the matrix of cross-products between concept-vectors, with the origin established at the centroid of the space. Although some of the latent roots associated with the factors were negative, and hence the concepts could not be considered to be perfectly represented in Euclidean space, the extent of this distortion was very slight, none of the four negative roots being higher in absolute value than the positive roots and only one of them being greater than .10. Wilson (1954) has suggested that, rather than equating $1 - p_{ij}$ with D as Rowan had done, it would be more consistent with both logical and empirical considerations to equate Rowan's function with D^2. When this was done by Wilson, using Rowan's data, the principal axis factor solution yielded only one negative root (i.e., a more satisfactory Euclidean solution). This is an important point because the assumption that the semantic space is Euclidean in nature is necessary for the use of D in representing the distances among concepts. The very slight distortion from Euclidean representation found by Rowan, and particularly by Wilson, increases our confidence in the validity of representing semantic relations with this model.

Rowan's factoring of the "similarity" and "semantic" spaces produced three reliable factors in each case — the orderings of concepts along these three dimensions in both cases were identical for the two subgroups of subjects. A fourth factor obtained with the triad method (accounting for only 3 per cent of the variance) did not give the same ordering for the subgroups and was discarded. Applying the coefficient of proportionality (see p. 44), Rowan found that only two of the factors in the "semantic" space were present in the "similarity" space, the coefficients being .86, .90, and .36. The first factor in the "similarity" space was clearly equivalent to the *evaluative* factor, but either the *potency* or the *activity* factor could be identified equally well with the second factor in the "similarity" space. The third factor in the "similarity" space was specific to METHODOLOGY, the concept not falling in any of the clusters. However, when the two identifiable factors were used to compute distances between concepts, and these distances were correlated across the two spaces, the resulting coefficient was .95, indicating almost identical structures. In other words, for this set of concepts at least two dimensions, *evaluation* and either *potency* or *activity*, or a combination of both (*"dynamism"*), are used "naturally" by subjects in their meaningful judgments. In Wilson's analysis, the factor solution could be rotated either to match Rowan's two-factor structure or equally well a three-factor solution which corresponded to those obtained in the Osgood-Suci factor work.

The factors along which subjects are forced to make judgments in the semantic differential correspond reasonably well with those which they use spontaneously in direct paired or triadic comparisons. These results, however, are limited to the particular set of concepts employed and more tests of this sort are called for. It may be asked why — if the method of triads involves fewer assumptions — do we not simply abandon the semantic differential as such? There are several reasons, the foremost being: (1) The method of triads and other methods of the same type are excessively laborious and time consuming, becoming prohibitive for both subject-time and analysis-time as the number of concepts increases much beyond 10 or 15; (2) Comparability tends to be lost because each study using a new set of concepts would require a completely new analysis; and (3) By providing the subject with dimensions, we probably tap available bases for comparison which the subject may not spontaneously think of, even though they may be valid bases — this may be the reason for the lack of separation of potency and activity factors in Rowan's "similarity" space. For these and other reasons, we feel that the "freer" but more laborious method of triads should be used to test the validity of more "restrictive" but simpler methods like the semantic differential.

Validity of Certain Scaling Assumptions

Use of the semantic differential involves several assumptions about the individual scales of which it is composed. When an integer score is assigned as a concept's scale position, for instance, the property of equal intervals within that scale is assumed. When D is taken over a set of scales, equal intervals between scales is assumed. In addition, the application of factor analytic techniques to the assigned scores involves assumptions about the scale origins, specifically that the zero point falls at the centroid of each scale. If the scales do not meet these assumptions, at least approximately, factor analyses of meaning based on such scales may yield distorted pictures of the underlying structure and differentials based on these analyses will be to some degree invalid.

In order to investigate these scaling properties,[2] the psychometric method of successive intervals (Gulliksen, 1954; Saffir, 1937) was applied separately to nine of the most frequently used scales: *good-bad, clean-dirty, valuable-worthless, large-small, strong-weak, heavy-light, active-passive, fast-slow*, and *hot-cold*. The analysis was based upon data originally gathered by the method of equal-appearing intervals, for factor analysis I (see pp. 33-39), and involved judgments of 20 concepts by 100 college student subjects. The two methods, of equal-appearing intervals and successive intervals, are identical with respect to data collection; they differ only in assumptions made to simplify the assignment of scale values.

By establishing a subjective metric, the method of successive intervals provides an estimate of interval length and thus permits an evaluation of the equality of intervals along a scale. The procedure used in the present investigation was an iterative, graphical, least squares solution developed by Diederich (see Diederich, Messick, and Tucker, 1955). In addition to providing scale values for stimuli, the method of successive intervals also yields scale values

---

[2] This study of the scaling properties of the semantic differential was made by Dr. Samuel J. Messick, at that time a Ford Fellow at the University of Illinois. The authors wish to express their gratitude to Dr. Messick for his skilled assistance on this problem and for his write-up of the results, which this report follows in the main.

for the boundaries separating response categories. Since seven response categories are used on the semantic differential scales, the successive intervals solution for each scale will yield six boundary values, which will be designated as t_g, where $g = 1, 2, \ldots 6$. Estimates of the size of intervals can then be found by subtracting successive boundary values.

The least squares solution entails certain restrictions which arbitrarily fix an origin and a unit for the scale. These restrictions set the origin of the scale so that

$$\sum_{g=1}^{k} t_g = 0,$$

i.e., the origin is placed at the centroid of the boundary values. The unit is set so that

$$\sum_{g=1}^{k} t_g^2 = k,$$

i.e., so that the variance of the boundary values is unity. It should be emphasized that this selection of a unit and origin is completely arbitrary and that any other origin and unit could be used, i.e., the scale values may be changed by a linear transformation. Under the above restrictions, the boundary values obtained from the successive intervals procedure will be such that their sum is zero and their variance is one, and hence they will not be directly comparable to boundary values on the equal-interval scale assumed with the semantic differential.

The numbers 3, 2, 1, 0, -1, -2, -3 are used as successive category mid-points on the assumed scale, so the assumed interval boundaries, designated by a_g, would be 2.5, 1.5, .5, $-.5$, -1.5, and -2.5. In making the t_g boundary values comparable to the assumed boundaries, it is desirable to leave the origin of the scale at the centroid, since this is also where it is placed on the assumed scale. The unit, however, should be multiplied by some constant c in order to make the obtained boundary values, t_g, the same order of magnitude as the assumed boundaries, a_g. The linear transformation appropriate for such a change would be $L_g = ct_g$, where L_g designates the transformed interval boundaries.

Since the choice of a unit is completely arbitrary, it would seem desirable to select the transforming constant according to some least squares criterion, so as to bring the successive intervals scale as close as possible to the assumed scale through a linear transformation. Accordingly, the following function was minimized:

$$\sum_{g=1}^{k} (a_g - ct_g)^2.$$

The value of c which made this function a minimum was

$$c = \frac{\sum_g a_g t_g}{\sum_g t_g^2}.$$

It should be noted that this constant is the coefficient for the regression of a on t, so that the computation of the above transformation also yields almost directly the correlation between assumed and scaled boundary values.

Accordingly, the method of successive intervals was applied to the nine bipolar scales to obtain six category boundary values, t_g, for each scale. Transformed scores, L_g, were computed using a separate c for each scale, thus making the scaled boundary values the same order of magnitude as the assumed boundaries on the equal-interval scale. Mid-points could then be found for the middle five categories of each scale by interpolation from the boundary values, and estimates of interval size could be obtained by subtracting successive boundaries. Table 22 presents the transformed interval boundaries, L_g, along with interpolated category midpoints, m_g, for each of the nine scales.

An examination of this table reveals some inequality of intervals within any one of the scales, e.g., the difference $L_5 - L_4$, which is the length of interval 5, is generally less than half the size of $L_2 - L_1$, the length of interval 2. However, interval sizes are fairly consistent between scales, i.e., the same categories tend to be too large or too small in similar amounts over all scales. Also, the origin falls in approximately the same place on all scales, the zero point being located so that the center category is always slightly negative.

In order to evaluate scale-to-scale variations in the placement of boundary positions, mean deviations between scales were computed by the following formula:

$$\text{Mean Dev.} = 1/6 \sum_g | L_{g\alpha} - L_{g\beta} |,$$

where α and β designate two different scales. These values are

Table 22

TRANSFORMED INTERVAL BOUNDARIES, L_k, OBTAINED BY THE METHOD OF SUCCESSIVE INTERVALS, ALONG WITH INTERPOLATED MID-POINTS

Scale	L_1	m_2	L_2	m_3	L_3	m_4	L_4	m_5	L_5	m_6	L_6
good-bad	2.74	2.06	1.38	.84	.30	−.21	−.72	−1.06	−1.40	−1.85	−2.30
clean-dirty	2.82	2.02	1.22	.69	.15	−.19	−.53	−.89	−1.25	−1.83	−2.41
valuable-worthless	2.81	2.10	1.39	.74	.09	−.33	−.74	−1.02	−1.31	−1.77	−2.23
large-small	2.71	2.06	1.40	.81	.21	−.18	−.58	−.95	−1.33	−1.88	−2.42
strong-weak	2.84	2.00	1.16	.62	.08	−.20	−.49	−.81	−1.14	−1.80	−2.46
heavy-light	2.72	2.06	1.40	.83	.26	−.19	−.64	−1.01	−1.38	−1.87	−2.36
active-passive	2.84	2.05	1.26	.65	.03	−.26	−.55	−.88	−1.21	−1.79	−2.37
fast-slow	2.67	2.02	1.38	.87	.37	−.11	−.60	−.98	−1.36	−1.91	−2.46
hot-cold	2.45	2.01	1.57	1.07	.56	−.10	−.76	−1.04	−1.33	−1.91	−2.50
Assumed Scale	2.50	2.00	1.50	1.00	.50	0	−.50	−1.00	−1.50	−2.00	−2.50

presented in Table 23, along with mean deviations between each bipolar scale and the assumed equal-interval scale. Table 23 indicates that, in general, deviations are less between two bipolar scales than between bipolar and assumed scales. This suggests a greater similarity of intervals between than within scales, i.e., the category boundaries are similarly placed on all nine scales but not exactly in the proper positions for equal intervals.

The question now arises as to whether or not these deviations can be considered to be only chance fluctuations in the placement of category boundaries. This question can be approached in several ways, but because of the paucity of appropriate statistical tests, none of the approaches is very direct. In the first place, the mean deviations presented in Table 23 are well within the limits of errors of measurement reported earlier in reliability studies (see p. 139). This indicates a possibility of the intervals actually being equal and the apparent differences being due to chance alone. However, this possibility seems unlikely because of the consistent placement of category boundaries between scales. Consistency is not a property of random fluctuations. Nevertheless, the deviations from equal intervals are small and, as has been pointed out before, within the error limits of the instrument.

Another factor which might contribute to an apparent inequality of intervals is the distribution of concepts over each scale. Twenty concepts were rated on the semantic differential in the study from which the present scaling data were obtained, and about three-quarters of these concepts were consistently rated on the positive side of the scale. This means that more estimates of the positive intervals were available in the scaling procedure than of negative ones. But since averages are taken in finding the interval size, the number of different estimates is not as important as their similarity. Since, even on those scales for which as few as four estimates of an end category were available, these estimates were found to be comparatively similar and presumably representative, the resulting distortions of interval size are probably not very marked in this case. There was also a tendency for the extreme categories, both positive and negative, to be large and the center ones small (the so-called "end effect"), which also argues against interval distortions solely from concentrations of positive ratings. However, the positive intervals were consistently larger on all scales than symmetric negative ones, so the possibility of such a distortion is at least plausible, if

Table 23

MEAN DEVIATIONS BETWEEN SCALES

$$\frac{1}{6}\sum_{g}\left|L_{g\alpha}-L_{g\beta}\right|$$

Scale	good	clean	valuable	large	strong	heavy	active	fast	hot	Equal Interval
good-bad		.14	.08	.08	.20	.04	.15	.08	.18	.18
clean-dirty	.14		.12	.08	.06	.11	.05	.13	.26	.22
valuable-worthless	.08	.12		.10	.15	.10	.11	.14	.22	.26
large-small	.08	.08	.10		.14	.04	.11	.05	.17	.16
strong-weak	.20	.06	.15	.14		.17	.06	.17	.30	.25
heavy-light	.04	.11	.10	.04	.17		.13	.06	.18	.16
active-passive	.15	.05	.11	.11	.06	.13		.15	.28	.25
fast-slow	.08	.13	.14	.05	.17	.06	.15		.14	.12
hot-cold	.18	.26	.22	.17	.30	.18	.28	.14		.10

difficult to evaluate. Later we shall note a similar effect in latency measurements (see p. 158).

Instead of trying to decide whether or not the intervals are "actually" equal, it may be more feasible to consider how far wrong one might go by assuming equality. In other words, how much distortion would be introduced by using the numbers 3, 2, 1, 0, −1, −2, −3 as category labels instead of the mid-points obtained from the scaling procedure? Some estimate of this distortion may be obtained from the correlations between assumed and scaled boundary position. Since the constant, c, used in obtaining the transformed scores, L_g, is the coefficient for the regression of assumed values, a_g, on scaled values, t_g, the correlation between a and t for each scale can be readily computed from corresponding constants. These correlations, in an order corresponding to the list of scales in Table 23, are .994, .990, .987, .995, .984, .995, .986, .998, .997. Due to restrictions on the variation of a and t values, these two estimates must be highly correlated, but these are exceedingly high correlations and indicate that little distortion would be introduced by using successive integers as category mid-points for these nine scales. _Considering this and the other indications of the present study,_ i.e., _an approximate equality of intervals between scales and a similar placement of origins across scales, it seems reasonable to conclude that the scaling properties assumed with the semantic differential have some basis other than mere assumption._[3]

There are other assumptions we make about scales which are not tested in the above study. One is that all scales used have a _common origin_, i.e., they intersect at the same point in the semantic space. We know that this is not true for some of the scales which have been occasionally used; for the scale _rugged-delicate_, for example, both polar terms, _rugged_ and _delicate_, are judged "good" when given as separate concepts — which could not be true if this

---

[3] A doctoral dissertation by Norman Cliff at Princeton University, entitled "The Relation of Adverb-adjective Combinations to Their Components" (1956), has provided particularly relevant evidence for our scaling assumptions. Cliff was able to show that adverbs like _very, somewhat, decidedly_ and so forth, combine multiplicatively with adjectives like _evil, ordinary, charming_ and the like in determining the scaling locations of judgment of their combinations along an 11-step scale running from "most unfavorable" to "most favorable." Most significant from our point of view was the fact that the adverbial quantifiers _slightly, quite,_ and _extremely_ (which define the three degrees of intensity in using the semantic differential) proved to yield almost perfectly equal increasing degrees of intensity, 0.50, 1.00, and 1.50 respectively. Our choice of these quantifiers in our instructions was thus most fortunate, although entirely intuitive.

scale went through the common origin and were linear. Another assumption is this matter of *linearity;* we assume that the line in semantic space representing each scale is a straight line, and further that the points representing the two polar terms are in opposite directions and equidistant from the origin.[4] One way of checking these assumptions is to have the polar terms themselves judged against a short form of the differential; "true" opposites (which fall at equal distances from a common origin along some straight line in the semantic space) would display perfectly reciprocal profiles in the differential — to whatever degree *rough* was displaced from the origin of scales like *good-bad* or *strong-weak* the term *smooth* would be displaced to an equal degree in the opposite direction. The obvious difficulty with this test is its circularity; it assumes the a priori linearity and centrality of the test scales themselves. We have not as yet figured out a way to test these assumptions.

Validity as an Index of Representational Mediation Processes

In the first chapter of this book an attempt was made to coordinate the two definitions of meaning provided by mediation learning theory analysis and by the measurement operations of the semantic differential respectively. In essence, the total representational mediating process elicited by a sign was analyzed into a set of bipolar components, the meaning of a sign corresponding to the pattern and intensity with which these components are elicited. The *direction* of a point in the semantic measurement space was assumed to index *what* mediator components are elicited and the *polarization* (distance from the origin) of the point was assumed to index *how intensely* these components are elicited. The total mediation process is also assumed to elicit adaptive encoding reactions, overt behaviors of various kinds as well as linguistic reactions, learned on the basis of differential reinforcement.

Experimental checks on this assumed coordination between learning theory and measurement models is admittedly one of the major

---

[4] Evidence on the linearity of the bipolar scales has recently been obtained by Drs. W. L. Taylor and H. Kumata. Four concepts were judged against ten scales in two ways: (1) unipolarly, against three-point scales defined by a single member of a pair of polar opposites; and (2) bipolarly, in the regular fashion. If the scales are linear, one would expect that an algebraic summation of the unipolar judgments should reproduce the judgment on the corresponding bipolar scale. Only four of the 40 judgments produced significant differences between the unipolar combination and the corresponding bipolar judgments. Thus the assumption of linearity is supported.

gaps in our work so far — although it can be fairly said that tight experimental designs here are not easily come by. The experiments described in this section are all attempts to validate these basic assumptions in the sense that they tie our semantic measurement results to the other behaviors of sign-using individuals. They are not all equally direct in their relevance, however, and some of them are only "in progress" at the time of this writing.

1 *Semantic Profile Similarity and Mediated Generalization.* The most direct check on the relation between the directions of points in the semantic space and kinds of mediating reactions elicited by signs would seem to arise in the *mediated generalization paradigm.* When a new reaction is associated with one meaningful sign (e.g., the word HAPPY) and is thence shown to transfer to other meaningful signs (e.g., JOYFUL, SMILE, HOPE, etc.) as a function of their meaningful similarity, generalization among the mediation processes characteristic of the signs is regularly invoked as an explanatory principle. Now, the more similar the patterns of bipolar mediators elicited by signs, (a) the greater should be the magnitude of mediated generalization and (b) the closer should be the profiles for these signs against the semantic differential, as measured by D. In other words, we should be able to predict at least the orders of magnitude of mediated generalization among signs from previous measurements with the semantic differential.[5] An extension of this design involves the use of *compound vs. coordinate bilinguals*: compound bilinguals have learned two languages in such a way that translation-equivalent signs are associated with a single set of meanings (e.g., ordinary language courses in schools, vocabulary lists, etc.); coordinate bilinguals have learned two languages in such a way that translation-equivalent signs are associated with a double set of somewhat different meanings (e.g., one language at home, the other at work, or one as a child, the other as an adult, etc.). From this it follows that both (a) the profile similarities for translation-equivalent terms on the semantic differential should be greater (smaller D) for compound as compared with coordinate bilinguals[6]

[5] James J. Jenkins, Wallace Russell, and others at the University of Minnesota have been collecting semantic profile data on a large number of words occurring as stimuli and responses in word association experiments. This is preparatory to studies on the prediction of generalization and association from semantic relationships.

[6] Just such a relation between size of D for translation-equivalent terms and type of bilingualism has recently been demonstrated by Wallace E. Lambert (McGill University).

and (b) the amounts of mediated generalization in an experimental setting between translation-equivalent terms should be greater for compound than for coordinate bilinguals. These experiments are in process at the time of this writing.

2 *Polarization of Judgment and Habit Strength.* The most direct check on the assumed relation between polarization of judgments on the semantic differential (distance from the origin) and intensity of mediating reactions would seem to lie in a correlation between extremeness of judgment and some index of overt reaction. An experiment of precisely this sort has been done,[7] using latency of judgmental reaction as the index.

The apparatus and procedure may be described briefly as follows: the subject sits before a screen and operates a single reaction device, a lever that can be thrown either to the left or to the right. The experimental items are projected onto the screen before him by means of a single-frame projector, each item requiring 15 seconds for presentation and involving the following sequence of frames: *Frame 1.* A pair of polar terms, such as *rough-smooth*, appears, one to the left and the other to the right with a space between them, and persists for two seconds. *Frame 2.* The same polar terms, in the same locations, appear again, but this time a concept, such as LADY, appears in the space between them, and this display persists for five seconds. The subject has been instructed to react as quickly as he can upon seeing the concept with a lever reaction, either to the left (LADY-*rough*) or to the right (LADY-*smooth*). The onset of this frame automatically starts a one-hundredth-of-a-second timer going and the subject's reaction stops it. The subject's lever reaction also turns on a light over one or the other of the polar terms and activates a single-frame recording camera. This camera takes a picture of the display, including the concept-scale item, the location of the light (indicating direction of judgment), the latency recorded on the timer, and chalked-in identification of the subject. If the subject fails to respond within five seconds, the recording camera automatically takes a picture showing no light and a five-second latency. *Frame 3.* This is a blank frame which persists for eight seconds, as a "rest" interval, after which the next item sequence begins.

A group of 40 subjects, 20 male and 20 female, first reacted in the

---

[7] The writers wish to thank Drs. Daniel Lyons and Lawrence Solomon, who conducted these latency experiments, and Mr. Milton Meux, who helped with some of the computations.

latency device to a set of 150 items (15 concepts × 10 scales) and subsequently to the same items in the usual graphic form of the differential. The scales were generally representative of the three major factors and the concepts were selected to include signs expected to elicit some degree of inherent anxiety (e.g., FINALS, PENIS, SWEAT, etc., as well as control concepts like STATUE, LAKE, DAD, etc.). The secondary purpose of this experiment was to investigate the effects of inherent sign-produced anxiety and of extraneous unpredictable-shock-produced anxiety upon meaningful judgments. A second group of 20 male subjects was subjected to the latter treatment. Since these data bear chiefly on personality factors, they are detailed in Chapter 6; here we concentrate on the relation between polarization and judgmental latency. For the purposes of this study, both the ordering of concepts and scales and the direction of scales (*good-bad* or *bad-good*) were randomized throughout; the graphic form of the differential matched exactly the sequence, directionality, etc., of items on the film strip for the latency experiment. (It may be noted in passing that in either the graphic or the reaction-time methods subjects are unable to recall their judgments on specific items — the rate of operation is too great and there is too much intra-serial confusion.)

Individual subjects were found to differ extremely in their average judgment times in the latency device, males ranging from 3.42 to 1.19 seconds and females from 3.16 to 0.97 seconds. The range for scales or for concepts, on the other hand, was only about .50 seconds. Subjects also differed markedly in the relative frequency with which the seven alternatives' positions on the graphic scales were checked. These data are given in Table 35, Chapter 6. For example, one female subject gives us 47 checks in the middle "4" position, but only four checks in the "3" and "5" positions combined, whereas another female subject has 75 checks in the "3" and "5" positions, but none at all in the "4" position. It is clear, then, that to determine the over-all relation between scale position and latency of judgment we cannot collect and average over either individual scales or over individual concepts. In both cases, subjects having markedly different average judgment times would be contributing unequally to the various scale positions. Rather, it is necessary to collect and average by individual *subjects*, so that each subject may serve as his own control in comparing the various scale positions.

Accordingly, we collected for each subject separately, his latency

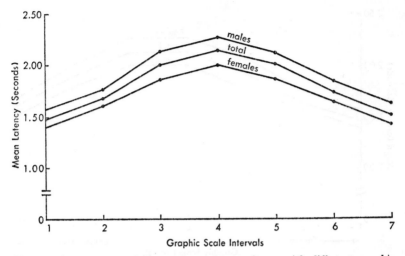

Fig. 14. Average mean latency of reactions to items with different graphic scale responses (evaluative direction not consistent on graphic scales).

scores for all items subsequently checked "1," for all items subsequently checked "2," and so on, and his average latencies for each scale position were then computed. The curves shown in Figure 14 were obtained by averaging these values over subjects. Data for males and females were kept separate because the females were consistently and significantly quicker than the males in making these meaningful judgments — the reason for this difference will be considered later (Chapter 6, pp. 234-35). For both sexes, however, and for their combined average, mean latency of judgment is shown to be a quite regular function of polarization or extremes of position checked on the usual graphic scales. Applying the sign test across subjects, differences in latency of judgment for positions "1" vs. "2" are significant at the 1 per cent level for both males and females (18/21 males, 17/18 females) ;[8] differences for positions "7" vs. "6" are also significant at the 1 per cent level (19/21 males, 19/19 females) ; differences between positions "2" and "3" are significant at the 1 per cent level for both (20/21 males, 17/18 females), and positions "6" vs. "5" at the 1 per cent level for males (21/21) and the 5 per cent level for females (14/18) ; differences between positions "3" and "4" and between "5" and "4" are in the predicted

[8] Twenty-one males were available for this analysis; the N for females sometimes drops below 20 because one or two of them failed to use certain categories entirely.

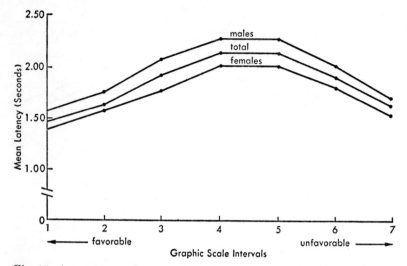

Fig. 15. Average mean latency of reactions to items with different graphic scale responses (evaluative direction consistently on the right on graphic scales).

direction in all cases but do not reach the 5 per cent level (14/21 and 14/21 for males, 13/18 and 12/18 respectively for females). None of the differences between corresponding scale positions ("1" vs. "7," "2" vs. "6," and "3" vs. "5") is significant; in other words, equivalent degrees of polarization in the two directions of our bipolar scales are associated with equal intensities of reaction as indexed by latency.

For the results presented so far, the *evaluative direction* has been random with respect to scale position, e.g., the *good* pole is as likely to be on the left side ("1") as on the right ("7"). It is possible to reanalyze the data in such a way that the favorable pole of each scale is consistently associated with "1" and the unfavorable pole with "7." In other words, in collecting the latency data we simply combine for each subject all instances where "extremely" *good, healthy, large, active,* etc., were checked and call them "1," regardless of the left-to-right alignment of the scales on the page — whatever loading each scale has on the evaluative factor determines its alignment in this analysis. As shown in Figure 15, a somewhat different picture results from such an analysis. Mean latency scores are now "tipped" in the direction of the favorable pole of the scales. In other words, latencies for *good, beautiful, fair, smooth, healthy, dry, strong, large, active,* and *hot* judgments tend to be somewhat shorter than latencies for their less favorable opposites. Sign tests show the "2" vs. "6" difference for males and the "1" vs. "7" and "2" vs. "6" differences for females to be significant at the 5 per cent level or better in the predicted direction. This finding is consistent with that reported earlier by Messick in his scaling analysis — that the intervals on the positive sides of the scales were slightly larger —and it suggests that the habits underlying favorable judgments are slightly stronger than those underlying unfavorable judgments. This, in turn, suggests somewhat greater practice or frequency in making favorable meaningful judgments about concepts in general; it is interesting in this connection that Bousfield (1944) has found that subjects produce significantly more pleasant sequential associates, and at a faster rate, than they do unpleasant associates.

The results of this comparison of graphic scale positions with judgmental latency generally support our basic theoretical assumption that the extremeness of judgment on the semantic differential is a valid measure of the strength with which signs are associated with representational processes. The fact that latencies are equivalent and the function symmetrical when the dominant evaluative polarity is randomized with respect to the graphic scale direction, suggests that the scales used in the semantic differential more nearly satisfy the assumption of equal units within scales than Messick concluded. In all cases but one (*heavy-light*), the scales Messick used in his analysis were aligned so that the favorable pole was assigned "1" and the unfavorable, "7." One of our remaining methodological problems, then, is to re-do Messick's analysis with evaluation randomized with respect to scalar direction.

3 *Some Other Behavioral Correlates.* We know that meaning is an important intervening variable in human behavior. If the semantic differential provides a reasonably faithful index of meanings, then many predictions about overt behavior to signs should be possible from measurements made with the differential or from the relationships indicated by our factor analyses. Similarly, as a dependent variable, scores on the differential or factorial relations should be predictable from the characteristics of signs being learned and the context in which they are learned. The following experiments all deal, in one way or another, with behavioral validity of this sort.

Verbal signs of pleasant connotation are typically heard and used in association with gratifying significates which we approach and reach for; verbal signs of unpleasant connotation are heard and used in association with punishing significates which we avoid and with-draw from. The mother uses words like "nice, sweet, and good" as the child reaches for and acquires an apple; she uses words like "bad, hurt, and nasty" as the child is hurt by and withdraws from a prickly bush. Given such a primitive and pervasive past history, one would expect it to be easier for subjects to learn to make approach movements to signs of favorable connotation than to signs of unfavorable connotation, and vice versa for making avoidance movements. Furthermore, if loading of polar opposites on our evaluative factor is a valid index of behavorial favorable-unfavorable meaning, then ease of learning approach vs. avoidant movements to verbal signs should be predictable from their loadings on the evaluative factor.

In one study,[9] an ingenious apparatus was devised in which the latency of initiating an approach or avoidant movement of the arm as well as the time required for executing it could be measured. An upright display panel, set on a short pole with a pressure switch, is placed in the center of a rack about two and one-half feet long; electrical contacts are placed close to the central position of the display panel and also at the ends of the rack. When the subject squeezes the hand holding the display panel, a new card drops into view on which is printed a single word (e.g., NICE); this squeezing movement also starts two timers. When the subject begins to move his arm (and the display panel) either toward or away from himself, one timer is stopped, recording the latency of initiating his response, and when the sliding display panel reaches one end or the other of the rack, the other timer is stopped, recording the total time required for response. In the experimental design, each subject must learn to associate a set of verbal signs (e.g., NICE, ROUGH, FRAGRANT, WHITE, SOUR, DOWN, etc.) with either approach or avoidant movements — by being told "right" or "wrong" after each response; by using four groups of subjects, each sign and its opposite is associated once with each type of response (e.g., NICE-*approach*, NICE-*avoid*; AWFUL-*approach*, AWFUL-*avoid*). The pairs of polar terms were selected in terms of their loadings on the evaluative factor in factor analysis I. The results were consistent with predictions: it proved easier for subjects to learn to move a word like SWEET toward themselves than away, and easier to move a word like SOUR away from than toward themselves.

---

[9] This study was conducted by Dr. A. Solarz at the University of Illinois in 1953.

In a similar, though independently conceived, experiment,[10] it was demonstrated that the guessing behavior of subjects — as to the relative frequency with which a pair of stimuli had been seen — could be influenced by associating certain evaluative signs with one or the other of the two stimuli. The stimuli were line-drawn facial profiles, given arbitrary names like "Jake" and "Clem." Two such profiles were presented 15 times each in a deck of 30 cards, shown one at a time to the subjects in random orders. The deck was gone through once as a training series and then once again as a guessing series, the subjects trying to anticipate which profile would appear on each succeeding card. The evaluative signs used were the following: in Experiments I and II the experimenter would move some object *toward* the subject for one profile and *away from* the subject for the other profile — these objects were varied in Experiment I (nickels, buttons, burnt matches, hairpins, etc.), but in Experiment II a valued object and a valueless object were compared (half-dollar vs. burnt match); in Experiment III an *upward-pointing* arrow was added to the cards bearing one profile and a *downward-pointing* arrow to the cards bearing the other profile; in Experiment IV a light was turned *on-bright* for one profile and turned *off-dark* for the other. In all experiments, half the subjects would have the "favorable" sign associated with one profile and the other half would have this sign associated with the other profile. In the results of our factorial studies (see unrotated Thesaurus analysis), the scale *near-far* has a loading of .31 on the evaluative factor, the scale *high-low* (e.g., *up-down*) a loading of .56, and the scale *bright-dark* a loading of .53; these loadings were used as indices of the favorableness of the signs being associated with the profiles.

For all of these experiments, the profile associated with the "favorable" sign, as determined from factor loadings of the relevant verbal scales, was over-guessed with a significance level of 5 per cent or better. However, the half-dollar was not superior to the burnt match in Experiment II — in fact, the reverse was true. This study, then, shows that even such a subtle semantic variable as moving objects toward a person rather than away or having a light come on or go off can measurably influence behavior like guessing the frequency with which one has seen something. Unfortunately, the experimenters did not find out if these manipulations had also influenced the evaluative tone of the profiles — the

---

[10] This study was conducted by Drs. C. Solley, S. Messick, and R. Jackson in 1955.

judged pleasantness, friendliness, and so on of the faces — as would be predicted.

Further evidence for the subtle influence of meaningful variables upon overt behavior is provided by another experiment on problem solving by Solley.[11] The materials consisted of the standard "pyramid puzzle," in which three rings of graduated size must be transferred from one peg to a third peg without ever violating the original arrangement of the rings — in the usual manner of presentation, this means never having a larger ring on top of a smaller one. There is a finite number of moves for the most efficient solution. Now, we know from our factor analytic work that *up, small, light-weight,* and *white* tend to go together in meaning and metaphor as opposed to *down, large, heavy,* and *black.* Solley devised hollow rings whose weights could be varied independent of size by loading them with varying amounts of buckshot, and whose shades could be varied from white through gray to black independent of both weight and size. The up-down dimension, of course, is constant because of the nature of the situation. All possible combinations of the other three dimensions, size, weight, and color, were used as ways of presenting this problem — from that in which all of the semantic relations are congruent (small, white, light-weight ring on top, and large, black, heavy-weight ring on bottom) to that in which there is a complete reversal of all relations with respect to up-down (large, black, heavy ring on top, and small, white, light-weight ring on bottom). Do variations in semantic congruence affect the ease of solving what is otherwise the same problem? Solley found that the time required for solution, the number of moves, and the number of errors all varied directly and significantly with the number of dimensions reversed from their normal correspondence with *up-down.*

In all of the work described in this book so far, we have simply used signs as fully learned processes in adult subjects, assuming that their meanings — the representational processes associated with them as stimuli — had been learned in the usual fashion. It should be possible, however, to take originally neutral stimuli and determine their meanings experimentally by associating them with certain significates or other signs. The question of validity of the semantic differential then becomes this: To what degree can the profile of such an arbitrary concept against the semantic differential be predicted from the pattern of experiential events presented in developing its meaning? In this case, the meaning of the concept,

---

[11] Conducted by Dr. C. Solley at the University of Illinois in 1952.

Table 24

**STATISTICAL STRUCTURES OF TWO CONCEPTS HAVING IDENTICAL
MARGINAL CHARACTERISTICS**

	Tribe A			Tribe B		
	happy	*sad*		*happy*	*sad*	
tall	10	2	*12*	6	6	*12*
short	0	8	*8*	4	4	*8*
	10	*10*		*10*	*10*	

as indexed by the semantic differential, is the dependent variable.
We have two studies of this sort available: One, by Solley and
Messick, developed from the investigators' interests in probability
learning in relation to the statistical structure of concepts, will
be described in the paragraphs immediately following. The other,
by Dodge (1955), developed from an interest in the formation of
assign meanings via the principle of congruity with primary signs;
this study will be described in a later chapter (7, pp. 286-90), after
the notion of congruity has been developed.

The former study[12] used as concepts various "tribes of stickmen,"
the members of which were line drawings of little men on decks of
20 cards. These "stickmen" could be either *tall* or *short*, either *fat*
or *skinny*, either *black* or *white*, and either *happy* or *sad* (up-turned
or down-turned mouths), each individual representing some combination of these traits (e.g., a *tall, fat, black, sad* stickman). The
authors were interested in the statistical structure of concepts and
what aspects of this structure are tapped by the semantic differential. It is possible to assemble "tribes" which have the same
marginal probabilities of traits, but quite different joint probabilities
of traits, as shown by the hypothetical tribes in Table 24, using
only two bipolar traits. Tribe A's members display a definite contingency or correlation between the two traits — the tall ones are
likely to be happy and the short ones sad; not so for Tribe B, where
height is independent of prevailing mood. Yet both tribes, as wholes,
are exactly alike in being somewhat more on the tall side and
neutral with respect to happy-sad. Which "aspect" of the meaning
of a concept — its marginal properties or its internal structure —
will the semantic differential reflect? Four "tribes" were assembled

---

[12] Conducted by Drs. C. Solley and S. Messick at the University of Illinois
in 1955.

for the experiment; two of them, A and B, had identical marginal characteristics for the four traits (height, shape, color, and mood) mentioned above, but differed in their joint probabilities, and similarly, tribes C and D had identical marginal characteristics (but different from A and B), but varied joint characteristics.

Forty subjects were assigned randomly to these four "tribes" as conditions for learning. The learning procedure was to have each subject guess which of the four bipolar traits characterized each of the 20 cards before it was turned up; the whole deck was gone through four times in this manner. Then these subjects marked a 20-scale semantic differential for the concept TRIBE OF STICKMEN, including the scales *tall-short*, *fat-skinny*, *white-black*, and *happy-sad*. Although the usual seven successive intervals were indicated on these scales, subjects were asked to make precise indications of degree which were later measured finely. That the subjects had learned both the joint and the marginal characteristics of the "tribes" was indicated by high correlation between the input probabilities (relative frequencies for the various combinations of traits in the stimulus cards) and the output probabilities at the fourth trial (relative frequency of guessing the various combinations of traits). There was one interesting exception here: tribe D had 12 *sad* vs. eight *happy*, yet the final guessing frequency was roughly 12 *happy* vs. eight *sad;* the authors suggest that this was due to the fact that this tribe also had 16 *fat* vs. four *skinny*, and the subjects persisted in expecting the stereotyped correlation of "fat people" with "happy people." The results given in Table 25 compare the theoretical scale positions for the tribes as wholes on each trait, based both on input ratios, $E(S)$, and on final output guessing ratios, $E(R)$, with the obtained mean scale positions checked on the differential, $\bar{\bar{X}}$.

Three conclusions seem warranted by these data: (1) The semantic differential provides a very accurate index of the final ratios (e.g., the *tall/short* guessing ratio as transformed to a -3 to $+3$ scale) of guesses by the subjects; it has high validity in this sense. (2) The semantic differential scores also reflect with considerable accuracy the input characteristics of the stimuli making up the arbitrary concept. In other words, when we experimentally produce a complex "meaning" for a concept — here a "tribe of stickmen" — the instrument faithfully reflects the learning experiences. (3) The semantic differential clearly indexes the marginal characteristics of the concept, but not the internal contingency structure — the se-

Table 25

THEORETICAL SCALE POSITIONS BASED ON STIMULUS INPUTS, E(S), AND FINAL OUTPUTS IN GUESSING, E(R), COMPARED WITH EMPIRICAL SCALE POSITIONS, X̄, ON SEMANTIC DIFFERENTIAL

	Tribe A			Tribe B		
	E(S)	E(R)	X̄	E(S)	E(R)	X̄
tall-short	1.5	1.2	2.2	1.5	1.8	2.0
happy-sad	.6	1.0	1.1	.6	.6	.5
black-white	−3.0	−3.0	−3.0	−3.0	−3.0	−3.0
fat-skinny	−1.7	−1.5	−1.7	−1.7	−1.8	−1.6

	Tribe C			Tribe D		
	E(S)	E(R)	X̄	E(S)	E(R)	X̄
tall-short	−1.5	−1.7	−2.1	−1.5	−1.3	−1.6
happy-sad	−.6	−.6	−1.5	−.6	.5	.9
black-white	3.0	2.6	2.6	3.0	3.0	3.0
fat-skinny	1.7	1.8	2.2	1.7	1.7	1.6

mantic profiles for tribes A and B and for tribes C and D are highly similar (with the exception of the *happy-sad* scale, as noted above). In a way, this would be expected because the concept being judged is the tribe-as-a-whole, and the authors present evidence to show that when the concepts "tall-stickmen" and "short-stickmen" are given, the joint probabilities tend to be reflected. It also seems likely that the joint probabilities, or contingencies between bipolar traits, when consistent in direction of relation over large numbers of concepts, are what determine the correlations between scales of judgment which we pick up in our factor work and which determine the structure of the semantic differential. Thus, *happy-sad* and *fat-skinny* would be correlated in our factor work because in many life experiences, real and fictional, roly-poly people like Santa Claus are found to be cheerful, and thin, angular people like Scrooge are found to be dismal.

Final mention may be made of what perhaps seems to be the most direct test of validity — the reversibility of the measurement operations. Given the profiles produced by a subject judging some number of concepts, can we discriminatively identify or label the concepts originally judged? When the set of concepts involved is both small and highly varied in meaning, this can be done with considerable success. When the set is large, or certainly when it includes concepts of very similar connotation, this cannot be done with any confidence. The bearing of this point on evaluation of our method as a measure of *meaning* will be discussed in a summary chapter (see pp. 320-25). One limitation on this reversibility criterion in the present case must be noted, however: Since the profiles obtained from different subjects for the same concept may vary markedly (e.g., for the concept SENATOR MCCARTHY), it would obviously be impossible to identify the McCarthy profile for a particular subject without already knowing his meaning (connotation) of the term. Therefore, this is not a necessary validity criterion for this type of measurement; its application would require that we reproduce the *meaning* of the concept from the profile, not the concept label.

SENSITIVITY

An instrument is sensitive to the degree that it renders discriminations commensurate with the natural units of the material being studied; ideally it should yield distinctions as fine, or even finer, than those made on common sense grounds. Sensitivity thus implies both reliability and validity. The procedure here is to take sets of closely similar, but discriminably different, word meanings and show that the distinctions made by the semantic differential correspond to those made independently by language users.

In a very early study, run prior to our factor analytic work, ten sets of near-synonymous adjectives, six in each set, were selected from materials originally scaled by Haagen (1949), on the basis of student judgments. Six groups of subjects, 20 in each group, differentiated a different adjective from each set against a 20-scale differential. Two control words, POLITE and CRAFTY, were differentiated by all six groups, with group differences on individual scales corresponding to the group reliabilities described earlier (see p. 139). The degrees of difference indicated by the semantic differential between closely similar adjectives did not correspond very well with the ordering determined by Haagen, and one reason seems to be that whereas Haagen had subjects judge the over-all similarities of the words by direct comparison in sets, our subjects rated the adjectives singly. For example, the word CRYING was included in a set with URGENT, ACUTE, REQUIRED and the like — when judged along with the others, CRYING means something quite different than it does when rated singly. Nevertheless, the discriminations made do seem to correspond well with common sense. The following are illustrations:

In the set GRACIOUS, GENIAL, PLEASANT, CHEERFUL, CORDIAL, FRIENDLY —

> CHEERFUL was the *loudest, happiest, healthiest,* and *youngest.*
> GRACIOUS and PLEASANT were the most *beautiful, softest, best,* most *peaceful* and *smoothest.*

In the set SKITTISH, FLIGHTY, FICKLE, GIDDY, FITFUL, and HEEDLESS —

> HEEDLESS was the *lowest, haziest,* most *passive,* and most *relaxed.*
> GIDDY was the *loudest, happiest,* and *youngest.*

In the set SAVAGE, BRUTAL, RUTHLESS, HEARTLESS, UNKIND, and CRUEL —

> BRUTAL was the *loudest, tensest, largest, roughest,* and *strongest.*
> HEARTLESS was the *coldest, emptiest,* and *sickest.*

In the set SOMBER, GLOOMY, DREARY, MURKY, DISMAL, and CHEERLESS —

> MURKY was the *wettest, haziest,* and *greenest.*
> SOMBER was the most favorable adjective (least *tense,* least *hazy,* least *low,* least *empty,* and least *stale*).

This evidence is very crude, of course, and relates only indirectly to the semantic differential forms, based on factorial studies, that are used at present.

Another way to get at the sensitivity of the instrument would be to see if pairs of words usually considered synonyms, but nevertheless used in different contexts by speakers, can be differentiated. Take, for example, the words GOOD and NICE: Most people we asked accepted them as synonymous, yet agreed that there was a difference, somehow, in their "feeling-tone" — most respondents were unable to verbalize this difference, however. Analysis with the differential indicates a marked difference between these two words on the *potency factor,* and when we investigate the linguistic contexts in which they are appropriate we find that GOOD is a "masculine" word and NICE a "feminine" word. Speakers of English agree that "nice man" differs from "good man" in that the former is rather soft, weak, and effeminate; on the other hand, while "nice girl" is appropriately feminine, "good girl" has a decidedly moral tone.

When the profiles for GOOD and NICE are compared with those for MALE and FEMALE, we find that wherever MALE and FEMALE separate sharply, so also do GOOD and NICE — GOOD like MALE is significantly *thicker, larger,* and *stronger* than NICE, but there are no significant differences on the *activity* and *evaluative factors.*

In a small scale study on this problem, four pairs of near-synonymous adjectives were hypothesized to differ as follows:

(1) GOOD and NICE differ in that the former is associated with masculinity and the latter with femininity; specifically, GOOD will be closer in meaning to MALE than to FEMALE, and NICE will be closer to FEMALE than to MALE.

(2) HANDSOME and PRETTY also differ in that the former is more masculine and the latter more feminine; therefore we predict that the profile for HANDSOME will be more similar to that for MALE than that for FEMALE and vice versa for PRETTY.

(3) BRIGHT (in the intellectual sense) and WISE differ on an age basis; BRIGHT should be closer to YOUNG in meaning than to OLD, and vice versa for WISE.

(4) SPRY and FRISKY also differ on an age basis; SPRY should be closer to OLD than to YOUNG, whereas FRISKY should be closer to YOUNG than to OLD.

The 12 words necessary to test these predictions (GOOD, NICE, HANDSOME, PRETTY, MALE, FEMALE, BRIGHT, WISE, SPRY, FRISKY, OLD, and YOUNG) were presented in randomized orders to 40 undergraduates who rated them on a set of scales which stressed the two factors, *activity* and *potency,* which were expected to differentiate the contextually determined synonyms — *fast-slow, hot-cold, sharp-dull, tense-relaxed, strong-weak, hard-soft, thick-thin, large-small, rough-smooth,* and *valuable-worthless.* For each subject, the D^2 values between each test word and each criterion word in the four sets above were determined by summing the squared differences over the ten scales. The appropriate arrays of D^2 values were then compared by a Wilcoxon paired-replicates analysis. For example, the array of squared distances between GOOD and MALE was compared with that between NICE and MALE, the prediction being that the former would be smaller in magnitude than the latter. The results of this analysis are given in Table 26. All but one of the comparisons was in the expected direction, and four were significant at the 5 per cent level or better. It is evident that we predicted better for the MALE-FEMALE contextual determinant than for the OLD-YOUNG determinant — it is possible, of course, that the experimenters' judg-

Table 26

RESULTS OF APPLYING WILCOXON'S PAIRED-REPLICATES TEST TO ARRAYS OF DISTANCES BETWEEN CONTEXTUALLY DIFFERENTIATED SYNONYMS AND THEIR CRITERION WORDS

	Direction of Difference (+ is predicted direction)	Significant at 5 Per Cent Level
GOOD-MALE < NICE-MALE	+	
GOOD-FEMALE > NICE-FEMALE	+	*
HANDSOME-MALE < PRETTY-MALE	+	*
HANDSOME-FEMALE > PRETTY-FEMALE	+	*
BRIGHT-YOUNG < WISE-YOUNG	+	
BRIGHT-OLD > WISE-OLD	+	*
SPRY-OLD < FRISKY-OLD	−	
SPRY-YOUNG > FRISKY-YOUNG	+	

ment that SPRY is more appropriate to older people and FRISKY to younger people was an incorrect assessment of English connotations. This study provides some evidence, then, for the sensitivity of the semantic differential. Parenthetically, it may also suggest a possible method for testing certain assumptions made by linguists about the contextual distribution of lexical morphemes.

COMPARABILITY

An instrument meets the criterion of comparability to the extent that it can be applied across the range of situations relevant to what is being measured and its results interpreted in constant fashion. This is again an extension of the notion of validity — over how broad a range of situations is the measuring instrument equally valid? In the case of the semantic differential, the range of "situations" in which we are interested is mainly *subjects* and *concepts*. Can the differential be applied with equal validity, and hence comparability, to men and women? To old people and young people? To "normals" and neurotics or psychotics? Does the same factor structure appear, and hence is the same scale system applicable, when political concepts are judged? With concrete objects as concepts? With highly abstract concepts? With the self-concept? And perhaps most interesting, can the same factors be shown to hold across different languages and different cultures?

Comparability Across Subjects

The most direct test of the comparability of the semantic differential across subjects would be to run a series of separate factor analyses on a random sample of *individual subjects*. The data collected in the Thesaurus factor analysis could be handled in this fashion, since we have the judgments of 20 concepts against 76 scales for each of 100 subjects, and correlations between all scales across concepts within individual subjects could be run. Even with electronic computers, this would be a laborious and time-consuming procedure; furthermore, since these subjects were all college undergraduates, positive results would not be as impressive as would the results of a more varied sample. We have made factorial comparisons in one individual case, however: Osgood and Luria (1954) reported an analysis of a case of triple personality with the differential and subsequently factor-analyzed scale structure within each of the several personalities — as will be reported in detail (see Chapter 6, pp. 260-63). Essentially the same factors seemed to be operating despite the gross overt differences in personality. It is also possible to compare *groups of subjects,* selected on some basis, in terms of their factorial structures. Another study in the personality area (Bopp, 1955) compared normal controls and schizophrenic patients (see pp. 223-24) — nearly identical factor structures were found. The 1952 election study, already reported (pp. 104 ff.), also provides evidence for comparability of the measuring instrument; despite gross differences between voting groups in meanings of political concepts, exactly the same set of characteristic attributes held for all groups — and it will be recalled that these characteristic attributes were derived from judgments against the same set of primary scales.[13]

Undoubtedly the most stringent test of the comparability of the semantic differential across subjects lies in comparisons made simultaneously across language and culture. When translation-equivalent terms are used to define the scales and concepts, will the members of other language-culture groups than our own be found to use essentially the same factors in their meaningful judgments?

---

[13] Jack Block (Institute of Personality Assessment and Research, University of California) had both male and female subjects judge the connotations of a sample of emotion terms against a form of the differential (forced-choice rather than scalar). Emotion-by-emotion correlation matrices were computed separately for men and women, and the two matrices were then correlated, by pairing corresponding cells. The r was .94, suggesting near identical correlation systems for males and females.

Table 27

CONCEPTS USED IN CROSS-CULTURAL STUDY OF THE GENERALITY OF SEMANTIC FACTORS (KUMATA AND SCHRAMM, 1956)

INDIA	SOUTH KOREAN PEOPLE	POLICE
UNITED STATES	EISENHOWER	ATOMIC WARFARE
SOVIET UNION	TRUMAN	LABOR UNION
CHINA	MACARTHUR	COLONIALISM
JAPAN	MAO TSE TUNG	CHRISTIANITY
SOUTH KOREA	CHIANG KAI SHEK	MAJORITY RULE
UNITED NATIONS	NEHRU	FATHER
AMERICAN PEOPLE	YOSHIDA	MYSELF
CHINESE PEOPLE	SYNGMAN RHEE	MALE
JAPANESE PEOPLE	COMMUNISM	WATERFALL

Were a positive answer found for this question, it would have implications far beyond the mere validation of our instrument: On the one hand, it would provide very basic evidence on the *Weltanschaung* problem stressed by Whorf (1949) and others, indicating that at one level, at least, the language code does not influence the thinking of its users; on the other hand, from the practical point of view of intercultural communication, such a positive result would indicate that the semantic differential can be used cross-culturally and cross-linguistically as a standardized measuring stick against which the meanings of the same concepts for differently nurtured people could be compared. In this section, studies both completed and in progress on this significant problem will be described.

Kumata and Schramm have worked with Japanese exchange students ($N = 25$) and Korean exchange students ($N = 22$), using American college students ($N = 24$) as controls. The relatively large number of 30 concepts was judged against a set of 20 scales, for the most part selected from our previous factorial studies to adequately represent the three dominant factors, but also selected to be relevant to the types of concepts being measured. Concepts are given in Table 27, scales in Table 28. In developing translation-equivalent differentials in both Japanese and Korean, three translator-judges in each language translated the concepts and polar terms and consensus was used in selecting the final translations. The standard instructions for using the differential were also translated into both Japanese and Korean. To provide an experimental check on the influence of the language-code per se — or alternatively to provide a reliability check if no code differences appeared — all three groups were given the complete test twice, with an interval of three weeks: the Japanese and Korean students, all of whom were to a considerable degree bilingual, took one test in their native language and the other in English, half of each group having the native language form first and the other half having the English version first; the American control subjects had the same English version twice as a straight reliability check.

Since Kumata and Schramm were chiefly interested in group comparisons, the means for items were computed for each group and these means were correlated to yield the interscale correlational matrix for each group (e.g., the r for Koreans between *fast-slow* and *hot-cold* was obtained across the means of the 30 concepts on these two scales for this group). The correlation matrices for the six conditions (Japanese in Japanese, Japanese in English, Korean in Korean, Korean in English, American in English I, and American in English II) were factored by the principal components method and rotated by the Quartimax method — all correlational and factorial operations were carried out with the ILLIAC. For all six conditions, the first and second factors were highly similar and corresponded to the *evaluative* factor and the *dynamism* factor (activity and potency combined) which we have already found to be characteristic of political concepts of this type; the remaining factors were much smaller in magnitude of variance and seemed to be "specifics" in nature (per cent variance for the third factors in each of six conditions were J-J, 13 per cent; J-E, 9 per cent; K-K, 9 per cent; K-E, 11 per cent; A-I, 7 per cent; and A-II, 5 per cent). The rotated factor loadings for all conditions for factors I and II are presented in Table 28. The per cent variance accounted for is given at the bottom of each column. Indices of factorial similarity were computed for every factor in each condition with every other factor in all conditions. The indices for factors I and II are given in Table 29; they can have a maximum of 1.00 and a minimum of zero.

Let us first consider the question of the effect of the language code per se upon semantic judgments. Running down the paired columns in Table 28 (J-J/J-E, K-K/K-E), we note that the loadings of scales on both *evaluative* and *dynamism* factors are highly similar for both native and English language forms, and the indices of factorial similarity are .99 and .98 for the Japanese students and .98 and .98 for the Korean students for the two factors. Exceptions are the scales *peaceful-belligerent* and *thick-thin* for the Japanese

Table 28

FACTORS I AND II AS ROTATED BY QUARTIMAX FOR JAPANESE STUDENTS IN JAPANESE LANGUAGE (J-J), JAPANESE IN ENGLISH (J-E), KOREAN STUDENTS IN KOREAN (K-K), KOREAN IN ENGLISH (K-E), AND FOR TEST AND RETEST OF AMERICAN STUDENTS IN ENGLISH (A-I, A-II)

Factor I

Scales	J-J	J-E	K-K	K-E	A-I	A-II
good-bad	.94	.93	.95	.93	.93	.94
clean-dirty	.83	.85	.93	.90	.86	.88
kind-cruel	.96	.97	.98	.94	.96	.96
happy-sad	.89	.87	.88	.85	.79	.86
honest-dishonest	.92	.93	.94	.94	.94	.92
fair-unfair	.95	.95	.94	.96	.94	.96
beautiful-ugly	.75	.66	.93	.91	.83	.83
peaceful-belligerent	.84	.91	.92	.94	.88	.86
rich-poor	.47	.38	.70	.68	.38	.49
brave-cowardly	.46	.55	.53	.01	.36	.37
relaxed-tense	.60	.79	.80	.81	.76	.63
strong-weak	.26	.12	.21	.27	−.04	.01
deep-shallow	.25	.34	.53	.27	.45	.23
thick-thin	.38	.31	.37	.27	−.18	−.22
rugged-delicate	−.44	−.64	−.76	−.85	−.31	−.20
active-passive	−.07	.08	.16	−.03	−.21	−.01
fast-slow	−.06	−.12	.08	.14	.00	−.12
hot-cold	.26	.28	.69	.79	.05	.17
angular-rounded	−.55	−.75	−.92	−.91	−.10	.16
sharp-dull	−.11	−.15	.00	−.09	−.01	−.13
Per Cent Variance	43	47	56	54	42	41

Factor II

Scales	J-J	J-E	K-K	K-E	A-I	A-II
good-bad	−.13	−.12	−.05	−.01	−.24	−.20
clean-dirty	.35	.34	.22	.28	.34	.33
kind-cruel	−.08	−.08	.00	−.13	−.11	−.12
happy-sad	.36	.43	.42	.42	.43	.34
honest-dishonest	.10	.09	.13	.11	−.03	−.01
fair-unfair	.04	.04	.19	.12	−.08	−.05
beautiful-ugly	−.05	.01	−.01	.15	.12	.02
peaceful-belligerent	−.22	.11	−.32	−.15	−.33	−.39
rich-poor	.71	.74	.46	.62	.69	.62
brave-cowardly	.37	.42	.62	.61	−.09	−.11
relaxed-tense	−.10	−.04	−.06	−.05	.10	.09
strong-weak	.83	.95	.89	.87	.93	.87
deep-shallow	.01	−.12	.13	.16	.12	.22
thick-thin	.01	.34	.14	.18	.25	.28
rugged-delicate	.25	.29	.12	.12	.43	.56
active-passive	.94	.91	.90	.96	.89	.93
fast-slow	.79	.83	.92	.93	.82	.85
hot-cold	−.29	−.28	.10	−.03	−.05	−.01
angular-rounded	.17	.08	.11	.23	.21	.39
sharp-dull	.56	.61	.61	.64	.81	.71
Per Cent Variance	20	22	20	22	24	24

Table 29

INDICES OF FACTORIAL SIMILARITY FOR FACTORS I AND II

Factor I

	J-J	J-E	K-K	K-E	A-I	A-II
J-J	1.00					
J-E	.99	1.00				
K-K	.97	.98	1.00			
K-E	.96	.96	.98	1.00		
A-I	.95	.94	.91	.89	1.00	
A-II	.93	.91	.88	.87	.98	1.00

Factor II

	J-J	J-E	K-K	K-E	A-I	A-II
J-J	1.00					
J-E	.98	1.00				
K-K	.94	.94	1.00			
K-E	.96	.96	.98	1.00		
A-I	.93	.93	.89	.90	1.00	
A-II	.91	.91	.87	.89	.99	1.00

on factor II (*peaceful* and *thick* seeming somewhat more dynamic when Japanese take the form in English) and the scale *brave-cowardly* for the Koreans on factor I (*brave* being favorable in their own language form but independent of evaluation in English). But these are relatively small differences, and as a whole, we can conclude that the language used by bilinguals in reacting to the semantic differential has little effect per se upon the semantic frame of reference. If this result can be consistently repeated across language groups, it will be a significant contribution to an understanding of the *Weltanschauung* problem.

Since the between-code comparisons yield no marked differences, we may treat the J-J/J-E and K-K/K-E indices of factorial similarity along with the A-I/A-II comparisons as reliability estimates. In other words, the higher the indices of factorial similarity between test and retest, the higher must be the reliability of the item means over which original correlations were made. These "reliability" coefficients are .99 and .98 for Japanese, .98 and .98 for Koreans, and .98 and .99 for Americans for factors I and II respectively. It is clear that these evaluative and dynamism factors reproduce themselves with an extremely high degree of consistency in all three groups of subjects.

Finally, we may consider the factorial similarities existing across cultures. The *evaluative factor* consists of the following scales in all three groups: *good-bad, clean-dirty, kind-cruel, happy-sad, honest-dishonest, fair-unfair, beautiful-ugly, peaceful-belligerent,* and *relaxed-tense.* We note certain differences between cultures — which make sense: for Koreans, *rich-poor* is a clearly evaluative scale; it is much less so for Japanese and Americans. The polar term *delicate* (as opposed to *rugged*) is highly evaluative for Koreans and Japanese, but not so for Americans. Interestingly enough, the scale *hot-cold* is highly evaluative for Koreans (*hot* being *good*), but this is not true for either Japanese or Americans. And the scale *angular-rounded* (*rounded* being favorable — like *delicate?*) is also highly evaluative for both Asiatic groups, but not for Americans. The *dynamism factor* consists of the following scales in all three groups: *strong-weak, active-passive, fast-slow,* and *sharp-dull.* Other scales having considerable loading on this factor for all groups are *rich-poor, happy-sad,* and *clean-dirty.* Here again there are some differences. *Brave-cowardly* is far more "dynamic" for Koreans than for either of the other two groups; *rugged-delicate* is more "dynamic" for Americans than for the Asiatics; similarly, being *belligerent* tends to be "dynamic" for Americans and Koreans, but not consistently, at least, for Japanese. It may also be noted in the "per cent variance" values that the Koreans display a larger *good-strong-active* general factor than either of the other two groups — they seem to have a more "sanguine" semantic orientation. It is also worth reporting that a "pure" potency variable (*thick-thin, deep-shallow, rugged-delicate,* and to some extent, *brave-cowardly*) appears as one of the secondary factors in all six of the analyses. The indices of factorial similarity (Table 29) are nearly as high across cultures as they are within.

We may conclude that as far as these concepts and scales provide an adequate sample, Korean and Japanese exchange students and American college students use the same major factors in their meaningful judgments. There is the possibility, of course, that these results merely reflect a high degree of acculturation on the part of the bilingual exchange students. Against this interpretation is the fact that certain individual scales are used in clearly different ways by the three groups — the evaluative significance of *rugged-delicate* for the Asiatics or of *hot-cold* for the Koreans, for example. Nevertheless, it will be necessary to demonstrate that the same communality in semantic factors holds *for monolinguals restricted to their own cultures.*[14]

Comparability Across Concepts

What information we have available, as summarized in the preceding section, indicates an encouraging degree of comparability across subjects. The situation is quite different with respect to comparability *across concepts*. Ideal or perfect comparability here would require that *individual scales* maintain the same meaning, and hence the same intercorrelations with other scales, regardless of the concepts being judged. This condition can definitely be shown not to hold. A less stringent condition would be that the *same factors* keep reappearing despite changes in the concept being judged, even though the particular scales contributing to these factors may vary. This condition is approached in our data, as we shall see. For purposes of generalized semantic measurement we would like to have a set of scales which consistently load heavily on a certain factor and are independent of other factors, despite variations in the concepts being judged. We have had difficulty trying to isolate a set of scales having these properties.

The first attempt to study the stability of scale relations across concepts (Shaw, 1955) was restricted to the *good-bad* scale and used the data on 100 subjects and 20 concepts on which factor analysis I was based. These data had been analyzed on an IBM machine in such a way that correlations between scales for single concepts could be readily obtained. Shaw computed the correlations for 34 scales with *good-bad* for all 20 concepts. These correlations varied greatly across concepts. For example, the correlation between *good-bad* and *strong-weak* varied from .67 on the concept GOD to —.03 on the concept of TORNADO. Shaw was interested in the reason for this variation. His original hypothesis was that it depended on

---

[14] Research on this problem is now under way: Kumata has collected data on monolingual Japanese students (in Japan); Harry C. Triandis (Cornell University) has run a parallel study in Greece in the summer of 1956; Phyllis Liu (University of Michigan) is doing a similar study on Chinese subjects; the research staff of the Southwest Project on Comparative Psycholinguistics, supported by the Social Science Research Council, is collecting similar data from samples of various American Indian communities (Hopi, Hopi Tewa, Navajo, and Zuni) as well as from Mexican Spanish speakers. It is to be hoped that these several studies on the cross-cultural generality of semantic factors will yield a consistent picture. Kumata's data for monolingual Japanese has been factor analyzed, and the structure proves to be very similar to that of Americans.

the *denotative relevance* of scales to concepts; if the scale *rough-smooth* is denotatively relevant to the concept BOULDER, but not to the concept of GOD, for example, the correlation with *good-bad* should be near zero in the first case, but significantly positive or negative in the second case. In other words, when scales are used metaphorically or connotatively, they should tend to rotate toward the dominant evaluative dimension. No support for this hypothesis was found — although it must be said that it proved difficult to assign scale-concept pairs to denotatively relevant vs. irrelevant categories on any basis other than intuition.

A second hypothesis was that the correlations of other scales with *good-bad* would depend upon the evaluativeness of the concept, e.g., in judging highly or lowly evaluated concepts like MOTHER, GOD, and SIN, all scales should tend to rotate toward a single, dominant evaluative dimension; i.e., the correlations of the scales with *good-bad* should increase. To obtain an independent index of concept evaluativeness, Shaw presented a new group of 169 subjects with the 20 concepts successively as stimuli for association, requesting descriptive adjectival responses. The index of evaluativeness was simply the frequency with which either *good* or *bad* were given as associates, and the concepts were rank-ordered in evaluativeness on this basis. This hypothesis was clearly supported. For all but five scales, the correlations with *good-bad* were higher when judging highly evaluative concepts than when judging less evaluative concepts, and ten scales exhibited significant differences as predicted.

Our most extensive check on comparability across concepts has been made in connection with the data collected for the Thesaurus factor analysis, involving judgments of 20 different concepts against 76 scales by 100 subjects. Here again the data was organized and analyzed so that separate 76/76 correlation matrices for the judgments of each concept were readily obtained. The matrices for the 20 concepts were factored by the Centroid Method and rotated by Quartimax, using the facilities of the ILLIAC. Blind rotation of this sort by a constant set of rules seemed to be the best preliminary, exploratory procedure. Although these data have not been completely analyzed at the time of this writing, enough work has been done to indicate the major results.

We may look first at the straightforward matter of variation in interscale correlation as a function of concept being judged. For each pair of scales (e.g., *soft-hard* with *intangible-tangible*) in the 76 × 76 matrix of scale relations we have 19 separate correlation coefficients,[15] one for each of the concepts. As an estimate of the variation in r across concepts we have used the simple *range* between the highest and lowest values; this seems legitimate in the present case, because each r is determined by 100 subjects and hence is quite stable. This range tells us empirically how large a variation in the r between two scales can occur within the concepts we have used. In the ideal case of perfect stability the variation in r across concepts should fall within the expected errors of estimate. With an N of 100 and an r of .00 (the most conservative estimate), another r which deviates by as much as .26 will be significant at the 1 per cent level — i.e., a range this large or larger is significantly beyond chance. For a sample of 52 of the 76 scales for which ranges in r across concepts were computed, the median range is .49, the largest being .99 and the smallest being .21. In other words, the vast majority of scales show significant variation in their correlations with other scales across concepts.

A few illustrations of this variation will provide some insight into what is happening. *Graceful (awkward)* goes positively with *soft (hard)* $+.34$ for FAMILY LIFE but negatively $-.26$ for KNIFE; *pleasurable* goes with *feminine* (.47) for MY MOTHER but with *masculine* (.36) for ADLAI STEVENSON; *sober* goes with *youthful* (.23) for DAWN but with *mature* (.33) for UNITED NATIONS; *feminine* goes with *clean* (.37) for MY MOTHER but *masculine* goes with *clean* (.32) for LEADERSHIP; *tenacious* goes with *successful* for UNITED NATIONS but *yielding* goes with *successful* for FAMILY LIFE; *sharp* and *healthy* go together (.31) for AMERICA but *sharp* and *sickly* go together (.22) for SIN; *soft* is *important* for MY MOTHER (.33) but *hard* is *important* for ENGINE (.31); *feminine* is *important* (.41) for MY MOTHER but *masculine* is *important* (.36) for ADLAI STEVENSON; *serious* is *sociable* (.55) for UNITED NATIONS but *humorous* is *sociable* (.42) for ME; and so forth. In most of these examples the scales *do* go together in different ways in experience for the different concepts; this is part of the *statistical structure of concepts* stressed by Solley and Messick (see pp. 163 ff.). It is also evident in our data that the meanings of certain scales may change with the concept being judged. For example, *sharp* as applied to concepts like ME and AMERICA has a dynamic, favorable meaning (the slang usage) and correlates highly with scales like successful, intentional, and progressive; on the other hand, *sharp* as applied to con-

---

[15] Because of machine failure the analyses for Concept 1 (MODERN ART) could not be used.

cepts like BOULDER and KNIFE has its ordinary denotative meaning and correlates with scales like angular and rough. In the last case we are probably dealing with what are functionally *homonyms*, words having the same form but different meanings.

The same dependence of scale correlation with *good-bad* upon evaluativeness of the concept being judged, demonstrated by Shaw, is found in these data, and the reason becomes evident. Although no external criterion of concept evaluativeness is available in this case, there is a definite internal criterion — the proportion of total variance accounted for by the evaluative factor. According to this criterion, the concepts ADLAI STEVENSON, UNITED NATIONS, FAMILY LIFE, and MY MOTHER are the most evaluative and the concepts TIME, ENGINE, BOULDER, ME, SNOW, and DAWN are the least evaluative (see Table 30). Inspection of the correlations of other scales with *good-bad* clearly shows that they are higher for the first set of the above concepts than for the second set; for example, comparing STEVENSON with ENGINE, we find that for 66 of the 75 correlations with *good-bad,* the *r* for the concept STEVENSON is higher than that for ENGINE. In a sense this is an artifact — the fact that the evaluative factor accounts for more than four times the variance in the former case necessarily means that many scales will have higher loadings on the evaluative factor and hence higher correlations with the *good-bad* scale — but in terms of the dynamics of human thinking, this still represents a tendency to collapse semantic dimensions toward a single evaluative factor when judging highly evaluative concepts.

Inspection of the ranges in correlation across concepts for various scales reveals another significant fact — evaluative scales are less stable, more susceptible to variation across concepts, than non-evaluative scales. For each pair of scales we have a range based on correlations for 19 concepts; for a given scale, such as *hot-cold*, we can compute its median range over all the other scales with which it is correlated (e.g., the median for the array of ranges, *hot-cold* with *graceful-awkward*, *hot-cold* with *true-false*, etc.). The median range for each scale will thus indicate how stable, in general, are its correlations with other scales. Now, in the sample of 52 scales analyzed in this fashion 18 were clearly evaluative, having loadings on the evaluative factor greater than .50, (*graceful, true, light* (*dark*), *believing, progressive, pleasurable, interesting, good, reputable, meaningful, sane, clean, successful, kind, important, beautiful, optimistic,* and *wise*). Since 15 of these 18 evaluative scales have median ranges greater than the over-all median range (.49), we may conclude that there is a significantly greater instability of evaluative scales. In other words, scales contributing to the evaluative factor are most susceptible to rotation as a function of the concept being judged.

Although the meanings of individual scales and their correlation with each other may vary considerably from concept to concept, as we have seen, can essentially the same general *factors* be shown to repeat themselves despite concept variation? In the over-all factor analysis of the Thesaurus data presented in Chapter 2, at least five factors appeared with sufficient clarity to warrant checking across these individual concept factorizations. These were *evaluation, potency, activity, stability,* and *receptivity.* The factors in the individual concept matrices, as rotated by Quartimax, were inspected for correspondence with these general factors, with the results tabulated in Table 32. In each instance only the five scales having highest loadings are given; the proportion of total variance accounted for by the factor as a whole is given below each column. For several concepts no factor in any way corresponding to a given general factor could be identified, and therefore no entries are made.

For every concept being judged a factor clearly identifiable as *evaluative* could be found. With the exceptions of the concepts BOULDER, TIME, and ME, this factor was the first in order of magnitude — and in the case of ME there were several factors of more or less equal evaluativeness, i.e., modes of self-evaluation, which warrant further study. However, the particular scales contributing to this factor vary markedly. In fact, the evaluative "direction" often rotates into alignment with other major factors. Rotation toward *receptivity* scales occurs for DAWN, FAMILY LIFE, and SYMPHONY; rotation toward *stability* scales occurs for MY MOTHER, ME, and ENGINE; rotation toward the combined *potency-activity* (or *dynamism*) factor occurs for HOSPITAL, DEBATE, BIRTH, UNITED NATIONS, LEADERSHIP, and ADLAI STEVENSON. This testifies to the instability of the evaluative factor which we have already noted. What is good depends heavily upon the concept being judged — *strong* may be good in judging athletes and politicians, but not in judging paintings and symphonies; *harmonious* may be good in judging organized processes like family life, symphony, and hospital, but not so much so in judging people or objects.

The *potency* factor fares as well as evaluation. A correlate of this dimension of judgment appears for all concepts but two (KNIFE

Table 30

EVIDENCE FOR GENERAL FACTORS IN SINGLE-CONCEPT ANALYSES

	Evaluation	Potency	Activity	Stability	Receptivity
KNIFE:	timely .73			sober .57	graceful .60
	sociable .72			sane .54	interesting .60
	reputable .64			insensitive .53	refreshed .57
	optimistic .61			dry .49	colorful .55
	good .60			cautious .48	high .54
	per cent V = .102			per cent V = .048	per cent V = .064
FOREIGNER:	grateful .73	healthy .66		masculine .49	interesting .70
	kind .72	strong .58		wise .47	meaningful .70
	sociable .68	fast .51		old .44	reputable .56
	true .62	aggressive .50		objective .43	colorful .46
	altruistic .61	refreshed .47		homogeneous .42	good .43
	per cent V = .102	per cent V = .052		per cent V = .038	per cent V = .051
HOSPITAL:	successful .81	hard .61		believing .52	sensitive .57
	important .67	unsociable .57		sober .48	wise .42
	progressive .67	severe .55		true .45	savory .40
	cooperative .66	angular .47		sharp .45	opaque .40
	harmonious .63	colorless .47		sane .44	generous .36
	per cent V = .125	per cent V = .062		per cent V = .035	per cent V = .033
DEBATE:	good .80	heavy .57	curved .63		ornate .67
	meaningful .75	masculine .56	active .51		colorful .51
	pleasurable .74	hard .54	excitable .49		hot .50
	successful .73	complex .44	erratic .49		light (dark) .50
	important .69	near .42	cruel .47		aggressive .47
	per cent V = .141	per cent V = .043	per cent V = .046		per cent V = .049

Table 30. Continued.

EVIDENCE FOR GENERAL FACTORS IN SINGLE-CONCEPT ANALYSES

	Evaluation		Potency		Activity		Stability		Receptivity	
SIN:	beautiful	.82	strong	.60			important	.50	ornate	.70
	kind	.72	tenacious	.54			weary	.48	colorful	.63
	good	.71	meaningful	.52			sober	.45	active	.60
	clean	.70	true	.51			serious	.44	interesting	.59
	reputable	.70	sharp	.50			tangible	.35	pleasurable	.55
	per cent V = .114		per cent V = .042				per cent V = .033		per cent V = .077	
BOULDER:	kind	.71	heavy	.63	active	.59	serious	.63	meaningful	.68
	grateful	.68	hard	.50	fast	.58	intentional	.62	colorful	.67
	optimistic	.61	believing	.49	progressive	.58	sane	.59	interesting	.67
	wise	.54	dark	.37	sensitive	.55	orthodox	.54	beautiful	.61
	cooperative	.52	old	.37	aggressive	.55	complete	.53	pleasurable	.54
	per cent V = .064		per cent V = .035		per cent V = .064		per cent V = .077		per cent V = .067	
MOTHER:	good	.81	heavy	.66	sophisticated	.58	humble	.65	savory	.53
	kind	.75	mature	.58	fast	.57	periodic	.47	hot	.48
	wise	.74	large	.54	ornate	.54	believing	.46	rounded	.46
	successful	.71	far	.39	strong	.53	calm	.44	sensitive	.41
	sane	.71	dark	.39	severe	.42	simple	.42	timely	.41
	per cent V = .185		per cent V = .034		per cent V = .039		per cent V = .038		per cent V = .039	
AMERICA:	interesting	.79	hard	.71	optimistic	.64	calm	.53		
	beautiful	.69	severe	.61	active	.59	stable	.47		
	good	.69	masculine	.50	angular	.51	homogeneous	.46		
	meaningful	.68	thrifty	.48	sociable	.49	wise	.44		
	high	.66	plain	.47	fast	.44	orthodox	.44		
	per cent V = .156		per cent V = .041		per cent V = .043		per cent V = .041			

Table 30. Continued.

EVIDENCE FOR GENERAL FACTORS IN SINGLE-CONCEPT ANALYSES

	Evaluation		Potency		Activity		Stability		Receptivity	
BIRTH:	meaningful	.72	large	.63	humorous	.63				
	good	.69	old	.56	fast	.51				
	successful	.67	strong	.42	curved	.48				
	important	.67	pleasurable	.40	colorful	.42				
	interesting	.65	healthy	.39	youthful	.38				
	per cent V = .127		per cent V = .037		per cent V = .039					
TIME:	interesting	.68	thrifty	.72			orthodox	.61		
	beautiful	.66	sharp	.62			inherent	.52		
	good	.64	severe	.61			positive	.52		
	pleasurable	.62	strong	.54			stable	.50		
	optimistic	.55	rational	.52			harmonious	.43		
	per cent V = .060		per cent V = .068				per cent V = .049			
SNOW:	kind	.78	hard	.68	excitable	.66	serious	.50	proud	.59
	sociable	.71	dirty	.53	fast	.57	objective	.44	healthy	.58
	pleasurable	.67	constrained	.53	dissonant	.56	usual	.43	sharp	.43
	good	.65	heavy	.50	active	.51	complete	.42	transparent	.43
	cooperative	.64	private	.50	changeable	.38	formed	.42	ornate	.40
	per cent V = .088		per cent V = .061		per cent V = .047		per cent V = .038		per cent V = .042	
ME:	sane	.65	hard	.73	sociable	.67	stable	.54	colorful	.69
	clean	.65	masculine	.58	pleasurable	.64	timely	.51	interesting	.66
	sober	.65	heavy	.53	active	.62	wise	.50	meaningful	.64
	good	.61	large	.51	positive	.59	calm	.48	sophisticated	.61
	reputable	.59	straight	.43	free	.58	blunt	.47	graceful	.61
	per cent V = .075		per cent V = .053		per cent V = .086		per cent V = .044		per cent V = .072	

Table 30. Continued.

EVIDENCE FOR GENERAL FACTORS IN SINGLE-CONCEPT ANALYSES

	Evaluation	Potency	Activity	Stability	Receptivity
DAWN:	good .75 successful .65 soft .59 interesting .57 clean .56 per cent V = .098			timely .62 periodic .55 calm .53 orthodox .47 colorful .43 per cent V = .044	sensitive .63 near .62 sharp .59 fast .51 youthful .47 per cent V = .046
UNITED NATIONS:	meaningful .76 successful .75 wise .75 positive .74 grateful .73 per cent V = .217	severe .67 hard .57 aggressive .52 tenacious .51 private .50 per cent V = .056			savory .60 sensitive .56 unusual .49 heretical .46 asymmetrical .34 per cent V = .038
LEADERSHIP:	wise .78 successful .78 important .72 meaningful .67 good .66 per cent V = .128	egotistic .60 strong .56 tenacious .54 rational .42 severe .40 per cent V = .045		calm .63 active .51 stable .46 tangible .44 timely .41 per cent V = .036	hot .59 colorful .46 new .44 savory .42 light (dark) .41 per cent V = .041
ENGINE:	good .68 meaningful .66 reputable .55 sane .50 positive .50 per cent V = .060	complex .63 important .58 strong .58 heavy .53 large .52 per cent V = .051		stable .57 periodic .41 cold .41 usual .40 formed .40 per cent V = .039	interesting .70 ornate .66 colorful .58 graceful .48 rash .48 per cent V = .051

Table 30. Concluded.

EVIDENCE FOR GENERAL FACTORS IN SINGLE-CONCEPT ANALYSES

	Evaluation	Potency	Activity	Stability	Receptivity
ADLAI STEVENSON:	important .86	hard .68			
	wise .84	severe .62			
	true .81	angular .53			
	good .80	masculine .51			
	meaningful .80	serious .39			
	per cent V = .253	per cent V = .044			
FAMILY LIFE:	harmonious .83	masculine .59		cautious .41	savory .50
	pleasurable .80	sharp .57		homogeneous .33	important .43
	successful .78	heavy .42		plain .32	meaningful .41
	kind .77	constricted .40		reputable .32	fast .41
	interesting .74	generous .33		constrained .32	near .40
	per cent V = .211	per cent V = .039		per cent V = .030	per cent V = .032
SYMPHONY:	pleasurable .80	mature .66	fast .64	objective .67	
	beautiful .78	heavy .63	rash .58	orthodox .60	
	interesting .77	generous .44	proud .51	constrained .46	
	successful .76	masculine .44	severe .48	constricted .43	
	meaningful .75	dark .42	changeable .46	intentional .41	
	per cent V = .172	per cent V = .037	per cent V = .054	per cent V = .039	

and DAWN) and there is a fair degree of consistency in the scales contributing (*masculine, hard, severe, heavy, strong, tenacious, mature, dark,* and *large*). Although it sometimes draws in certain specific scales (e.g., *unsociable* in the case of HOSPITAL, *complex* in the case of DEBATE, and *thrifty* in the case of TIME), it does not become aligned with other factors as was the case with evaluation. The *activity* factor, on the other hand, fares very poorly in these single-concept analyses. It was considered identifiable in only eight of the 19 concepts (DEBATE, BOULDER, MOTHER, AMERICA, BIRTH, SNOW, ME, and SYMPHONY), and in some of these it is dubious. Actually, the activity characteristic seems to be distributed about other factors in these analyses — as *receptivity* in DAWN and FAMILY LIFE, as *stability* (or rather its converse) in LEADERSHIP, as *potency* (*dynamism*) in FOREIGNER, and so forth. It should be remembered here, however, that we are dealing with the results of a blind and automatic rotation, and it is possible that a more deliberate rotation (e.g., selecting representatives of already identified factors as principal axes) would sharpen these factorial structures without reducing the proportions of variance accounted for by the same number of factors. This remains to be tried.

The *stability* and *receptivity* factors appear with rather surprising regularity and consistency as to composition. A factor resembling *stability* can be identified with some assurance in all but four of the single-concept matrices (DEBATE, BIRTH, UNITED NATIONS, and STEVENSON). The typical scales here are *sane, sober, serious, orthodox, periodic, calm, stable,* and *wise*. A *receptivity* (or sensory orientation) factor could be identified in all but four concepts (BIRTH, TIME, STEVENSON, and SYMPHONY), and in all of these but STEVENSON it probably did not appear because evaluation had rotated into alignment with receptivity. However, this factor seems somewhat more diffuse in scale composition. The most common scales are *interesting, colorful, meaningful, sensitive, savory, ornate, hot,* and *graceful*.

For an ideal semantic measuring instrument we would like to select a small set of scales having the following properties: (a) high loading on the factor they represent, (b) high correlation with the other scales representing the same factor, (c) low correlation with scales representing other factors (and hence low loading on other factors), and (d) a high degree of stability across the various concepts judged. A careful inspection of both the single-concept correlation matrices and the single-concept factor loadings with these criteria in mind was not particularly successful. Although it was possible to select about two scales to represent each of ten factors which met the criterion of independence from other factors, these pairs of scales did not prove to have sufficiently high correlations with each other across the 19 concepts. On the other hand, scales displaying high within-factor correlations (e.g., *interesting* and *meaningful* for the receptivity factor) typically were not independent of other factors (in this example, not independent of evaluation).

It proved most difficult to isolate anything resembling "pure" evaluative scales. Scales which we think of as being most generally and abstractly evaluative, like *good-bad, positive-negative,* and *optimistic-pessimistic,* proved to be the most unstable, in some concepts being aligned with receptivity, in others with stability, and in yet others with dynamism (potency-activity). Other evaluative scales display consistent secondary loading on some other factor: *progressive, successful, high,* and *important* usually "lean" toward the activity dimension; *reputable, wise, harmonious,* and *formed* usually fall toward the stability dimension; and *graceful, near, pleasurable, healthy, clean, beautiful, sociable,* and *grateful* usually tend toward the receptivity factor. The only evaluative scales we were able to specify as essentially independent of other factors were *true-false, believing-skeptical,* and *timely-untimely,* and this may have been simply a function of the particular set of concepts used in this study.

Several conclusions seem justified by these studies of comparability across concepts. In the first place, it is clear that there is a high degree of concept-scale interaction; the meanings of scales and their relations to other scales vary considerably with the concept being judged. This is in direct contrast to subject-scale interaction, which we have found to be minimal. One general principle governing this concept-scale interaction seems to be that the more evaluative (emotionally loaded?) the concept being judged, the more the meaning of all scales shifts toward evaluative connotation. This may be phrased as a more general hypothesis: *In the process of human judgment, all scales tend to shift in meaning toward parallelism with the dominant (characteristic) attribute of the concept being judged.* Thus, in judging ATHLETES, whose dominant attribute we may assume to be active-potent dynamism, all scales will display some tendency to rotate toward this dominant dimension, terms like *clean, successful,* and even *timely* and *colorful* becoming more potent and active in meaning. We suspect that this phenomenon may reflect a very general principle of cognitive interaction to be described in the next chapter, the principle of congruity. In any case, we have still to extend our tests of this hypothesis beyond the evaluative factor. We may also conclude from these data that evaluative scales are more susceptible to these rotational effects than are non-evaluative scales. Evaluation thus appears as a highly generalizable attribute which may align itself with almost any other dimension of meaning, depending on the concept being judged — and it is most often the dominant attribute of judgment. A final conclusion is that despite instability of individual scales, there is considerable repeatability (and hence comparability) of the major *factors* across the concepts being judged. A more deliberate type of rotation than that used here might well strengthen this conclusion.

Obviously these results raise serious practical problems in connection with the construction of generalized semantic measuring instruments. It appears that it will be difficult to locate specific scales which have the ideal properties of high within-factor relationship, low between-factor relationship, and stability across concepts judged. However, in our work so far we have only sampled some 100 or so scales, and then on a deliberately random basis. At this point, knowing the general natures of several major factors, we need to select sets of scales presumably representative of these factors and test them for the necessary properties. In the last analysis it may prove necessary to construct separate measuring instruments for each class of concepts being judged, but for both theoretical and practical reasons we hope this will not be the case.

5

One of the significant by-products of our work in experimental semantics, we believe, has been a new approach and rationale for attitude measurement. It has been feasible to identify "attitude" as one of the major dimensions of meaning-in-general and thus to extend the measurement procedures of the semantic differential to an important area of social psychology. In working in this area with the differential we have also found evidence for a general principle governing some aspects of cognitive processes — a *principle of congruity*. Although the operation of this principle is not necessarily limited to the attitudinal dimension of the meaning space, we first encountered it in connection with research on attitude measurement and will therefore introduce it in this context.

ATTITUDE MEASUREMENT

A Definition of Attitude

Despite a plethora of definitions of "attitude" in contemporary social science, some consensus and agreement is evident, particularly with respect to the major properties that attitudes are assumed to possess. Most authorities are agreed that attitudes are learned and implicit — they are inferred states of the organism that are presumably acquired in much the same manner that other such internal learned activity is acquired. Further, they are predispositions to respond, but are distinguished from other such states of readiness in that they predispose toward an *evaluative* response. Thus, attitudes are referred to as "tendencies of approach or avoidance," or as "favorable or unfavorable," and so on. This notion is related to another shared view — that attitudes can be ascribed to some basic bipolar continuum with a neutral or zero reference point, implying that they have both direction and intensity and providing a basis for the quantitative indexing of attitudes. Or, to use a somewhat different nomenclature, attitudes are implicit processes having reciprocally antagonistic properties and varying in intensity.

This characterization of attitude as a learned implicit process which is potentially bipolar, varies in its intensity, and mediates evaluative behavior, suggests that attitude is part — to some authorities, the paramount part — of the internal mediational activity that operates between most stimulus and response patterns. This identification of attitude with anticipatory mediating activity has been made most explicit by Doob (1947), who, casting attitude within the framework of Hullian behavior theory, identified it with the "pure stimulus act" as a mediating mechanism.

Still lacking, however, is an identification and localization of attitude per se within this general system of mediational activity. Our work in semantic measurement appears to suggest such an identification: If attitude is, indeed, some portion of the internal mediational activity, it is, by inference from our theoretical model, part of the semantic structure of an individual, and may be correspondingly indexed. The factor analyses of meaning may then provide a basis for extracting this attitudinal component of meaning.

In all of the factor analyses we have done to date (see particularly Chapter 2) a factor readily identifiable as evaluative in nature has invariably appeared; usually it has been the dominant factor, that accounting for the largest proportion of the total variance. Despite different concepts and different criteria for selecting scales, high and restricted loadings on this factor were consistently obtained for scales like *good-bad, fair-unfair,* and *valuable-worthless,* while scales which were intuitively non-evaluative in nature, like *fast-slow, stable-changeable,* and *heavy-light,* usually had small or negligible loadings on this factor. It seems reasonable to identify attitude, as it is ordinarly conceived in both lay and scientific language, with the evaluative dimension of the total semantic space, as this is isolated in the factorization of meaningful judgments.

In terms of the operations of measurement with the semantic differential, we have defined the *meaning* of a concept as its allocation to a point in the multidimensional semantic space. We then define *attitude* toward a concept as the projection of this point onto the evaluative dimension of that space. Obviously every point in semantic space has an evaluative component (even though the component may be of zero magnitude, when the evaluative judgments are neutral), and, therefore, every concept must involve an attitudinal component as part of its total meaning. This does not imply that the evaluative or attitudinal dimension is necessarily stable in orientation with respect to other dimensions of the space; as we found in the last chapter (pp. 179-80), depending upon the concept or set of concepts being judged, "purely" evaluative scales, like *good-bad*, may rotate so as to correspond in alignment with the potency factor, the sensory adiency factor, and so on. In other words, the kind of evaluation may shift with the frame of reference determined by the concepts (e.g., political, aesthetic, and so on).

Measurement Procedure with the Semantic Differential

Following the definition and rationale above, to index attitude we would use sets of scales which have high loadings on the evaluative factor across concepts generally and negligible loadings on other factors, as determined from our various factor analytic studies. Thus, scales like *good-bad, optimistic-pessimistic,* and *positive-negative* should be used rather than scales like *kind-cruel, strong-weak,* or *beautiful-ugly* because the latter would prove less generally evaluative as the concept being judged is varied. However, since the concept-by-concept factoring work on which the present rationale is based was not done at the time most of the attitude measurement reported here was undertaken, we have not always satisfied this ideal criterion. For purposes of scoring consistency, we have uniformly assigned the unfavorable poles of our evaluative scales (e.g., *bad, unfair, worthless,* etc.) the score "1" and the favorable poles (*good, fair, valuable*) the score "7" — this regardless of the presentation of the scales to subjects in the graphic differential, where they should be randomized in direction. We then merely sum over all evaluative ratings to obtain the attitude "score." A more refined method would be to weight each scale in terms of its evaluative factor loading for the concepts being judged, but this would be extremely laborious and, if the scales are "purely" evaluative as defined above, would probably add little to the precision of the instrument. It should also be noted that in practice we usually include a considerable number of scales representing other factors — this is done both to obscure somewhat the purpose of the measurement and to provide additional information on the meaning of the concept as a whole, aside from the attitude toward it.

The major properties of attitude that any measurement technique is expected to index are readily accommodated by this procedure. *Direction* of attitude, favorable or unfavorable, is simply indicated by the selection of polar terms by the subject; if the score falls more toward the favorable poles, then the attitude is taken to be favorable, and vice versa. A score that falls at the origin, defined by "4" on the scales, is taken as an index of neutrality of attitude. *Intensity* of attitude is indexed by how far out along the evaluative dimension from the origin the score lies, i.e., the polarization of the attitude score. Although on a single scale there are only three levels of intensity, "slightly," "quite," and "extremely" in either direction, summing over several evaluative scales yields finer degrees of intensity. If six scales are used, for example, we have a range of possible scores from six (most unfavorable), through 24 (exactly neutral), to 42 (most favorable), there being 18 degrees of intensity of attitude score in each direction. On the basis of earlier work (see Katz, 1944; Cantril, 1946) it is assumed that a neutral rating is one of least intensity in terms of attitude. *Unidimensionality* of the attitude scale is provided automatically in the factor analytic procedures from which the scales are selected. If the scales used are selected on the basis that they all have high and pure loadings on the same factor — ideally maintaining this consistency across various factor analyses — unidimensionality must obtain. In other words, factor analysis is itself a method for testing the dimensionality of the items or scales entering into a test.

Evaluation of the Differential as a Measure of Attitude

1 *Reliability.* Test-retest reliability data have been obtained by Tannenbaum (1953). Each of six concepts (LABOR LEADERS, THE CHICAGO TRIBUNE, SENATOR ROBERT TAFT, LEGALIZED GAMBLING, ABSTRACT ART, and ACCELERATED COLLEGE PROGRAMS) was judged against six evaluative scales (*good-bad, fair-unfair, valuable-worthless, tasty-distasteful, clean-dirty,* and *pleasant-unpleasant*) by 135 subjects on two occasions separated by five weeks. Attitude scores were computed by summing over the six scales, after realignment according to a constant evaluative direction. The test-retest coefficients ranged from .87 to .93, with a mean r (computed by z-transformation) of .91. Additional reliability data, which confirm this, were obtained in another study and are given in Table 31.

2 *Validity.* The evaluative dimension of the semantic differential

displays reasonable face-validity as a measure of attitude. For example, Suci (1952) was able to differentiate between high and low ethnocentrics, as determined independently from the E-scale of the Authoritarian Personality studies, on the basis of their ratings of various ethnic concepts on the evaluative scales of the differential. Similarly, evaluative scale ratings were found to discriminate in expected ways between shades of political preference, by Suci in his study of voting behavior (see pp. 104-24) and by Tannenbaum and Kerrick in their pictorial political symbolism study (see pp. 296-99). However, unlike the measurement of meaning in general, in the case of attitude we have other, independently devised measuring instruments which have been used and against which the present technique can be evaluated. We report two such comparisons, the first with Thurstone scales and the second with a Guttman-type scale.

a *Comparison with Thurstone scales.* Each of three concepts (THE NEGRO, THE CHURCH, and CAPITAL PUNISHMENT) was rated against a series of scales, including five purely evaluative ones (*fair-unfair, valuable-worthless, pleasant-unpleasant, clean-dirty,* and *good-bad*). In addition, subjects indicated their attitudes on Thurstone scales specifically designed to scale these attitude objects — the standard scale for the Church, Form B of the Negro scale, and Form A of the Capital Punishment scale (see Thurstone, 1931). Subjects were divided into two groups for testing purposes: one group (N = 23) was given the semantic differential form first, followed approximately one hour later by the Thurstone tests, and the other group (N = 27) had the reverse order. Two weeks after this initial session, the subjects again took both tests, except that this time their respective orders were reversed. The latter session was run to obtain reliability information on both types of attitude measuring instruments. Columns (1) and (2) of Table 31 present the product-moment correlations between the semantic differential (s) and Thurstone (t) scale scores for each of the three objects of judgment, on the initial test session ($r_{s_1 t_1}$) and on the second test session ($r_{s_2 t_2}$); columns (3) and (4) present the test-retest reliability coefficients for the Thurstone scales ($r_{t_1 t_2}$) and for the evaluative scorés on the differential ($r_{s_1 s_2}$), again for each of the three concepts judged. It may be seen that the reliabilities of the two instruments are both high and equivalent. The correlation between the semantic differential scores and the corresponding Thurstone scores is significantly greater than chance (p < .01) in each case,

Table 31

VALIDITY AND RELIABILITY COEFFICIENTS FOR SEMANTIC DIFFERENTIAL ATTITUDE SCORES (S) AND THURSTONE SCALE SCORES (T)

	(1) $r_{s_1 t_1}{}^*$	(2) $r_{s_2 t_2}$	(3) $r_{t_1 t_2}$	(4) $t_{s_1 s_2}$
Attitude Object				
The Church	.74	.76	.81	.83
Capital Punishment	.81	.77	.78	.91
The Negro	.82	.81	.87	.87

* The subscripts 1 and 2 refer to the first and second testing, respectively.

and in no case is the across-techniques correlation significantly lower than the reliability coefficient for the Thurstone test. The differences in the between-techniques correlations from first to second testing sessions are well within chance limits. It is apparent, then, that whatever the Thurstone scales measure, the evaluative factor of the semantic differential measures just about as well. Indeed, when the six validity coefficients are corrected for attenuation, each is raised to the order of .90 or better.

b *Comparison with a Guttman scale.* Recently, an opportunity to test the validity of the evaluative factor of the differential as a measure of attitude against a scale of the Guttman type arose. A 14-item Guttman-type scale (reproducibility coefficient: .92) had been developed, at the expense of some time and labor, to assess the attitudes of farmers toward the agricultural practice of crop rotation. At approximately the same time, the semantic differential was being used in connection with a series of television programs dealing with agricultural practices, and one of the concepts included was CROP ROTATION. Although these studies were conducted independently, 28 subjects were found who had been exposed to both testing instruments. The Guttman scale had been administered first in all cases and the time between the two tests varied considerably, from only three days to almost four weeks. With attitude scores on the differential obtained by summing over the three evaluative scales used (*good-bad, fair-unfair,* and *valuable-worthless*), the rank order correlation between the two instruments was highly significant (rho =.78; p <.01). Again we may say that the Guttman scale and the evaluative scales of the differential are measuring the same thing to a considerable degree.

The findings of both of these studies support the notion that the evaluative factor of the semantic differential is an index of attitude. It is, moreover, a method of attitude assessment that is relatively easy to administer and easy to score. Although it does not tap much of the *content* of an attitude in the denotative sense (e.g., the specific reactions which people having various attitudes might make, the specific statements that they might accept), it does seem to provide an index to the location of the attitude object along a general evaluative continuum. That the semantic differential *in toto* may provide a richer picture of the meaning of the attitude object than just the evaluative dimension is a point to which we return momentarily.

The Question of Generalized Attitude Scales

It is apparent that the semantic differential may be used as a generalized attitude scale. Using exactly the *same* set of evaluative scales, we have seen that correlation between our scores and those obtained with specific Thurstone scales are *equally* high for such diverse attitude objects as WAR, NEGRO, and CAPITAL PUNISHMENT. If we were careful to select as our evaluative scales those which maintain high and pure loading on the evaluative factor regardless of the concept class being judged, it is probable that such high correlations with standard attitude-measuring instruments would be obtained regularly. The question, however, is whether the use of generalized attitude scales is justified and valuable.

Attitude scales of the generalized type were introduced some two decades ago by Remmers and his associates (see Remmers, 1934; Remmers and Silance, 1934) in an attempt to overcome the laborious work involved in developing scales by the Thurstone equal-appearing-interval technique. The same basic procedure was followed, but instead of having statements referring to single attitude objects, they were couched in terminology designed to be applicable to a variety of objects. A number of such "master" scales were developed, each applicable to a particular class of objects — e.g., a scale for attitude toward any social institution, toward any proposed social action, and so forth. Most of these master scales were fairly reliable (median coefficient, .70) and, on the whole they compared favorably with specific Thurstone scales.

These Remmers scales were criticized on many grounds and from many quarters, however: that generalized statements cannot apply with equivalent meaning to different attitude objects (see Krech and Crutchfield, 1948; Clark, 1953), that generality is achieved with a loss of detailed information about the structure of the attitude (see Campbell, 1953), that subjects are responding to the abstracted symbol and not in terms of the content of the issue as such (see Newcomb, 1941), and so on. All of these arguments, in one way or another, aim at the question of validity, as does Mc-Nemar's (1946) scathing criticism based on lack of correlation in some cases with Thurstone scales; for example, Dunlap and Kroll (1939) found that a generalized scale correlated only .28 with specific Droba scale for attitudes toward war. On the other hand, Campbell (1953) reported that in four of five direct comparisons, the correlations between Remmers and Thurstone scales were as high as the reliability coefficients of the latter themselves.

At any rate, such generalized scales have fallen into disuse. Nevertheless, they have some very definite values which warrant their further development. For one thing, they are *economical* — if their validity can be assumed in new situations, they make unnecessary the development and standardization of specific scales for every attitude object, saving money, time, and effort. For another thing, they are *available at the proverbial moment's notice* — Remmers (1954) cites the case where the master scale for attitude toward any proposed social action was applied immediately following President Roosevelt's announcement of the proposed enlargement of the Supreme Court. But unquestionably, the major scientific value of generalized attitude scales is the matter of *comparability:* When a subject has one attitude score on a Thurstone scale for WAR and another score on a Thurstone scale for CAPITAL PUNISHMENT, we can conclude only in a most tenuous manner, if at all, that he is less favorably disposed toward one than the other. When exactly the same yardstick is used to measure both attitudes, however — again assuming that the generality of the instrument is valid — such direct comparison becomes much more tenable. In later portions of this book, particularly in experiments testing the congruity hypothesis, several examples will be given of studies which would be impossible without the use of generalized, standard measuring instruments, in this case the semantic differential.

When used as a measure of attitude, the semantic differential carries even further the logic used by Remmers in developing his generalized scales. Rather than having different "master" scales for different classes of attitude objects, exactly the same set of evaluative dimensions would be used for all objects of judgment. Rather than using "statements" of any sort with which the subject must agree or disagree, scales defined by pure, abstracted linguistic evaluators would be used. These are at present *ideal* conditions, because we have not as yet done the systematic research necessary to select such scales. From our available factorial data on single concepts we need to select those scales which maintain a high loading on the evaluative factor, regardless of its orientation for judgments of particular concepts; then we need to test the generality of these scales by comparing them with a battery of varied, specific attitude-measuring instruments, demonstrating (a) that these scales maintain high intercorrelation among themselves across the objects being evaluated and (b) that the summation scores derived from them jointly display high and roughly equal correlations with the various specific attitude-measuring instruments used as criteria. The evidence we have collected so far indicates that this will be a likely conclusion.

Such an instrument, if developed, will still face many of the criticisms aimed at Remmers' scales. Krech and Crutchfield's argument that generalized scales cannot apply with equivalent meaning to varieties of specific objects or concepts would be met by the procedures of developing our evaluative matrix — i.e., by the demonstration that the scales selected do maintain their high and pure evaluative loading despite the nature of the concept being judged. Campbell's argument that generality is achieved at the cost of losing richer information about the structure of the attitude does not seem to us to be a criticism of an instrument *as a measure of attitude,* assumed to be a unidimensional attribute. Other methods can be used to get at the more detailed structure of a concept's meaning; indeed, the semantic differential as a whole (e.g., the profile of the object against the n-dimensional differential) is designed to get at just such information, as we suggest in the next section. Finally, there is Newcomb's criticism that in using such scales, subjects react in terms of symbols and not in terms of issue content — he cited the case where people who rate symbols like FASCISM very unfavorably may actually agree with many of the beliefs of Fascists. This is not as much a criticism of generalized attitude scales as it is of *the phrasing of the concept* judged; these subjects did have unfavorable attitudes toward the concept FASCISM and simultaneously favorable attitudes toward statements of authoritarian polices — if subjects are illogical and inconsistent, this is not a fault of the measuring instrument. In fact, comparison of the evaluative locations of concepts like FASCIST and SENATOR MC CARTHY, or even a phrase like CENTRALIZATION OF POWER IN THE HANDS OF A STRONG LEADER, would reveal just such logical inconsistencies. One of the advantages of the semantic differential in this regard is its flexibility with respect to the nature of the concept judged — ordinary nouns, phrases, pictures, cartoons, and even sonar signals have been used at one time or another.

Meaning vs. Attitude in the Prediction of Behavior

One of the most common criticisms of attitude scales of all types is that they do not allow us to predict actual behavior in real-life situations. Like most such arguments, this one is overdrawn. Most proponents of attitude measurement have agreed that attitude scores indicate only a *disposition* toward certain *classes* of behaviors, broadly defined, and that what overt response actually occurs in a real-life situation depends also upon the context provided by that situation. We may say, for example, that a person with an extremely unfavorable attitude toward NEGRO may be expected to make some negatively evaluating overt response to an object of this attitude if he is in a situation in which he does not anticipate punishment from others about him. As Doob (1947) has put it, "overt behavior can seldom be predicted from knowledge of attitude alone." But there is more involved here than this: It can also be said that the attitudinal disposition itself accounts for only part of the intervening state which mediates between situations and behaviors, albeit perhaps the dominant part. The *meaning* of NEGRO to the individual subject is richer by far than what is revealed by his attitude score. Within the framework of the theoretical model underlying our own research, attitude is one — but only one — of the dimensions of meaning, and hence provides only part of the information necessary for prediction.

By combining judgments derived from scales representing other dimensions with those derived from the evaluative factor alone, additional information can be obtained and prediction presumably improved. Two people may have identical *attitudes* toward a concept (as determined by allocation to the evaluative dimension alone), and yet have quite different meanings of the concept (as determined by the profiles as wholes). Consider, for example, one of Tannenbaum's observations in the Thurstone comparison study reported above: One subject rated THE NEGRO as *unfavorable*, *strong,* and *active;* another subject rated THE NEGRO as equally *unfavorable,* but also as *weak* and *passive.* Although no behavioral criteria were available in this study, it seems likely that the former subject would behave differently in a real-life situation (e.g., with fear and avoidance) than the latter. While it is true that different attitudes imply different behaviors toward the objects signified, at least in some contexts, it is not true that the same attitude automatically implies the same behaviors.

A recent pilot study by Tannenbaum demonstrates how increasing the dimensionality of judgment utilized within the differential can increase predictability. This does not, unfortunately, involve direct, overt behavior toward the objects of attitude, but it does approach closer to that real-life situation. Subjects (N = 40) were asked to judge three nationality concepts — GERMANS, CHINESE, and HINDUS — against a series of semantic differential scales representative of the three major factors of meaning repeatedly obtained in factor analysis. In addition, these subjects also rated each of the nationalities on a modified Bogardus Social Distance Scale. Separate factor scores were computed for each subject on each concept, and correlation coefficients were then computed both between these scores (e.g., evaluation/potency, potency/activity, etc.) and between them and the Bogardus ratings. While the evaluative factor correlated most highly with the Bogardus ratings — as might be expected — multiple correlation analysis showed that the predictability of the social distance ratings was significantly enhanced by addition of information from the other factors. On the concept GERMANS, for example, evaluative scores correlated only .22 with the Bogardus scale, yet combining all three yielded a multiple correlation of .78. The increases in predictability for the other two concepts were not so great — from .62 to .80 for CHINESE and from .59 to .72 for HINDUS — but support the same conclusion.

THE PRINCIPLE OF CONGRUITY

So far in this book we have been dealing essentially with a descriptive analysis of the dimensionality of the meaning space and the development of techniques for allocating concepts to this space. But cognitive events such as are involved in meaning formation and change do not transpire in isolation from one another; human learning and thinking, the acquisition and modification of the significance of signs, involve continuous interactions among cognitive events. In this section we turn our attention to analysis of the manner in which meanings interact and are thereby changed. In the course of our work on the nature and measurement of meaning we have gradually formulated a very general principle of cognitive interaction, which we call *the principle of congruity*. Although we first discussed it in connection with the prediction of attitude change (see Osgood and Tannenbaum, 1955), and therefore include it in the present chapter, we think it is broader than this in implication, and therefore try to give it in as general form as we can at this time.

Nature of the Congruity Principle

According to the rationale in Chapter 1, any sign presented in isolation elicits its characteristic mediation process, this total process being made up of some number of bipolar reaction components which are elicited at various intensities. The total representational process is assumed to be coordinate with a point in the semantic measurement space, this point projecting onto the several dimensions of the space in correspondence with the kinds and intensities of the reaction components elicited. Thus, two signs having different meanings, such as ATHLETE and LAZY, must elicit different mediation processes, produce different profiles against the semantic differential, and thus be associated with different points in the semantic space. But what happens when two (or more) signs are presented simultaneously, e.g., when the subject sees the phrase LAZY ATHLETE? Common sense tells us that some interaction takes place — certainly a *lazy* athlete is much less active, perhaps less potent, and probably less valuable than he would be otherwise. If interactions of this sort are lawful, and we can get some understanding of the laws, then it should be possible to predict the results of word combination like this and related phenomena.

Since the various dimensions of the semantic space are assumed to be independent, we may deal with a single dimension for simplicity in analysis and then generalize the argument to all dimensions. Also, for the sake of simplicity, we shall treat only the minimum case of interaction between two signs, again assuming that the formulation can be generalized to any number of interacting signs. The general congruity principle may be stated as follows: *Whenever two signs are related by an assertion, the mediating re-*

action characteristic of each shifts toward congruence with that characteristic of the other, the magnitude of the shift being inversely proportional to intensities of the interacting reactions. This "shift," obviously, may be in intensity, direction, or both. Thus, if sign A elicits an intensely favorable evaluative component and sign B only a slightly unfavorable evaluative component, the compromise will be such that the reaction to A will be only slightly modified, but that to B relatively more modified. For this principle to acquire some usefulness, it is necessary to be explicit about what is meant by "assertion" and by "congruence."

Assertion as a Condition for Cognitive Interaction. Individuals have varied meanings for a near infinity of signs, yet there is no interaction among them, and no consequent meaning change, except when they are brought into the peculiar evaluative relation to one another that we shall call an *assertion.* As anthropologists well know, members of a culture may entertain logically incompatible attitudes toward objects in their culture (e.g., ancestor worship and fear of the spirits of the dead; Christian and business ethics, etc.), as long as these ideas are not brought into direct relation. But an assertion is more than simple contiguity in time and/or space (although these factors are presumably also necessary). Take for example, the following utterance: "Tom has the reputation of being an angel; Sam, on the other hand, is a devil." Although SAM and ANGEL are more contiguous as signs, the linguistic structure is such that TOM and ANGEL are associated as signs — i.e., they are related by an assertion, and will interact. Nor is this a phenomenon solely of language structure. If we see Tom standing in a crowd on a station platform, waving and smiling at the distant figure of a girl on the departing train, although Tom is closer physically to other people in the crowd, there is an assertion implicit in "waving and smiling at" which relates TOM and GIRL-ON-TRAIN. Just as the copula in the basic English sentence (A *is* B) relates subject and object and is a condition for cognitive interaction, so does the *action* of objects and people with respect to each other serve to relate them and set up pressures toward congruity. A news photo of Mrs. Roosevelt smiling and shaking hands with a little colored boy is just as effective in setting up the conditions for attitude change as would be a policy statement on her part.

Now such assertions, or coupling actions, may be either *associative* or *dissociative,* which corresponds to the basic distinction in all languages between affirmation and negation. The basic form in

English for *association* is the paradigm /A *is* B/, e.g., LAZY ATH-
LETE equals /ATHLETE *is* LAZY/, but there are innumerable variations on this theme — A *is an instance of* B, A *loves* B, A *helps* B,
A *goes with* B, A *shakes hands with* B, and so on, whether occurring
as perceptual events or language signs, are assertions which associate the included objects of judgment. The basic form in English for
dissociation is the paradigm /A *is not* B/, and again there are innumerable variations — A *is not an instance of* B, A *hates* B, A
hinders B, A *avoids* B, A *strikes* B, and so on, are assertions which
dissociate the included objects of judgment.

The forms that assertions may take, as we have seen, are highly
variable: *simple linguistic qualification* (lazy athlete / or walks
gracefully); *simple perceptual contiguity* (e.g., an advertisement
showing a pretty girl with her hand possessively on the hood of a
new automobile); *statements of classification* ("Tom is an ex-con,"
"Mr. Frank Smith is a Democrat," "Cigarettes contain nicotine")
where to the extent that there is difference in meaning between
member and class some pressure toward congruity is assumed to
exist; *source-object assertions* ("University president bans research on krebiozen," "Communists dislike strong labor unions,"
and Mrs. Roosevelt shaking hands with the little colored boy); and
of course, more complex statements which may include several
overlapping assertions (e.g., "The fun-loving people of New Orleans
love their colorful Mardi Gras," where we have /people of New
Orleans *are* fun-loving/, /Mardi Gras *is* colorful/ and /people of
New Orleans (as modified) *love* Mardi Gras (as modified)/). In
terms of our theory, the signs included in messages embodying such
assertions are in constant interaction and are constantly being
modified in meaning by the principle of congruity — in the last
example, the strait-laced Puritan, who takes a very dim view of
FUN-LOVING will arrive at a much less favorable evaluation of both
the PEOPLE OF NEW ORLEANS and MARDI GRAS.

We realize that these examples do not provide a precise definition
of "assertion." Although we are able to distinguish situations involving assertions (and hence dynamic interaction among sign-
processes) from situations not involving assertions on an intuitive
basis, so far we have not been able to make explicit the criteria on
which we operate.

The Direction and Location of Congruence. If we were unable to
state the direction and location of congruence in cognitive interactions, our principle would be of little value. By taking into

account the nature of the assertion, whether associative (+) or dissociative (−), and the original, pre-interaction locations or the meanings of the signs being related (as measured by some such instrument as the semantic differential), however, we can make specific statements about congruence and hence make predictions about change in attitude or meaning. The general statement is as follows: *Whenever two signs are related by an assertion, they are congruent to the extent that their mediating reactions are equally intense, either in the same* (compatible) *direction of excitation in the case of associative assertions or in opposite* (reciprocally antagonistic) *directions in the case of dissociative assertions.* It should be kept in mind that we are referring to a single dimension or component of the cognitive system taken at a time here, and that "intensity" or reaction of a component is assumed to be coordinate with "polarization" (extremeness) of judgment in the measurement space. We state the principle in mediation theory terms principally in the interest of generality.

Let us first take an example where both signs are equally intense in the same, compatible direction: EISENHOWER *is in favor of* FREEDOM OF THE PRESS. Assuming that on the evaluative factor, at least, EISENHOWER and FREEDOM OF THE PRESS are equally favorable, the assertion is already perfectly congruent and no pressure toward meaning change is expected. A similar situation for typical members of our culture would exist for the statement HITLER *was in favor of* MASS EXTERMINATION, except for the unfavorable locations of both signs. But what about the statement EISENHOWER *stifles* FREEDOM OF THE PRESS (or the equivalent, HITLER *favored* FREEDOM OF THE PRESS) — assuming the subject is completely credulous? Here we have equally favorable signs *dissociated,* and the point of congruity for each would be an equally intense, but reciprocally antagonistic reaction (e.g., a strongly unfavorable reaction to either EISENHOWER or to FREEDOM OF THE PRESS); since the signs are equally polarized, the result should be a cancellation to zero evaluation of both. A similar situation exists when oppositely evaluated signs are related by an *associative* assertion, and the subject is credulous, e.g., HITLER *favored* FREEDOM OF THE PRESS. The case in which a highly favored source is against a highly disfavored object is again perfectly congruent, e.g., EISENHOWER *condemns* MASS EXTERMINATION. We expect sources we like to sponsor ideas we favor and denounce ideas we are against, and vice versa.

Now let us suppose that one of the signs included in an assertion is *neutral* on the dimension being dealt with — EISENHOWER *is cordial to* the MINISTER FROM SIAM. Here we must ask what reaction to the unknown or neutral item *would be* congruent. Since EISENHOWER is highly positive and since we have an associative assertion, a perfectly congruous state of affairs would exist *if* MINISTER FROM SIAM were also highly favorable in meaning. Following our principles, (a) the congruent position for EISENHOWER is neutrality and the congruent position for MINISTER FROM SIAM is extreme favor, and (b) the shift toward congruence is inversely proportional to the existing intensities of the reaction to the signs; therefore, all of the shift in meaning is concentrated upon the MINISTER FROM SIAM, who becomes highly favored. Similar situations and resolutions apply to all cases where one member is neutral, e.g., EISENHOWER *strikes out at* the JASON JONES POLICY, COMMUNISTS *welcome* ABRIGOTO *with open arms,* PROFESSOR SO-AND-SO *favors* PREMARITAL SEXUAL RELATIONS, etc. The familiar "I am against sin" technique, of course, is another case in point, where the unknown political aspirant strives to raise his own evaluation by assertions dissociating himself from various unsavory persons and policies.

Coordination with Measurement Operations

To handle cases that are not polar in nature and to make quantitative prediction and analysis possible, it is now necessary to coordinate the congruity principle with the operations of measurement by the semantic differential. Knowing the direction of the assertion, either associative or dissociative, we need to determine the projections or locations of the two signs *in isolation* in order to predict what the effects of their interaction will be in combination — on as many dimensions as we wish to predict. Since intensity of a reaction component is coordinate with *polarization* on a factor of the differential, we may assign to each sign included in an assertion a value p representing its factor score on a given dimension, expressed as a deviation from the neutral point. For the evaluative factor we arbitrarily assign $+$ to the favorable direction and $-$ to the unfavorable direction. Thus p has a range from -3 to $+3$. Utilizing our principle, we may now define the *location of congruence, p_c,* for each sign as follows:

$$\text{for associative assertions,} \quad p_{c_1} = p_2 \text{ and,}$$
$$p_{c_2} = p_1;$$

for dissociative assertions, $p_{c_1} = -p_2$ and,
$$p_{c_2} = -p_1,$$

where the subscripts refer to signs 1 and 2 respectively. Figure 16 provides some graphic illustrations. In example (1) we have a positive assertion relating two equally favorable signs (the nature of the assertion, associative or dissociative, is indicated by the + or − sign on the bar connecting the concepts); in this case the positions of perfect congruity already exist. In all other cases the existing locations are not those of maximum congruity, and the latter position is indicated by a dashed circle for each concept (in this figure, in anticipation of the following experimental report on the prediction of attitude change, one sign in each assertion is called S for *source* and the other C for *concept*). Note that in keeping with the principle, the position of congruity is always that equal in degree of polarization to the other sign, in either the same (associative) or opposite (dissociative) directions.

The total amount of "pressure of incongruity" existing in the cognitive system for any given assertion is always equal to the difference (expressed in scale units) between the existing location of each concept and its location of maximal congruity. That is, symbolizing this "pressure" by P,

$$P_1 = p_{c_1} - p_1 \text{ and,}$$
$$P_2 = p_{c_2} - p_2.$$

And therefore, substituting from the equations given earlier,

for associative assertions, $P_1 = p_2 - p_1$ and,
$$P_2 = p_1 - p_2;$$

for dissociative assertions, $P_1 = -p_2 - p_1$ and,
$$P_2 = -p_1 - p_2$$

the resulting signs of these equations giving the direction of P, either yielding shift in a favorable direction (+) or in an unfavorable direction (−) in the case of the evaluative factor. For example (2) in Figure 16, the pressures toward congruity are −2 and +2 respectively for the source and concept. Inspection of the other examples indicates that the magnitudes of pressure on the signs included in the same assertion are always equal, although they may be different in direction (i.e., $|P_1| = |P_2|$).

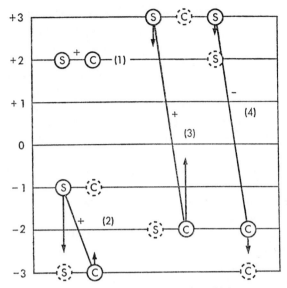

Fig. 16. Graphic examples of four situations in which a source (s) makes an assertion (+ or —) about a concept (c). Positions of maximum congruity are indicated by broken circles; predicted changes in attitude are indicated by arrows.

It will be recalled, however, that this total "pressure" toward congruity is not distributed equally among the signs included in an assertion. Rather, the principle states that the shift in reaction toward congruity is *inversely* proportional to the original intensities of the reactions to the signs — the more polarized one sign relative to the other, the less change it undergoes. Letting the symbol C stand for *change*, the following equations take into account this inverse proportionality and predict the amount and direction of the shift to be expected from each sign when they are related in an assertion:

$$C_1 = \frac{|p_2|}{|p_1| + |p_2|} \, P_1 \text{ and,}$$

$$C_2 = \frac{|p_1|}{|p_1| + |p_2|} \, P_2,$$

where the polarizations of the signs are taken at their absolute values regardless of sign and hence the sign of the equation as a whole (i.e., the direction of change predicted) depends upon the sign of P — the change is always in the direction of increased congruity. The solid arrows in Figure 16 represent the magnitudes and directions of change to be expected in each of the cases given; note that in every case the less polarized member is shifted more than the more polarized member. (The arrows for case (3) do not meet at a common point as they should according to this equation in an associative assertion. This is because the magnitudes of change have been corrected for the *incredulity* inherent in this situation; see Osgood and Tannenbaum, 1955.) When we are dealing with associative assertions only, in which the resolution of congruity is necessarily to a single, common point along the dimension, and when we are interested in the point of resolution rather than the amount of change, the following formula may be used:

$$p_R = \frac{|p_1|}{|p_1| + |p_2|} p_1 + \frac{|p_2|}{|p_1| + |p_2|} p_2$$

where p_R is the degree of polarization, in one direction or the other, of the point of resolution. In a study on the effects of word mixture, for example (cf. p. 278), we use this formula to predict the meanings of word combinations like LAZY ATHLETE from the measured meanings of the components.

Congruity and Learning

The congruity principle as stated above strictly applies only to that *momentary* situation in which the decoding of two signs of different meanings is simultaneous. At this point, the theory says, the interaction is such that the meaning of each sign is completely shifted to the point of mutual congruence. Such a situation is closely approached in the word-mixture case where an adjective modifies a noun, in the perceptual situation where one object is perceived in immediate assertive contiguity with another. As the relation diverges from this perfect simultaneity among mediation process, the magnitude of the congruity effect presumably decreases — perhaps as a negatively accelerated function of the time interval, in common with other similar relations — but the effects should still be proportionate to those predicted at simultaneity. In other words, we would expect the effect of one sign upon another to decrease as the time interval between them increases, e.g., as the time between perceiving LAZY and perceiving ATHLETE increases. We have no evidence on this in relation to congruity per se, but Howes and Osgood (1954) have demonstrated what is certainly a correlated effect of time interval upon associations made to combinations of signs.

Even though the effect of synchronous presentation of two signs like LAZY and ATHLETE may be such as to shift them completely toward a point of mutual congruity, it is certain that this effect is not permanent — word meanings would be as fluid as quicksilver if this were the case! After each such cognitive interaction, we assume that the meanings of the related signs tend to "bounce" back to their original locus — the representational process elicited in isolation is again much as it was before. However, this does not mean that repeated cognitive interactions have no effect which persists; like the bough that is repeatedly bent in a particular direction, the mediation process characteristic of a sign will gradually change toward congruence with the other signs with which it is associated. This is the basis, we suspect, for *semantic change* in languages over time, and even in the short run we can note such effects — FIFTH AMENDMENT has become a somewhat unfavorable term, even to college students we have studied, presumably as a result of persistent and pernicious associative relation with COMMUNIST.

It is clear that we are dealing here with *learning* — the modification in mediation processes as a result of "experience" in cognitive interaction. The underlying notion is much like that of ordinary conditioning, in fact may easily incorporate conditioning. We have a situation in which the reaction elicited by a stimulus (sign) is different from what it was previously, due to congruity effects; if this new reaction is repeatedly elicited by this sign, because it appears persistently in interaction with the same other signs, then this new reaction will gradually supersede the original reaction produced in isolation. Let us now phrase this as a *congruity-learning principle: Each time two signs are related in an assertion, the intensity of the mediating reaction characteristic of each in isolation is shifted toward that characteristic of each in interaction, by a constant fraction of the difference in intensity.* Since the difference in intensity (or location along the dimension) decreases with each "trial," this means that the reactions characteristic of both signs must approach a point of common intensity (of the same or antagonistic reactions), which is the point of congruity, according to a negatively accelerated function. In other words, this generates a typical learning curve, for which the terminal point or asymptote is predictable from the initial locations of the signs. Again, it is assumed that this principle operates identically but independently along all dimensions of the cognitive system and that it can be generalized to any number of interacting signs. It should be reiterated, however, that all this is by way of tentative theorizing, still to be verified by experimental investigation.

Congruity and the Prediction of Attitude Change

Perhaps the most typical situation in which one expects to find changes in attitude is that in which some *source* makes some evaluative statement about some object or *concept* in a message that is received and decoded by a receiver. If we consider the source as one sign, the concept evaluated as another sign, and the evaluative statement as an assertion which relates them, then we have the necessary conditions for operation of the congruity principle. Although the theoretical model presented above does not pretend to take into account all of the variables that influence attitude change, it does cover those which are most significant with respect to both the direction (favorable or unfavorable) and the *relative* magnitude of change to be expected in any given situation. These variables are the existing attitude of the subject toward the source, the existing attitude toward the concept, and the nature of the assertion relating them. The predictions generated by the theory apply to attitude changes toward both sources and the concepts they evaluate.

Tannenbaum (1953) devised an experimental situation in which these predictions could be directly tested. On the basis of a pretest, three source-concept pairs were selected which met the following criteria: (a) approximately equal numbers of subjects holding favorable, neutral, and unfavorable original attitudes toward them; (b) lack of correlation between attitude toward the source and toward the concept making up each pair. The three source-concept pairs thus selected were LABOR LEADERS with LEGALIZED GAMBLING, CHICAGO *Tribune* with ABSTRACT ART, and SENATOR ROBERT TAFT with ACCELERATED COLLEGE PROGRAMS. One of the standard attitude-change testing designs was used in the experiment proper: A group of 405 college students was given a *before-test*, in which the six experimental concepts, along with four "filler" concepts, were judged against a form of the semantic differential including six highly and purely evaluative scales. Five weeks later the same subjects were given very realistic news articles and editorials to read (made up like clippings from actual newspapers); both in the headlines and in the body of these short articles assertions relating source and concept were given several times, associative assertions being made in the story for each source-concept pair given to one-half of the subjects and dissociative assertions being made for the same source-concept pair for the other half of the subjects. Immediately after reading the three news items, subjects were given the *after-test*, again judging the same sources and concepts against the same semantic differential. Original attitude scores, ranging from six (most unfavorable) to 42 (most favorable), toward each source and concept were determined from the *before-test* results; subjects distributed into nine cells on each story: source $+$, concept $+$; source $+$, concept 0; source $+$, concept $-$; source 0, concept $+$; etc.

Before reporting the results of this experiment, let us consider the nature of the situation theoretically and the way in which predictions were generated. Since measurement of the meanings of the signs is made in isolation and after the assertions relating them have been presented and removed, it is apparent that we are dealing with the persisting aftereffects of congruity, e.g., with a learning situation rather than a momentary interaction situation such as occurs in judging the meaning of LAZY ATHLETE. However, since the exact number of assertions relating source with concept varied in the news items, and since we do not know the constants of the congruity-learning function in any case, we cannot predict the exact magnitude of the effect on attitude change — except that it will be something less than the maximum. We can, however, predict the *relative* magnitude of attitude change for subjects falling in the various cells above. Knowing the original scale locations for source and concept (e.g., $+2$, -1) and the nature of the assertion presented (associative or dissociative), we can apply the formulae for C given above to both source and concept to predict the amount of attitude change that would be expected under simultaneous conditions. Then to take into account the fact that this is a learning situation, we may take some constant fraction of C — we used $\frac{1}{5}$ arbitrarily to approximate the observed values — as the predicted attitude change in the experiment. The direction and order of magnitude of the predictions are not affected by this procedure.

On each of three stories under each of the two assertion conditions, it was possible to assign 15 subjects to each of the nine cells mentioned above as representing a different combination of original source-concept attitudes. The average expected C and average ob-

Table 32

PREDICTED (UPPER VALUES IN CELLS) AND OBTAINED (LOWER VALUES IN CELLS) CHANGES IN ATTITUDE

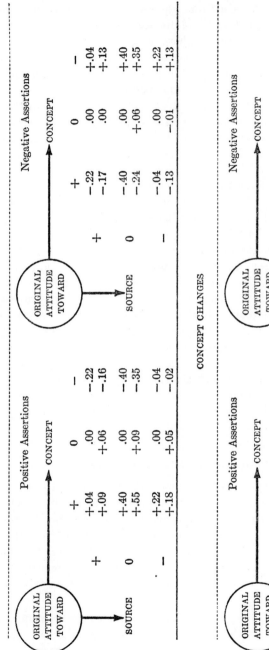
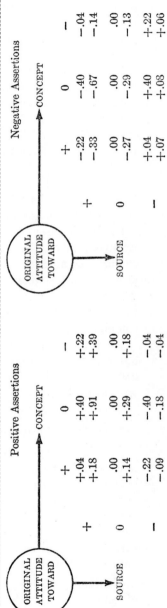

tained C (*after-test* score minus *before-test* score) was computed for each cell. These predicted and obtained attitude-change scores, expressed in seven-step scale values, are presented in Table 32.[1] (The article by Osgood and Tannenbaum, 1955, previously referred to gives tables from which values of C for all possible combinations of original scale values can be read.) The first thing to note is that in every case where a direction of attitude change is predicted (e.g., cases where something other than zero is predicted), the sign of the obtained change corresponds to that predicted — there are 24 such cases in the table. To get at the success with which the principle predicts the relative magnitude of effect, we may correlate predicted and obtained changes; correlation over this table is .91.[2]

For the results of this experiment, then, the principle of congruity yields reasonably accurate predictions. Methodologically it should be emphasized that it is the use of the semantic differential *as a generalized attitude scale* that makes it possible to test this principle. In all cases of cognitive interaction, two or more signs are involved; only to the extent that we are able to measure them in common, comparable units can we test the implications of the congruity principle quantitatively. Other experiments bearing on the validity of this principle will be reported in subsequent chapters; particularly relevant are an experiment on the meanings of word combinations (pp. 275-84), on the effects of color upon the meanings of advertised products and abstract three-dimensional forms (pp. 301-2), on the development of the meaning of nonsense assigns (pp. 286-90), and on the interaction of anxiety-level and intelligence with attitude change (pp. 235-36).

Some Limiting and Parametric Conditions of Congruity

Both in the experiment just reported and in several to be covered later we have been made aware of a number of factors which affect operation of the principle of congruity — it seldom operates in a pure, uncomplicated fashion, as might be expected from the complexity of human cognitive processes. Here we shall indicate our awareness of at least some of these factors, as reference points for further research for the most part. In some cases we have a little data to contribute.

1 *Contiguity of signs in assertions.* Whether measurement is made of compromises at the time of assertion (e.g., the LAZY ATHLETE

---

[1] As corrected for incredulity, see Osgood and Tannenbaum, 1955.

[2] As corrected by an assertion constant, see Osgood and Tannenbaum, 1955.

case) or of the signs in isolation following assertion (e.g., congruity-learning effects), the degree of contiguity in both time and space should affect the magnitude of congruity effect predicted. In the latter case it should appear in the fractional constant by which the meaning of the sign is shifted on each trial, but this in turn presumably depends upon the shift produced at the moment of assertion. We expect to be able to show that, for example, as the modifier LAZY is displaced from the nominal object ATHLETE in syntactical constructions of various types, the effect upon the meaning of ATHLETE will diminish according to some lawful function.

2 *Intensity of assertion.* By operating on the copula of English statements or on the kind of assertive action in perceptual situations, the intensity of either associative or dissociative assertions can be modified. In language, for example, it seems intuitively true that A *gives 100 per cent support to* B is a stronger assertion than A *is cordial to* B, and that therefore the congruity effect should be greater in the former case. We have done no experiments on this, but they should be relatively straightforward.

3 *Credulity of assertions.* The congruity hypothesis in its pure form as presented above assumes complete credulity of assertions on the part of subjects. Presented with the statement, EISENHOWER *is an exponent of* COMMUNISM, it assumes the typical American receiver will "believe" this assertion and be affected accordingly. But this is not the way human receivers handle grossly incongruous messages: one typical way of "getting out of the field" cognitively is to *discredit the given or implied source* of the assertion as a whole — "This is a trick by some subversive columnist designed to deceive us," "This is obviously part of an experiment on us by some crazy professor," etc. Another type of resolution, allowing the subject to retain his existing frame of reference, is to *rationalize* the assertion — this is a typical Amercian reaction to Russian "peace overtures" ("Look out, it's a trick to get us to relax our defenses"), and vice versa, no doubt. Another reaction to highly incongruent assertions is blank bewilderment and failure to comprehend what was said; and this may, of course, be accompanied by adjustive "mis-cognition" in which the subject swears the statement said EISENHOWER *is an opponent of* COMMUNISM.

In a very rough and preliminary attempt to make adjustments for incredulity, we have simply subtracted from incongruous assertions (+ favors −, + against +, − favors +, and − against −) a value which increases according to a negatively accelerated function with the degree of such incongruity. In other words, we assumed on intuitive grounds that an extremely incongruous assertion like EISENHOWER (+3) *sponsors* COMMUNISM (−3) is disproportionately much less credulous than a mildly incongruous assertion like EISENHOWER (+3) *praises* BULGARIA (−1). The arbitrary function used for making such corrections is given in Osgood and Tannenbaum (1955). Actually, it should be possible to ascertain the incredulity function independently of attitude change and thus determine the relationship empirically. A proposed experiment might take the following form: Subjects are presented with a large number of assertions and are told that some are "fake" and some are "valid" (e.g., come from acceptable sources); we would predict that the frequency of "fake" judgments would be some increasing function of the previously measured incongruity of the signs related in the assertions. The shape of this function would be our main interest here.

4 *Relevance of the assertion.* Quite apart from the purely evaluative locations of the signs, it appears that the *relevance* of the signs related to each other influences the magnitude of the congruity effect. Even though the sources in the following assertions may be equally favorable in general evaluation — DR. X *attacks* U.S. PUBLIC HEALTH SERVICE *on polio program* vs. AIR PILOT Y *attacks* U.S. PUBLIC HEALTH SERVICE *on polio program* — it certainly seems likely that the congruity effect will be greater in the former than in the latter case. It is possible that "relevance" here is akin to the sharing of characteristic attributes (or frame of reference) in the sense developed by Suci and described earlier (see pp. 116-20); this relation, however, has not been investigated.

The data from one experiment bearing directly on this question of relevancy in relation to the amount of attitude change are available.[3] On the basis of a pre-test, four relevant source-concept pairs were selected—HENRY WALLACE with PROTECTIVE FARM TARIFFS; MUSEUM OF MODERN ART with ABSTRACT ART; U.S. DEPARTMENT OF AGRICULTURE with FLEXIBLE PRICE SUPPORTS, and JOHN FOSTER DULLES with RECOGNITION OF RED CHINA. All subjects (undergraduates) indicated their attitudes toward these objects on six evaluative scales of the semantic differential, both before and after exposure to the appropriate material. There were two groups of 40 subjects each. One group was exposed to two stories in which the sources were relevant to the concepts (e.g., WALLACE with PROTECTIVE TARIFFS,

[3] This study was conducted by Dr. Jean S. Kerrick at the University of California in 1955.

Table 33

PER CENT OF TOTAL ATTITUDE SHIFT BY INDIVIDUAL SUBJECTS PREDICTED BY PRINCIPLE OF CONGRUITY*

Sources	Per Cent as Predicted in Relevant Situation	Per Cent as Predicted in Non-relevant Situation	$p_{diff.}$
U.S. Department of Agriculture	79	67	.05
Museum of Modern Art	90	92	NS
Henry Wallace	81	56	.01
John Foster Dulles	82	73	NS
Combined Sources	83	71	.01
Concepts			
FLEXIBLE PRICE SUPPORTS	99	87	.01
PROTECTIVE TARIFFS	98	86	.01
ABSTRACT ART	87	63	.01
RED CHINA	85	97	.01
COMBINED CONCEPTS	92	82	.01

* All figures are rounded to the nearest per cent.

and DULLES with RED CHINA), and two stories where the source-concept association was "non-relevant" (e.g., MUSEUM with FLEXIBLE PRICE SUPPORTS, and U.S. DEPARTMENT OF AGRICULTURE with ABSTRACT ART.) The second group also had two relevant and two non-relevant situations, but the reverse of those as in the first group.

As indicated in Table 33, the principle of congruity was able to predict much more efficiently (over-all $p < .01$) under relevant conditions than non-relevant ones. Only with the concept RECOGNITION OF RED CHINA were the non-relevant predictions significantly greater than the relevant ones. It is of interest to note too, that even under non-relevant conditions, congruity predicted significantly better than chance.

5 *Meaning of the copula or action itself as a variable.* In many cases the linguistic copula or the assertive action itself has meaning apart from its associative or dissociative function. Take for example the linguistic assertion JONES *lied about* SMITH or the behavioral situation in which A *saves the life of* B. Not only do we have a dissociative relation between JONES and SMITH and an associative one between A and B indicated, but we also have the implied assertions that JONES *is* A LIAR and A *is* A LIFESAVER. By the congruity

principle, then, we should expect attitude toward JONES to be less favorable and attitude toward A to be more favorable, quite apart from their relations with the third members of the assertions. What we are saying is that all lexical (meaningful) members in assertions, whether they occur as subjects, copulas, or objects, participate in cognitive congruity interactions. Although we have done no direct experiments on this, these notions have been utilized fruitfully in a new method of content analysis (see Osgood, Saporta, and Nunnally, 1956). Also, the effect of the copula of assertions upon congruity predictions was noted by Osgood and Tannenbaum (1955) in the attitude-change study reported above, and had to be taken into account. In this case — where a source makes an assertion about a concept (SENATOR TAFT *sponsors* ACCELERATED COLLEGE PROGRAMS) — it seemed likely that the concept would absorb more of the copula effect (e.g., being sponsored vs. being denounced) than the source. In any event, analysis showed that in every case but one where direct comparisons were possible, concepts showed greater magnitudes of attitude change than did sources (17/18 cases).

Summary

The congruity principle appears to be a very general process operating whenever cognitive events interact. These interactions are such that the representational processes characteristic of related signs are modified toward congruity with each other, degree of modification being inversely proportional to the original intensities of the processes in isolation. The effects of such interactions persist and accumulate as do other learning phenomena, resulting in changes in the meanings of the signs when measured in isolation. So far our experiments have dealt mainly with congruity phenomena as they occur in language behavior, in the attitude area, in word meanings, and in the aesthetics area. But it seems likely to us that congruity will also apply to overt behavioral situations, e.g., to changes in the like-dislike structure of interacting groups (sociometry and group dynamics) and to the interactions between individuals and objects in their environment. Using notions very much like these, Festinger (in a forthcoming book) has done many experiments in this behavioral area. Newcomb (1953) has also utilized similar notions in his theoretical analysis of interpersonal communication. The earliest expression of ideas dealing with "congruity" in human thinking, at least in contemporary psychology, may be found in a paper by Heider (1946).

6

MEANING AND PERSONALITY STRUCTURE

Individual differences in the meanings of signs lie at the base of many diagnostic instruments in this field. The Picture Frustration Test, the Blackie Test, the Rorschach, the Thematic Apperception Test — the so-called projective tests — are merely more extreme examples. Agreements and disagreements of subjects with statements like "I am more sensitive to criticism than most people," as found in inventories like the Minnesota Multiphasic or the Bernreuter, also depend upon the meanings subjects have of other people and themselves. Psychodynamic mechanisms like repression, projection, and identification can be analyzed as involving representational processes or meanings as critical components and hence may be amenable to semantic measurement. Also within this framework, it seems fruitful to view mental illness as involving a disordering of meanings or ways of perceiving significant persons and situations, and psychotherapy as involving a re-ordering and alteration of these meanings in the direction of consistency with those of other people considered normal.

An approach to the measurement of personality and to psychotherapy which, although independently developed, bears many similarities to our own has recently been described by George A. Kelly in *The Psychology of Personal Constructs* (1955). Starting from the basic postulate that "a person's processes are psychologically channelized by the ways in which he anticipates events" (which, as elaborated, proves similar to our conception of the formation and nature of representational mediating processes) and further postulating that "a person's construction system is composed of a finite number of dichotomous constructs" (where "constructs" are similar to our bipolar semantic scales), Kelly develops a "Repertory

Test" that has some resemblance to the semantic differential. It is different in that (a) individual subjects produce their own dimensions (or constructs) by indicating in what way two of three known persons are similar to each other and different from the third person and (b) it is therefore limited by intent to the personality measurement area. But there are sufficient similarities in both the theory and the measurement operations to warrant comparative study. For example, would the clusterings of significant persons obtained by Kelly for a particular subject, through factorization of his data, correspond to clusterings we might obtain for the same subject judging the same person-concepts against the differential? This must remain at present as an invitation to future study, but Kelly's work does indicate the fruitfulness of this type of approach to the personality area.

Personality Traits

What is a "personality trait?" At the conclusion of a chapter in which this term is analyzed in penetrating detail, Gordon Allport (1937) defined "trait," in essence, as some implicit state of the individual which renders equivalent classes of situations and classes of behaviors. Although it is not necessary that all traits be learned (e.g., certain temperamental, stylistic, aptitudinal characteristics), it is certainly the learned characteristics that are of greatest interest to clinicians because, being learned, they are potentially modifiable. It is also not necessary that the class of behaviors mediated be evaluative in nature — although Allport and Odbert in their dictionary of trait-names (1936) do find an evaluative reference to dominate all others. In other words, most traits seem to involve a common mediation process elicited by a class of signs and mediating a class of overt behaviors — very much akin to the general paradigm for mediated semantic generalization. Thus, for a person with an "inferiority complex," a competitive situation may signify "threat" and he responds by avoidance, by "big talk," or by compensating with some other activity in which he excels, and so on — selection among the alternative response skills depending upon contextual cues.

When the members of a society *share* a common representational process to a common set of signs, it seems legitimate to speak of a *culture trait*. When, for example, the members of a given society agree in perceiving spirits in natural objects like trees and lakes and agree in behaving toward these objects by ceremonial avoidance of some and ceremonial propitiation of others, we have a culture trait. Or, closer to home, when members of our culture agree in perceiving FATHERS as strongminded, MOTHERS as warm, COMMUNISM as evil, etc., we are dealing with similar phenomena. In other words, here on a cultural level, we have shared significances which render equivalent classes of stimuli and classes of responses and which mediate between these classes.

How does semantic measurement apply to this situation? The semantic differential is designed to tap variations in representational mediation processes (meanings, significances). Thus, the trait of "stinginess" should be identifiable from the common meanings (profiles against the differential) to the individual of an appropriate set of situations as well as from his overt behavior in these situations — the latter being very difficult to get at. Similarly, when subjects differ in their meanings of concepts like MYSELF, LOVE, MOTHER, ATHLETICS, and PUNCTUALITY we assume that personality differences of some sort are being tapped. Furthermore, aspects of the semantic measurement operation other than the meanings of concepts per se may be relevant to personality variables. The number of factors employed in making judgments and their relative weights may be related to traits like "authoritarianism," and even the way the subject checks the scales (e.g., the dispersion of his checks toward the extremes) may relate to a trait like "constriction," as we shall see.

Psychodynamic Mechanisms

The term "psychodynamics" is frequently used to refer to those aspects of personality that arise from situations of *frustration* and *conflict*. Frustration situations and the aggression generated, particularly when persistent or repetitive, are assumed to lead to the learning of reaction patterns (progression, regression, withdrawal, compensation, etc.) which become characteristics of the individual personality. Similarly, persisting conflict situations, and the anxiety generated, often give rise to various substitute reactions (repression, projection, obsessions, compulsions, etc.) which are learned on the basis of anxiety reduction, and also become traits of the personality. It is possible to make a fairly rigorous theoretical analysis of such personality dynamics in terms of learning theory (see Dollard and Miller, 1950). In any case, the existence of disturbed or deviant significances for signs is evident in most phenomena of this type. The person with a "phobia" certainly has different meanings for a certain class of objects or situations than most of us. The person who "projects" his trait of stinginess judges other people, in general, as more stingy than most of us do. The person with a "withdrawal" trait will perceive certain situations as more laden with threat and anxiety connotations than will most of us — and all this could conceivably show up in semantic measurement.

Differences in meaning to be expected from such personality dynamisms will show up mainly in *comparisons*, i.e., in the test of differences between individuals or between groups. The typical procedure here will be to either (a) make predictions (from some theory or model) about the differences in meanings of certain signs to be expected between two groups and then test the prediction against the semantic differential, or (b) measure differences in meanings of concepts with the differential, make predictions about overt behavior in certain situations from these measurements, and test the accuracy of these predictions. The first procedure involves meaning as a dependent variable, and the second involves meaning as an independent variable. As an illustration of the first approach, it might be predicted that students scoring high on the Taylor Manifest Anxiety Scale would have more nearly neutral (ambivalent) meanings for their SELF CONCEPT. As an example of the second, it might be predicted that people whose SELF CONCEPTS are closer in meaning to those they hold for their like-sex parent, either MOTHER or FATHER, will have a lower divorce rate, i.e., the greater the identification with the like-sex parent, the greater the probability of successful marriage.

Change in Personality: Psychotherapy

The significance of meaning as a critical variable in personality is most apparent perhaps in the process of therapy itself, where the principal changes that occur appear to be in the meanings that various persons, events, and situations have for the patient, and changes in the interrelationships between these significances. The self-concept is one of the more important concepts here, but there are others equally crucial, the meanings of which provide the focus for the therapeutic process. The changes that take place during therapy, then, should be reflected by changes in the patient's meanings of such relevant concepts, which, in turn, should be reflected in judgments on the semantic differential. There have been many attempts with many techniques — including such formal language measures as the type-token ratio, adjective-verb ratio, discomfort-relief quotient, and the like — to uncover indices which are sensitive to such "movement" in therapy. These techniques, however, have not been altogether successful, particularly when the more intimate details of this "movement" are sought. There is reason to believe that the semantic differential possesses such sensitivity, as some of the findings on the following pages will indicate.

There appear to be many potential points of application of such an instrument to problems in the clinical and psychotherapeutic area. Consider, for example, the matter of diagnosis: We have some data to show that disturbed individuals can be selected from a sample in terms of meanings of certain key concepts (particularly the self-concept). Is it possible that both in meanings of specific concepts and in their clustering, a more refined diagnosis into types of disturbance could be made? The systematic job here is still to be done. On the matter of "movement" in the course of therapy itself we have a considerable amount of data to show that the instrument is sensitive to some rather critical changes in meaning — of ME, of THERAPIST, of MY FATHER, of SEX, etc. And the therapists who have cooperated in these studies generally express the feeling that the measured changes "make sense" in terms of their own intimate knowledge of the cases. In one instance, for example, a sharp "dip" in the evaluative location of the self-concept foreshadowed a sudden outpouring of self-criticism a few sessions later; in others, shifts in the measured distances between ME and MOTHER vs. ME and FATHER corresponded to changes taking place in identification patterns in the course of therapy, according to the therapist involved (see Mowrer, 1953).

To the extent, then, that the semantic differential is able to index the meanings of relevant concepts, it seems capable of providing insights into the variables at work in personality and psychotherapy. On the following pages we report a number of studies in which the semantic differential is applied to these areas. They are not complete reports, only highlights of investigations that the interested student may wish to explore in greater detail himself.[1]

---

[1] Studies going on elsewhere which the reader interested in this area may wish to check include the following: A study by E. Lowell Kelly (University of Michigan) on marital compatibility, in which a form of the semantic differential is included with other tests administered to 182 husband-wife pairs; a study by Paul McCullough (VA Hospital, Fort Douglas Station, Salt Lake City, Utah), in which the differential is used as a means of clustering groups of patients receiving sepasil drugs; and a study by Warren W. Webb (VA Hospital, Roanoke, Virginia) on attitudes toward groups in a hospital setting, in which doctors, psychologists, social workers, nurses, aides, and patients rated their own group and the others (as labels) as well as ME against five evaluative scales.

APPLICATIONS IN PERSONALITY AND PSYCHOTHERAPY RESEARCH

Comparison of Factorial Structures

One of the most basic ways in which individuals or groups could differ cognitively would be in terms of the underlying dimensions of judgment they use in differentiating among concepts. They could differ (1) in the *number* of factors required to account for their judgments, (2) in the relative *weights* given to the same set of factors (e.g., one group giving much more weight to the evaluative factor), or (3) in the *nature* of the factors used. In Chapter 4 some data relevant to this problem were given; it was shown by Kumata and Schramm, for example, that even groups as divergent in language and culture as Americans, Japanese, and Koreans seemed to use the same major factors in closely the same relative weights. It is still possible, however, that subgroups selected within a single culture on some basis might differ in these respects. It seems likely, for example, that in the development of meaning in children, differentiations will appear earliest in the dominant evaluative factor, gradually progressing into other, more diversified dimensions. We have no data on this particular question ourselves, but several studies in progress are aimed in this direction. It also seems likely that groups selected (a) in terms of extremeness as personality types or (b) in terms of normalcy vs. diagnosed schizophrenia should show differences in factorial structure, and here we do have some experimental data.

Factorial Structures of High vs. Low Ethnocentrics. Suci (1952) compared the factor structures of high and low ethnocentrics, as determined by scores on the *F*-scale (see Adorno *et al.*, 1950), when judging a sample of ethnic concepts (FRENCHMAN, ENGLISHMAN, GERMAN, MEXICAN, JEW, and NEGRO) against a set of 16 scales. These scales were drawn from Cattell's (1946) personality inventory (*cooperative-obstructive, intelligent-stupid, calm-excitable, childish-mature, hostile-friendly, sociable-unsociable, honest-dishonest, trusting-suspicious, wasteful-thrifty, slow-quick,* and *artistic-inartistic*), from Adorno *et al.* (*safe-dangerous* and *passionate-frigid*), from Stagner and Osgood's (1946) study of social stereotypes (*happy-sad* and *strong-weak*), and from our previous factor work (*large-small*). On the basis of the Adorno *et al.*, conclusions about the differences between high and low ethnocentrics, it was predicted that these two groups should differ markedly in their use of the evaluative factor, the high ethnocentrics showing relatively more variance on evaluation than on other dimensions. Therefore, rotation of the two factorial structures into simple structures was undertaken only in terms of the first factor, which turned out to be clearly evaluative in both groups (represented by scales like *cooperative, friendly, sociable, safe, honest,* and *trusting*).

Contrary to the hypothesis, high and low ethnocentrics showed equal dependence on the first, *evaluative* factor (approximately 46 per cent of the total variance for this set of concepts). The second and third factors for the low ethnocentric group accounted for 15 per cent and 13 per cent respectively of the total variance and showed some correspondence to our *potency* and *activity* factors. Scales loading on the second factor in order of magnitude were *mature, thrifty, calm, intelligent, large, cooperative, sociable,* and *strong;* scales loading on the third factor in order of magnitude were *artistic, quick, mature, intelligent, passionate,* and *strong.* The high ethnocentrics displayed a more definite fusion of the second and third factors into a single *dynamism* factor (21 percent of the total variance) — *mature, intelligent, strong, quick, artistic,* and *large.* Thus we have some suggestion of a difference in the nature of the factors employed by high and low ethnocentrics, but it is very slight and could be due to the type of rotation. The major hypothesis, that high ethnocentrics rely more heavily on general evaluation, definitely does not hold up.

Factorial Structures of Normal vs. Schizophrenic Subjects. In her thesis research, Bopp (1955) first set out to test the hypothesis that the factorial bases of schizophrenic judgments are different from those of normals — it was necessary to reject this hypothesis in order to test subsequent notions about associative processes. A review of the literature relating to schizophrenic thinking strongly suggested that there would be differences in the number, nature, or at least clarity of semantic factors, as compared with normals. Sixteen concepts were selected to sample those areas of meaning in which, on a priori grounds, schizophrenics might be expected to deviate from normals, as well as control areas. These words served as the stimuli in a standard free-association test. Subjects took the word association test and then rated both the stimulus words and their *own* responses (32 concepts in all) against a 13-scale form of the differential (including 7 evaluative scales and 3 each of scales loading mainly on the potency or activity factors). The experimental subjects consisted of 40 schizophrenics in all diagnostic subclasses who were found (after testing of a much larger number) to be both able and willing to cooperate throughout the testing procedure; the control group consisted of 40 non-schizophrenics — who were, however, hospitalized in tubercular or broken-bone wards — selected to match the experimental group in terms of sex, age, and education.

To test the first hypothesis, Bopp randomly divided each of the groups in half. Separate factor analyses were made on the semantic data of these four resulting groups, restricting analysis to the 16 stimulus words to which they responded in common. Product-moment correlations over the means of the concepts on the 13 scales were computed for each group and factor analyzed by the method of principle components. The results of this analysis are shown in Table 34, the upper portion of the table giving the proportions of total variance accounted for by each of the first four factors in each of the four groups and the lower portion giving the indices of factorial similarity. Looking first at the proportions of total variance accounted for by the first four factors in each group, we find no evidence for differences in the weights given. The order — approximately 61 per cent, 21 per cent, 6 per cent, and 5 per cent — is duplicated almost exactly within and between normal and schizophrenic groups. Nor do the natures of the factors vary either within or between groups: factor 1 was clearly *evaluative* in all groups; factor 2 was clearly *activity* in all groups, *active-passive* and *fast-slow* showing high and pure loadings; factor 3 was less clearly a *potency* variable, *large-small* having high loadings in all groups and *strong-weak* considerable loadings. The scales *hot-cold* and *heavy-light* yielded specific factors in all groups, the former as factor 4. The extremely high correspondence across groups in the content of these factors is also supported by the indices of similarity in the lower half of Table 34. On the basis of these findings we must reject the notion that the semantic frame of reference for schizophrenics differs from that of normals. Also worth noting here are the high reliabilities of the factorial structure for both normals and schizophrenics and the fact that as much as 90 per cent of the total variance is accounted for by only the first three factors.

Having demonstrated a lack of factorial structure differences between normal and schizophrenic subjects, Bopp was able to test her second hypothesis — that the association processes of schizophrenics are more determined by semantic (similarity) variables than by transitional (sequences frequently encountered in experience, like BREAD-BUTTER) variables. This hypothesis also has its roots in the

Table 34

PROPORTIONS OF TOTAL VARIANCE AND INDICES OF FACTORIAL SIMILARITY FOR FIRST FOUR FACTORS IN ORDER OF MAGNITUDE (UNROTATED) FOR CONTROL (A AND B) AND EXPERIMENTAL (C AND D) SUBGROUPS

Proportions of Total Variance

Factors	Control Groups (in per cent)		Experimental Groups (in per cent)	
	A	B	C	D
1	61	63	59	64
2	22	21	20	21
3	7	6	7	5
4	5	4	6	6

Indices of Factorial Similarity

Factors	Normals	Schizophrenics	Normals vs. Schizophrenics			
	A with B	C with D	A with C	A with D	B with C	B with D
1	.95	.93	.98	.95	.98	.85
2	.95	.92	.96	.95	.95	.83
3	.88	.93	.73	.68	.91	.79
4	.87	.97	.77	.79	.94	.94

literature of this field. It will be recalled that Bopp obtained semantic differential profiles for both the stimulus words and the free-associated response words from both control and experimental subjects. The most straightforward test of the present hypothesis would seem to be to show that the D between profiles for S and R words is significantly smaller for schizophrenics than for normals, e.g., that the meanings of schizophrenic response words are more like their meanings for the stimulus words. The difference here was in the expected direction and significant at the 2 per cent level by the Mann-Whitney U-test.[2] However, any conclusion from this result assumed (1) that normals and schizophrenics are equally reliable in their semantic judgments on the scales, or at least that degrees of unreliability are not correlated with S-R distances, and (2) that they use the alternative scale positions with equal frequencies, or at least that differences here are not correlated with S-R distances. Bopp found that there were, in fact, differences between normals and schizophrenics in both immediate test-retest reliabilities and in delayed test-retest reliabilities (or meaning stability), and that these differences were correlated with the measured distances (D) between stimulus and response profiles. She also found that although there were marked differences between normals and schizophrenics in the use of scale positions (see next section below), these differences were not correlated with S-R distances. Another implication of the same general hypothesis is that schizophrenics should give relatively fewer opposite associates — this was verified at the .002 level. There is suggestive evidence, then, that schizophrenic thinking is more determined by similarity than by transitional factors.

Comparison of Scale-checking Styles

As early in our work on semantic measurement as the studies on social stereotypes by Stagner and Osgood (1946) very marked differences in what might be called personal "styles" in checking semantic differential scales were noted. Although the matter was not tested statistically at that time, it appeared that more intelligent subjects, or perhaps better educated (i.e., college students

---

[2] In a personal communication James M. Anker (Perry Point VA Hospital, Perry Point, Maryland) reports that he is engaged in a very similar study with schizophrenics using the semantic differential as a measuring device. Norman Garmezy (Duke University), with Roland Englehart and Robert Alverez, is also using the instrument in studies on schizophrenics.

vs. laymen), used the intermediary positions (2, 3, 5, and 6) relatively more frequently than the polar (1, 7) or neutral (4) positions
on the scales. It also seemed likely that the *emotionality* of the subject with respect to the judgment being made was a variable operating here — in any event, subjects identified in the Stagner and
Osgood samples as members of the American Legion displayed a
very definite tendency to use only the most polar 1 and 7 positions,
or perhaps 1, 4, or 7 (i.e., things were either all-or-nothing, or
neither, for them). It has also been noted that *age* is a variable
here — children of grade school ages seem to operate better with a
five-step than with a seven-step scale, for example. Although we
have many large samples of data from which such tests could (and
should) be made, we have not as yet tested any specific hypotheses
relating scale-checking styles to personality variables.[3]

Scale-checking Style and Mental Disorder. In the Bopp study
(1955) already described, a direct comparison of the scale-checking
styles of normals and schizophrenics (for the same concepts) was
made. For the normal group, 36 per cent of the checks occurred in
the extremes (1 and 7), 29 per cent in the neutral category (4),
and 35 per cent in the more discriminative intermediary positions
(2, 3, 5, and 6); for the schizophrenic group, 41 per cent were extremes (1, 7), 39 per cent were neutral (4), and only 20 per cent
were intermediary (2, 3, 5, and 6). When tested for significance,
the difference for extreme 1 and 7 judgments is not significant, but
that for the neutral 4 position is significant at the 6 per cent level
and that for the more discriminatory positions is highly significant
at the .002 level. It appears, then, that schizophrenic patients are
far less discriminatory in their use of semantic scales. The reason
for this difference — whether due to intellectual deficits or to emotional factors in the testing situation — cannot be determined from
these data.

Scale-checking Style and Intelligence. There is some evidence that
I.Q. score is related to these "position habits" in responding to the
differential. In connection with her study on relations of anxiety
and intelligence to congruity effects in attitude change, Kerrick
(1954) had high school students of known I.Q. rate a number of

---

[3] One such test has been made elsewhere, however. Julian Wohl (University
of Nebraska) correlated personality "constriction" as judged by peers with the
dispersion of judgments over the semantic differential scales, finding the expected inverse relation, e.g., subjects judged to be more "constricted" tended
to compress their checking operations in toward the neutral points of the
scales, avoiding the polar extremes.

concepts against a form of the semantic differential. Comparing upper and lower quartiles in I.Q. in terms of scale-checking behavior, she found that whereas the high I.Q. subjects used 39 per cent 1 and 7 judgments, low I.Q. subjects used 48 per cent; whereas the highs gave 30 per cent neutral judgments, the lows gave 26 per cent; and whereas the highs gave 31 per cent judgments in the discriminatory positions, lows gave 26 per cent. In other words, in this situation at least, subjects of lower intelligence tended to be more polarized in their judgments. The over-all difference in scale-checking styles was significant at beyond the 1 per cent level by Chi-square test. Kerrick's study also provides evidence bearing on the relation of anxiety to scale-checking style, but first we need to look more closely at the psychological significance of the scale positions.

Scale-checking and Response Conflict. In an earlier chapter (4, pp. 155-59), a near-linear relation was demonstrated between extremeness of position checked on the graphic scales and judgmental *latency* in a reaction device. This was interpreted as evidence that polarization on the scales is a function of the intensity of mediating reactions. It is also possible, however, that the recorded latency reflects the degree of *conflict* between competing mediators, i.e., between the reciprocally antagonistic reactions assumed to mediate judgments on our bipolar scales. The more nearly equal the reaction tendencies, the slower the judgments and the nearer to the center of the scale the check-mark. Although this would explain the near-linear relation between extremeness and judgmental latency, there are other data which indicate that the situation is not so simple. For one thing, when Tannenbaum (1953) plotted the amount of attitude change toward a concept against the original (i.e., before the pressure to change was initiated) attitude toward that concept, an interesting function was generated. The amount of change was least at the extremes of attitude — most favorable and most unfavorable — and increased in a linear progression as the original attitude became less intense (i.e., approached neutrality). But there was one important exception: At the point of least intensity, instead of the expected maximum of attitude change, there was a pronounced and significant dip in the curve.

More to the point was an early study by Osgood (1941) where latencies were measured with a voice-key under conditions where the subject could select the neutral position, 4, something not possible in the latency study previously reported (where the response lever could only be moved toward one polar term or the other). Presented aurally with a scale (polar terms only) and then with the concept to be judged (which started the voice-key timer in motion), the subject called out one number from 1 to 7 to indicate his judgment. Extreme 1 and 7 judgments gave the shortest mean latencies and the intermediary positions the longest, *with the neutral position, 4, falling between these levels.* In other words, when subjects are allowed to select a neutral position, they do so with judgment times shorter than those required for the more discriminatory 2, 3, 5, and 6 positions. In terms of response conflict, this suggests that one resolution of a judgmental conflict situation is to rather promptly select a "neither" or "don't know" alternative. Osgood interpreted these data as evidence for three "difficulty levels" of the judgment process — an all-or-nothing "black-white" decision being easiest, a "neither" judgment as intermediate in difficulty, and more finely graded judgments of degree as being most difficult. This is certainly consistent with the data on American Legion members, schizophrenics, and people of low I.Q. that we have already reviewed. Psychologically, polar judgments mean lack of conflict, judgments nearer the center position mean increasing response conflict, and judgments on the center position mean maximum conflict — conflict which can be resolved, however, by "going out of the field" with a prompt "4" judgment. But what happens when the subject is not allowed to "go out of the field," when he has no "neither" alternative as in the latency experiment reported earlier?

Scale-checking Style and Anxiety. The latency experiment conducted by Lyons and Solomon reported in Chapter 4 was designed to yield data on the relation of anxiety to semantic judgment processes as well as on the relation between extremeness and reaction latency. Although the data in this study go beyond the question of scale-checking types, it has bearing here and so will be reported in full at this point. It will be recalled that 20 male and 20 female undergraduates served as subjects in the original phase of the experiment. The 15 concepts were selected to include various possible areas of what we may call *sign-specific anxiety* (PENIS, TAMPAX, SWEAT, JEW, NEGRO, FINALS, FRATERNITY, SORORITY, ME) as well as ones it was thought would serve as controls (MOM, DAD, NUN, FIRE, STATUE, and LAKE). The scales used were *good-bad, healthy-sickly, fair-unfair, beautiful-ugly, smooth-rough, large-small, strong-weak, active-passive, hot-cold,* and *dry-wet.* It will also be recalled that these subjects first reacted individually to the 150 items projected in the latency device, and then checked the same items, in exactly the same order and orientation, on the usual graphic differential form. To augment what we may call *generalized situational anxiety*, each female subject had a male observer (along with a female experimenter) and each male subject had a female observer (along with a male experimenter).

The over-all results of this experiment, it will be remembered, showed that female subjects made their judgments with significantly shorter latencies, consistently for all scale positions (see Figures 14 and 15 in Chapter 4). Was this simply a sex difference in the language area or was it due to the fact that *the females experienced greater generalized situational anxiety* when faced with these items in this situation? What would happen to male subjects if they were subjected to increased generalized anxiety in the same situation? To answer these questions, another group of 20 male undergraduates was run through the 150-item judgment-time experiment, but in this case, 15 *unpredictable electric shocks* of 50 volts A.C. were administered to the left hand at intervals during the testing (the right hand manipulated the bi-directional reaction lever). It was reasoned that this treatment would augment the generalized anxiety drive under which these male subjects were operating. Figure 17 compares the average judgmental latencies for individual concepts, for male controls (solid line), male shock (dashed line) and female subjects (dotted line). Not only is the reduction in reaction latency for males with unpredictable shock highly significant and consistent for all concepts, but the over-all mean latency across all concepts for these males turns out to be the same as that for the females in the original analysis (1.72 seconds for these males and 1.73 seconds for the females). This is consistent with the interpretation that the female subjects in the original experiment were laboring under higher generalized anxiety than the males.

It is apparent from the above results that increasing *generalized drive* (here, anxiety) serves to increase the over-all speed with which meaningful judgments are made. What about *sign-specific anxiety*? In Figure 17 the concepts judged are arranged according to the mean latencies of the male control group. The five concepts yielding the quickest judgments are LAKE, DAD, MOM, FIRE, and STATUE, all viewed on a priori grounds as relatively non-anxiety-producing in nature; the five concepts yielding the slowest judgments are JEW, TAMPAX, FINALS, SWEAT, and NEGRO, all considered as rela-

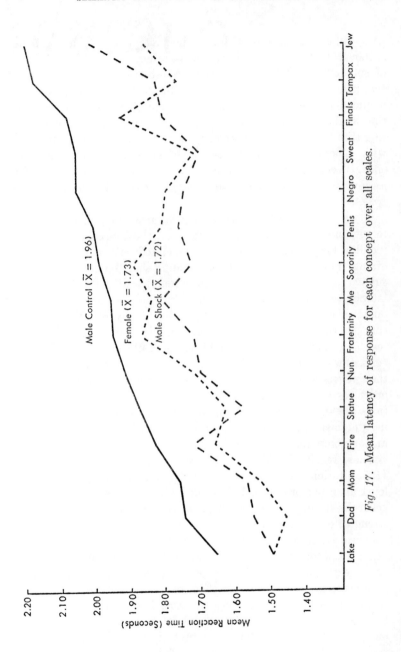

Fig. 17. Mean latency of response for each concept over all scales.

tively likely to be anxiety-producing, again on a priori grounds. Although there are some inversions in order for the different groups of subjects, the differences between these two sets of concepts are significant in all cases. It is not possible to claim that the concepts included in these two sets are equivalent in recognition time and this weakens the case somewhat; but, on the other hand, recognition threshholds of the order of .10 seconds should have little to do with semantic judgment times which range from 1.50 to 2.20 seconds. It seems legitimate to conclude, then, that *sign-specific anxiety*, as contrasted with generalized anxiety, *tends to lengthen judgment time.*

If, as we have hypothesized, long latencies of judgment are due to response competition or ambivalence, the concepts in Figure 17 yielding long latencies should be associated with more reversals in direction of judgment than those yielding short latencies. Since each subject in the original phase both reacted with the lever in the latency test and checked the same items on the graphic form, this question can be answered directly — by simply counting, for each concept, the number of subjects giving one response on the latency test (e.g., JEW — *beautiful*) and the opposite on the graphic form (e.g., JEW — *ugly*). Correlating the mean latencies for concepts with their reversal frequencies showed that for male subjects, the rank-order correlation is .49; for female subjects it is .48. Both correlations are significant though not too high, and indicate that increasing judgment times may be associated with increasing ambivalence among competing reactions.

These results would seem to have bearing on the Taylor-Spence (1952) rationale regarding the relation of anxiety-produced drive level upon performance. Following Hull, they argue that increased generalized drive, by multiplicative combination with habit strength, operates to increase excitatory potential and hence overt response strength. They argue further that if the behavioral situation is one in which a single dominant response is being strengthened (e.g., conditioning, or in our case where polarized 1 and 7 judgments are involved), the effect of increased drive level will be facilitative on behavior; if the situation is one in which competing responses are operating (e.g., serial or trial-and-error learning, or our case where intermediary, compromise judgments are involved), the effect of increased drive level will be to produce even greater interference, since the response competition is intensified. This argument seems to lead inevitably to the prediction in our case

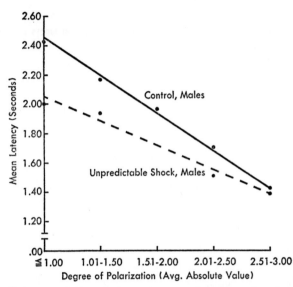

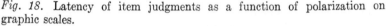

Fig. 18. Latency of item judgments as a function of polarization on graphic scales.

that giving unpredictable electric shock should shorten the judgment times for highly polarized items most and those for ambivalent items least, if at all. *Just the reverse result was obtained.* In the first place, comparing the solid and dashed curves in Figure 17 (control vs. shocked males), we note that the decreases in judgment time tend to be greater for the long-latency items, which we have just seen are associated with greater response ambivalence — the rank correlation here is .54, which is significant.

A more direct procedure, however, is to deal with individual items (judgments of particular concepts against particular scales) and plot judgmental latency against degree of polarization. This is done in Figure 18 — separately for male-control and male-shock groups. As is clearly shown, the reduction in latency of judgment attributable to generalized drive level (unpredictable shock) is progressively smaller as the degree of graphic polarization of the item increases. Augmenting anxiety had almost no effect upon the most polarized items (presumably the most uncomplicated, single reaction tendencies). How this is to be explained is not clear: it is possible, though not likely, that we have a "ceiling" on speed of judgment that is approximated by the polarized items. It is also possible, and more likely, that the effects of generalized drive upon

Table 35

USES OF ALTERNATIVE SCALE POSITIONS BY MALE AND FEMALE SUBJECTS UNDER ANXIETY-PROVOKING CONDITIONS

	1	2	3	4	5	6	7
Males	.13	.18	.17	.10	.14	.18	.10
Females	.18	.11	.09	.23	.10	.13	.16

performance in a situation where learning is already maximal (which we have here) is different from its effect upon *learning* (which has been involved in most tests of the Taylor-Spence hypothesis). Looking at these data from a common sense basis, and recalling that sign-specific anxiety has been shown to slow down judgment time, the following seems a plausible explanation: when faced with an anxiety-producing item under ordinary circumstances, the subject tends to hesitate and rationalize his judgment; when energized by additional *generalized* drive, however, he tends to retreat immediately into whatever anxiety-reducing, face-saving alternative is available to him.

This leads us back to the question with which we began our study of this experiment: How is a subject's scale-checking style affected by anxiety and what does he do in the latency apparatus where no neutral 4 position is provided? Unfortunately, as it turned out, the male-shock subjects were not required to fill in the graphic forms. (In preparing Figure 18 it was assumed that this group of 20 males under ordinary conditions would have checked items on the graphic form essentially as the control group did. This seems justified by our reliability data showing that the means for successive groups of 20-25 subjects can be expected to deviate by no more than one-third of a scale unit at the 5 per cent level of confidence.) We do have data for the female subjects, however, and presumptive evidence that they were under higher generalized anxiety than the males. Table 35 compares male and female subjects in terms of how they distributed their judgments over the seven-step graphic scales. It is apparent that whereas the males tend to use the more discriminatory intermediary positions, the females pile up heavily in the polar and neutral positions (1, 4, and 7). On the polar 1 and 7 positions, 14/20 females are above the median frequency for males, which barely misses significance at the 5 per cent level; on the neutral 4 position, we find 16/20 females exceeding the median male frequency, which is significant beyond the 5 per cent level.

On the other hand, for the intermediary 2, 3, 5, and 6 positions we find 18/20 males exceeding the female median, which is significant at the 1 per cent level.

We may conclude, then, that there are real differences between men and women in their use of scale positions here. Whether this is due to heightened anxiety effects in the women in this situation, or perhaps a general sex difference, we cannot say for sure from these data — but we have not observed such distinctions between the sexes in other, non-anxiety-provoking situations. We also have some hint as to what subjects do under anxiety conditions where no "escapist" 4 judgment is possible. For both males and females we have analyzed what direction the lever in the latency situation is thrown when a subject has judged an item as neutral (or 4) on the graphic scales. Assigning each scale a *good-bad* polarity in terms of its factor loadings, we find a highly significant tendency in female subjects to throw the lever toward the *good* side for items they later mark as 4 — 29/34 items which had sufficient data go in this direction, or 244 individual reactions toward *good* as compared with only 86 toward *bad*. As might be expected from the assumption that the females were under greater anxiety than the males, the latter show only 16/24 items toward the favorable sides of scales, or 73 individual reactions toward *good* as compared with 44 toward *bad*. In other words, when subjects are placed in judgmental situations where they cannot give a neutral "don't know" or "neither" response, and particularly when they are under the added impetus of generalized anxiety (the females), they will often "get out of it" by quickly giving a favorable response, one more likely to be socially acceptable. This seems to serve much the same function as a quick, polite smile in an ambiguous and potentially threatening social situation.

Finally, we may take up Kerrick's (1954) results on this question at the point where we left them. She had found significant differences in the scale-checking behavior of high vs. low I.Q. subjects, the lows showing generally greater polarization. When a similar analysis was made in terms of anxiety-level (as indexed by the Taylor Manifest Anxiety Scale), however, no differences whatsoever were found between high and low anxiety groups — contrary to our expectations. Analysis of the *interaction* between I.Q. and anxiety-level yielded an interesting result, however. The effect of greater anxiety-level upon *high* I.Q. subjects was to make them use the polar positions more often; the effect upon *low* I.Q. subjects was to make them use discriminatory positions relatively more often and the polar or neutral positions less often. All of the differences were significant at the 5 per cent level or better by Chi-square test. To generalize, it appears that the effect of making intelligent people anxious is to make them less discriminating in their judgments, more prone to either extreme "black-and-white" decisions or sheer "escapism." The effect of making people of lower intelligence anxious, on the other hand, is to make them more cautious, more wary, more seeking of distinctions.

All this, of course, raises a serious methodological issue. Should we standardize each subject's scores before doing further computations like r and D? We have definite evidence that subjects differ in their scale-checking behavior, but there are two ways of interpreting this: (1) If we standardize scores, we are assuming that despite the definitions of the scale positions and the instructions the same scale positions have different meanings to different subjects, e.g., that a 2 really means the same thing as a 1 to a subject who rarely uses extreme judgments. (2) If we do not standardize scores, we are assuming that the definitions and instructions guarantee consistent meanings of the scale positions, but people display real individual differences (due to personality factors, intellectual factors, and so on) in reaction to the scales, e.g., that the person who rarely uses 1 and 7 is "constricted" in outlook and is cautious about making extreme judgments. In most of our work we have favored the second alternative, believing that standardization in this case may involve loss of valuable information. To the extent that scale-checking styles can be shown to relate to personality, intellectual, situational, etc., variables, this choice seems justified.

Use as a Device for Quantifying Subjective Testing Instruments

Many of the most penetrating diagnostic instruments in the personality and psychotherapeutic area are essentially subjective in nature. By "subjective" we refer to the operations whereby the investigator or therapist arrives at the scores or values assigned the subject on the test. This is particularly true of the projective tests. Consider the Rorschach, for example: The subject looks at an ink-blot, presumably perceives it in certain ways, makes verbal comments on it which may or may not accurately reflect his perceptions, and the investigator, using these verbalizations and what general rules and intuitions are at his command, assigns scores in various categories. Experiments have shown that scores depend not only upon the personality of the subject, but also upon that of the investigator, upon his meanings of the ink-blots and of the patient's words and perhaps actions. It is also true that clinicians differ markedly in their ability to use such instruments sensitively, that they often have little confidence in the interpretations of others from such tests, and that patients differ markedly in their ability to cooperate.

The semantic differential could be considered as a technique for at least providing a quantitative index of such introspective data — if not one for objectifying such data. When a patient looks at an ink-blot, a TAT picture, or some other projective display and reacts with meanings and significances which (we hope) reflect aspects of his personality, it should be possible to index such reactions by having him make judgments against the differential. There are several potential advantages to such a procedure, assuming the validity of the measurement can be established: (1) the personality, intuitions, and biases of the observer (investigator, clinician) are removed from the process whereby a score is obtained and at least pushed further back in the interpretive process; (2) some standardization in the scores from a variety of tests would be accomplished; (3) the possibility of group administration (e.g., in military situations) is enhanced; (4) subjects who ordinarily have trouble communicating could be studied; (5) the quantification of scores would facilitate research designed to test the validity of such instruments. We have only two, rather preliminary studies to report, but the results are encouraging and more research along these lines is under way.

Application to the Thematic Apperception Test. Reeves (1954), as part of her doctoral dissertation, was concerned with the validity of the semantic differential as a means of quantifying TAT results, particularly on the evaluative factor. Undergraduate subjects were shown ten TAT pictures one at a time via a slide projector; they rated each of these pictures against a 20-scale form of the differential. They were then shown the same pictures in the same order, but were asked to write "a brief statement of the plot of a story that might be told about this picture," a typical story with a major theme such as might be obtained in a clinical setting. The stories for all pictures were classified as to major theme, and each theme represented by at least eight subjects was judged on a positive-negative continuum by a set of 20 experts, professionals who had used the TAT clinically. For each picture, the most positive and most negative theme was selected; the two groups of subjects giving these extreme themes were then compared on the basis of their summed ratings over five clearly evaluative scales of the differential. In all cases, the *direction* of the difference in evaluative ratings corresponded to the ratings of experts, and on seven of the ten pictures the difference was significant at the 5 per cent level by the Mann-Whitney U Test. There was a low but significant correlation ($r = .25$; $p < .05$) between evaluative scores on the differential and distress-relief quotients (DRQ) on the stories told. There was also interesting evidence for specific meanings being reflected on the differential, e.g., stories including reference to "hot sun" showing greater polarization on the *hot-cold* scale, stories including reference to "young" or "old" in relation to characters showing appropriate scores on the *young-old* scale, etc.

Application to the Rorschach. In a recent experiment,[4] the relationship between certain key Rorschach cards and certain concepts, as hypothesized by a number of Rorschach experts, was investigated. In the course of this investigation the feasibility of using the semantic differential as a means of quantifying data of this type was also demonstrated. The specific hypotheses concerned the designation of Card IV as the "Father Card," Card VII as the "Mother Card," and Card VI as the "Sex Card." If these designations were valid clinically, the semantic profiles for concept FATHER and for Card IV should be similar, those for MOTHER and Card VII similar, and so forth.

The ten cards of the Rorschach Test, as projected via a lantern slide, were judged against a ten-scale form of the differential, which included scales representative of the three major factors, by 20 undergraduates. They then rated a set of ten verbal concepts, including the three under consideration, against the same differential. Rather than using the D statistic, McQuitty's agreement-analysis score (1956) served as an index of the relationship between all possible pairings of concepts with cards. For the present situation, this score can range from 0 (no agreement) to 10 (maximum agreement), there being 10 scales used, and the summation over subjects yields scores from 0 to 200. The results uniformly failed

---

[4] Conducted by Mr. Aaron Smith at the University of Illinois in 1955. Albert I. Rabin (Michigan State University) and Ephraim Rosen (University of Minnesota) are both currently studying the validity of Rorschach indices by means of judgment of cards, verbal symbols, etc., against forms of the differential.

to verify the hypothesized relations. The concept MY FATHER ranked only seventh (out of ten) in profile agreement with Card IV; MY MOTHER ranked only fifth in profile agreement with Card VII; SEX ranked only sixth in profile agreement with Card VI. Analysis in the other direction gave similar results: Card IV ranked tenth in agreement with MY FATHER, Card VII ranked fifth in agreement with MY MOTHER, and Card VI ranked fourth in agreement with SEX. Despite the negative findings with respect to these particular hypotheses, this experiment indicates that it is feasible to use the semantic differential as a means of "scoring" the Rorschach.

Use as a Hypothesis-testing Device

The semantic differential can be employed in a large number of hypothesis-testing situations in personality and psychotherapy research. The only apparent restriction is that some aspect of meaning be functioning as either the dependent variable or the independent variable. Some of the experiments we have already reviewed have been of this type. In this section we describe two studies: in the first, dealing with the effects of intelligence and anxiety-level upon attitude change, meaning is the dependent variable; in the second, dealing with the effect of ego-satisfaction upon manifest anxiety scores, meaning is the independent variable.

Effects of Intelligence and Anxiety-Level upon Attitude Change. Some of the data from Kerrick's (1954) thesis — those relating specifically to scale-checking behavior — have already been presented. Her main hypotheses, however, concerned the effects of both intelligence and anxiety-level (as indexed by the Taylor Scale) upon the magnitude of pressure toward congruity in producing attitude change. The general nature of the congruity principle has already been discussed (Chapter 5, pp. 199 ff.). Her first hypothesis was simply a check on the congruity notion: *Given an assertion by a source about a concept, attitude change resulting from that assertion will always be in the direction of greater congruity.* Her second hypothesis concerned the special effect of intelligence: *The lower the I.Q. of the individual, the more susceptible he will be to pressure toward congruity.* There is considerable evidence in the literature showing that intelligent people are more aware of incongruities — witness the use of logical incongruities as tests of intelligence — and as such, they should resist pressures toward cognitive simplification more effectively. Kerrick's third hypothesis dealt with the special effect of manifest anxiety: *The greater the manifest anxiety displayed by an individual, the more susceptible he will be to pressure toward congruity.* This prediction derives from experimental evidence showing that anxiety hinders discrimination in complex learning tasks, as well as from common sense notions about the effect of anxiety on seeking quick, simple solutions to problems.

On the basis of a pretest, Kerrick selected four *sources* for her communication materials, two that were most often judged favorably and two that were most often judged unfavorably, and two *concepts*, the two nearest neutrality and hence capable of the most potential change. AMERICAN COUNCIL OF CHURCHES (+) and THE COMMUNIST PARTY (−) with the concept MENTAL HYGIENE CLINICS served as the materials for one set of stories, and THE PUBLIC HEALTH SERVICE (+) and THE KU KLUX KLAN (−) with COMIC BOOKS as the materials for a second set of stories. For each of these two sets of material, four versions were written: (1) a positive assertion by the positive source; (2) a negative assertion by the same positive source; (3) a positive assertion by the negative source; and (4) a negative assertion by the negative source — all about the same concept. High school students served as subjects in two testing sessions: on the first, they were given the Taylor Manifest Anxiety Scale and the pretest for attitudes toward all sources and concepts; on the second, they were given a booklet containing the experimental stories (which they were to read and indicate interest in) and then the post-test on attitudes toward the sources and concepts. Otis I.Q. scores were already available for the students used.

Data relating to the first (congruity) hypothesis were analyzed both in terms of the number of individual subjects shifting in the predicted direction under all conditions and in terms of the mean magnitudes (and directions) of change. The individual subject analysis was discouraging — although the changes in attitude toward the source tended to be in the direction predicted from the congruity principle (63 per cent on Story 1, and 62 per cent on Story 2), they did not reach the 5 per cent level of confidence, and changes toward the concepts were only chance in direction (50 per cent and 51 per cent for Stories 1 and 2 respectively). Treating the algebraic sums of individual subjects, however, gave a more satisfactory picture: of the 16 predictions of direction made (two types of assertion times two sources times two loci of measurement, source-change and concept-change, times two stories), 12 were correct in terms of the congruity principle, which is significantly better than chance at the .02 level. Again, the errors were concentrated in the predictions of concept-change, and in every case they consisted in shifts *in the direction of the assertion* regardless of the source. Inspection of the data shows that in the story for which the large errors occurred, *the source was mentioned only once and then in a small by-line* at the top of the article. Kerrick concludes that for the congruity mechanism to operate effectively, source and concept must be closely associated, and probably with some frequency.

The failure of the congruity hypothesis to be cleanly supported in these data makes it difficult to test the hypotheses relating to intelligence and anxiety, of course. There was no evidence that low I.Q. subjects were more susceptible to congruity effects, but this was confounded by the fact that on all sources and concepts the low I.Q. subjects were more polarized in their judgments to start with — and it has already been shown (Tannenbaum, 1953, and others) that susceptibility to attitude change varies inversely with the intensity with which original attitudes are held. When Kerrick matched her high and low I.Q. subjects on the basis of polarization of original attitudes, a difference in magnitude of attitude change in the direction predicted (i.e., low I.Q. changing more than high I.Q.) was obtained which was significant at the 10 per cent level. There is some support, then, for the notion that people of low intelligence are more susceptible to pressures toward congruity or cognitive simplification, but it certainly needs further checking. The third hypothesis — that people displaying high manifest anxiety should be more susceptible to congruity effects — failed to be confirmed completely, even when subjects in various anxiety categories were matched for initial polarization.

Effect of Ego-Satisfaction upon Anxiety Level. The concept of self or ego is central in personality theory — how people judge themselves in relation to others, in relation to how they would like to be, and so on. There are several ways in which attitudes (and meanings) of the self can be measured with the semantic differential: one measure is simply the location of ME, MY ACTUAL SELF, THE REAL ME, or however one phrases the concept, against the coordinates of the differential. An example of this index will be given in connection with our study of a case of triple personality.[5] Another way is to measure the distance, D, between MY ACTUAL SELF and the labels for a variety of personality traits, e.g., aggressiveness, submissiveness, extroverted, introverted, etc., the assumption being that if MY ACTUAL SELF is close profile-wise to COMPETITIVE and EXTROVERTED, say, this characterizes the subject's personality in terms of his own meanings of various traits.[6] Yet another method is to index the evaluation of the self-concept along a scale provided by the subject's own judgments of the presumably polar concepts, MY IDEAL SELF and MY LEAST LIKED SELF, e.g., the distance from MY ACTUAL SELF (AS) to MY IDEAL SELF (IS) as a ratio to the distance from MY LEAST LIKED SELF (LLS) to MY IDEAL SELF. Or, if we wish the value to increase in size with ego-satisfaction, we may take the distance from AS to LLS as a ratio to the total distance IS to LLS.

This last index was the one used in a study[7] on the relation of manifest anxiety level (as measured by the Taylor Scale) to ego-satisfaction. The subjects were 124 college students in introductory psychology. The scales used included nine representative of the evaluative factor (*happy-sad, beautiful-ugly, clean-dirty, honest-dishonest, valuable-worthless, good-bad, pleasant-unpleasant, fair-unfair,* and *healthy-sick*), three for the potency factor (*large-small, deep-shallow,* and *strong-weak*), four for the activity factor (*active-passive, sharp-dull, hot-cold,* and *fast-slow*), and three from Cattell's personality inventory (1950) presumed to be particularly relevant (*calm-excitable, adaptable-inflexible,* and *self-assertive-submissive*). The scale *tense-relaxed* was also included because of

[5] In this connection, James S. Peters (Purdue University) has compared the semantic ratings of the self-concept and other-concepts by delinquent and non-delinquent youths. There were significant differences between these groups in the meanings of the self-concept; evaluation of the self was positively correlated with evaluation of others.

[6] A similar method has been used by David Ricks (University of Chicago). Student nurses judged MYSELF WITH PATIENT, MYSELF WITH MY MOTHER, etc., to study role variations (MYSELF WITH PATIENT was found to be closest in meaning to MYSELF WITH A CHILD). On another study, Ricks found that patients in a group therapy situation came to judge themselves as less different from others in the group.

[7] Conducted by James Dyal at the University of Illinois in 1955. Henry Raymaker, Jr. (Fulton County Health Department, Atlanta, Georgia) has used the D^2-scores between MYSELF and MY IDEAL SELF, obtained from 60 scales, as an index of *maladjustment,* this index then being correlated with certain MMPI variables (positively) and with certain Rorschach indicators (chance-wise).

its relevance. Now the ratio, LLS — AS/LLS — IS, approaches 1.00 as the location of AS approaches that of IS, i.e., as one's ego-satisfaction increases. Dyal ran rank-order correlations between this ego-satisfaction index and scores on the Taylor Scale: the correlation for all scales combined was small but significant (.29; p <.05); when the scales representing various factors of the differential and the Cattell scales were analyzed separately, only Cattell's scales and the activity scales were found to be significantly related to manifest anxiety. Although it is understandable that the Cattell scales, being based on factor analysis of personality variables, should correlate with anxiety scores, it is surprising that the activity rather than evaluative factor should show this relation. The only interpretation we can offer is that scales like *hot-cold*, *fast-slow*, and *sharp-dull* offer a more subtle index of self-satisfaction, as compared with very direct, non-subtle scales like *good-bad* and *valuable-worthless* on which all subjects may have given a socially acceptable response for both IS and AS.

Dyal reports another very interesting observation: He reasoned that the experience of taking the Taylor Scale — and of agreeing with a number of self-derogatory statements in the course of this experience — should temporarily increase ego-anxiety, hence set in motion ego-defensive mechanisms, and therefore result in an increased favorableness toward AS as measured. To test this hypothesis, an experimental group judged the AS, IS, LLS, and other concepts against the differential, then took the Taylor Scale, and finally rejudged the concepts against the scales; a control group judged the concepts, rested for the same interval, and then rejudged the concepts (i.e., a straight reliability test). The sum of the deviations, *d*, on individual scales, taking account of sign in the favorable or unfavorable direction, between test and retest were computed for individual subjects. Eliminating subjects showing zero change, he found that 39/70 experimental subjects shifted in the positive direction as compared with 12/34 cases in the control group, a difference significant at the 3 per cent level by Chi-square test. However, since most of the change was due to a *negative* shift (22/34 cases) in the control group, it is difficult to draw any firm conclusion. Dyal also found no significant differences between high and low anxiety groups in this respect, contrary to his expectations.

Comparison of Individual Conceptual Structures

When a subject or patient has judged a set of concepts against the same form of the differential, we may compute the distances (D) between every concept and every other concept in the semantic space, i.e., obtain a *D-matrix* which represents this much, at least, of the person's conceptual structure. If desired, these distances can be plotted as a model having the same dimensionality as the factors operating in the differential employed. Such models have the

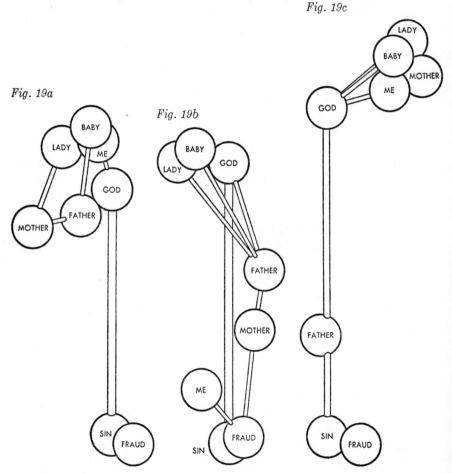

Fig. 19. Semantic space for female patient at beginning of therapy (A); middle of therapy (B); and shortly after termination of therapy (C).

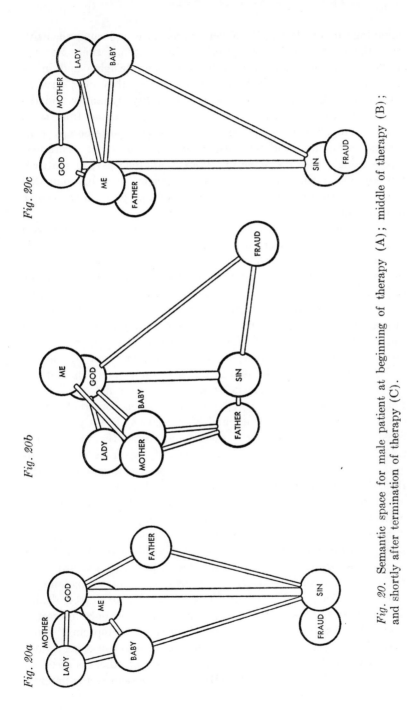

Fig. 20. Semantic space for male patient at beginning of therapy (A); middle of therapy (B); and shortly after termination of therapy (C).

advantage of displaying, in a very immediate and comprehensive way, the entire set of conceptual relations at one time. For the therapist, they often provide a basis for new insights and inferences about his patient; for the experimentalist, they may serve as the basis for new hypotheses about personality dynamics and the therapy process. *D-matrices* or the models constructed from them can be compared across people (e.g., pre- and post-therapy conceptual structures for patients treated by different therapists representing either the same or different approaches), or matrices representing a time series for a single person may be compared (e.g., as a means of studying what changes take place in the course of therapy).

The earliest study of this sort was done in collaboration with Dr. O. Hobart Mowrer, using data collected from two of his patients, a young woman and a young man both suffering from forms of agoraphobia. These patients responded to a form of the differential three times — first at a point very near the beginning of therapy, second at a point near the middle of the therapy process, and third at a point shortly after therapy, judged successful, had been discontinued. The form used included eight concepts (ME, MOTHER, FATHER, BABY, LADY, GOD, SIN, and FRAUD) and 20 scales (a sub-set of those used in our first factor analysis, but not chosen on the basis of factorial results which were not available at that time). Figure 19 (A, B, C) gives the models constructed from the data for the young woman and Figure 20 (A, B, C) gives those constructed from data for the young man. Since the validity and usefulness of this technique depends heavily upon its correspondence with intimate clinical observation, we shall quote liberally from Mowrer's own discussion of these models in relation to his own interpretations of the cases (see Mowrer, 1953, pp. 532-35).

In both cases we note the extreme polarization (evaluative dimension) between concepts like GOD, MOTHER, and ME, on the one hand, and SIN and FRAUD on the other. According to Mowrer, "the neurotic is typically a person who has repudiated his own self-criticisms . . . refused to accept his own sense of wrongdoing or 'sin.' The result is that the self-critical faculty or forces, denied direct access to consciousness, can assert themselves only indirectly, deviously, bizarrely, in the form of so-called symptoms." That part of the impact of therapy is "readmission into conscious awareness of the self-criticisms" as well as criticism of others is certainly suggested by the second models (B) for each patient — the parental concepts, MOTHER and FATHER, and the self-concept, ME, show marked drops in evaluation during this middle period of therapy. Mowrer points out that this period was accompanied by alleviation of symptoms. In the case of the female patient it is interesting to note that violent self-criticism in the therapy sessions appeared about a month after semantic measurement had revealed the sharp drop in self-evaluation.

Also evident in the data for both patients is a complete shift in *parental identifications* between the beginning of therapy and its conclusion: the young woman first perceives herself, ME, as closer in meaning to FATHER than to MOTHER, but after therapy, ME is found within the "womanly" cluster of LADY, MOTHER, and BABY; the young man originally sees himself very close to MOTHER as compared with FATHER, but again, by the end of therapy, ME, FATHER, and GOD form a cluster opposed to MOTHER, LADY, and BABY. According to Mowrer, "these changes correspond remarkably well to the clinical facts. One of the (female) patient's main difficulties had been her 'alliance' with her father against her mother. . . . During therapy this situation was explored and repudiated. . . . The (male) patient . . . spoke very warmly of his mother and indicated that he had consciously been relieved when his father had died some years earlier." This situation in the male patient was again explored in therapy with the result shown in the models. These cases illustrate the generation of hypotheses from such models — in this case, that therapy in neurosis may involve shift in parental identification as a typical process. However, from these data we cannot determine whether this is characteristic of all neurosis, or cases of agoraphobia, or perhaps of cases treated by a particular therapist. A test of this hypothesis on a larger number of cases by Luria will be reported in the next section.

One of the more intriguing uses of the semantic differential in clinical work is as a standard tool in the therapist's kit bag, so to speak, which, like free-association, dream analysis and the like, can be applied when needed. It is possible that occasional and repeated testing of significant concepts against a standard form of the differential as the case progresses would both provide a running check on progress as well as a source of interpretive insights. The only work along this line that we know of has been done by Moss (1953), in connection with two of his own cases. These two cases provide a sort of control on each other, however. Both were diagnosed as cases of "conversion hysteria," both were young men with strong (unconscious) conflicts with their dominant fathers, and both were in unsuccessful rivalry with older brothers; but whereas the first case continued to a conclusion that was successful by all criteria, the second case was terminated in midcourse clearly without improvement. Moss obtained semantic differential measurements on certain standard concepts at several points during the course of therapy — these concepts related to the significant persons and situations in their lives (PEOPLE, MOTHER, FATHER, BROTHER, WIFE (Case 1), ACTUAL SELF, IDEAL SELF, NEGATIVE SELF, THERAPIST, and THERAPY). Also, at irregular intervals in connection with dream materials, Moss collected data on various other concepts (the study of dream symbolism was actually the focus of his research and will be reported later in this chapter.)

An innovation which Moss introduced was to obtain from these patients differential ratings *under the hypnotic state* which, as a presumed index of unconscious meanings, could be compared with ratings made in the waking state, as an index of conscious meanings. To obtain these hypnotic ratings Moss placed his subjects in the trance state and told them they would see a series of seven-step scales projected against a screen as he called them out; as each concept to be judged was called out, they would see a pointer (hallucinated, of course) drift along the scale, stopping involuntarily at that place indicating the patient's "true" meaning. That this hypnotic procedure "worked" is indicated both by the fact that gross differences between waking and hypnotic ratings were obtained and by the fact that these differences were consistent with clinical data on the cases.

Moss hypothesized that (a) *semantic discrepancies between waking and hypnotic ratings would be greater for clinically defined conflict areas than for other areas* (e.g., the psychological conflicts underlying neurosis are reflected in discrepancies between conscious and unconscious meanings), and (b) *successful therapy is paralleled by reduction in discrepancy between waking and hypnotic ratings* (e.g., by reduction conflict between conscious and unconscious meanings). Using the set of standard concepts listed above as a sample (independence of the errors of measurement being assumed), the hypothesis that the distances (D) between waking and hypnotic profiles should be smaller at the end of the successful therapy than at the beginning was tested by the Wilcoxon Signed Ranks test; it was significant at the 1 per cent level. For the unsuccessful case, on the other hand, not only was the difference here not significant, but there were more increases in semantic discrepancy than decreases between the beginning of the case and its termination some 23 sessions later. In the successful case, furthermore, the concepts showing greatest reduction in D between waking and hypnotic ratings were mainly those judged clinically to represent conflict areas — FATHER, BROTHER, WIFE, and ACTUAL SELF. It is also worth reporting that whereas during roughly the first half of the successful therapy it was the waking (conscious) meanings that shifted toward the hypnotic (unconscious) meanings, during the second half of therapy the hypnotic ratings tended to move toward the waking ratings — the greatest movement in all cases being on the evaluative scales.

Comparison of Concept Meanings and Distances Across Groups

Work on individual cases like those of Mowrer and Moss described above often leads to new hypotheses about the nature of the therapeutic process or about personality that can be tested in group data by the comparison of concept meanings and distances. The work of Moss, for example, leads to certain hypotheses about semantic differences between successful and unsuccessful cases. The work of Mowrer, as was noted, leads to certain hypotheses concerning typical changes in the meaning of the self-concept and concerning distances between ME and MOTHER vs. ME and FATHER (parental identifications) at the beginning of therapy as compared with its successful conclusion. As part of her research on therapy patients in comparison with normal controls, and with the generous cooperation of a number of therapists,[8] Dr. Zella Luria (unpublished research) has checked a number of hypotheses of this nature.

Her preliminary results do not support the hypothesis derived from Mowrer's notions, that neurotics characteristically suffer from inadequate identification with the parent of the same sex. In the evaluative sphere, normals, both male and female, are characteristically close to both parents. They judge themselves as being almost as good as the parent figures. The average neurotic, on the other hand, while seeing himself and his parents as less valued than the normal, perceives greater evaluative semantic distance between ME and MOTHER and between MOTHER and FATHER.

Patients tended to judge themselves and their parents as weaker,

---

[8] Dr. O. H. Mowrer, Dr. Carl Rogers, Miss Harriet P. Ray, and the staffs of the University of Chicago Counseling Center and the University of Illinois Student Counseling Bureau.

tenser, more passive, and less valuable than do normal college students. The results suggest that normal subjects show little variance in how highly they value themselves and their parents; patients, on the other hand, showed relatively greater variance. If neurotics tend to vilify authority in the person of parent figures, as suggested by Mowrer, they vilify themselves in the process, too. This suggests that they see themselves as inadequate and identify their parental models as inadequate too.

No support was found for the explanation by Wendell Johnson (1946) that neurosis is a semantic disorder characterized by extremely dichotomized meanings. Johnson sees neurotics as people who see white and black, but not shades of grey. Luria's results, based on an analysis of the frequency of extreme scores (1 and 7), showed that the average neurotic used 1 and 7 only 45 times (out of 150 opportunities) as compared with an average of 57 uses by normal controls. The tendency of the normal controls to use the extremes shows up in greater reliability too. Luria found a correlation of .81 between extremity of judgment and test-retest reliability. If anything, Luria's results suggest that normals are more comfortable in neat dichotomies than are neurotics.

In like manner, Luria examined the data for evidence of Mowrer's concept of "neurotic evasiveness." Using frequency of use of 4 as an index of evasiveness, she found no differences between the two groups.

A measure of "self-criticalness" of patients was also studied. Luria reasoned that if a patient rates ME closer to the "good" concepts than to the "bad" ones, and if there is no overlap in the ratings of such concepts, the patient is not critical of himself. If he rates ME closer to the bad concepts, he is said to be self-critical. If there is overlap of ME with good and bad concepts, the case is considered indeterminate. A test of the role of "self-criticalness" as a possible basis for patient acceptance by therapists indicated that five of nine of Mowrer's patients were self-critical, while only two of six of the patients in Rogers' group were. Obviously, more data of this kind need to be analyzed before this index can be effectively gauged.

THREE ILLUSTRATIVE STUDIES IN THE PERSONALITY AREA

The studies reported so far serve to illustrate various ways in which the semantic differential can be used in this area. The three studies we present here serve the same function, but their uniqueness and unitary character justify separate treatment. In the first, the semantic differential is used to test certain hypotheses about *identification* deriving from mediation learning theory. In the second, it is applied in testing some Freudian notions about *dream symbolism*. And in the third, it is used in an analysis of a very unusual case of *triple personality*.

On the Nature of Identification

The process whereby children identify with their parents is of central significance in personality development and maldevelopment. Lazowick (1955), on the basis of theoretical analysis in mediation learning theory terms, defined identification as the sharing of common meanings between parent and child and then proceeded with the semantic differential to measure degrees of identification between college students and their parents as a means of testing certain hypotheses. His findings, although somewhat contrary to most contemporary viewpoints, seem sensible and have been substantiated in at least one additional experiment.

Let us first briefly review his theoretical analysis. Following the Miller and Dollard (1941) analysis of *imitation* on the basis of matched dependency, the child in the home is assumed to learn generalized imitative tendencies with respect to both parents. As shown in the paradigm in Figure 21, the parental model reacts to various signs ($\boxed{S}_x$) with various adjustive responses (R_X, etc.) as mediated by representation processes ($r_m \dashrightarrow s_m$). The child, without knowing the significance of these signs, nevertheless responds to

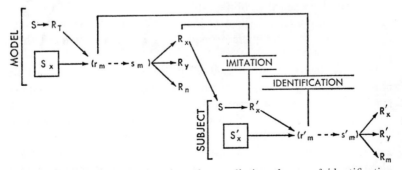

Fig. 21. Schematic representation of a mediation theory of identification (Lazowick).

the parent's *behavior* as a stimulus (S) and makes imitative responses (R_X'). Portions of this total imitative behavior become associated with the same or similar signs ($\boxed{s}x'$) as the child's representational process ($r_m' \dashrightarrow s_m'$) which is at once the *child's* meaning of the sign and the mediator for various adjustive acts (R_X'). As shown in the figure, imitation refers to similarities of overt behaviors between model and subject, but *identification refers to similarities of meanings.* It is not necessary, in terms of this analysis, that the overt behavior of a child identifying with a parent be similar to that of the parent, merely that his ways of perceiving people and situations be similar.

Lazowick was concerned with testing the validity of current opinion on identification — namely that normal people tend to identify with the like-sex parent more than with the unlike-sex parent while neurotics show confused, divided, or converse sexual identification. He was also interested in the notion that the parents of normal children should show greater "semantic harmony" than the parents of neurotic children. To obtain two groups of students differing at least potentially in neuroticism, Lazowick used the Taylor Manifest Anxiety Scale — the upper 10 per cent of 268 male students and 150 female students on this test were called "neurotic" and the lower 10 per cent called "normal." The index of identification was the D between profiles for the same concepts, ten being used: MYSELF, FATHER, MOTHER, FAMILY, HUSBAND, WIFE, MAN, WOMAN, PLEASANT, and UNPLEASANT. Differentials were rated by the male and female college student subjects and by as many of their parents as could be induced to cooperate. Two measures were thus available: *direct identification* (profile similarities between the child's concepts and parent's concepts) and *inferred identification* (profile similarities between the child's ratings of ME and the child's ratings of MOTHER or FATHER, which is analogous to the observations ordinarily made by therapists depending on communications of their patients).

We may deal first with *direct identification.* The hypothesis that normal children should identify more closely with the like-sex parent than neurotic children was clearly borne out, low-anxiety subjects, male or female, showing greater semantic similarity with their like-sex parent than high-anxiety subjects (significant at the 1 per cent level by Mann-Whitney test). Contrary to expectations, although not significantly so, normal men showed greater semantic similarity to their mothers, as well as their fathers, than did normal women. Lazowick also matched parents with children at random and compared the semantic distances of these pairs with those for parents and their own children; except for low-anxiety males with their own mothers, the over-all similarities of children with their own parents were not significantly greater than those between parents and children matched at random. This suggests that there is a very stable cultural norm determining the meanings of these concepts, a norm from which high-anxiety subjects may deviate, however.

The data for *inferred identification* yield much the same picture. Low-anxiety males show greater profile similarities in their ratings of MYSELF and FATHER than do high-anxiety males, and low-anxiety females show greater profile similarities between MYSELF and MOTHER than do high-anxiety females — both significant at the 1 per cent level. But whereas normal college men see more similarity between MYSELF and FATHER than they do between MYSELF and MOTHER, normal college women do not make the corresponding distinction — this may reflect the greater "masculinity" of professional women as compared with other women.[9] It was also found that high-anxiety (potentially neurotic) subjects of both sexes perceived a significantly greater similarity between UNPLEASANT and each of the following, FATHER, MOTHER, and FAMILY, than did normal, low-anxiety subjects. Further testimony to the close relation between anxiety-level, identification, and family discord was provided by direct profile comparisons between the two parents. Lazowick found that the parents of low-anxiety male subjects show greater "semantic harmony" between themselves than do the parents of high-anxiety male subjects; the anxiety-level of female subjects, however, was not related to the "semantic harmony" of their parents. He also found a trend, though not highly significant, for married couples to show greater "semantic harmony" than couples matched at random.

In an experiment by Dyal already reported (pp. 242-43), the Taylor Scale was also given to college subjects, and concepts were included (MY ACTUAL SELF, MY MOTHER, and MY FATHER) which made possible a check on Lazowick's findings with respect to inferred identification. Dyal agreed in finding greater identification of normal males with the same-sexed parent than of high-anxiety males. Such a difference between anxiety groups was not significant

---

[9] Martin Capell (VA Hospital, Fort Douglas Station, Salt Lake City, Utah) reports a similar study on identification.

for the females, however. Dyal was also able to show that it was the *potency scales* and the *tense-relaxed scale* which contributed mainly to this difference between high- and low-anxiety males in inferred identification with FATHER. There was also a marked correlation between identification of male subjects with their fathers and the closeness of their ratings of MY FATHER to those of AN IDEAL FATHER (rank $p = .873$); consistent with this was the finding that low-anxiety men perceived MY FATHER as significantly closer in meaning to AN IDEAL FATHER than did high-anxiety men. In other words, boys who like their fathers tend to like themselves.

The parental identification picture we get as a whole is one in which young men fit the expected pattern fairly well — normal men identifying more with their fathers than their mothers, more with both parents than do neurotic men, and seeing their fathers as nearer the ideal. But this is not the case with the women subjects in these studies. Young women seem to identify as much with their fathers as their mothers, the distinctions between normal and neurotic women is not so clear, and the parents of normal women show no greater "semantic harmony" than the parents of neurotic women. Whether this is a reflection of the male-dominance of our culture, is characteristic of "professional" women or women of high intelligence, or perhaps represents an inadequacy of our definition of identification in terms of semantic similarity between parent and child remain as problems for future study.

Quantitative Analysis of Dream Symbolism

According to Freud, the true symbol was believed to possess universal (usually sexual) meaning and to represent unconscious content, i.e., "only what is repressed need be symbolized." In dreams, symbolism was supposed to serve the purpose of censorship by rendering the dream strange and incomprehensible. Moss (1953) made an analysis of symbolism, particularly dream symbolism, in mediation learning theory terms and proceeded to check certain hypotheses bearing on both Freudian and learning theory predictions. Since this book is concerned with measurement more than theory, only a brief sketch of the theoretical analysis will be given here.

Let us represent what is symbolized, the *latent content* (e.g., PENIS), as $⑤_1$, a sign associated with its characteristic representational mediation process, $r_{m_1} \dashrightarrow s_{m_1}$; let us represent the symbol, the *manifest content* (e.g., METAL STOVE POKER), as $⑤_2$, another sign

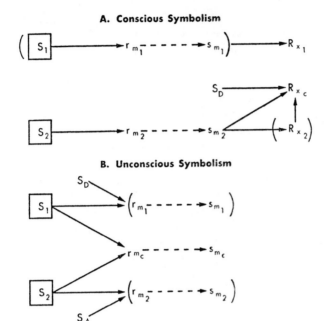

Fig. 22. Schema of theoretical analysis of dream symbolism (Moss).

ordinarily associated with its own characteristic mediation process, $r_{m_2} \rightarrow s_{m_1}$. Let us also postulate two basic types of motivational state, *need for expression* or "approach drive," S_D, and *need for disguise* or "escape (anxiety) drive," S_A. We shall assume that S_D combines multiplicatively with $\boxed{S}_1$ to increase the tendency to react cognitively with the meaning characteristic of the thing symbolized and that S_A, in effect, combines multiplicatively with $\boxed{S}_2$ to increase the tendency to react cognitively with the meaning characteristic of the symbol. We must distinguish between the conscious and unconscious use of symbols: in the *conscious use of symbols*, as shown diagrammatically in Figure 22 (A), the need for expression combines with the self-stimulation characteristic of the mediator for the symbol to modify overt behavior in the direction of that associated with the thing symbolized (R_{x_c}) — but the meaning of the symbol as such is unchanged. An example would be a child using a PENCIL ($\boxed{S}_2$) *as if* it were a GUN ($\boxed{S}_1$), or an adult using a flag as a symbol for his nation and behaving respectfully — both child and adult ordinarily are aware that the pencil is a wooden writing instrument and that the flag is a colored piece of cloth. But we also know that under the stress of emotion the child tends to lose his awareness of the pencil as such and the adult his awareness of the flag as a piece of cloth, and presumably the effect of sleep may be similar. In the *unconscious use of symbols*, as shown in Figure 22 (B), the mediation process or meaning characteristic of the symbol is shifted toward that characteristic of the thing symbolized. For the dreamer, the symbol METAL STOVE POKER ($[S]_2$) acquires a *meaning* to some degree characteristic of PENIS ($[S]_1$) — it is perceived in the dream as reddish rather than black, as pliable rather than rigid, as somewhat evil and threatening rather than evaluatively neutral.

Moss had available as material the dreams of two patients whom he had treated intensively himself. The things symbolized were typically the significant persons and situations (SELF, THERAPY, THERAPIST, WIFE, FATHER, BROTHER, MOTHER, etc.) in the patients' lives, for which Moss obtained both waking (conscious) and hypnotic (unconscious) ratings on the semantic differential. The meanings of the symbols, *as used in the dream state*, were obtained from the patients by having them differentiate the symbols immediately after hypnotic revivification of the dream, but the measurement was in the waking state. The meanings of the symbols, as used in ordinary experience, were obtained several weeks later by inserting them as concepts in general materials the patients were judging. All of the quantitative tests of hypotheses about dream symbolism deal with *semantic distances* (D's) between profiles of either symbols-as-symbols (e.g., dream state) or symbols-as-signs (ordinary usage), and either the waking (conscious) or hypnotic (unconscious) meanings of the things symbolized.

Now we may review Moss's hypotheses and the evidence bearing on them. *Hypothesis I: When dreams emanate from a conflict area, the meanings of symbols correspond more closely to unconscious than to conscious meanings of the things symbolized.* To test this hypothesis we must compare the profile distances of symbols (as used in dreams) from the waking latent content with those of these symbols from the hypnotic latent content. For 19 of 21 cases clearly meeting the criterion of emanating from a conflict area the meaning of the dream symbol was semantically closer to the hypnotic or unconscious meaning of the thing symbolized, as predicted — a result significant at the 1 per cent level of confidence. This finding is consistent with the Freudian view and not inconsistent with the learning theory approach, which has nothing to say about the distinction between waking and hypnotic meanings.

Hypothesis II: The greater the anxiety potential of the thing being symbolized, the greater the semantic distance between the ordinary meaning of the symbol chosen and the hypnotic meaning of the thing symbolized (latent content). This hypothesis is consistent with the Freudian view (disguise function), but not the learning theory view (displacement in approach-avoidance conflict), according to Moss. This is because in approach-avoidance conflicts, as they appear in the course of therapy, increases in anxiety are paralleled by increases in need for expression — or else there is no conflict. To test this hypothesis it is not necessary to index different levels of anxiety. For his successful case, Moss had ample evidence (clinical observation as well as objective Taylor Scale scores) that his patient was operating under higher anxiety during the first half of therapy than during the second half. Contrary to the hypothesis, the distances between the ordinary meanings of the dream symbols and the hypnotic meanings of the things symbolized were not significantly different for the first as compared with the second half of therapy.

Hypothesis III: The distortion which a sign undergoes when used as a dream symbol is toward the meaning of the thing symbolized when anxiety is low but away from the meaning of the thing symbolized when anxiety is high. According to Moss, this follows from the Freudian notion of censorship when combined with the need for expression. According to the learning theory analysis (or the congruity principle), the distortion must *always be toward the meaning of the latent content.* To test this hypothesis we need to compare two sets of distances — those between ordinary meanings of the symbol and meanings of latent content vs. those between dream-state meanings of the symbol and meanings of latent content — in both the first half and in the second half of therapy (e.g., two levels of inferred anxiety). If the hypothesis is valid, then during the first half of therapy, at least, the dream-state meanings of symbols should be *further* away (larger D) from the meanings of the things symbolized than the ordinary meanings for these signs. This was not the case. In both halves of therapy (9/12 cases in the first half, 6/7 in the second half) the dream-state meanings were distorted *toward* the meanings of the latent contents.

Hypothesis IV: Dream symbols should be closer to the things symbolized in evaluative meaning (affect) than in other semantic dimensions. This derives from the notion of Freud (and other psychoanalysts) that distortion takes place in the denotative (identifying) dimensions of meaning, but not in the connotative (emotional) dimensions. Learning and congruity principles would presumably make no distinction between the various factors or dimensions of meaning. To test this hypothesis, Moss selected eight highly evaluative scales (*healthy-sick, good-bad, happy-sad, beautiful-ugly, fresh-stale, sweet-sour, valuable-worthless,* and *kind-cruel*) and matched them with eight largely denotative scales having low loadings on the evaluative factor (*strong-weak, active-passive, large-small, hot-cold, sharp-dull, light-heavy, angular-rounded,* and *fast-slow*). D-values for dream symbols vs. latent content were computed separately for the evaluative set and for the non-evaluative set. Contrary to the hypothesis, there were no differences whatsoever in the D's based on evaluative scales and those based on non-evaluative scales. This, again, is contrary to the Freudian notion but consistent with the learning theory and congruity notions.

Quite apart from the bearing of these results upon Freudian vs. learning thories as applied to the dynamics of dream symbolism — and it is difficult in both cases to define terms and state principles with sufficient rigor to feel confident that the theories are really being tested — the results themselves are interesting and contribute to our understanding of "dream-work." We find that the meanings of symbols in dreams correspond more closely to unconscious than to conscious meanings of the things symbolized, that anxiety associated with latent content does not apparently determine the semantic distance between the ordinary meaning of the sign selected as a symbol and the meaning of the thing being symbolized, that the distortion produced in the meaning of a sign when being used as a symbol is always toward the meaning of the thing symbolized, and that distortion seems to be equally likely along all semantic dimensions, including the emotionally evaluative one. Furthermore, we have here a demonstration of the usefulness of the semantic differential in quantifying a novel and highly subjective phenomenon, dream symbolism.[10]

Blind Analysis of a Case of Triple Personality

During the fall of 1953, Osgood and Luria (1954) were presented with an unusual opportunity to test the validity and usefulness of

---

[10] Bernard S. Aaronson (Indiana Village for Epileptics, New Castle, Indiana) has had subjects judge universal dream symbols on the differential and has used cluster analysis to determine what manifest contents jibe with what latent contents.

the semantic differential as a clinical tool. The editor of *The Journal of Abnormal and Social Psychology* (Dr. J. McV. Hunt) had received a manuscript entitled "A Case of Multiple Personality," by Drs. Thigpen and Cleckley (1954). Without our knowledge he had suggested to these therapists that it would be interesting to collect semantic data from each of the personalities of their patient and have us interpret them on a blind basis. Thigpen and Cleckley kindly consented to cooperate in this venture and administered a form of the differential twice (at intervals of about two to three months) to each of these three personalities. The form, which had already been used by Luria in some research in psychotherapy, included 15 concepts (LOVE, CHILD, MY DOCTOR, ME, MY JOB, MENTAL SICKNESS, MY MOTHER, PEACE OF MIND, FRAUD, MY SPOUSE, SELF-CONTROL, HATRED, MY FATHER, CONFUSION, and SEX) and ten scales (*valuable-worthless, clean-dirty, tasty-distasteful, large-small, strong-weak, deep-shallow, fast-slow, active-passive, hot-cold,* and *tense-relaxed*).

Before going into the treatment and interpretation of the data, we should state exactly what information we had about this case. We knew that we were dealing with a case of triple personality, and these had been labeled for us as "Eve White," "Eve Black," and "Jane." We also knew, of course, that the patient was a woman, presumably participating in some kind of therapy — but we did not know the stage of therapy or whether or not the woman was hospitalized. To make the interpretation of data on certain concepts meaningful, we also considered it fair to ask (of J. McV. Hunt) if the patient had a child (she did), if she was married (she was), if her parents were alive (the mother was, but he wasn't sure about the father), and if she had a job outside of homekeeping (she did). This was the sum total of our external information about the case. The semantic data consisted of two testings, which we shall identify by the roman numerals I and II, on each of the three personalities. On the basis of these data, we attempted a description of the salient characteristics of each of the three personalities and an interpretation and prognosis about the case as a whole.

Let us look first at the comparative reliabilities with which judgments were made by these several personalities. It so happened that double (reliability) forms were sent to Thigpen and Cleckley, i.e., forms in which the 150 items were immediately repeated in the same assemblage, and we can therefore get a reliability estimate for each personality at each testing. The test-retest reliability coefficients taken over the 150 items were as follows: Eve White I, .82; Eve White II, .90; Eve Black I, .65; Eve Black II, .89; Jane I, .89; Jane II, .94. We note a tendency for increasing stability through time in all three personalities (which may, of course, represent some adaptation to the test procedure); we also note that Eve Black I is the least reliable.

In all subsequent computations we used the average of the immediate test and retest scores for each testing. From these values the factor scores for each concept were determined (i.e., its location in the semantic space) as an index of its meaning. The D-matrices for each personality on each testing (i.e., the distances from each concept to every other concept), six altogether, were computed in two ways: (1) from the factor scores, which would necessarily plot in three dimensions since there were only three factors represented (*tense-relaxed* omitted); (2) from the raw data on all ten scales. To check the amount of distortion or error introduced by using factor scores, we correlated the D-matrices based on factor scores with those based on all ten scales; these correlations, across pairs of corresponding cells in the D-matrices, ran as follows: Eve White I, .91; Eve White II, .93; Eve Black I, .96; Eve Black II, .98; Jane I, .86; Jane II, .92. In other words, a large part of the variance in this woman's judgments in all of her personalities can be accounted for in terms of only three factors.

Do the factors employed in these three personalities correspond closely in terms of both nature and relative weight? The total data for the initial testing for all three personalities were subjected to factor analysis and rotated by Quartimax on the ILLIAC. Table 36 gives the rotated factor loadings for each of the ten scales for each personality, with the proportion of total variance accounted for by each factor below. The first factor in all three personalities is clearly evaluative (*valuable, clean,* and *tasty*), but what is remarkable is the immense slice of variance taken out by this dimension of judgment, 49 per cent in Eve White I, 59 per cent in Eve Black I, and 48 per cent in Jane I. It can also be seen that certain other scales, ordinarily not evaluative, become so for all three of these personalities — this is particularly true of *hot-cold* and to lesser degrees for the potency scales, *strong-weak, large-small,* and *deep-shallow.* For Eve Black I this general evaluative factor tends to envelop all scales to a considerable degree. It is possible to identify the second factor in all three personalities as a kind of potency factor, but the scale *relaxed-tense* (with *relaxed* being potent, perhaps reflecting

Table 36

ROTATED FACTOR LOADINGS AND PROPORTIONS OF VARIANCE FOR TRIPLE PERSONALITY CASE

	Eve White I			Eve Black I			Jane I		
	I	II	III	I	II	III	I	II	III
valuable	.86	-.11	.11	.98	.08	.09	.92	.05	-.11
clean	.98	-.02	-.01	.83	-.03	.05	.93	-.05	-.03
tasty	.89	-.22	-.01	.96	.06	-.07	.73	.59	.05
hot	.86	.16	-.16	.94	-.02	-.18	.93	-.17	.17
large	.66	.23	.14	.26	.88	.13	.83	.21	-.08
strong	.74	.43	-.17	.54	.74	.02	.84	.27	-.09
deep	.77	.25	.41	.67	.53	.12	-.12	-.14	-.05
relaxed	.20	.90	.02	.67	.57	.03	.44	.84	-.06
fast	-.19	-.16	.14	.57	.32	.75	-.05	-.03	.99
active	.07	-.01	.96	.92	.02	.23	.29	-.16	.25
Per Cent Variance	.49	.12	.12	.59	.20	.07	.48	.13	.11

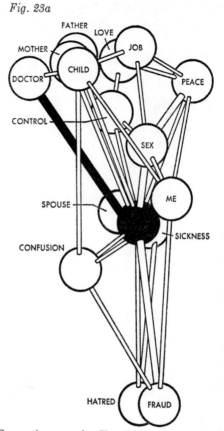

Fig. 23a

Fig. 23. Semantic space for Eve White (Osgood and Luria).

the therapy context) must be included in this category. Thus the scales loading highest on factor II for Eve White I are *relaxed, strong, deep,* and *large;* for Eve Black I are *large, strong, relaxed,* and *deep;* and for Jane I are *relaxed, tasty, strong,* and *large.* Similarly, the third factor in each personality can be identified as a kind of activity factor by virtue of the relatively high loadings of *fast* and *active* on it — but for Eve White I, at least, *deep-shallow* also has high loading on this factor. We have evidence, then, for essentially the same three major factors operating in the several personalities of this disturbed patient, although there is considerable shifting in the meanings of specific scales between personalities and considerable divergence of this patient in general from most people

Fig. 23b

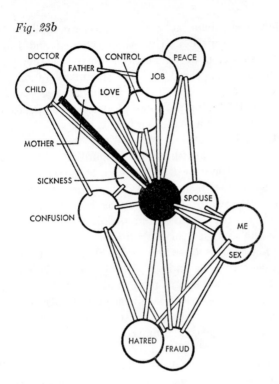

on whom we have data (e.g., in the use of *hot-cold* and *relaxed-tense*).

The models displayed in Figures 23, 24, and 25 were constructed from the *D*-matrices computed from factor scores. Within the limits of our type of measurement and our sampling of concepts, the locations and relations among concepts shown here can be thought of as pictures of how this woman perceives herself, the significant people about her, and certain modes of action — when functioning in her several personalities. For purposes of ready comparison, all of the models are oriented in respect to the concept MY DOCTOR, which stays almost constant in meaning (*good, strong,* and *quite active*) throughout both time and personalities; spatially in these figures, *good* is up and *bad* down, *active* is to the left and *passive* to the right, and *strong* is away from the viewer while *weak* is toward the viewer; the solid ball represents the origin of the space, i.e., a hypothetical "meaningless" concept that would result from checking all 4's on the scales. Since the descriptions and interpretations which follow were made on a blind basis, we shall quote entirely from the article written at that time (Osgood and Luria, 1954). Following submission of our article for publication, the clinical study of the case appeared in print and many of our statements could be checked. Materials taken from this case study (Thigpen and Cleckley, 1954) for purposes of present comparison, but unknown to us at the time are given below.

(From Osgood and Luria): *"Eve White.* Semantic structures for Eve White I and II are shown in [Figure 23]. The most general characterization would be that Eve White perceives 'the world' in an essentially normal fashion, is well socialized, but has an unsatisfactory attitude toward herself. ME (the self-concept) is considered a little bad, a little passive, and definitely weak. Substantiating evidence is the weakness of her CHILD and the essential meaninglessness to her of MY SPOUSE and SEX. Note also the wide evaluative separation between LOVE and SEX. In the interval between testings I and II, ME and SEX become more bad and passive and simultaneously become almost identical in meaning to her — and note that her conceptions of LOVE (a good, strong thing) and SEX (a bad, weak thing like herself) have moved still further apart."

The above was largely descriptive; in a sense we merely put into words what this woman indicated by her check-marks. The treatment of the data from check-marks to these models is completely objective and any investigator starting from the same checks and following the rules must end up with the same pictures. What follows was, of course, more speculative and interpretive; not only was it on a blind basis, but neither of the authors was a clinician by training.

(From Osgood and Luria): "Eve White is simultaneously the most in contact with social reality and under the greatest emotional stress. She is aware of both the demands of society and her own inadequacies in meeting them. She is concerned and ambivalent about her CHILD, but apparently is not aware of her own ambivalent attitudes toward her MOTHER. Those psychoanalytically inclined may wish to identify EVE WHITE with dominance of the *superego*: certainly, the superego seems to view the world from the eyes of Eve White, accepting the mores or values of others (particularly her mother) but continuously criticizing and punishing herself. If this case came to the psychotherapists with a voluntary, self-initiated plea for help, then it seems likely that Eve White was dominant at the time."

(From Thigpen and Cleckley): "One of us (C. H. T.) had for several months been treating a twenty-five-year-old married woman who was referred because of 'severe and blinding headaches.' . . . To the therapist, Eve White — as we shall call her — was an ordinary case with commonplace symptoms and a relatively complex but familiar constellation of marital conflicts and personal frustrations." Now Thigpen and Cleckley describe the sudden appearance of Eve Black on the scene, and contrast her with Eve White: "As if seized by a sudden pain she put both hands to her head. After a tense moment of silence, her hands dropped. There was a quick, reckless smile and, in a bright voice that sparkled, she said, 'Hi there, Doc!' The demure and constrained posture of Eve White had melted into bouyant repose. . . . Instead of that retiring and gently conventional figure, there was in the newcomer a childishly daredevil air, an erotically mischievous glance, a face marvelously free from the habitual signs of care, seriousness, and underlying distress, so long familiar in her predecessor." Other incidental evidence about Eve White can be culled from the case history given by Thigpen and Cleckley: "Mrs. White admits difficulty in her relation with her mother, and her performance on the Rorschach and drawings indicate conflict and resulting anxiety in her role as a wife and mother. . . . Demure, retiring, in some respects almost saintly. . . . Voice always softly modulated, always influenced by a specifically feminine restraint. . . . An industrious and able worker; also a competent housekeeper and a skillful cook. Not colorful or glamorous. Limited in spontaneity. . . . Consistently uncritical of others."

(From Osgood and Luria): "*Eve Black.* Semantic structures for Eve Black I and II are shown in [Figure 24]. The most general characterization would be that Eve Black has achieved a violent kind of adjustment in which she perceives herself as literally perfect, but, to accomplish this break, her way of perceiving 'the world' becomes completely disoriented from the norm. The only exceptions are MY DOCTOR and PEACE OF MIND, which maintain their good and strong characteristics, the latter, interestingly enough, becoming also active on II. But if Eve Black perceives herself as good, then she also has to accept HATRED and FRAUD as positive values, since (we assume) she has strong hatred, and is socially fraudulent. What are positive values for most people — CHILD, MY SPOUSE, MY JOB, LOVE, and SEX — are completely rejected as bad and passive, and all of these except CHILD are also weak. Note that it is MOTHER in this personality that becomes relatively meaningless; FATHER, on

Fig. 24a

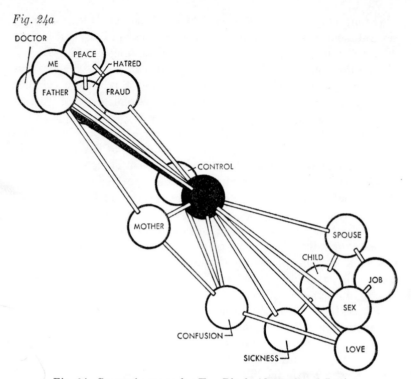

Fig. 24. Semantic space for Eve Black (Osgood and Luria).

the other hand, stays good but shifts completely from strong (in Eve White) to weak." Continuing more interpretively: "Eve Black is clearly the most out of contact with social reality and simultaneously the most self-assured. She sees herself as a dominant, active wonder-woman and is in no way self-critical. Those psychoanalytically inclined could say that the *id* looks out at the world through the eyes of Eve Black. Like a completely selfish infant, this personality is entirely oriented around the assumption of its own perfection — personal perfection is apparently the demand acceded to rather than sexuality."

(From Thigpen and Cleckley): "Eve Black's career has been traced back to early childhood. She herself freely tells us of episodes when she emerged, usually to engage in acts of mischief or disobedience. She lies glibly and without compunction, so her account alone can never be taken as reliable evidence." Note the essential masculinity of the following reported by the therapists: " 'When I go out and get drunk,' Eve Black with an easy wink once said to

Fig. 24b

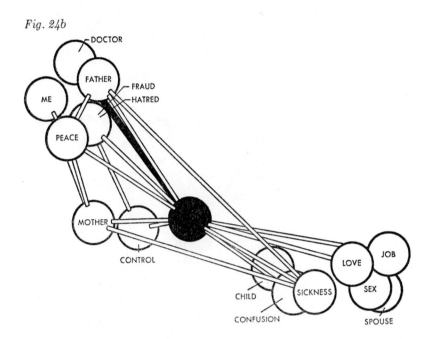

both of us, 'she wakes up with the hangover. She wonders what in the hell's made her so sick.' " And further characterization: "Obviously a party girl. Shrewd, childishly vain, and egocentric. . . . Voice a little coarsened, 'discultured,' with echoes or implications of mirth and teasing. Speech richly vernacular and liberally seasoned with spontaneous gusts of rowdy wit. . . . A touch of sexiness seasons every word and gesture." But that this trait of sexiness was superficial in Eve Black is indicated by her relations with a temporary husband, which she finally admitted to the therapists: "Apparently she had no. desire for sexual relations but often enjoyed frustrating her supposed husband by denying herself to him."

(From Osgood and Luria): *"Jane.* The general characterization is that Jane displays the most 'healthy' meaning pattern, in which she accepts the usual evaluations of concepts by her society yet still maintains a satisfactory evaluation of herself. Most of the significant persons in her life are seen as good, strong and active. The major modes of behavior, PEACE OF MIND, LOVE, SELF-CONTROL, and MY JOB are seen as equally good and strong, but somewhat passive — as if these ways of behaving and thinking were simply accepted without stress. The self-concept, ME, while still not strong (but not weak, either) is nearer the good and active directions of

Fig. 25a

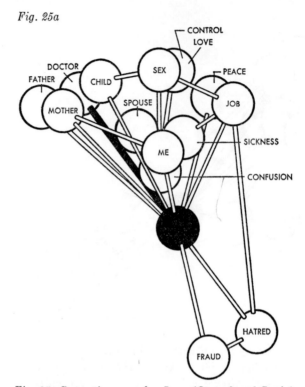

Fig. 25. Semantic space for Jane (Osgood and Luria).

the semantic space. Her attitude toward her husband, MY SPOUSE, is for the first time meaningful (unlike Eve White) and tending toward the good, strong, active directions, like the other significant persons (unlike Eve Black). And LOVE and SEX (quite unlike Eve White) are both favorable and quite closely identified. The changes from testings to I and II are simply such as to strengthen the 'healthy' pattern." The models for Jane are given in Figure 25. Now, in a more interpretive vein: "Superficially, Jane is a very healthy personality — 'all's well with the world, and day by day I'm getting better and better.' Her SPOUSE is becoming more like the noble DOCTOR all the time, and she is coming to perceive herself, even, as a pleasant and reasonably active (if somewhat weak and submissive) person. But all this is a little too rosy, a little too pat. We note that Jane is becoming more and more 'simple-minded' — all of her judgments tending to fall along a single factor of good-strong vs. bad-weak — which makes the Jane II model the most

Fig. 25b

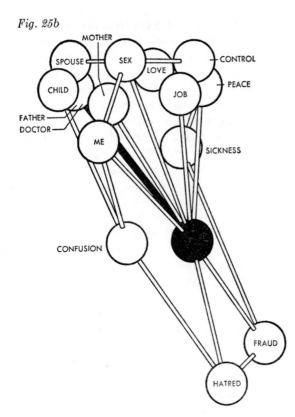

restricted and undiversified of all. Those psychoanalytically inclined may wish to view this personality as representing dominance of a self-deceptive *ego* which has woven a web of repression as to the state of reality; or, they may wish to view Jane as an essentially strong, healthy, and improving ego-dominated personality."

According to Thigpen and Cleckley: "It is easy to sense in her (Jane) a capacity for accomplishment and fulfillment far beyond that of the sweet and retiring Eve White, who, beside this genuinely impressive newcomer, appears colorless and limited. In her are indications of initiative and powerful resources never shown by the other. . . . Apparently she is capable of compassion, and, we feel likely, of devotion and valid love. She has cooperated with sincerity, and with judgment and originality beyond that of the others." Jane's charitableness toward the other personality (Eve White) whose life and role she was taking appears in a letter she wrote to the therapist: "She must not die yet. There's so much I must know, and so very much I must learn from her. She is the substance of, 'this above all to thine own self be true.' In her, too, 'the quality of mercy is not strained.' I want her to live — not me!'"

Also on the basis of the semantic data, the following guesses about the development of the case were made by Osgood and Luria: ". . . Jane is both the original personality which broke apart and the terminal personality which is being developed out of therapy. . . . The picture of Eve Black is certainly suggestive of an *Electra complex* as the underlying dynamism. In 'real' life, her MOTHER is or was the dominant, threatening figure — moralizing, demanding standards and SELF-CONTROL — and in Eve Black this woman escapes the pressure by rendering both MOTHER and SELF-CONTROL meaningless and simultaneously identifying with and taking her FATHER's place. Suggestive evidence may be found in (that) MOTHER is consistently *colder* than FATHER and usually more *tense* and *fast*. . . . We must assume strong and about equal pressures toward solving the Electra complex, (a) by identifying with FATHER and asserting the self (id?), and (b) by identifying with MOTHER and devaluating herself (superego?). This produces a two-way split from the Jane pattern, one into Eve Black where selfish needs for superiority and playing the father role are achieved and another into Eve White where societal needs for submission and playing the mother role are achieved . . . the effect of therapy may be to strengthen the self-deceptive organization of Jane without resolving the underlying conflicts dramatized by Eve White and Eve Black. The over-simplified, Pollyanna-like ways of perceiving herself as good along with all the other significant persons in her life yields a superficially happy person who views the world in an acceptable, if rigidly stereotyped, fashion. If (this) interpretation approximates the actual situation, then we feel compelled to predict another breakdown at some later period in this person's life."

Thigpen and Cleckley carefully, and perhaps wisely, avoided any attempt at interpreting the dynamics of their case. Nevertheless, considerable incidental evidence that seems at least consistent with the above interpretation can be culled from their report. (From Thigpen and Cleckley): "Eve Black, so far as we can tell, has enjoyed an independent life since Mrs. White's early childhood. She is not the product of disruptive emotional stresses which the patient has suffered during recent years. . . . The parents had had to punish their ordinarily good and conforming six-year-old girl for having disobeyed their specific rule against wandering through the woods. . . . On her return Eve received a hearty whipping despite her desperate denials of wrongdoing or disobedience." It had been Eve Black, of course, who wandered off. "The patient is the oldest of three siblings, having twin sisters." In other words, she had a model for a split into Eve White and Eve Black. "Actually the problem started at a much earlier period of life, with a strong feeling of rejection by her parents, especially after the birth of her twin sisters. Mrs. White loves them dearly, Mrs. Black despises them." Of special interest and relevance is the therapists' description of the conditions under which Jane first appeared in therapy. (From Thigpen and Cleckley): "At this point the situation changed for the worse. Eve White's headaches returned. With them also returned the 'blackouts.'. . . . Attempts were made with each Eve to work back step by step into early childhood. . . . It was hoped that some link or bridge might be found on which additional contact and coalition could grow or be built. . . . Sometime after the return of headaches and blackouts, with Eve White's maladjustment still growing worse generally, a very early recollection was being discussed with her. The incident focused about a painful injury she had sustained when scalded by water from a wash pot. As she spoke her eyes shut sleepily. . . . After remaining in this sleep or trance for perhaps two minutes her eyes opened. Blankly she stared about the room . . . her eyes finally met those of the therapist, and stopped. Slowly, with an unknown husky voice and with immeasurable poise, she spoke. 'Who are you?' " [Jane had appeared at this point.]

It is clear from their report that Thigpen and Cleckley feel that the new Jane is a successful resolution of the personality disturbance, and having developed some identification with this patient ourselves, even though remotely, we certainly hope they are correct. Our reason for doubt on this score was essentially the extreme lack of conceptual differentiation in Jane II — her tendency to judge all persons and roles in simple blacks and whites. (It may be added here that since our write-up of the case we have received three more samplings of Jane extending over a period of more than a year; these data show development of even further rigidity in this respect.) Yet, in personal communications we have had from the therapists it appears that Jane is adjusting satisfactorily to her role as mother and wife. In any case this study seems to demonstrate the potential usefulness of the semantic differential as a research instrument in this area.

7

SEMANTIC MEASUREMENT
IN COMMUNICATIONS RESEARCH

Speaking in most general terms, we have communication whenever one system, a *source*, influences the states or actions of another system, the *destination* or *receiver*, by selecting among the alternative signals that can be carried in the *channel* connecting them. In dealing with human communication systems we usually refer to signal sets as *messages*; and these are most often, though not necessarily, *language* messages. It is the job of the linguist to describe the structure or *code* according to which these messages are organized. Also, in dealing with human communication, it is necessary to further analyze both source and receiver into integrated subsystems. The individual human communicator is equipped both to receive and transmit messages more-or-less simultaneously — indeed, he is regularly the receiver of the messages he himself produces, via feedback mechanisms. But beyond such sensory reception skills and motor transmitting skills, the human communicator is equipped to learn symbolic, representational processes, or meanings. On the input side, certain patterns of signals in the channel, as *signs*, acquire association with certain representational mediators and hence have *significance*; on the output side, these mediators acquire selective association with certain motor skills (speaking, writing, etc.), which thereby express *intentions*. We refer to the process whereby signs in messages select among representational mediators as *decoding*; the process whereby representational mediators select among motor expressions in messages is referred to as *encoding*.

The types of human communication systems are many and varied. At one extreme we have the *one-to-many* system, e.g., when the President of the United States encodes a message which is amplified via the mass media of radio, TV, and the press into the receptive field of many millions of citizen receivers, each of whom decodes according to his own fashion. At another extreme we have the *many-to-one* system, e.g., the dependence of the meanings, attitudes, and beliefs of some particular individual upon the sum total of messages received from parents, from friends, from school, from magazines, from TV, and so on. At yet a different extreme we have the *one-to-himself* system, e.g., an individual solving a problem, working out a theory, ruminating, or even dreaming — being stimulated by the symbols he produces himself. Between these (and other) extremes there are all kinds of variations — the interactions in a small face-to-face group like a boys' gang, the communication of a relatively small group (institution like a newspaper staff) to a relatively large group (the readership), cross-culture and cross-language communication via the mediation of an interpreter, and so on.

Nor is it necessary that the communication channel be "linguistic" in the usual sense. The language channel is admittedly the most finely coded and important coupling between human communicators, but it is not the only channel. There is also, for example, the *visuo-gestural channel* of facial and postural expressions — one may study the efficiency of communication between intentions of "actors" and significances in "judges" via this medium (see Osgood, 1956). Similarly, *aesthetics* may be studied as a kind of communication: the source (artist, composer, writer, poet) encodes in the medium of his special talent, presumably expressing his own meanings or intentions by his selection among alternatives (colors, texture, tempo, harmonics, metaphor, word-choice, etc.); there is aesthetic communication to the extent to which receivers (the audience) experience corresponding meanings or significances upon decoding the signs produced by the source. If the artist skillfully employs rough-textured reds to convey aggression, for example, and those viewing his canvas (message) experience appropriate feelings and meanings, then to this extent, at least, there has been aesthetic communication. Bordering between aesthetics and "ordinary" communication are many of the communications in contemporary society — the use of color in advertising, application of captions to pictorial matter, the effects of political cartoons, and so forth.

Where does semantic measurement enter this communications picture? The semantic differential is proposed as an index of certain aspects of *meaning*, particularly connotative aspects. In human communication, be it via linguistic, aesthetic, or other channels, meaning is critically involved at both the initiation (the intentions being encoded by the source) and the termination (the significances being decoded by the receiver) of any communicative act. Most often the researcher will be interested in the significances derived from messages by receivers, i.e., *effect studies* (What effect does this pictorial display have upon the meaning of this advertised product? What effect upon changing attitudes toward this candidate does this particular cartoon have? What are the connotations of various technical devices in abstract art?), because, if our general model is correct, upon such semantic effects depend the overt behaviors and decisions of audiences. It was obviously the significance of Orson Welles' "Invasion of Mars" broadcast, uncritically accepted, that led some receivers to make a mad dash for the Jersey hills. Less often, perhaps, but equally important, the researcher in communications may be interested in the intentions of sources, the meanings behind the signs selected by the source for communication. How facile, for example, are various speakers at encoding words which accurately express their own meanings for objects and situations? Could the significance of a scene to a poet or artist be estimated with the differential and this profile compared with the meanings derived by the audience from his aesthetic product?

The applications of semantic measurement to human communications problems are potentially as broad and varied as the communication area itself. In this chapter we report a number of applications which have been made, but they by no means exhaust the possibilities and should be considered as illustrative samples. The chapter is organized quite arbitrarily in terms of subject matter rather than method: (1) *Psycholinguistic studies* — more-or-less "pure" research on the nature, development, and combination of signs in relation to the semantic states of language users; (2) *Studies in experimental aesthetics* — focusing on the dimensionality of the aesthetic meaning space for artists and non-artists and the effects of color in visual abstraction and in advertising; (3) *Communication effect studies* — attitude and meaning change in political, advertising, and other areas, as produced by messages carried in the mass media.

APPLICATIONS TO RESEARCH IN PSYCHOLINGUISTICS

In the broadest sense — and one which would include most of human communication — the relatively new discipline of psycho-

linguistics deals with relations between messages and the characteristics of those who issue and interpret them. The term is usually
applied, however, to analysis of language mechanisms in individual
communicators rather than analysis of mass media manipulations
and effects. Even within this limitation, the variety of research
problems encompassed is tremendous. There is, for example, *content analysis* — attempts to infer the characteristics and intentions
of sources from inspection of the messages they produce. There is
the question of *onomatopoeia* — do the sounds of speech per se
have meaningful connotations to the hearer and are these connotations consistent across languages and cultures? Yet another psycholinguistic problem is that of *semantic units* — what segments of
messages correspond to semantic decisions in the speaker and
hearer? Are the units the same for speaker and hearer? Do long
pauses, "ums" and "ahs," serve to index these units? A recent mono-
graph (*Psycholinguistics,* Osgood and Sebeok, eds., 1954) sketches
many of the research problems in this area, and others — particularly on relations between language and cognition — which are
currently being investigated in the Southwest Project on Cross-
cultural Psycholinguistics sponsored by the Social Science Research
Council. Strictly speaking, the semantic differential is a psycholinguistic tool, designed as it is to measure the meanings (states of
language users) of signs (units of messages). In this section we
report several typical psycholinguistic applications.

The Semantic Effects of Word Combination[1]

The meaning of a word in ordinary speech is influenced by the
context of other words with which it occurs. Speakers select adjectives to modify nouns and adverbs to modify verbs, and they arrange word sequences to change meanings in desired directions and
to desired degrees, thereby greatly expanding the discriminatory
power of the communication system. An AGGRESSIVE LEADER is somewhat different in meaning from a POWERFUL LEADER, and both in
turn are quite different from a SYMPATHETIC LEADER. An experiment
by Howes and Osgood (1954) demonstrated that the probabilities
of various associative responses to a given stimulus word can be
changed by varying the antecedent verbal context; while this is
evidence that meaning is influenced by linguistic context, it provides

[1] Mr. Donald C. Ferguson collaborated with the senior author on this
research, supported by an Undergraduate Research Fellowship with the Social
Science Research Council. We gratefully acknowledge this support.

no insight into the laws that might be operating. In the present study, a set of adjectives is combined with a set of nouns in all possible pairs, and we are interested in the degree to which the meanings of these combinations are predictable from knowing the meanings of their components.

Materials and Procedure. It was necessary to select verbal materials whose meanings would be as widely distributed throughout the semantic space as possible and whose combinations, therefore, would yield as wide a variety of amounts and directions of change as possible. It was also necessary to have components whose combinations would be as "natural" and credulous as possible. The combination of adjective and noun into the nominal phrase seemed to be the linguistic form most suited to our purpose. To satisfy the credulity criterion, we tried to avoid nouns having a rigid connotative significance, e.g., a HAPPY BOULDER would be rather hard to swallow cognitively! Nouns referring denotively to classes of persons were finally selected: NURSE, SCIENTIST, THUG, PROSTITUTE, HUSBAND, COMEDIAN, IMP, and SECRETARY. The following adjectives were selected on a priori grounds as giving a fairly wide coverage of the semantic space: ARTISTIC, HAIRY, LISTLESS, AVERAGE, SINCERE, SHY, TREACHEROUS, and BREEZY. To make the prediction situation as rigorous as possible, and to avoid any bias in choosing particular combinations, the eight adjectives were combined in all possible ways with the eight nouns, i.e., 64 word mixtures.

Since it was desirable not to have a subject judge more than one combination using the same component, it was necessary to employ eight groups of subjects. These groups ranged from an N of 21 to an N of 29, averaging an N of 25. Each group differentiated the meanings of all 16 component words (the eight adjectives and eight nouns) and then subsequently differentiated the meanings of eight of the 64 possible combinations. Group I had ARTISTIC NURSE, Group II had BREEZY NURSE, Group III had TREACHEROUS NURSE, and so on.

The scales used in this study were nine in number, three to represent each of the major factors isolated in our factor analytic work: evaluation *(valuable-worthless, admirable-deplorable, good-bad)*; potency *(robust-delicate, intense-mild, powerful-powerless)*; and activity *(quick-slow, active-passive, and restless-quiet)*. These scales appeared on mimeographed sheets with the component term or combination to be judged printed at the top; the order of the components and combinations was randomized in the booklets handed out to the subjects. Beyond the standard instructions, the following special instructions for judging the combinations were given:

On the following pages you will find descriptive pairs of words such as PIOUS THIEF, which you might find easier to judge if you try to recall some character who seems to fit the description — for example, one from a movie, play, or book. Here, too, do NOT look back and forth through the booklet or try to remember how you marked similar items earlier, but make each item a separate and independent judgment.

The Basis for Prediction. The problem of predicting the meaning of word mixtures is somewhat analogous to that of predicting the color of wave-length mixtures. In both cases we are dealing with the locations of component stimuli in an n-dimensional space and are seeking general principles governing their interaction. The direction of a point from the origin of our semantic space is analogous to the wave-length of a visual stimulus; the distance from the origin out to the point is analogous to the colorimetric purity of a visual stimulus. Thus we might speak of AGGRESSIVE as being *strong, active,* and *slightly good* in "hue" and quite intense or "saturated." One of the laws of color mixture is that if two component stimuli lie on the same straight line through the origin and on opposite sides of it (complementary colors), their mixture will merely cancel toward neutral gray. Will the combination of words of opposed meaning also tend toward a meaningless "neutral gray," e.g., the meaning of a SUBTLE OAF? Another law is that the hues of mixtures must always lie between those of the components. Will the point in semantic space corresponding to a CATLIKE WRESTLER necessarily fall somewhere on a line between the points representing CATLIKE and WRESTLER? In color mixture the saturation of a mixture cannot be greater than that of the most saturated component. Must the meaning of STURDY TREE be equally or less polarized than STURDY?

In predicting the semantic effects of word mixture, use was made of *the congruity principle,* which is similar to, but not identical with, the laws governing color mixture. This principle and the formulae deriving from it have been discussed in detail in Chapter 5 (see pp. 199 ff.). The essence of the principle is that when two cognitive events are simultaneously elicited, each exerts a modifying pressure on the other, in proportion to its own degree of polarization and in the direction of the other's position of perfect congruence. If such a principle can be shown to operate along one of the dimensions of meaning (the attitudinal or evaluative dimension), it seems reasonable to expect that it will operate simultaneously along all semantic dimensions. The present study, in part, may be considered a test of this expectation.

If two words of known meaning (i.e., measured meaning), such as the adjective SINCERE and the noun PROSTITUTE are combined in a linguistic phrase, SINCERE PROSTITUTE, the meaning of the compound should be predictable by applying the congruity formula simultaneously along all three dimensions, *evaluation, potency,* and *activity.* There are several ways in which this situation differs from that described for attitude change in Chapter 5, however: (1) Here we assume that we are always dealing with a positive, associative assertion, i.e., that the modification of a noun by an adjective is equivalent to the assertion that the noun *is associated with* the adjectival characteristic. (2) We also assume that the subject is always credulous of the combination, that he accepts any adjectival characterization of any noun. (3) And rather than dealing with *change* in the meaning of a concept due to interaction, we deal with the resolution of component meanings into the "new meaning" of the compound. The formula we use is

$$d_m = \frac{|d_a|}{|d_a| + |d_n|} (d_a) + \frac{|d_n|}{|d_a| + |d_n|} (d_n)$$

where $|d|$ is deviation or polarization from neutrality on the scales regardless of sign, d is deviation from neutrality with respect to sign (i.e., location along a continuum from -3 to $+3$), and the subscripts m, a, and n refer to *mixture, adjective,* and *noun* respectively (see p. 207). This formula is applied separately to each of the three semantic dimensions.

Results. The raw data were first transformed to factor scores by averaging over the three scales representing each factor; for each subject's judgment of each component word we then had three scores. Using the congruity formula above, a table was generated giving the predicted scale values for all combinations of these factor scores; entering this table with a particular subject's scores for the adjective and noun components contributing to a given combination, the predicted factor scores for the combination were read off and listed. The obtained factor scores were computed directly from the same subjects' actual judgments of the word combinations. The main concern of the experiment is with the accuracy of prediction, i.e., how close the obtained meanings of the

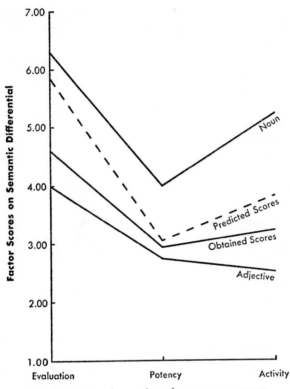

Fig. 26. Cultural meanings for SHY SECRETARY.

word combinations are to those predicted from the component terms.

We may look first at analyses based on the *means for groups.* The reliabilities of the meanings of the component words (replication across the eight groups) have already been presented in Chapter 4 (see pp. 139-40); deviations in mean score as small as one-half of a scale unit prove to be significant at the 5 per cent level. Figure 26 illustrates the prediction problem: the upper solid line gives the mean factor scores for the noun, SECRETARY, and the lower solid line the means for the adjective, SHY; the dashed line gives the means of the predicted factor scores for the combination, SHY SECRETARY, and the remaining solid line gives the means of the obtained factor scores for this combination. It will be noted that the measured meaning of SHY SECRETARY consistently deviates from the prediction in the direction of the adjective; this dominance of the adjectival component is typical of our data.

There are several ways in which the accuracy of prediction can be estimated from these means. One estimate — perhaps the crudest — is how often the obtained factor scores for the combinations fall between the factor scores for the components, a result required by the congruity formula. In every case where the obtained mean for the combination fell outside the limits set by the two components, a sign test was run across the approximately 25 subjects in the group between the mean of the combination and the mean of the nearest component. Of the 192 possible cases (three factors times 64 word combinations), only three show a significant failure of prediction by this criterion.

Another estimate of the accuracy of prediction is the average magnitude of deviation (across all 64 items) between predicted and obtained scores for word combinations. The mean deviation in scale units for the evaluative factor is .92, for the potency factor .29, and for the activity factor .35. The average errors in prediction are well within reliability estimates for potency and activity factors, but the error is significantly greater for the evaluative factor. Still another, and perhaps the best, estimate of prediction accuracy here is the correlation between predicted and obtained mean factor scores across the 64 word combinations. For the evaluative factor, $r = .86$; for the potency factor, $r = .86$; and for the activity factor, $r = .90$ — all highly significant. Summarizing these results on the "cultural meanings" of word mixtures, we find that the obtained factor scores, as predicted with the congruity formula, are consistently within the limits set by the meanings of the components, deviate from predictions on the average by amounts attributable to unreliability (except for the evaluative factor), and correlate very highly with predicted factor scores.

More sensitive tests of the accuracy of predictions can be obtained from the data on individual subjects. Two such tests were made: (1) *Constant errors as determined by sign test.* For each word combination on each of the three factors we have approximately 25 pairs of obtained and predicted scores. If there were no constant error in prediction (the null hypothesis here), then the obtained factor score for each subject should have a 50/50 chance of being larger or smaller than his predicted factor score. The Dixon-Mood Sign Test was run separately for each word combination on each factor, to determine if predictions were significantly displaced from obtained meanings. Constant errors were plainly occurring for the evaluative factor, 40/64 items having errors sig-

Table 37

COMBINATION OF CONSTANT ERROR AND SUBJECT RELIABILITY CRITERIA IN DETERMINING PREDICTION SUCCESSES AND FAILURES

| | Factors | | |
Classes of Results	I	II	III
A. No constant error; S's within limits: ("perfect prediction")	16	55	45
B. No constant error; S's outside limits:	7	2	5
C. Constant error; S's within limits:	8	5	11
D. Constant error; S's outside limits: ("clear failure")	33	2	3

nificant at the 5 per cent level or better; this was not true of the other two factors, only 7/64 items for the potency factor and 14/64 items for the activity factor showing significant constant errors. (2) *Number of subjects showing reliable difference between predicted and obtained factor scores.* It will be recalled that in test-retest reliability data (see Chapter 4, pp. 138-39) the factor scores of individual subjects may be expected to vary by as much as 1.00 scale unit on factor I, 1.50 scale units on Factor II, and 1.33 scale units on factor III only 5 per cent of the time. Actually, the subjects on whom these estimates were based are the same as those contributing the data for this word mixture study. Assuming that these values establish 5 per cent confidence limits, we may ask of each factor for each word combination if a significant (by sign test) number of subjects show reliable errors in prediction based on congruity. By this criterion, also, prediction is shown to be poorest for the evaluative factor, 42 of 64 combinations failing to meet this criterion of good prediction; for the potency factor, only 4 of 64 combinations fail, and for the activity factor, only 8 of 64 combinations show significant prediction failure. Table 37 combines these two criteria as a summary evaluation of the success of prediction. For both potency and activity factors, the vast majority of word combinations are "perfectly predicted" by the congruity formula — there is no constant error and the deviations of subjects fall within their own reliability limits. For the evaluation factor, however, a majority of word combinations show "clear failure" of prediction — there is both a significant constant error and a significant number of subjects yielding measured meanings reliably deviant from the predicted meanings.

Nature of Prediction Failures. Restricting our attention to the 38 cases where "clear failures" of prediction were recorded, we may try to discover some lawfulness. In the first place, it is clear that most errors occur on the evaluative factor. In the second place, these errors are almost always in the direction of the adjective (31 of the 38 cases) — and only three nouns, seemingly the most "loaded," THUG, PROSTITUTE, and IMP, account for the seven exceptions to this rule. Finally, inspection of the direction of error shows that in every case deviation is in the unfavorable direction of the semantic space, i.e., toward the *bad, weak,* and *passive* directions. These results are consistent with what might be dubbed the "evaluative stickiness" of some concepts — resistance of concepts having strong evaluative loading to meaning change. Thus every combination made with LISTLESS deviates from the predicted meaning toward the location of this adjective; all combinations made with THUG (except with the adjectives LISTLESS and SHY) deviate toward the location of this noun. However, it is really *"pessimistic* evaluative stickiness" that seems to be operating. It is as if the more unfavorable, unpleasant, or socially derogatory component were always dominant in word mixtures. Whereas the meaning of NURSE can easily be devalued by attaching TREACHEROUS to it, attaching SINCERE to PROSTITUTE fails to budge the immoral connotation of the fallen woman. A TREACHEROUS NURSE is definitely not to be trusted, but a SINCERE PROSTITUTE is still a prostitute!

But isn't there some simpler, or at least less esoteric, way of accounting for these errors? For one thing, the variability in mean evaluative factor scores for the 16 components is much greater than for the other factors — is the greater error in predicting the evaluative meaning of mixtures simply a function of the greater distances between the components? To check this possibility the 64 combinations on each factor were ordered according to the distance between adjective and noun means, and separate correlations between predicted and obtained factor scores were run for the upper and lower halves of this distribution. The results were as follows: *evaluative factor,* small disparities, $r = .96$, large disparities, $r = .84$; *potency factor,* small disparities, $r = .87$, large disparities, $r = .87$; *activity factor,* small disparities, $r = .78$, and large disparities, $r = .92$. There is little evidence here that large disparities in meanings of components tend to be accompanied by decreasing accuracy in prediction.

What about the *angle* in the semantic space between the components contributing to a combination? It will be recalled that Suci has argued that concepts are comparable to the extent that they share the same characteristic attributes (see Chapter 3, pp. 116-20). If this is a general condition for cognitive interactions, then congruity effects should also operate to the degree that the inter-acting concepts share characteristic attributes. Since concepts will share the same attributes in proportion to how close they lie to a common dimension through the semantic space, accuracy of predic-tion should vary inversely with the cosine of the angle between adjective and noun components. Accordingly, cosines of the angles between all adjective and noun pairs were computed from the mean factor scores of these components when judged separately, and these values were then correlated with the accuracy of predicting the meanings of their combinations via congruity (as estimated from the numbers of subjects showing reliable errors). A significant negative correlation, .69, was obtained, indicating that errors in prediction do, in fact, increase with the angular displacement of the components in the semantic space.

Summary. Quite apart from the validity of the congruity principle as a basis for predicting the meanings of word mixtures, this experi-ment demonstrates the usefulness of the semantic differential as a tool for testing certain psycholinguistic notions. In this case it was possible to measure in comparable units at least certain aspects of the meanings of both individual words and of phrases in which they were combined, and thereby to test for the lawfulness of semantic change under conditions of combination. The results of this study show that the semantic effects of word combination are neither haphazard nor unique. In terms of the average meanings of the word combinations, semantic effects follow the expectations from a congruity principle quite closely. Analysis of the data from individual subjects, however, reveals consistent errors in prediction with the congruity formula: particularly on the evaluative factor, the measured meanings of combinations regularly deviate by being more unfavorable (*bad, weak,* and *passive*) than predicted. It was also shown that the congruity formula predicts less and less well as the angular displacement of word components in the semantic space increases. In other words, the less comparable two signs that are put in combination, in terms of the sharing of characteristic at-tributes, the less congruity interaction they display; and the failure of congruity under these conditions typically appears as dominance of the unfavorably evaluative component. It is entirely possible, of course, that some formula other than that derived from the congruity principle would incorporate these word mixture results more adequately.

An Experimental Study of Individual Encoding Fidelity

As indicated earlier, decoding is regarded as the process whereby the stimulus patterns we call signs elicit distinctive representational mediators (significances) and encoding refers to the process whereby the self-stimulation produced by these mediators (intentions) elicits distinctive patterns of instrumental skills, linguistic or otherwise. Both of these communication processes are *learned*, and presumably, as in other learned activities, individuals differ from one another in facility, i.e., in the precision and flexibility with which signs call forth appropriate mediators and with which mediators call forth appropriate behaviors. To the extent that the semantic differential provides a valid and sensitive index of states in the mediational system, it should be useful in gauging individual differences here. At least two types of estimate can be envisaged in this connection: *individual fidelity*, the degree to which an individual's decoded significances or encoded intentions correspond to his own criterion; and *social fidelity*, the degree to which his decoding and encoding correspond to a social psycholinguistic norm. There are thus four distinct classes of language facility implied — individual decoding fidelity, individual encoding fidelity, social decoding fidelity, and social encoding fidelity.

To date, only the second of these — individual encoding fidelity — has been investigated, and here only to a limited degree.[2] The general procedure followed by Finfgeld (1953) was as follows: a sample of 160 undergraduate students rated ten familiar but diversified concepts (HITLER, DIAMOND, STALIN, ORCHID, FLORENCE NIGHTINGALE, BAYONET, ABRAHAM LINCOLN, DOOR, JESUS CHRIST, and TELEVISION) against 12 semantic differential scales selected so as to give roughly equal loading on the three major semantic dimensions isolated in factor analysis. At the same time, each subject was also given two minutes to select (i.e., encode) that one

---

[2] Roger E. Nebergall (Department of Speech, University of Oklahoma) has recently completed a thesis on the measurement of individual differences in *fidelity of message transmission*. Various speakers view abstract paintings, rate them on the differential and encode a description of them. Groups listen to these verbal descriptions and rate the "pictures" as understood from the descriptions. Fidelity is measured in terms of correspondence between speaker and audience profiles.

adjective which, to him, best represented *his own meaning* of each concept. Approximately one week later, each subject rated his own resulting ten descriptive adjectives against the same 12-scale semantic differential. The average D^2 for each subject's ten concept-adjective profile comparisons was taken as that subject's "intentional adequacy (or fidelity) score" — i.e., the degree to which he was able to encode an adjective whose meaning (for him) corresponded to the meaning of the concept being described (again, for him).

The results showed wide individual differences in these intentional fidelity scores, the distribution of these differences closely approximating a normal one. However, when Finfgeld ran Pearson product-moment correlations between these fidelity scores and three attributes which he hypothesized should correlate highly — intelligence (ACE test), verbal reasoning, and vocabulary — the results were entirely negative ($-.10$ with intelligence; $-.13$ with verbal reasoning, and $-.11$ with vocabulary — all nonsignificant). Similarly, there was no significant difference on these scores between students who had had no training in speech and students majoring in speech.

But these findings do not imply that intentional fidelity measures derived in this manner are invalid. Finfgeld demonstrated this in two ways: (a) 20 subjects were selected at random, and, for each concept, the D^2 between the profile for that concept and its selected adjective was compared with the D^2 between that same concept and the nine other adjectives that had been selected to describe the nine other concepts. For 19 out of 20 such comparisons (by Chi-square) the null hypothesis was rejected at the 1 per cent level (the D^2 of the concept with the selected adjective always being smaller; (b) experts (18 speech and rhetoric instructors) rated the five most frequently given adjectives for each concept on a number of scales reflecting traditional criteria of communication effectiveness (clarity, semantic effectiveness, and the like). There was an almost perfect correspondence (beyond the .01 level) between these ratings and the selection frequency.

Much remains to be done along these lines, of course. For one thing, it would be useful to know with what other characteristics individual encoding fidelity *does* correlate. Its failure to correlate with intelligence is perhaps not too surprising — it is not uncommon to observe highly intelligent people who are not able to "express themselves" well, while other people of relatively low intelligence may display a high degree of verbal fluency. The low correlation with vocabulary may be due to the fact that many vocabulary tests, such as the one used here, are basically *decoding*, not encoding, operations — given a set of possible synonyms for a test word, the subject must select the most appropriate in meaning.

Then, other aspects of the more general area of language facility may be investigated. A test for *individual decoding fidelity* might possibly take this form: after differentiating the meanings of a fairly large sample of words, subjects would be asked to select from the set (a) words most similar in meaning to a given test word, and (b) words most opposed in meaning. The subject's score would then be how closely his selections match his own profile similarities. It would be expected that this would correlate highly with intelligence. A test for *social decoding fidelity* might involve measuring the differences between individual profiles for a set of words and normative profiles for a given language community. Measuring *social encoding fidelity* is a somewhat different and more difficult matter. It would require judgments of a number of concepts (objects and situations, etc.) by a group of subjects, selection by the same subjects of words to label or describe these situations, and finally measurement of the similarity in semantic profile between the words chosen by individuals and the meanings, for other people, of the concept. In short, this gets down to the basis of communication per se — the ability to select words that will produce in other people significances which correspond to one's own. There is a practical side to all this, of course. Many potential applications of such language measures can be envisaged: to predict success in certain types of occupations (e.g., newspaper reporting, advertising copy writing, selling), to study creative literary activities, to provide norms for vocabulary development in children, and so on.

A Study on the Experimental Production of Assign Meanings

Analysis of the formation of both sign and assign meanings in terms of mediation theory was given in Chapter 1 (pp. 5-9). *Primary signs* (e.g., the adjective GOOD) acquire meaning through direct association with significates (e.g., gratifying situations), a representational portion of the total behavior to the significate becoming associated with the sign as its mediation process. In the case of *assigns*, however, there is little if any direct association with significates — if, indeed, there is any referent in the behavioral sense (e.g., the assign FASCISM). Rather, the assign is consistently associated with a certain sample of primary signs and gradually acquires as its mediation process the most common elements of mediators for the signs with which it appears. In other words, the meanings of assigns develop out of the *context* of primary signs with which they occur. As the child who has learned to read with some facility moves through a story, the matrix of familiar signs limits the possible meanings which the new and unfamiliar words can have. And since the adult story writers are reasonably consistent in the signs they put together (PRIESTS are *kind* and *calm*, LIBERTY is *good* and *free*, VICIOUS is something characteristic of *wild animals, bad men,* and so on), a reasonably stable assign-meaning develops. Certainly, the vast majority of lexical items employed and understood by adult humans are assigns in this sense.

The interesting theoretical and empirical problem here is to make explicit the functions whereby assigns acquire meanings from sign contexts. Werner and Kaplan (1950) studied the development of meanings of nonsense assigns imbedded in meaningful contexts, on the part of children of various ages, and generalized in most interesting ways to the nature of semantic change in languages. Although mainly empirical, this work is full of implications for theory. The research of Dodge (1955), to be described here, employed a method somewhat similar to that used by Werner and Kaplan, but the hypotheses tested derived from mediation learning theory and the congruity principle.

The general procedure was to associate nonsense words (assigns) with other words whose meanings were familiar (signs). Stories were written in which simple adjectives (signs) were used to describe the characteristics of a hypothetical — but entirely believable, to the subjects — native tribe, e.g., the MEBLU (assign). These stories were written after the style of *The National Geographic Magazine,* describing a trip through strange terrain, an encounter with a MEBLU tribesman, and subsequent discussion of this tribe around the campfire. Prior to exposure to the story, subjects rated both the signs and assigns to be used later against a typical nine-scale form of the semantic differential. After exposure to the experimental materials, these ratings were repeated. A control group made both sets of judgments, but was given no intervening material.

Both ordinary *conditioning theory* (in which the signs are analogous to unconditioned stimuli and the assigns to conditionable stimuli) and the *congruity principle* (in which we are predicting the resolution of the interaction of more-or-less polarized signs and essentially neutral assigns) lead to the following predictions: (a) the meaning of the assign will shift from a position of neutrality toward the locations in the semantic space of the signs with which it is associated. Since we assume an associative assertion to be operating here, the point in the space toward which the assign should move is defined by the same formula (extended to a set of three signs) as that used above to predict the effects of word mixture (see p. 278); (b) the terminal degree of polarization of the assign on any one dimension of the space will be a negatively accelerated positive function of the frequency of association between sign and assign and a linear function of the initial degree of polarization of the sign. In other words, an ordinary growth curve of learning is postulated here as elsewhere in habit formation (see pp. 207-9 where the relation of congruity to learning is discussed). The only differential prediction as between ordinary conditioning theory and congruity theory concerns the effect of contextual association upon the meaning of the signs themselves; whereas conditioning theory predicts no change in the meaning of the signs (adjectives) as a result of being associated with the neutral assign, the congruity principle necessarily predicts a slight but progressive decrease in polarization of the signs under conditions of successive association with the assign.

Dodge employed two designs. In Design I, the degree of polarization of the signs was held constant and the *frequency* of association with the assign was varied, e.g., in the story given to one group, subjects would encounter the *friendly* MEBLU (evaluative) four times, the *brawny* MEBLU (potency) two times, and the *excitable* MEBLU (activity) one time — other groups getting other combinations. In Design II, frequency of association was held constant and the *degree of polarization* of the signs associated with the assign was varied, e.g., in the story for one group it would be the *very friendly* MEBLU, but no intensifiers would be used for the adjectives representing other factors — again, other groups getting other combinations.

The results supported the main predictions. When the data from Design I were analyzed by the sign test, with each subject as his own control, the following results were obtained: the difference between one and four successive exposures of a particular sign-assign association was significant at the 1 per cent level; the difference between two and four exposures was significant at the 5 per cent level. These results held for each dimension considered separately. The difference between one and two exposures was not significant, except for the evaluative dimension. Dodge also used these data to test the prediction from the congruity principle that when an assign (neutral) is repeatedly associated with a polarized sign, the *sign* should become somewhat less polarized on any given dimension. Contrary to expectations, the largest reductions in polarization for the signs occurred under conditions of only one or two associations, although none of the differences were significant. However, in terms of the direction of change in signs, all of the shifts but one (i.e., eight out of nine) were as predicted.

The results of Design II were quite impressive. Considering each dimension of meaning separately, the more intense signs produced greater change in the assigns associated with them, and in the predicted direction, at a significance beyond the 1 per cent level. When all dimensions are considered simultaneously, the significance level goes to .001. Another way to demonstrate the dependence of assign shift upon original intensity of associated signs, using individual subjects as their own controls, is to correlate the amount of assign change on a given dimension (pre- to post-test) with the original distance or discrepancy between sign and assign on the pretest for the same dimension. Treating only changes in the predicted direction, the correlation here is .79, which is highly significant.

To summarize the results of this study on assign development, we find that the meaning an assign will acquire can be estimated from the measured meanings of the signs with which it is associated. Furthermore, the development of assign meanings, like any other learned process, is a function both of the frequency of association with signs and of the intensity of the signs with which they are associated. This study, of course, represents only a beginning in the quantitative study of the development of semantic decoding processes. The area — which is really that of concept *formation*, as contrasted with concept *utilization*, studied in most cases — is replete with tantalizing possibilities for experimental research. It should be possible, for example, to study the development of meanings for true linguistic assigns like JUSTICE (rather than nonsense terms) in children of various age levels by similar means.[3] Another

---

[3] John W. Donahoe (University of Kentucky) has reported just such a study on the acquisition of meanings in children. Using *five*-step scales, and subjects ranging from first grade to college level, he was able to demonstrate a negatively accelerated curve, reaching the "adult asymptote" at the 9-year level. Judgments on the evaluative factor were the first to reach the adult norm.

study on the planning boards will compare the congruity predictions regarding shift in polarization of assigns under two conditions: first, where several signs, all heavily polarized on one dimension, are associated with the assign simultaneously (in a single phrase), and second, where the same signs are associated with the assign in sequence and with some time interval separating each association, as in the Dodge study.

APPLICATIONS TO EXPERIMENTAL AESTHETICS AND RELATED PROBLEMS

Although it is by no means the only fruitful approach, aesthetics can be studied as a form of communication. The message in this case is the aesthetic product itself — the musical composition as performed, the painting as viewed, the poem or essay as read, or even the advertisement as seen in a national magazine. Like ordinary linguistic messages, the aesthetic product is a Janus-faced affair; it has the dual character of being at once the result of responses encoded by one participant in the communicative act (the creator) and the stimulus to be decoded by the other participants (the appreciators). Aesthetic products differ, perhaps, from linguistic messages by being more continuously than discretely coded (e.g., colors and forms in a painting can be varied continuously whereas the phonemes that discriminate among word-forms vary by all-or-nothing quanta called distinctive features). They also differ, perhaps, in being associated more with connotative, emotional reactions in sources and receivers than with denotative reactions. It also seems likely that the individual variations in both encoding and decoding — in the ways creators express intentions and in the ways appreciators derive significances — are much greater than in language per se. But nevertheless, to the extent that the creators of aesthetic products are able to influence the meanings and emotions experienced by their audiences by manipulations in the media of their talent, we are dealing with communication.

It is precisely because the semantic differential taps the connotative aspects of meaning more immediately than the highly diversified denotative aspects that it should be readily applicable to aesthetic studies. Indeed, as the reader will recall from Chapter 1, the semantic differential had its origins in an essentially aesthetic context — studies of color-music synesthesia. To date, applications of the instrument in the field of aesthetics have been modest in scope. One fairly extensive study of the factor structure of aesthetic judgments (in the visual arts) has been undertaken; a series of studies on the connotative meanings of colors, in both abstract art forms and in advertised products, has been done; and a number of more remote studies on interactions of music with dramatic productions and on pictorial and cartoon symbolism can be reported. Again, these researches have more value as illustrations of the potential usefulness of the measuring technique than they do as contributions to a "science of aesthetics," if we may use such a term.

There are, of course, many people who shudder at the thought of bringing a quantitative measuring instrument into the domain of aesthetics, who are dismayed at any attempt to make a science out of art. It is necessary to draw a sharp distinction between study of the process of aesthetics as a kind of human communication and the creation of aesthetic products. Whereas the latter should, and undoubtedly will, remain in the domain of art, the former is a perfectly legitimate area of scientific study, and any instruments, quantitative or otherwise, which facilitate this study are to be welcomed.

Factorial Studies on the Structure of Aesthetic Judgments

Problem. To apply the semantic differential technique effectively in the study of aesthetics, it is first necessary to determine the major factors or dimensions underlying aesthetic meanings. The particular instruments used, the specific scales selected, etc., depend upon such analysis. The factors operating in aesthetic judgments may be the same as those that appear in ordinary semantic judgments of linguistic signs, or they may be quite different; the factors operating for visual art objects may differ from those for musical or poetic objects, although it would be hoped that this would not be the case. Restricting his attention to the visual arts (painting), Tucker (1955) first studied the factor structures apparent in the judgments of both artists and non-artists — hypothesizing that there would be differences between these groups. To demonstrate differences, however, he found it necessary to analyze separately the judgments of representational as compared with nonrepresentational (abstract) paintings. Using a reduced sample of scales, selected on the basis of his factor work, Tucker then undertook to investigate what artistic techniques are related to what semantic factors.

Method. Tucker's methods have already been briefly described in connection with the generality of semantic factors (see Chapter 2, pp. 68-70). The 40 scales finally used in his factor studies were selected in a variety of ways: from the spontaneous comments of art students when viewing large numbers of slides, from the comments of visitors to an art exhibition, and from the previous factor studies of Osgood and Suci (particularly to include reference scales for the factors they had isolated). The complete list is given in Table 7 in Chapter 2. The paintings finally chosen as the objects for judgment included seven representational paintings and four nonrepresentational paintings or abstracts. These stimuli were presented on projected slides to 33 non-artists (juniors and sophomores in the College of Commerce) and ten artists (graduate students and faculty members of the Art Department). The subjects were allowed one minute to view the picture (without marking judgments); then the stimulus was removed and all judgments about it were made on the usual graphic form of the differential. The D² method of factoring (see the Appendix) was used to get at the structuring of aesthetic judgments.

Results of Factor Analyses. The judgments of both artists and non-artists, when analyzed over *all 11 paintings,* generated three major factors which were quite comparable in nature to those originally obtained by Osgood and Suci for verbal concepts. For artists, an *activity factor* (characterized by scales like *active-passive, vibrant-still,* and *dynamic-static*) accounted for 46 per cent of the variance, an *evaluative factor* (characterized by scales like *ordered-chaotic, controlled-accidental, clear-hazy,* and *pleasant-unpleasant*) accounted for 17 per cent, and a *potency factor* (characterized by scales like *hard-soft, masculine-feminine,* and *formal-informal*) accounted for 10 per cent of the variance. The non-artists showed essentially the same factors, but in more nearly equal weights. When the judgments on representational paintings were analyzed separately, an even closer approximation to the Osgood-Suci results on verbal materials was obtained, for both artists and non-artists. The data for representational paintings judged by non-artists are given as Table 7 on page 69.

On the other hand, when the judgments on abstract paintings were factor analyzed separately, artists and non-artists displayed completely different structures. The judgments of abstract paintings by artists are accounted for by a single, overwhelming evaluative factor which reflects 79 per cent of the total variance. Judging from other research (particularly studies by Suci on political and ethnic judgments), this suggests that artists have highly polarized and emotional reactions to abstract paintings which collapses the semantic space about a dominant single dimension. All scales of judgment tend to rotate toward this dominant dimension of evaluation; if an abstract is liked it is also *smooth, dynamic, vibrant, serious, intimate,* and so on through the favorable poles of the various scales. It also suggests that artists have explicitly worked out and agreed upon systems of evaluation; otherwise individual differences in scale allocation would wash out such a dominant factor. The situation for non-artists judging abstract paintings is quite the reverse. Here, what could best be described as semantic chaos results. Although two factors accounted for a large part of the variance, the factors made no semantic sense whatsoever. The graphic plot of the variables in terms of the two factors was a nearly homogeneous circle, and the factors could have been placed equally well in any orientation. In other words, when non-artists judge a set of abstract paintings, there is very little structuring of the judgments — as if they had no frame of reference for the task.

Relation of Artistic Techniques to Semantic Judgments. What uses of color and form by artists are correlated with what types of semantic judgment? To get at this question, Tucker first studied the encoding operations of student artists and then the decoding operations of non-artist viewers of their work. In the first part of the experiment, 52 art students at the University of Georgia served. Each student was asked to create an abstract pastel appropriate to one of the following phrases: *extreme activity, extreme passivity, extreme chaos, extreme orderliness, extreme strength, extreme weakness* — these terms, of course, representing the poles of the three major factors found in representational paintings. The students, without exception, were enthusiastic over this problem. In general, paintings made to represent *activity* employed the warm colors (red, orange, and yellow) and jagged lines; paintings representing *passivity* were typically large and simple curvilinear shapes, smoothly drawn and using pale rather than intense colors; *chaos* was like activity in representation as far as form was concerned, but there was greater use of dark colors and mass patterns; *orderliness* paintings were almost always geometric in character (straight lines, simple forms) and made use of few colors (an average of three vs. seven colors in paintings for chaos); to represent *strength,* several modalities were employed — extreme color and/or bright-

Table 38

SELECTION OF ADJECTIVES TO DESCRIBE PASTELS DRAWN TO REPRESENT POLES OF AESTHETIC SEMANTIC FACTORS

Drawings	Adjectives					
	orderly	chaotic	active	passive	strong	weak
Extreme orderliness	12	0	1	1	2	1
Extreme chaos	0	10	4	0	3	0
Extreme activity	0	10	3	0	2	2
Extreme passivity	1	0	2	5	0	9
Extreme strength	4	0	1	1	10	1
Extreme weakness	0	2	4	6	1	4

ness contrast along with the use of massive forms were common to most, however; *weakness* was typically displayed by uncertain, amorphous lines and/or by faintly blanked out patches having slight contrast and indefinite pattern. These relationships will be recognized as having their counterparts in language metaphor.

To complete the communicative act, we must inquire whether the viewers of these student pastels, in decoding their significances, could recreate the original intentions (activity, strength, orderliness, etc.) of the artists. The answer, as indicated by the results in Table 38 was a qualified "yes." A group of 17 commerce students (University of Georgia) was asked to select one of six adjectives — *active, passive, chaotic, orderly, strong,* and *weak* — with each of six pastels chosen from the group done by the artists. The paintings to represent *orderliness, chaos,* and *strength* yielded the expected judgments with a high degree of accuracy; the painting drawn to represent *passivity* tended to be judged *weak,* and vice versa; and that drawn to represent *activity* tended to be judged *chaotic.* Recalling the lack of factor structure in the judgments of abstract paintings by non-artists, however, these confusions are not too surprising.

Summary. When either artists or non-artists judge representational paintings against a large number of scales, the dominant factors to appear are recognizable as the same as those derived from judgments of verbal concepts, *evaluation, potency,* and *activity,* although the particular scales which represent these factors best in judging aesthetic objects are not necessarily the same and the activity factor has relatively more weight. When we consider that highly representational drawings of objects and scenes are facsimiles of perceptual signs, and hence approach functional equivalence to linguistic signs in their capacity to evoke the same mediation processes, this result is to be expected. The essential equivalence of pictorial and verbal signs will be demonstrated again in the next study in this section. When artists and non-artists judge abstract paintings, however, the former display a single, dominant factor (evidence that they have very definite and polarized meanings for these stimuli) whereas the latter display a relatively unstructured system (suggestive evidence that abstracts are essentially meaningless to them). This finding, too, is reasonable. When presented with terms defining the poles of the major aesthetic factors (for representational paintings), student artists were able to produce pastel drawings which not only differed in expected ways but also elicited the original polar adjectives with a fair degree of accuracy. These results were obtained on rather small numbers of subjects, however, and need confirmation; further, we would like to extend this type of semantic analysis to other aesthetic modes.

Pictorial Signs and Symbols

Let us reflect a moment on the probable development of sign processes in the young individual. It is evident that for most of the common objects and situations in the child's environment *perceptual signs* are established prior to *linguistic signs*. The perceptual patterns generated by seeing a BALL or a SPOON, hearing a BARK or a CAR HORN, and feeling a BUTTON or a STRING acquire significance long before the words we use to refer to these objects — we know this because the pre-verbal child displays appropriate meaningful behaviors to these objects, as perceived. Later, the arbitrarily coded noises that constitute vocal signs, and still later, the arbitrarily coded visual patterns that constitute orthographic signs, come to be associated with the same or very similar mediation processes. When a set of physically different stimuli are associated with a process which mediates common overt behavior, we speak of a class of signs having the same significance.

What about *pictorial signs?* Is the outline drawing on a white card of a dog, say, simply a substitute for a perceptual sign? Does the mediation process already associated with DOG as perceived simply generalize to this similar visual presentation? Although generalization may play some role, particularly in highly representational artistic products (see Tucker's research above) which skillfully duplicate the conditions of visual perception, this is certainly not true for ordinary pictorial representations. The outline drawing of DOG on a small white card is far removed from the perception of this object; such drawings are actually a very arbitrary class of visual signs (two-dimensional, untrue in color stimulation, etc.) whose significance must be learned, just as the meaning of orthographic signs on the printed page must be learned. Anthropologists are made aware of this arbitrariness when they show drawings or even photographs of common objects to primitive subjects; what is "obviously" a picture of a horse to the Western white investigator proves to be a complete mystery to the Bantu Negro!

The direct visual perception of an object, the spoken word which labels the object, the printed word for the object, and the conventional picture (outline drawing, painting, photograph, etc.) of the object, then, become a class of alternative *signs* of the object, by virtue of association through learning with the same or similar mediation process. But what about a *pictorial symbol?* What is the status, semantically, of the political cartoon of the Democratic DONKEY? Here we have something new — a sign (picture of donkey) which already has its own characteristic meaning being used to represent something other than itself. Our discussion of the basic nature of symbolism in connection with Moss's research on dream symbolism may be recalled (Chapter 6, pp. 254-58). When a person reacts overtly to one sign with the behaviors ordinarily made to another sign, e.g., when he sees his youngster point his forefinger at him and he agreeably simulates fear and raises his hands, he is behaving symbolically. If he maintains the meaningful distinction between the sign and the thing symbolized — recognizing the pointed finger as such and merely behaving *as if* it were a gun — we may speak of *conscious symbolism*. If he does not maintain this distinction, and actually perceives the pointed finger as a gun, as in dream symbolism, we may speak of *unconscious symbolism*. The distinction theoretically lies in whether the sign elicits merely the overt behavior appropriate to the thing symbolized or the mediation process characteristic of the thing symbolized as well.

The experiment described below was designed to study the degree to which the meanings of pictorial signs and pictorial symbols (specifically, political cartoons) replicate the meanings of the things symbolized. Is an outline drawing of an ordinary elephant semantically equivalent to the word ELEPHANT? Is a political cartoon of the Republican elephant, clearly identified as such,

Table 39

MEAN D-SCORES (UPPER VALUES) AND CORRELATIONS (LOWER VALUES) BETWEEN VARIOUS EXPERIMENTAL CONDITIONS

Animal	1 a vs. b	2 b vs. c	3 b vs. d	4 c vs. d	5 d vs. e
Eagle	1.15	1.29	5.31	7.00	1.81
	.94*	.95*	.41	.12	.98*
Lion	.73	2.97	2.74	5.79	2.48
	.99*	.81*	.76*	.41	.25
Bear	1.09	3.65	4.48	7.67	.92
	.97*	.56*	.59	−.16	.99*
Elephant	1.02	3.11	3.98	7.34	1.03
	.96*	.79*	.43	.11	.93*
Donkey	.96	3.35	4.67	6.71	.97
	.92*	.44	.33	−.08	.91*
Average D	.990	2.874	4.236	6.902	1.442
Average r	.965*	.785*	.525	.085	.930*

* p < .01.

semantically equivalent to the words REPUBLICAN PARTY, or is there some degree of compromise in which the meaning of elephant per se interacts with that of REPUBLICAN PARTY? One study[4] employed the semantic differential to investigate these problems. Five groups of 20 undergraduate subjects each, arranged in a Latin-square design, rated each of five classes of animal objects in five different modes of presentation. The animals were BEAR, EAGLE, LION, ELEPHANT, and DONKEY. The modes of sign presentation were as follows: (a) the *orthographic sign* for the animal (e.g., the printed word ELEPHANT); (b) a *pictorial sign* of the animal (e.g., an outline drawing of an ordinary elephant); (c) a *nonpolitical stereotypical pictorial symbol* of the animal (e.g., outline drawing of the elephant cowering before a mouse); (d) as a *political symbol* (e.g., outline drawing of the Republican elephant clearly identified as such); and (e) the *orthographic sign of the thing symbolized* (e.g., the printed words REPUBLICAN PARTY). Ten semantic scales were used — four for the evaluative factor and three each for the potency and activity factors. Each subject rated all 25 stimuli; the order of modes of presentation (types of signs) was held constant, but the order of presentation of the animals was varied from group to group.

[4] Conducted by Drs. P. H. Tannenbaum and Jean S. Kerrick at the University of Illinois in 1952.

Analysis of the data was in terms of profile similarities for the various modes of presentation, as indicated in terms of both D-scores and correlation. Table 39 presents both these indices of similarity for the various types of comparison that will concern us here. Our first question is directed at the *essential equivalance in meaning between the orthographic and pictorial signs for the same object.* The main test here lies in comparing conditions a vs. b (e.g., the word ELEPHANT with the plain drawing of an elephant). Inspection of column (1) in Table 39 shows that the mean D for these comparisons is smaller than those for the other comparisons, and in each case there is a high and significant correlation between the profiles.

A second question is concerned with whether *the meaning of the nonpolitical stereotypical symbol represents some compromise between the meaning of the sign itself and the meaning of the stereotype.* The data in column (2) shows the comparison between the plain drawing of the animal and the drawing of the animal in a nonpolitical stereotyped situation. The mean D's here are somewhat larger for that in column (1), but there is still some basis for a strong similarity between the profiles, as indicated by the significant correlations. This suggests that the meaning of the nonpolitical stereotyped situation did represent some compromise — e.g., the elephant remains essentially an elephant, although there are shifts on scales appropriate to the stereotypical situation. Indeed, such specific shifts are readily apparent when one examines the scale-by-scale profiles of judgment, not included here for purposes of economy.

What about the *use of the animal cartoon as a political symbol?* Unlike the above findings, here we have practically no evidence of compromise. The D's between conditions d and e, as shown in column (5), are all lower than those between conditions d and the other drawings, i.e., in columns (3) and (4). Also, the correlations between the political drawing and the political word are, with one exception, high and significant. Only in the case of the lion as a symbol of Great Britain did this relation fall down — one possible explanation of this is that midwestern undergraduates failed to perceive a drawing of a lion with a Union Jack flag on its chest as a symbol of Britain.

These results support the conclusion that for certain pictorial symbols, at least, the meaning of the symbol may be shifted completely to that of the thing symbolized. The standard political cartoon symbols carry very little of the original meaning of the sign being used as a symbol — the elephant as a symbol of the Republican party bears little resemblance to the judgment of an elephant per se. That this is not a universal characteristic of symbols is at least suggested by the results with the nonpolitical pictorial symbols; here there is evidence for compromise between sign-meaning per se and meaning-as-symbol, although the case would have been stronger had Tannenbaum and Kerrick also presented words referring to the stereotyped characteristics for rating (e.g., the word COWARDLY in the case of the elephant set). Finally, it is clear that, at least for the sign classes used here, ordinary pictorial signs are semantically equivalent to linguistic signs.

Studies in Color Meanings

The field of color perception occupies an honored place in the history of psychology. We know a great deal about the dimensions of color vision and its physiology, this area probably being as extensively researched as any other single area of psychology. But we know very little about the communication values of colors. Do different colors have different meanings? Can different colors alter the meanings of objects with which they are associated? There are many intriguing questions here from the standpoint of communication theory. Two studies on this problem have been conducted with the semantic differential technique, and a third is now in progress.

Effects of Color on the Meanings of Advertised Products. One of the important questions in contemporary advertising practice concerns the role of color. Beyond the naturalness or appropriateness of colors to a particular product being advertised, do colors have different emotional and meaningful effects in general? Can they alter the judgment of the product with which they are associated? Is blue generally *stronger* than, say, yellow? Do bright colors generally make products appear *cheaper* than pale, pastel ones? This will become an even more pressing problem for advertising research with the advent of color television.

The following experiment[5] was conducted: A Latin-square analysis of variance design was set up in which five nationally advertised products (a SHIRT, an ICE CREAM, a RUG, an AUTOMOBILE, and a CAKE MIX) and a control COLOR SPOT appeared randomly in each of six

[5] Conducted by Drs. Tannenbaum and Osgood, in 1952, with the support of a grant from Young and Rubicam, Inc. We gratefully acknowledge this aid.

different colors (red, yellow, green, blue, violet, and black-and-white). These were particular brands appearing in regular magazine advertisements. Four replications of this design were conducted — one with the color intense in the product only, with the rest of the ad in neutral gray; a second with the color pale in the product; a third with the product gray but the background intensely colored; and the fourth with the background in pastel. Six different groups of 20 subjects each were used in each of the four replications, each group seeing each product with each color, in particular combinations, only once. Subjects were asked to judge the *product*, as such, against a set of 20 scales, no reference to color being made. Separate analyses were conducted for each scale under each condition, or 80 analyses of variance in all.

The major findings of this study may be summarized as follows: (a) On several scales, typically non-evaluative ones such as *warm-cool, heavy-light,* and *exciting-dull,* over-all (i.e., over all six products) significant differences between colors were obtained, e.g., red invariably made the product appear *warmer,* blue and green shifted the judgment toward *cool.* Evaluative scales, however, failed to show such consistent effects. (b) Particularly on the evaluative scales, it was the *interaction* between color and product that proved to be statistically significant, testifying, for one thing, to the importance of selecting appropriate, culturally accepted colors to go with particular products — a violet auto was favorably judged, but not so a violet cake. (c) Pastel colors on products, as well as in the backgrounds, produced small but consistently more favorable judgments than intense colors. This was not true for all scales, nor for all products, but is justified as a general conclusion. (d) Similarly, color-in-background was somewhat more favorable than color-in-product on the evaluative dimensions — again, on a general, over-all basis.

The data for the intense color-in-product condition was also analyzed within each of the three semantic dimensions. This was done by conducting an analysis of variance by ranks of the color judgments, using the number of scales within each factor as "replications." For example, there were seven clearly evaluative scales (as indicated by earlier factor analyses); on each of these the six colors were ranked from most favorable to least favorable, and then the analysis conducted across all seven scales. The findings were quite intriguing: (a) On *evaluation,* yellow proved to be the most favorable color ($p = .05$), but there were no differences among the other colors; this, of course, may be a function of the particular products used in this experiment. (b) On *activity* (across four scales), the resulting Chi-square was significant beyond the 2 per cent level, and the ordering of colors generally followed the *hue* dimension, i.e., red and yellow toward the *active* end, then black-and-white occupying a more or less neutral position, and swinging around to green, violet, and blue toward the *passive* end. (c) On *potency*, the colors ordered more along the *saturation* dimension, and again to a degree significant beyond the 2 per cent level. We defer comment on these findings until a later point.

The data from this study yielded another interesting finding: Some two years after the study was conducted, the data were re-analyzed in terms of predictions of direction of change in meaning from the congruity principle. That is, given the judgment for a black-and-white version of a particular *product* and the judgment of a particular *color* appearing as a simple color-spot, it was possible to predict the direction of the change in judgment of that product when it appeared in a particular color, as an instance of interaction via congruity. It was found that 77 per cent of all changes were in the predicted direction, which, with the large N available here, was highly significant.

Effects of Color on the Meanings of Sculptured Objects. The same basic Latin-square design used in the above advertising study was also used in a study of the meanings of colors in abstract sculptures. The reason for using such abstractions was to avoid the contamination of recognized, familiar objects having very stable meanings, as had been the case with the advertised products like shirts and ice cream used in the previous study. This time, however, only four colors were used (green and violet being omitted for reasons of economy), only the color-on-objects condition was studied, and a few changes were made in the selection of scales — mainly greater sampling of non-evaluative scales. On the scale-by-scale analysis, again only certain non-evaluative scales showed significant over-all between-color differences — e.g., *warm-cool, serious-humorous, masculine-feminine.* And also again, the object-color interaction was highly significant on the essentially evaluative scales.

These data were also analyzed within factors in the same manner as in the advertising study: across seven scales for evaluation, across five scales for activity, and across four scales for potency. Significant differences were obtained on all three dimensions. The ordering of colors on the activity and potency dimensions were identical with those found in the previous study — *activity* judgments paralleled the *hue* dimension of color experience, and *potency* judgments paralleled the *saturation* dimension — but on the *evaluative* factor, blue proved to be the most favorable color. The data from this study were finally analyzed for the accuracy of predictions from the congruity principle; the results were remarkably like those for the advertising study, that is 75 per cent of the changes were in the predicted direction, again a significant result.

Summary. The results of these two studies on the connotative meanings of colors are consistent and suggest the following conclusions: The effects of colors upon the *evaluation* of the objects with which they are associated — whether familiar commercial products or sculptured abstractions — are not systematic; rather, the evaluative effect of the color interacts with the nature of the object. Whereas a blue color may make an automobile more favorable, a yellow may have this effect upon a shirt. This dependence of what is "good" upon the concept being judged is entirely consistent with what we have discovered about evaluation in other studies reported in this book. Evaluative scales display the least stability semantically. On the other hand, the effects of color upon the judged *activity* and *potency* of the objects with which they are associated are remarkably systematic; regardless of the object being judged, colors toward the red end of the spectrum increase the "activity" perceived in the object and colors toward the blue increase the "passivity" perceived, and in general, the more saturated (intense) the color, the more potent becomes the object being judged. These parallelisms between meaningful connotation and the hue and saturation of colors may well be general cross-culturally; research is now under way to check this possibility. Finally, the fact that the direction of the resolution between object meanings and color meanings has been shown to be consistent with predictions from the congruity principle gives further evidence of the generality of this principle. The study in this area mentioned as being "in progress" is a more detailed test of the principle: subjects first rated the three colors and the three uncolored sculptures independently against a ten-scale differential; subsequently they rated all nine possible combinations of colors with objects, the predicted meanings of these combinations being arrived at through application of the congruity formula to the original ratings. These data are presently being analyzed.

Effects of a Musical Background in Stage and TV Drama

Given at least a basic communicative function for music and a similar one for drama (along the lines outlined at the beginning of this section), a significant problem for research is posed by the situation where an appropriate — begging the question as to what "appropriate" means here — musical score is used as background to a dramatic presentation: Can the presence of such a musical score significantly influence the judgment of that drama? Certainly when one judges by the criterion of use, music background is believed to play a most significant role, both in drama on the legitimate stage and via the mass media of radio, television, and the motion picture. There has been much speculation as to the role such music can have, but, as is generally characteristic of aesthetic communication, there has been little in the way of experimental research. Similarly, the effects of alternate forms of dramatic presentation have been a subject for conjecture, but little, if any, research.

Tannenbaum (1956) selected an original one-act play as the subject matter for his experiment. The play was performed in two versions by the same cast — a *stage version,* in the form that the play was originally written, and a *TV-studio version,* consisting of a two-camera studio adaptation of the play making full use of the television technique. For purposes of the study, a third version was added: a television recording of the stage version, made at the same time that the stage version was performed, with a camera situated in the middle of the audience (the *TV-theater version*). Three separate groups of subjects were exposed to these three versions; three additional groups of subjects were exposed to the same three versions, except that a continuous musical score, especially selected for this particular drama, was heard in the background. After exposure, all subjects rated the drama on a semantic differential consisting of four evaluative scales and three scales each from the activity and potency factors. Ratings on each dimension were summed to obtain three separate factor scores for each subject.

The data were analyzed within each factor separately by a standard analysis of variance, followed up by *t*-tests wherever appropriate. On the *evaluative* dimension, the form of presentation proved to be a highly significant variable. There was no real difference between the stage and TV-studio versions, but both were judged significantly more favorable than the TV-theater version. The addition of the musical background had a negligible effect, and the interaction between these two variables was also insignificant. On the *potency* dimension, both the form of presentation and the musical background variables were highly significant, but not their interaction. On the form of presentation the TV-studio version was judged the most powerful and significantly more so than the stage version, which was judged only slightly more powerful than the TV-theater version. The addition of musical background made the play being judged more powerful in each of the three versions. On the *activity* dimension, the only significant difference was on the musical background variable, which caused the play to be judged as much more active. This effect, again, was general to all three versions, but was most pronounced on the TV-theater version and least for the stage version. The addition of a musical background is shown to have a significant effect upon the judgments of a play, then, but this effect appears in the activity and potency dimensions of meaning, not in the evaluation of the play, and hence would not have appeared in the results of ordinary attitude scales, in all probability.

APPLICATION TO COMMUNICATIONS EFFECT STUDIES

The dividing line between aesthetic and communications effects is not always clear — certainly both the experiment on color in advertising and that on musical background for a play could have been included as studies in communication effects. In both of these experiments it was the greater dimensionality of judgment provided by the semantic differential that enriched the results obtained. From the point of view followed here, communication effects are changes in the meaning of concepts central to the message, changes in the location of these concepts in the (potentially) n-dimensional space provided by a semantic differential. Such changes may be measured *in toto* by applying the D measure between pre- and post-message scores on all factors, or they may be assayed on a unidimensional (or even single scale) basis. In either case, a greater wealth of information derives from such a multidimensional instrument.

However, many of the studies on communication effects to be reported here have been limited to the single evaluative dimension and hence are properly to be considered experiments on attitude change. The usual procedure in these cases has been to use a number of purely evaluative scales (as determined by factor analyses), sometimes imbedded among scales tapping other factors which merely serve a masking purpose, and to sum over these evaluative scales for an "attitude score." The analysis is then conducted as it would be with any other unidimensional measure. In this section are included studies ranging from the effects of TV coverage of a congressional hearing to the influence of verbal captions upon response to pictures, but all having in common the fact that they deal with the effects of messages in the mass media upon the meanings and attitudes of people receiving them.

Effects of TV Coverage of a Congressional Hearing

In early May, 1954, a subcommittee of the House Committee on Un-American Activities convened in Lansing, Michigan, at a two-day public hearing. According to the subcommittee chairman, ex-Representative Kit Clardy, the hearings were held to "investigate Communist infiltration into local educational and labor institutions." About a dozen witnesses were called, most of whom invoked the fifth amendment at some point during their testimony.

A complete coverage of these hearings was carried by WKAR-TV, the Michigan State University television station, as "a public service." As conceived by the station personnel, the purpose of the telecast was "to present an objective study of this one phase of governmental activity — the proceedings of a congressional investigating sub-committee." Toward this end, two major ingredients were included in the telecast: (a) A straightforward camera-eye's view and microphone-ear's report of the proceedings. This reportorial function was restricted somewhat by the request of several witnesses that no telecast of them be made during their testimony — a right that is guaranteed by the procedural rules of the committee. This restriction applied only to the visual element of the coverage and not to the witnesses' oral testimony. (b) Background and interpretative commentary by two qualified political scientists before and after the hearings and during the periodic recesses. This commentary included discussions of the rights of witnesses, the fifth amendment, functions of congressional investigating committees, and so on, and was designed to provide a framework for following the hearings.

In order to investigate certain assumptions often made in connection with such televised coverage of committee proceedings, a

Table 40

**COMPARISON BETWEEN TV GROUP AND NON-TV GROUP ON TOTAL AMOUNT
OF CHANGE ON SEMANTIC DIFFERENTIAL RATINGS**

Concept	Sum of Ranks TV Group	Non-TV Group	p
KIT CLARDY	1347.5	998.5	.05
CONGRESSIONAL INVESTIGATING COMMITTEES	1277.5	1068.5	.20
COMMUNIST INFILTRATION INTO LOCAL INSTITUTIONS	1214.0	1132.0	.60
FIFTH AMENDMENT	1356.0	990.0	.05
TELEVISING OF COMMITTEE HEARINGS	1369.0	977.0	.02

program of research was conducted in conjunction with the broad-cast (Tannenbaum, 1955). Here we report only on that part of the research which utilized the semantic differential.

Procedure. Prior to the hearings, a panel of 68 persons was estab-lished. Each panel member was told the purpose of the study and was asked to keep a record of his communication exposure to the hearings over the two-day period. Among other things, he also rated five concepts (KIT CLARDY, CONGRESSIONAL INVESTIGATING COMMIT-TEES, COMMUNIST INFILTRATION INTO LOCAL INSTITUTIONS, THE FIFTH AMENDMENT, and TELEVISING OF COMMITTEE HEARINGS — all be-lieved, on a priori grounds, to have relation to the hearings) against ten semantic differential scales. Four scales (*good-bad, valuable-worthless, fair-unfair,* and *pleasant-unpleasant*) were representative of the evaluative factor, three (*weak-strong, heavy-light,* and *large-small*) of the potency factor, and three (*active-passive, fast-slow,* and *calm-agitated*) of the activity factor. During the three days immediately following the hearings, panel members were again contacted and repeated the same ratings.

For purposes of analysis, the panel was divided into two groups according to the kinds of communications exposure experienced: The *TV Group* consisted of subjects who had at least one and one-half hours of exposure to the WKAR-TV telecast, including some exposure to the background commentary (most subjects here had considerably more than this minimum). The *Non-TV Group* was composed of those subjects who had seen little or none of the TV coverage (most subjects here had not seen it at all, while only a few had fleeting glimpses; but all had followed the hearings via the newspaper). There were 34 subjects in each group.

Table 41

CHANGE FROM PRE-TEST TO POST-TEST IN SEMANTIC DIFFERENTIAL JUDGMENTS FOR TV GROUP

(The sign represents the direction of change and the value represents the significance of the change.)

Concept	Change on Evaluation	Potency	Activity
KIT CLARDY	−(.20)	+(.10)	+(.30)
CONGRESSIONAL INVESTIGATING COMMITTEES	−(.20)	−(.20)	+(.50)
COMMUNIST INFILTRATION INTO LOCAL INSTITUTIONS	−(.90)	+(.05)	+(.20)
FIFTH AMENDMENT	−(.05)	−(.10)	+(.30)
TELEVISING OF COMMITTEE HEARINGS	−(.10)	−(.05)	−(.70)

Results. The analysis was directed at two main questions: First, did the TV Group change more in their over-all judgment for each concept than did the Non-TV Group? Second, what was the direction and magnitude of change for each concept on each of the three factors within the TV Group?

To answer the first question, D scores between the pre-test and post-test ratings across the ten scales were computed for each subject in each group, and separately for each concept. Thus, for any one concept, there were 68 D-scores — 34 in each group. The two groups were then compared on each concept by means of the Wilcoxon Unpaired Replicates Test. The results, as summarized in Table 40, show significantly greater (at or beyond the 5 per cent level) changes in meaning for the TV Group on three concepts (CLARDY, FIFTH AMENDMENT, and TELEVISING COMMITTEE HEARINGS). On the other two concepts, the differences are in the same direction (i.e., a greater shift for the TV Group), but are not significant. Testing across all five concepts at once (by means of analysis of variance by ranks) indicates a significant over-all difference.

To answer the second question, separate factor scores were computed on each concept for each subject in the TV Group — an *evaluative* score by summing over the four evaluative scales (possible range of scores, 4-28); a *potency* score over the three potency scales (range, 3-21), and an *activity* score over the three activity scales (range, 3-21). This was done both for the pre-exposure ratings, and for the post-exposure ratings. Table 41 presents both the directions and levels of magnitude of the changes for each concept. The sign (+ or −) represents the direction of change, a plus (+) sign indicating the mean judgment of the post-rating to be more favorable, more powerful, or more active, respectively, than on the pre-ratings, and conversely for the minus (−) sign. The approximate significance level (as determined by a Wilcoxon Paired Replicates Test) of the magnitude of change is indicated by the parenthetically enclosed value associated with each directional index — the lower the value, the more significant the change. Although only three of the changes reached the 5 per cent level of significance, some of the other changes were quite substantial, indicating that the TV coverage was not without its effects.

Some observations of these changes in meaning on each concept may be of interest:

1 KIT CLARDY: The changes on this concept were all quite substantial, although none reaches the 5 per cent level. Clardy was perceived as more powerful than before the hearings, but also less favorable. Some of the changes in evaluation were quite extensive, including complete reversals from originally favorable ratings to equally unfavorable ones. One may speculate whether this was a harbinger of things to follow six months later when Clardy, whose constituency included the television coverage area, was defeated in his bid for re-election.

2 CONGRESSIONAL INVESTIGATING COMMITTEES: Apparently, these particular hearings did not endear those exposed to them to the general notion of congressional investigating committees. This concept was judged less favorable and weaker than prior to the hearings, with no real change on the activity factor. It is possible, however, that these changes were as much a carry-over of other public hearings (particularly the "Army-McCarthy" hearings then still in the public eye) as they were a function of the Lansing hearings, with the latter serving to precipitate already existing predispositions. The design of the present research unfortunately did not include provisions for studying this and related factors systematically.

3 COMMUNIST INFILTRATION: This was the alleged main focus of the hearings, and the greatest single change noted on this concept was its being judged much more potent. One reason no real change was noted in evaluation may be that most of the initial, pre-exposure judgments were so extremely unfavorable that there was no room on the scale for further unfavorable shift.

4 FIFTH AMENDMENT: This concept showed the most change on the average, becoming much more unfavorable, less strong, and somewhat more active. No doubt, these changes were largely a

reflection of the relatively high frequency of application of the fifth amendment during the current hearings. Equally probable, they were also a manifestation of latent dissatisfaction brought to the surface by the TV viewing. If the present hearings are any criterion, then, public exposure to such proceedings can apparently do as much to undermine judgment of the fifth amendment as it can encourage the perception of Communism as a menace.

5 TELEVISING COMMITTEE HEARINGS: When this concept was presented, it was emphasized that the general idea of televising this type of governmental activity, and not the Lansing hearings in particular, was to be judged. If these instructions were followed, the effect of the Lansing coverage was quite detrimental to the general notion. The lackluster nature of these particular hearings may have been a major factor influencing these changes; the television coverage, as such, appeared to be quite adequate.

Summary. From the practical communications point of view, this study has shown that televising a congressional hearing may have significant effects upon the attitudes and meanings of relevant concepts in the public mind. TV viewers were found to be changed more than those who got their information from other channels. The semantic changes engendered in TV viewers were in part those which may have been intended by the committee chairman, Kit Clardy (the concept of COMMUNIST INFILTRATION INTO LOCAL INSTITUTIONS became stronger and more active, and FIFTH AMENDMENT became less favorable and weaker), but in part they were certainly not those intended (KIT CLARDY, although becoming somewhat stronger, became less favorable also, and both CONGRESSIONAL INVESTIGATING COMMITTEES and TELEVISING OF COMMITTEE HEARINGS became less favorable and less potent in connotation). Although the urge to generalize these findings, e.g., to the Army-McCarthy hearings of not so long ago, is inviting, it would be open to serious question.

From the methodological point of view, this study gives some indication of the kind of information that can be obtained from the semantic differential when applied in a situation of this type. The instrument revealed many effects that might otherwise have been completely overlooked in straight polling-type questions or ordinary attitude scales. Indeed, many of the critical changes revealed were not in attitude per se (the evaluative factor) but along other dimensions of meaning — the dimension showing the largest changes over all five concepts was the potency dimension. The greater the dimensionality of judgment sampled, the more likely is the investigator to detect the effects of communications and the more readily interpretable are these effects. It follows, too, that the development of a theory of communication effects will be considerably enhanced by determining the full dimensionality that such effects assume in given situations.

Experimental Studies in Attitude Change

In this area, except for one study which measured attitude change resulting from a bona fide communication message, the main focus has been on investigating the effect of different variables on the direction and amount of attitude change produced by deliberately prepared communication messages. As such, they are very much along the lines of the work of Hovland and his group at Yale (see Hovland, Janis, and Kelley, 1953), differing principally in the measure of attitude employed. We will first report on the study dealing with the straightforward effects analysis, and then proceed to reports of several investigations of a more experimental nature. It might be mentioned in passing that at least two investigations already reported — those of Tannenbaum (1953) and Kerrick (1954) — also may be included within this latter category.

Attitude Change from a Radio Satire. When the program "The Investigator," a biting radio satire on Senator Joseph McCarthy and McCarthyism, was performed by the Canadian Broadcasting Corporation some years back, it aroused considerable comment on both sides of the border. The program was in the form of an allegorical satire in which no specific verbal identification was made of the two main issues — McCarthy and Congressional investigations — but only to the most naïve listener would these not be apparent. Like most such satires, it had its humorous moments, but it also carried a message of some importance.

Berlo and Kumata (1956) had 45 subjects (undergraduates) rate each of eight concepts against nine evaluative semantic differential scales before and after exposure to a recording of "The Investigator." A control group ($N = 37$) did both sets of ratings but was not exposed to the recording. The concepts rated included: SOCRATES, JEFFERSON, MILTON, and MACKENZIE (persons who were "deported" from Heaven by the investigating committee); SENATOR MCCARTHY (the Investigator); CANADIAN BROADCASTING CORPORATION (the source of the message); CONGRESSIONAL INVESTIGATIONS and SECURITY CLEARANCES (two concepts felt to be related to the general tenor of the program). Subjects also answered selected items from the F-scale, but no correlation was noted between F-scores and ratings of any single concept.

After exposure, the experimental group showed only two significant changes in attitude — on the concept CONGRESSIONAL INVESTIGATIONS, which became much less favorable, and on MACKENZIE, who changed in a favorable direction. Near significant changes $(.10 > p > .05)$ were obtained for CBC and SECURITY CLEARANCES, both in a negative direction. No other concepts changed significantly, although there was a substantial shift on MCCARTHY toward a more *favorable* attitude $(p = .10)$. The congruity hypothesis was also applied to these data, using CBC as the source and MCCARTHY and CONGRESSIONAL INVESTIGATIONS as the respective concepts. For the CBC-MCCARTHY combination, the results indicated a "boomerang" effect as hinted at in the attitude change above — CBC became less favorable and MCCARTHY more favorable, instead of the reverse as predicted. For the CBC-CONGRESSIONAL INVESTIGATIONS combination, however, the direction of attitude change was significant and as predicted. To interpret these results, it appears that the subjects felt the satire was unfair to MCCARTHY (already something of an underdog by the time of the experiment), but were affected in the intended way toward CONGRESSIONAL HEARINGS. MACKENZIE — an unknown to most of these subjects — became definitely more favorable by virtue of his association with MILTON, JEFFERSON, *et al.*, and his dissociation from MCCARTHY and inquisitions in general.

"One-sided" vs. "Two-sided" Communication. The comparative effectiveness of one-sided messages (i.e., where the source directly favors one side of a controversial issue) vs. two-sided messages (where the source favors the same side, but also outlines the arguments of the other side) was investigated by Hovland, Lumsdaine, and Sheffield (1949), with the focus on change in opinion toward the issue of the message. A recent study by Wolfinger (1955) measured attitude change toward both the issue (or concept) and the perceived source of the message, as a function of the same presentation variable.

College freshmen rated the concepts FIFTH AMENDMENT and an imaginary GEORGE HASTINGS against a semantic differential form including five evaluative scales. Immediately following this pretest, one group of subjects $(N = 125)$ was exposed to the two-sided version of a tape-recorded speech, by one GEORGE HASTINGS, on the FIFTH AMENDMENT, with this source indicating his favoring of the concept. A second group ($N = 124$) received the one-sided version, which was identical with the two-sided one except that all opposing arguments had been deleted from the tape. A control group ($N = 56$) heard another speech unrelated to the experimental topic. After exposure, all subjects again rated the source and concept.

Both experimental versions produced attitude changes toward both the concept and the source which was significantly greater ($p < .01$ in each case) than the change in the control group. Regarding attitude change toward FIFTH AMENDMENT, subjects originally favorable to the concept were affected more by the two-sided presentation than by the one-sided one; subjects originally unfavorable to the concept were more affected by the one-sided message. These findings are contrary to predictions arising from the Hovland et al. work, but they do not reach satisfactory statistical significance. It may be, also, that differences in intelligence were operating here. With respect to attitude change toward the source (which, being more-or-less hypothetical, was initially judged neutral by almost every subject), the following results were obtained: Subjects originally favoring the position advocated by the source were more favorably affected by the one-sided message than by the two-sided one; the difference here was significant at the .10 level. However, the hypothesis that subjects originally unfavorable to the source's position would become relatively more favorable toward the source as a result of the two-sided message was not upheld by the data, the difference between the two groups being well within chance limits. Considering change in attitude toward both source and concept simultaneously, the one-sided presentation produced significantly more favorable changes than did the two-sided version.

Effects of Message Order and Structure. One experimental study[6] was directed at the problem of the serial order of arguments in an oral message in terms of producing the desired attitude change. Two variables were investigated: one consisted of three orders of argumentation — *climactic* (from weakest to strongest); *anticlimactic* (strongest to weakest); and *pyramidal* (strongest assertion at the middle of the message, weakest at both beginning and end); the other variable referred to the position of the assertion in relation to its supporting evidence — *deductive structure*, where the assertion precedes the evidence, and *inductive structure*, where the assertion follows the evidence. This led to a two-variable, three-by-two factorial design, with six separate groups of experimental

---

[6] Conducted by Dr. H. E. Gulley and Mr. David K. Berlo at the University of Illinois in 1955.

subjects ($N = 29$ in each group). A control group ($N = 27$) was also used.

Each experimental group was exposed to its respective version of a tape recording on the merits of general education courses in the college curriculum, with the various assertions selected from relevant literature. Pre- and post-exposure attitudes toward the concepts GENERAL EDUCATION COURSES and RESEARCH PROFESSOR (the ostensible message source) were obtained. Each experimental group showed a significant shift in attitude toward the proposition when compared with the control group. An analysis of variance between the six groups, however, showed no significant differences for either the orders or argumentation or the deductive vs. inductive structures, nor was the interaction significant. When the data were analyzed in terms of prediction from the congruity model, it was found that approximately 70 per cent of the changes were in the predicted direction — a significantly greater than chance prediction. In terms of magnitude of change, the Pearson product-moment correlations between predicted (via congruity) and obtained results were .63 on the source, and .71 for the concept — both highly significant.

Being essentially unrelated studies, these experiments permit no substantive summary. Methodologically, they further extend the types of research problems to which the semantic differential may be applied;[7] theoretically, they include some additional tests of the congruity principle.

Influence of Verbal Captions on Picture Identification

Another study which can be considered within the general realm of communications research with the semantic differential has been contributed by Kerrick (1955). It was designed to test the effect of different captions on the significance of pictures. It has often been claimed that the meaning of a particular photograph can be entirely altered by ingenious choice of words in the caption accompanying it — the expression on a face can be made to seem calm or irritated, a street scene can be made shabby or neat, a charge may be turned into a retreat, and so on.

---

[7] Walter B. Essman (University of North Dakota) has reported to us a study in which the degree of self-confidence (indexed by self-ratings on a *stable-unstable* scale) was found to be inversely related to the amount of attitude change toward ESP induced by a lecture on that topic. Helen Peak (University of Michigan) is presently using the semantic differential in an investigation of the structure of attitudes.

Kerrick selected five pictures from the Thematic Apperception Test for their somewhat ambiguous qualities. She had different groups of subjects rate each picture (1) without a caption, (2) with a caption loading the meaning in one direction, and (3) with a caption loading the meaning in the opposite direction. The results showed a significant effect of the caption in altering the judgment on the intended scales (e.g., toward *happy* in the case of a picture captioned *At the Station: Reunion,* and toward *sad* when the same picture was captioned *At the Station: Parting*). Moreover, the effect of the caption generalized to other scales *within the same factor,* so that the total interpretation was congruent with that aspect made explicit in the caption. Although, generally, a caption that was quite opposite to the basic pictorial content failed to shift judgment, there were several instances where this caption effect was sufficient to cause a complete reversal in meaning on certain scales. Unfortunately, independent judgments for the captions alone were not obtained, so no check on the possible operation of congruity can be made with these data.

Studies on Advertising Effects

The semantic differential technique has had considerable application to advertising research. Most of the applications to date have been restricted to the use of the evaluative factor, but this is not a necessary limitation. Indeed, it seems likely, on an intuitive basis, that many of the significant changes that result from advertising campaigns would be reflected on semantic dimensions other than the evaluative one. One instance of the use of the semantic differential in this field — on the effects of color on product meanings — has already been reported in some detail (see pp. 299-301). In this section we report on several studies that have been conducted in or through our own research center.[8]

The Comparative Effectiveness of Five Advertising Appeals. Mindak (1955) used eight evaluative scales of the semantic differential to compare the effectiveness of five different types of radio appeals dealing with a new hand lotion that was being readied for marketing. Five one-minute radio commercials were written, emphasizing

---

[8] Applications of the semantic differential to advertising research being made elsewhere include studies by Mary Jane Grunsfeld (Weiss and Geller, Inc., Chicago, Illinois) on brand comparisons, appeal comparisons, blind product testing, etc. Miss Grunsfeld has prepared a "manual" for the use of semantic measurement in advertising.

each of these five appeals: *negative appeal* (emphasis on symptoms of cracked skin, calloused hands, etc.) ; *testimonial appeal* (Marilyn Monroe suggests use of product because of her own personal success with it) ; *scientific appeal* (emphasis on the scientific newness of product, using several pseudo-scientific terms) ; *"romance despite work" appeal* (emphasis on maintaining lovely hands despite their use in household tasks) ; and the *"zany" appeal* (whimsical appeal with considerable use of puns). Each of these five versions was imbedded at the opening and closing of a 15-minute, musical comedy highlight radio program, especially produced for the experiment. These five versions were presented to different groups of subjects (female undergraduates) who rated a number of concepts associated with the content of the commercials (e.g., IDEAL HAND LOTION, MARILYN MONROE, ROMANCE, etc.) against the eight-scale differential, both before and after the program.

The results showed that each of the five appeals produced significant change in attitude toward the product (when tested by Wilcoxon's Paired Replicates Test), but on only one version — the scientific one — was the change in a favorable direction. All other appeals produced unfavorable changes, with the testimonial appeal producing the largest negative change (of course the fact that the subjects were female undergraduates and the testimonial source was Miss Monroe is probably the main reason for this).

Believability of Beer Advertising. In another study reported by Mindak (1955), a selected sample of 100 male beer drinkers rated the slogans used by four different brands of beer, including one being pretested for marketing purposes, and the concepts BEER ADVERTISING and ADVERTISING IN GENERAL on a series of semantic differential-type scales especially constructed to measure the believability of the advertising. Among the findings were the following: (1) The slogans used were generally rated more favorable than the concept BEER ADVERTISING. (2) The slogans for the "new" beer were judged significantly more favorable than the others. (3) BEER ADVERTISING was judged generally more *exaggerated,* more *dishonest,* and more *untrue* than ADVERTISING IN GENERAL. All of these findings, and several specific ones of less importance for our purposes here, were then used in constructing the advertising campaign for the new beer when it was placed on the market.

Effect of Slogans on Attitude Toward Products. Another problem in the advertising field concerns the effects of slogans upon attitudes toward the products they represent — entirely apart from the sheer frequency effect upon recall and association. This problem was investigated in a study[9] which had subjects in an introductory course in advertising first try to recall the product names associated with a number of slogans — e.g., "Man of Distinction" with Calvert's Whiskey. The subjects then rated both the products and the slogans against the same form of the semantic differential which included 12 evaluative scales, mostly selected on the basis of available factor loadings, but also including several that were thought to have direct bearing on advertising. The most significant finding was that while most products were more favorably rated by those subjects who recognized their slogans, for others just the reverse was true. For Calvert's Whiskey, for example, subjects who did *not* associate the slogan "Man of Distinction" with the product gave significantly *more* favorable mean ratings of the product than subjects who did make the association — evidence that for this college population, at least, the slogan was working against acceptance of the product.

Evaluation of the Components of an Ad. In another study,[10] subjects rated the different components (copy, illustration, headline, trade-mark, and signature) of four different and diverse advertisements against nine scales selected (on a subjective basis) to represent three supposed sub-factors of general evaluation — utility, pleasurableness, and morality. However, subsequent factor analysis failed to reveal anything but a single, general evaluative factor. In addition subjects also rated the advertisements as wholes, the products being advertised, and the specific product brands advertised.

Among other things, Richmond found that in each of the four cases, the illustration was judged significantly more favorable than the copy, when each was judged separately. Another interesting result was that the evaluation of the *product itself* — whether presented in terms of the generic product class (e.g., AUTOMOBILES) or in terms of a specific brand of that product (e.g., OLDSMOBILE) — was consistently more favorable than the evaluation of the respective *advertisements* for these products. Richmond also applied the congruity principle to predict the evaluative judgment of the total advertisement from knowledge of the judgment of the several components. Although this situation was admittedly a crude approximation to an ideal one (for purposes of prediction), he found that the predicted results correlated significantly with the obtained ones (when the subjects judged the advertisement per se).

---

[9] Conducted by Dr. W. A. Mindak at the University of Illinois in 1953.
[10] Conducted by Mr. D. Richmond at the University of Illinois in 1953.

Summary. The above examples help point out one of the values of the semantic differential for advertising research. Here the need very often is for some instrument that allows for *comparability,* and the generality of the technique lends itself to such purposes. The same set of scales — whether selected on the basis of the factor analysis or developed for a particular study — can be used to get judgments of different products, different brands of a single product, different ads on a single brand, or even different segments of a single ad. For example, the instrument may be used to determine which of a number of alternate ads, as a unit, best gets across the intended message, and which does best on a certain dimension of judgment, or, if desired, on a certain single scale. Analysis of such data may indicate, for example, that a revamping may be in order wherein a completely new ad would be constructed incorporating the best features of each of the test ads. In much the same manner variations of the components of an ad may be pretested individually and in combination, to determine the best single aggregate.

Another feature of the technique that might be important for advertising research is its ability to get at connotative judgments so difficult to obtain otherwise. For example, the instrument may be used to determine how close the profile of judgment for a particular brand of beer, say, approximates that for the concept IDEAL BEER in comparison with other competing brands. As one pilot study showed, the instrument was able to differentiate between different brands of beer tasted blindly by subjects, according to their smoothness, mellowness, and so on — all richly connotative terms which may be useful in constructing an advertising campaign.

So far, the research has been concentrated on the use of the semantic differential in judging specific brands or products. There is another kind of advertising to which it might be fruitfully applied — so-called *institutional advertising.* A study that has been proposed in this area would deal with the meanings of various *corporate personalities* — e.g., GENERAL MOTORS, SEARS ROEBUCK, U.S. STEEL, etc. As lawyers who represent such corporations know, the subtle connotations of such terms as "bigness," "power," "fairness," and "honesty" associated with these stereotypes can have substantial effects on public relations and even courtroom decisions. The differential may also be applied in this respect to compare judgments of such concepts across different population groups, and to index the effectiveness of advertising designed to alter these stereotypes.

8

It must be evident by now that this book is a progress report and not any final statement. We feel that we have come far enough along to be confident that there is some sort of path here, but just what may be its actual course and destination remains obscured. We believe that we are validly measuring at least certain aspects of a very important variable in human behavior, *meaning*, and that therefore our type of instrument has many valuable applications. But it has also become increasingly clear that our original conceptions were insufficient, that human semantic processes are very complex, and that problems of meaning are inextricably confounded with more general problems of human thinking or cognition. Certainly, when viewed from some future vantage point, our theoretical notions and measuring operations will seem very crude and inadequate — but we have come far enough along to think that we are more or less on the right track. In this final chapter we will try to define where we stand at present (as a kind of summary) and thereby be better able to say where we should go in the future (as a kind of prospectus of contemplated research).

The Semantic Differential as an Index of Meaning States

In Chapter 1 we identified the aspect of meaning in which we were interested as a strictly psychological one: those cognitive states of human language users which are necessary antecedent conditions for selective encoding of lexical signs and necessary subsequent conditions in selective decoding of lexical signs in messages. Within the general framework of learning theory, the meaning of a sign was identified as a representational mediation process — representational by virtue of comprising some portion of the total behavior elicited by the significate and mediating because this process, as a kind of self-stimulation, serves to elicit overt behaviors, both linguistic and non-linguistic, that are appropriate to the things signified. In semantic decoding, stimulus patterns (signs as stimuli) selectively elicit representational processes as reactions; in semantic encoding, vocal, orthographic, gestural, and other response patterns (signs as responses) are selectively elicited by representational processes as stimuli. Thus we have a two-stage, mediational mechanism.

To provide a coherent rationale for our proposed measuring technique, we have tried to show how such a theory of meaning as this could be coordinated with the actual operations of measurement with the semantic differential. To accomplish this it was necessary to assume that the representational mediation process is a complex affair, a compound reaction made up of some n bipolar reaction components. Within each such set of bipolar components we assume reciprocal antagonism — given some support by retroactive interference studies using verbal opposites — which corresponds to the bipolar character of our measurement dimensions; between each such set of components we assume functional independence, which corresponds to the statistical independence of the factors of the semantic space. When the subject decodes a given sign, we assume that a complex mediating reaction occurs, consisting of a pattern of these alternative bipolar reactions elicited with varying intensities; when the subject encodes this semantic state against the differential, we assume that his selection of directions in the semantic space (toward *good* vs. *bad,* toward *active* vs. *passive,* etc.) is coordinate with what reactions are elicited by the sign and that his degree of polarization or extremeness in the space (how far out along the scales he checks) is coordinate with how intensely these reactions are made.

Some readers will consider this rationale to be an unnecessary *tour de force,* quite arbitrary, and certainly not essential to the usefulness of the measuring instrument as such. They are quite correct in this, but there are other considerations. For one thing, the behavior of a subject reacting to the semantic differential is lawful and, somewhere along the line, must be coordinated with behavior theory — which may not be of the sort offered here, of course. For another thing, the authors find it awkward and uncomfortable to have on the one hand a fairly elaborate and rigorous theory of meaning and, on the other, a fairly elaborate and reasonably effective method of measuring it and yet have them proceeding on completely independent paths. Finally, it is possible to generate many hypotheses about sign behavior from learning theory; these can only be tested with measurements on the semantic differential to the extent that this instrument is coordinated with theory.

It therefore follows that one of the most challenging tasks facing us in the future is to make even more explicit this coordination of measurement with theory, and test various implications which can be derived. A few steps in this direction have already been taken: Using a judgmental latency device, we have been able to show that extremeness of judgment against the graphic form of the differential corresponds very closely to intensity of judgment as indexed by latency. Since this apparatus prevents the subject from rationalizing his judgments — or rather provides a record of such time-consuming rationalizations — more work with it should be done. For example, more consistent data on word mixture effects might be obtained in this way. Work by some of our colleagues (e.g., Solley and Messick) has shown that frequencies of input experiences with experimental concepts are reflected faithfully by the differential, which is another step in the coordination of learning theory with measurement. On the planning boards at the time of this writing are perhaps the most direct tests of the implied coordination: first, an experiment to determine if amounts of mediated generalization are predictable from the similarity of signs as measured with the semantic differential, and second, an experiment comparing mediated generalization in compound and coordinate bilinguals, again against predictions from the differential. Many other predictions about the meanings of signs (e.g., about the development of assign meanings, as in Dodge's study) can be derived from learning theory, and these can be tested with the semantic differential.

In What Sense Is the Semantic Differential a Measure of Meaning?

One of the most serious criticisms of this book probably could have been anticipated at the outset: "Although we understand pretty well what you are measuring and appreciate its value," many readers may say, "why do you call it *meaning?* Aren't you really measuring the emotive reaction to words rather than 'meaning' as I have understood the term?" In the first chapter we tried to indicate, at least roughly, that aspect of meaning in which we were interested. And at that time we promised to return to the question after our findings had been presented.

As psychologists we find it necessary to focus on that "state of" or "event in" a sign-using organism that is at once a necessary sub-sequent condition (r_m) in the decoding of signs and a necessary antecedent condition (s_m) in the encoding of signs. Note carefully that we do not say necessary *and sufficient*. Although it may be trivial in one sense to insist that all discriminable events in messages must ultimately be correlated with discriminable events in language users, this must be the case if we are to avoid mysticism in our interpretation of language behavior. When a language user comes out with sequences of linguistic responses which are ordered both as to structural and semantic characteristics, we must assume that there is some ordered, selective system operating within the organism. Ultimately it is the job of the psycholinguist to make a science out of the correlations between message events and states of the organism. In our work on what we have been calling "meaning," we have mapped only a small region of this complex set of correlations, and that rather sketchily.

But is it justifiable to use the term *meaning* for the kinds of correlations between signs and organismic states indexed by the semantic differential? We can best indicate the issue here, perhaps, by setting up two questions that have frequently been put to us. Both involve the distinction between what has variously been called denotative, designative, or referential "meaning" and what has been called connotative, emotive, or metaphorical "meaning."

1 *How can there be interpersonal communication despite connotative disagreement?* Many linguists and philosophers would say (and have, to us) that two people must first agree on the "meaning" of a sign before they can disagree on their diverse emotive and other reactions to it. For example, man A may find THUNDER (object) challenging and exciting while man B finds it extremely frightening, but before they can communicate about this state of affairs they must agree on the *referent* of the linguistic sign "thunder" in their common language. As a matter of fact, our data are replete with cases where individuals differ in their semantic differential profiles for the same sign-vehicles — one of the major uses of the instrument is to measure such differences between people. What, then, is the problem here? If we agree that the "meaning" of "thunder" for A and B must in some sense be the same because they are obviously referring to the same object or event, and if we were to claim that the representational mediation process as we have defined it is a *sufficient* antecedent condition for language encoding, then the semantic differential profiles we derive from A and

B should correspond in some way. A few moments' consideration shows that we can not make this claim: Men A and B will probably experience no more referential confusion on "thunder" (where their profiles disagree on most factors) than they do on "blueberry pie" (where their profiles agree closely, let us say). In other words, we must admit that distances in our semantic space as between individuals judging the same concepts are not indicative of degrees of *referential* agreement — if, indeed, one can speak of "degrees" of such agreement.

How can you have referential agreement despite lack of correspondence in the psychological states we index with the differential? A color-blind person may go through his whole life correctly labeling and referring to most colored objects and yet in a test case (e.g., choosing between particular orange vs. brown ties) show conclusively that he cannot be "seeing things" the way the rest of us do — what looks obviously different to us looks just the same to him! Let us postulate two hypothetical people: F (father) is normal; S (son) is not only red-green blind, but he is also allergic to what are commonly called "apples" — they make him deathly sick. We shall assume that F has an evaluatively favorable "meaning" of "apple": part of the gratifying reaction to APPLES-as-eaten has become associated with the perceptual and linguistic signs of this object. Now, on repeated occasions S is stimulated by APPLE visually (and necessarily has experiences different from F because he is color-blind); he also sees F point to this rounded patch of stimulation and say "apple" and point to this and other similar patches and say "red." Given human learning capacity and language facility, S rapidly learns to say "apple" to recurrent appearances of this object and to say "red" to radiant patches similar to the ones F calls "red" — even though, we must agree, the internal states of F and S cannot be identical. But even beyond this, F encourages S to bite into the APPLE object, saying it is "tasty" and "good" — to S it tastes horrible and makes him sick.

On the basis of a number of such experiences, and following the behavioral principles governing the formation of representational mediation processes discussed in Chapter 1, S must develop a "meaning" (in our sense) of "apple" which is quite different from that of F — and he would check it quite differently on many of the scales of the semantic differential as well as displaying different behavior in response to the object. Here, we have two users of the same language, F and S, who, despite their manifest differences in mediation processes, will point to the same things and say to each other, "Oh, I know what you mean," when they employ the noises "apple" and "red." Similarly, returning to our original example, it is clear that men A and B may agree on what "thunder" refers to *even though* the distinctive representational states in each may differ.

We may summarize our argument on Question 1 as follows: Agreement on the referents of signs implies nothing whatsoever about similarity of the representational states associated with these signs, but rather that these states have entered into the same sets of relations between situations and verbal responses. It therefore follows that agreement on the reference of signs despite lack of profile correspondence on the semantic differential is not evidence for insufficiency of the instrument as a psychological measuring device.

2 *How can there be discriminative encoding despite connotative indiscriminability?* This problem becomes apparent when one considers the lack of perfect reversibility of our measurement operations with the semantic differential. Given only the profile produced by a subject in judging a particular concept, or the point in the space specified by this profile, we are unable to work the system backwards and identify that concept. The force of the argument really is this: Many denotatively distinct concepts may occupy essentially the same region of our semantic space, i.e., may have highly similar profiles — "hero" and "success" and "nurse" and "sincere" would be examples. If the state of the speaker which the semantic differential presumably indexes were a *sufficient* condition for selective encoding, how could we account for discriminative selection of "nurse" rather than "sincere," of "hero" rather than "success," when the states in each case are essentially the same?

One possible answer to this problem would be to take the position that the factors or dimensions of the semantic space we have isolated so far are insufficient. Increase the number of factors, this argument goes, and any two concepts would have to be distinguished on at least one dimension. Although we admit the insufficiency of present factors even for our purposes, this solution seems to envisage an almost infinite proliferation of dimensions and becomes practically infeasible. Furthermore, it takes it for granted that variations among representational processes must be a sufficient condition for selective encoding.

A better answer, we think, takes off from the assumption that the representational state indexed by the semantic differential is not the only determinant operating in lexical encoding. It is a necessary but not a sufficient condition. In the simplest cases, this is obvious: given essentially the same semantic process, the speaker will encode "eats" in one linguistic context and "eat" in another, depending on whether the subject of the sentence is singular or plural. Here we have selection among two word alternatives on the basis of something other than semantic factors. Going a step further, it has been shown in word association experiments that the form class of the stimulus word markedly influences the form class of the response word from the subject, e.g., given MAN he'll say "woman" but given MEN he'll say "women," given COME he'll say "go" but given CAME he'll say "went." Again, we assume that the "meaning" (in the sense of our measurements) of the stimulus terms stays constant. Coming now to the examples given above, it seems likely that, even with near identical representational states of the sort we hypothesize and try to measure, a speaker will encode "hero" in the context, "The villain was vanquished by the . . . ," rather than "success"; conversely he will encode "success" in the context, "He is always striving for . . . ," rather than "hero."

In other words, we believe that *habits of usage and association* serve to refine the relatively gross differentiations of which the representational system is capable. Although lexical items *a, b, c,* and *d* may be associated with the same representational process, *X,* indiscriminately, context 1 plus *X* selects *a,* context 2 plus *X* selects *b,* and so forth. To summarize our argument on Question 2, then: Self-stimulation from the representational system $(r_m \dashrightarrow s_m)$, as indexed by the semantic differential, provides a necessary but not sufficient condition for encoding lexical items; cues from both the linguistic and the situational context combine with those from the representational system to select more discriminatively among alternative responses. By way of analogy, there are some classic experiments in the psychology of the emotions in which the subject is given an injection of adrenalin in a completely neutral, non-arousing situation; the subject typically reports experiencing a vague, stirred-up feeling, a sort of objectless, nameless emotion, as if "something were about to happen." If we could get inside the speaker somehow and produce a particular $r_m \dashrightarrow s_m$ without any context, it is possible that he too would experience a kind of "reference-less," "denotation-less" meaning, referable to some

region of the semantic space but non-specific as to designation —
"something bad, strong, and active, but *what* I do not know."

In what sense, then, are we measuring meaning with the semantic
differential? It is certain that we are not providing an index of
what signs refer to, and if reference or designation is the *sine qua
non* of meaning, as some readers will insist, then they will conclude
that this book is badly mistitled. On the other hand, language users
do develop representation processes in association with signs and
these processes are intimately concerned with their behavior. The
psychologist quite naturally focuses his attention on processes that
are relevant to the prediction and interpretation of differential behaviors, and, as we have tried to demonstrate, agreement in the
reference of signs carries no necessary implication of relatedness of
representational states. As we also tried to show, however, the representational states indexed by the semantic differential are not the
only determinants operating in language production; linguistic and
situational variables also contribute to selective encoding. Perhaps
we should admit that the word "meaning" is used in several senses;
whether or not it is *meaning* that we are measuring, then, would
seem to be merely a matter of choice of terms.

The Dimensionality of the Semantic Space

We began our research on the measurement of meaning with the
simplest — and most naïve — conceptual model. We hoped that
most of the variance in human semantic judgments could be explained in terms of a relatively small number of orthogonal factors,
these factors being completely general over both subjects and concepts and always represented by the same set of scales — i.e., we
wanted to set up a perfectly general and simple measuring instrument. What is perhaps surprising is how close to the truth this
naïve model actually seems to be. The same three major factors
of *evaluation, potency,* and *activity* (which were empirically rather
than theoretically derived) have reappeared in a wide variety of
judgmental situations, particularly where the sampling of concepts
has been broad. The relative weights of these factors have been
fairly consistent: evaluation accounting for approximately double
the amount of variance due to either potency or activity, these two
in turn being approximately double the weight of any subsequent
factors. But since a large portion of the total variance remains unaccounted for, we assume that there must be other factors operating;

since their individual contributions to the total variance are small, we assume their number must be large — i.e., a large number of relatively specific semantic factors.

Just how general are the factors isolated so far? When we sample across sets of subjects with the concepts judged held constant, a very high degree of consistency in factor structure is revealed — essentially the same factors appearing in the judgments of such diverse groups as normals vs. schizophrenics or Americans vs. Japanese or Koreans. When we sample across sets of concepts, however, it becomes evident that the scales of judgment and the concepts being judged interact, this interaction influencing the relative weights and even appearance of identifiable factors and certainly determining what specific scales contribute to factors. Despite variation in scale composition, the factors which can be identified over most (though not all) concepts judged are *evaluation, potency, stability,* and *receptivity* (or *sensory adiency*); the *activity* factor, at least in the blind rotations of individual concept matrices we have used so far, seems to vary in alignment with other dimensions.

How are we to account for this instability of individual scales in relation to each other? There seems to be a general principle operating here: all scales of judgment, to the extent that they have correlation with the dominant attribute for a particular concept, tend to rotate toward this dominant attribute. It also seems that the greater the emotionality involved in the concept, the greater this rotational tendency, leading to a tight, single factor of judgment in some extreme cases. The scales representing the evaluative factor appear to be most susceptible to this rotational effect, i.e., what is "good," scale-wise, depends heavily upon the concept being judged. These explanations stand pretty much as hunches at present; there is much that we can do, both with our available data on single-concept correlational matrices and by means of more experimental procedures, to test the validity of these hunches. It should also be remarked that this is but one of the many points where our work on experimental semantics leads us into basic problems about the nature of human thought and judgment.

What do these findings have to say about the practical problems of semantic measurement? For one thing, it now seems less likely that we will be able to discover a single set of scales which represent an adequate set of factors and which are stable across whatever concepts may be judged. On the other hand, it may be possible to identify classes of concepts for which general instruments may be used, and perhaps, in course, the principles which operate in determining a common semantic frame of reference can be discovered. Here the work of Suci on determining the characteristic attributes of concept sets seems promising. Also on the agenda is further research directed at the isolation of additional factors; but rather than further general factorial studies with random samples of scales, it now seems better to deliberately put together sets of scales to represent potential factors and test them within a matrix of scales representing known factors; i.e., the new scales, or at least some of them, must maintain high correlations with each other and insignificant correlations with scales representing other factors. We have sufficient materials from the Thesaurus Study to begin this work.

Construction and Evaluation of Semantic Differentials

Among the "constants" in our work have been the use of *seven-step scale*s having a *bipolar* (verbal opposites) form and defined by *adjectives*. Is this type of instrument necessarily the "natural" grid against which to differentiate the meanings of concepts? We have fairly satisfying evidence that our seven-step scales, defined by the linguistic quantifiers "extremely," "quite," and "slightly," in both directions from a neutral "meaningless" origin, do yield nearly equal psychological units in the process of judgment, and we intend to assemble additional evidence on this point. But what about the use of bipolar scales defined by verbal opposites? We have been following a more or less implicit assumption that thinking in terms of opposites *is* "natural" to the human species; data presently being collected on Indians in the Southwest seem to support this assumption, and the ethnolinguists we have talked to — after due consideration and checking with their own experiences — usually agree that semantic opposition is common to most, if not all, language systems. However, it still might be true that unidirectional scales would serve as well as those we now use. One of the difficult methodological problems we have faced — unsuccessfully so far — is to demonstrate that the polar terms we now use are true psychological opposites, i.e., fall at equal distances from the origin of the semantic space and in opposite directions along a single straight line passing through the origin. The use of unidirectional scales might eliminate this problem, but it would probably involve us in another: if there is a "natural" human tendency to think in terms of opposites, the so-called neutral point at one extreme of unidirectional scales would probably tend to take on the semantic properties of opposition.

And why the use of adjectives? We assume that it is the lexical (root) meanings of our polar terms that determine judgments; adjectives are merely the most general and natural qualifiers *in English*. We think that scales could be made up with polar terms defined by nouns (*good* vs. *evil*, *strength* vs. *weakness*, etc.) or verbs (*loving* vs. *hating*, *going* vs. *stopping*, etc.) and yield the same dimensionality, but this remains to be demonstrated.

Much of our energy to date has been spent on evaluation of the instrument. Evaluation and refinement of the measuring technique seems to be more our job than application. We have amassed a considerable amount of data on reliability. The evidence shows that for individual subjects a shift of more than two scale units probably represents a significant change or difference in meaning, and a shift of more than 1.00 to 1.50 scale units in factor score (depending on the particular factor) is probably significant. For group data ("cultural meanings"), changes or differences in measured meaning as small as one-half of a scale unit are significant at the 5 per cent level. These levels of reliability should be satisfactory for most applications of the instrument. Regarding validity, there seems to be little question about the general face validity of the differential, because it obviously differentiates among and clusters concepts much the way most of us do spontaneously. There are at least two validity issues on which we need more evidence. One of these concerns the use of the method of triads (where the subject determines his own dimensions of judgment) as a way of validating the dimensions arrived at through factor analysis: Does the semantic differential force the subject to use unnatural bases of judgment? The data we have show considerable correspondence, but more research of this type is needed. However, this method can probably only validate the major factors, i.e., the differential probably does force the subject to attend to some dimensions he would not use otherwise in addition to those used spontaneously. The second issue concerns behavioral validity: Does the semantic differential accurately predict meaningful behaviors in test situations? We have meager amounts of data here — on the prediction of voting behavior in the 1952 election and on certain phenomena of problem-solving — and again more evidence of this sort is needed.

The Congruity Principle

This is another instance where our work with experimental semantics has led us into problems of human thinking. The congruity principle deals with the interaction of cognitive events that occur more or less simultaneously. It states, in effect, that along each semantic dimension these events modify each other in proportion to their relative intensities, yielding changes in meaning or resolutions into new combined meanings that are predictable from the congruity formulae. There is no necessary dependence of this principle upon the semantic differential as a kind of measurement operation (witness the work of Leon Festinger with a very similar notion but very different measures), but to the extent that the differential provides an index of cognitive events, it provides a "natural" means of testing the principle. Thus, we have tested predictions about attitude change, about the effects of colors upon the meanings of advertised products and sculptured abstractions, about the development of assign meanings from association with signs, and about the semantic effects of combining adjectives and nouns into nominal phrases — all against measurements obtained with the semantic differential. The range of prediction situations covered testifies to the potential range of such a principle of human thinking. But it is very clear that congruity does not operate in a vacuum. We have evidence that its operation is conditioned by such variables as the relevance of the two or more concepts to each other, the intensity of the assertions made, and the psychological comparability of the concepts. These and other parameters affecting the operation of congruity in human thinking need to be further studied.

Applications of Semantic Measurement

A fairly representative sample of applications of semantic measurement has been reported in this book. It includes attitude assessment, the study of personality traits and dynamisms, measurement of the course of psychotherapy, studies in psycholinguistics, in aesthetics, in advertising, and in other mass communications. There is nothing surprising or remarkable about this. Meaning is one of the most significant pivotal variables in human behavior, and even a crude and very provisional measure of it, such as the semantic differential now is, readily finds uses. As a matter of fact, we are now more concerned that its applications — and claims for it —

will outstrip development and evaluation of the basic methodology, and this is one reason why our own staff has been concentrating more on these methodological matters.

There are, of course, many applications we intend to make ourselves. In the area of personality and psychotherapy, for example, we think that with sufficient trial and effort it should be possible to develop a semantic tool for use in psychotherapy that would sensitively and accurately gauge the course of treatment and differences between treatments. Also, our factor analysis of the single concept, MYSELF, revealed a number of dimensions of self-evaluation which could lead to a useful personality test. In the social area, the generalized character of our attitude index makes feasible the development of a standardized "social attitude index" which could be very useful to sociologists, political scientists, and the like. The field of experimental aesthetics begs for quantitative studies with an instrument like the differential — extension of factor analysis to other aesthetic modes than painting, color-music synesthesia, and color TV (which are closely related problems), development of tests of aesthetic appreciation and communication, to name only a few — but a great deal of preliminary digging around needs to be done first.

In psycholinguistics, the semantic differential finds its place in the tool bin quite naturally, for it is at base a psycholinguistic instrument. We think that our work on word mixture (which could be extended to larger units than the adjective-noun phrase) will lead to a method of identifying lexical units (e.g., the combination HOT DOG is functionally a new lexical unit because its meaning is not predictable from the meanings of the components HOT and DOG). The differential seems to open new ways of studying onomatopoeia, both within and across cultures. And the study of the cross-cultural generality of semantic factors, which is already under way, certainly deserves extension because of its potential contribution to international communication and understanding. One can also envisage the gradual construction of "a functional dictionary of connotative meanings" — a quantized Thesaurus — in which the writer would find nouns, adjectives, verbs, and adverbs (all lexical items) listed according to their locations in the semantic space, as determined from the judgments of representative samples of the population; wishing to find an adjective which would be like WARRIOR in meaning (21134XXX), but derogatory, he might search under the listing 71134XXX and find words like *vicious, savage,* and *barbaric.* A variety of potential uses of semantic measurement in advertising and other mass communications has been suggested in the last chapter.

But many of these applications must wait upon further refinement of the measuring instrument. It would, for example, be foolish to begin collecting data for a functional dictionary of connotative meanings when the factor structure remains unclear and obviously insufficient, and the nature of the concept-scale interaction is still obscure. Therefore we shall continue to concentrate on further development, evaluation, and refinement of the measuring technique itself. In this work, and in further extending the range of application, we welcome the help and advice of students and colleagues both at Illinois and at other institutions.

THE D-METHOD OF FACTORING

This technique of factoring is essentially equivalent to Thurstone's diagonal method (1947). The diagonal method begins with correlation coefficients; this technique begins with raw scores. The proof that the two methods are equivalent under certain conditions will be omitted.

The D-method has been applied to matrices of correlation as well as to matrices of raw scores. Such application requires that the correlation matrix be filled out on both sides of the main diagonal and that the correlation coefficients then be used as if they were raw scores. Empirically, factoring matrices of correlation coefficients as if they were matrices of raw scores by the D-method yields factors which are highly similar to the factors given by more conventional methods, e.g., the centroid method.

Below we give the D-method, first in terms of the distances, D; then in terms of sums of cross-products and squares of the original scores; and finally in terms of an example wherein each step in factoring a small matrix of scores is given.

We begin with the score matrix:

concepts

$$1 \ldots f \ldots g \ldots h \ldots i \ldots m$$

$$
\begin{array}{c|cccccc}
1 & X_{11} \ldots & X_{1f} \ldots & X_{1g} \ldots & X_{1h} \ldots & X_{1i} \ldots & X_{1m} \\
\text{scales} \quad j & X_{j1} \ldots & X_{jf} \ldots & X_{jg} \ldots & X_{jh} \ldots & X_{ji} \ldots & X_{jm} \\
k & X_{k1} \ldots & X_{kf} \ldots & X_{kg} \ldots & X_{kh} \ldots & X_{ki} \ldots & X_{km}
\end{array}
$$

The elements of the matrix are semantic differential ratings by an individual, or the mean ratings by a group of individuals, scored in the system $-3, -2, -1, 0, 1, 2, 3$. (Of course, the same technique may be applied to other data whose range is not $+3$ to -3. This is done in the example below.) The assumption is made that the matrix defines a space of k dimensions such that each concept i has coordinates $(X_{1i} \ldots X_{ji} \ldots X_{ki})$ on the k dimensions.

The goal is to find the coordinates on a new set of k' dimensions where $k' < k$.

For k-dimensional space the following definitions are made (all summations are over j, where $j = 1, 2, \ldots, k$):

$D_{oi}^2 = \sum X_{ji}^2$; the squared distance between concept i and the origin o; (1)

$D_{hi}^2 = \sum (X_{jh} - X_{ji})^2$; the squared distance between any two concepts h and i; (2)

θ_{hi}; the angle between two vectors where one vector extends from o to h and another from o to i. (3)

In k-dimensional space:

$$D_{hi}^2 = D_{oh}^2 + D_{oi}^2 - 2D_{oh}D_{oi} \cos \theta_{hi}; \qquad (4)$$

therefore,

$$D_{oi} \cos \theta_{hi} = \frac{D_{hi}^2 - D_{oh}^2 - D_{oi}^2}{-2D_{oh}} = c_{Ii}. \qquad (5)$$

This is the coordinate of concept i on a dimension passing through h. The dimensions are symbolized by I, II, III, $\ldots$, and the coordinate of i on the first dimension is symbolized as c_{Ii}.

To find the coordinates on a second dimension, II, orthogonal to I, the distances in k-space must be reduced to their $k-1$ values by subtracting from the D^2 values their squared components on I. The reduced distances $(D')^2$ may be substituted in equation (5) to find c_{IIi}. The components of the D_{oi} are c_{Ii}, and the components of the D_{hi} are $(c_{Ih} - c_{Ii})$.

Selecting a concept g through which II is to pass in $k-1$ space:

$$c_{IIi} = \frac{(D_{gi}')^2 - (D_{og}')^2 - (D_{oi}')^2}{-2D_{og}'}, \text{ where} \qquad (6)$$

$$(D_{gi}')^2 = D_{gi}^2 - (c_{Ig} - c_{Ii})^2, \qquad (7)$$

$$(D_{oi}')^2 = D_{oi}^2 - c_{Ii}^2, \text{ and} \qquad (8)$$

$$(D_{og}')^2 = D_{og}^2 - c_{Ig}^2. \qquad (9)$$

To find a third dimension, orthogonal to I and II, select a concept f through which III will pass in $k-2$ space. Find the distances D'' in $k-2$ space by subtracting their components on I and II, and substitute in (5) to find the coordinates on the third dimension:

$$c_{IIIi} = \frac{(D_{fi}'')^2 - (D_{of}'')^2 - (D_{oi}'')^2}{-2D_{of}''} \qquad (10)$$

where

$$(D_{fi}'')^2 = D_{fi}^2 - (c_{If} - c_{Ii})^2 - (c_{IIf} - c_{IIi})^2, \qquad (11)$$

$$(D_{oi}'')^2 = D_{oi}^2 - c_{Ii}^2 - c_{IIi}^2, \text{ and} \qquad (12)$$

$$(D_{of}'')^2 = D_{of}^2 - c_{If}^2 - c_{IIf}^2. \tag{13}$$

This process is continued until the coordinates are reduced to zero or to a negligible amount.

In practice it is more convenient to work with sums of cross-products and squares than with distances. By substitution of the equivalences given in (1) and (2) into equation (5), and by reducing, we find:

$$c_{Ii} = \frac{\sum X_{jh} X_{ji}}{\sqrt{\sum X_{jh}^2}} . \tag{14}$$

Similarly, we find c_{III} by substituting into (6) and reducing to:

$$c_{IIi} = \frac{\sum X_{jg} X_{ji} - c_{Ig} c_{Ii}}{\sqrt{\sum X_{jg}^2 - c_{Ig}^2}} . \tag{15}$$

For a third dimension, substitution is made into (10), and reducing, we find:

$$c_{IIIi} = \frac{\sum X_{jf} X_{ji} - c_{If} c_{Ii} - c_{IIf} c_{IIi}}{\sqrt{\sum X_{jf}^2 - c_{If}^2 - c_{IIf}^2}} . \tag{16}$$

This process is continued until coordinates are zero or a negligible amount.

An example is given below showing each step in finding the coordinates of five concepts on three dimensions, I, II, and III. It should be noted that the selection of concepts h, g, and f through which dimensions I, II, and III, respectively, pass, is based on the magnitude of the sum of squares at each step. The highest sum of squares determines which concept is chosen.

		concepts				
		1	2	3	4	5
	1	−3.0	0.0	4.5	0.0	3.0
	2	−1.0	1.0	1.5	2.0	0.5
	3	2.0	2.0	−3.0	4.0	2.0
scales	4	1.0	2.5	−1.5	5.0	−0.5
	5	4.0	1.5	−6.0	3.0	1.0
	6	−2.0	0.5	3.0	1.0	−1.0

$\sum X_{ji}^2$	35.00	13.75	78.75	55.00	15.50	$\sqrt{78.75} = 8.874$
$\sum X_{j3}X_{ji}$	−52.50	−15.75	78.75	−31.50	0.00	
Applying equation (14), $c_{Ii} =$	−5.92	−1.77	8.87	−3.55	0.00	
$\sum X_{ji}^2 - c_{Ii}^2$	−.05	10.62	.07	42.40	15.50	$\sqrt{42.40} = 6.512$
$\sum X_{j4}X_{ji}$	21.00	27.50	−31.50	55.00	8.50	
$c_{I4}c_{Ii}$	21.02	6.28	−31.49	12.60	0.00	
$\sum X_{i4}X_{ji} - c_{I4}c_{Ii}$	−.02	21.22	.01	42.40	8.50	
Applying equation (15), $c_{IIi} =$	0.00	3.26	0.00	6.51	1.31	
$\sum X_{ji}^2 - c_{Ii}^2 - c_{IIi}^2$	−.05	−.01	.07	.02	13.78	$\sqrt{13.78} = 3.712$
$\sum_{j5}X_{ji}$	0.00	4.25	0.00	8.50	15.50	
$c_{I5}c_{Ii}$	0.00	0.00	0.00	0.00	0.00	
$c_{II5}c_{IIi}$	0.00	4.27	0.00	8.53	1.72	
$\sum X_{j5}X_{ji} - c_{I5}c_{Ii} - c_{II5}c_{IIi}$	0.00	−.02	0.00	−.03	13.78	
Applying equation (16), $c_{IIIi} =$	0.00	0.00	0.00	0.00	3.71	

REFERENCES

ADORNO, T. W., ELSE FRENKEL-BRUNSWICK, *et al.* (1950). *The authoritarian personality.* New York: Harpers.

ALLPORT, G. W. (1937). *Personality: a psychological interpretation.* New York: Holt.

————, AND H. S. ODBERT. (1936). Trait-names: a psycho-lexical study. *Psychol. Monog.,* No. 211.

BARTLETT, F. C. (1932). *Remembering.* Cambridge, England: Cambridge University Press.

BERLO, D. K., AND H. KUMATA. (1956). The investigator: the impact of a satirical radio drama. *Journ. Quart., 33,* 287-98.

BINGHAM, W. E. (1943). A study of the relations which the galvanic skin response and sensory reference bear to judgments of the meaningfulness, significance, and importance of 72 words. *J. Psychol., 16,* 21-34.

BLOCH, B., AND G. L. TRAGER. (1942). *Outline of linguistic analysis.* Baltimore: Linguistic Society of America.

BLOOMFIELD, L. (1933). *Language.* New York: Holt.

BOPP, JOAN. (1955). A quantitative semantic analysis of word association in schizophrenia. Unpublished doctor's dissertation, University of Illinois.

BOUSFIELD, W. A. (1944). An empirical study of the production of affectively toned items. *J. gen. Psychol., 30,* 205-15.

————. (1950). The relationship between mood and the production of affectively toned associates. *J. gen. Psychol., 42,* 67-85.

BRUNER, J. S., AND C. C. GOODMAN. (1947). Value and need as organizing factors in perception. *J. abnorm. soc. Psychol., 42,* 33-44.

BURT, C. (1948). The factorial study of temperamental traits. *Brit. J. Psychol. Statist. Sect., 1,* 178-203.

CAMPBELL, D. T. (1953). Generalized attitude scales. In O. K. Buros (ed.), *The fourth mental measurements yearbook.* Highland Park, N. J.: Gryphen Press, pp. 90-91.

CANTRIL, H. (1946). The intensity of an attitude. *J. abnorm. soc. Psychol., 41,* 129-36.

CARMICHAEL, L., H. P. HOGAN, AND A. A. WALTER. (1932). An experimental study of the effect of language on the reproduction of visual perceived form. *J. exp. Psychol., 15,* 73-86.

CATTELL, R. B. (1946). *Description and measurement of personality*. New York: World Books.

———. (1950). *Personality: a systematic theoretical and factual study*. New York: McGraw-Hill.

CLARK, E. K. (1953). Generalized attitude scales. In O. K. Buros (ed.), *The fourth mental measurements yearbook*. Highland Park, N. J.: Gryphen Press, pp. 91-92.

COFER, C. N., AND J. P. FOLEY. (1942). Mediated generalization and the interpretation of verbal behavior. I. Prolegomena. *Psychol. Rev.*, *49*, 513-40.

———, M. G. JANIS, AND M. M. ROWELL. (1943). Mediated generalization and the interpretation of verbal behavior. III. Experiments. *J. exp. Psychol.*, *32*, 266-69.

CRONBACH, L. J., AND GOLDINE C. GLESER. (1953). Assessing similarity between profiles. *Psychol. Bull.*, *50*, 456-73.

DIEDRICH, G. W., S. J. MESSICK, AND L. R. TUCKER. (1955). *A general least squares solution for successive intervals*. Princeton: Educational Testing Service. (Mimeographed.)

DODGE, JOAN S. (1955). A quantitative investigation of the relation between meaning development and context. Unpublished doctor's dissertation, University of Illinois.

DOLLARD, J., AND N. E. MILLER. (1950). *Personality and psychotherapy*. New York: McGraw-Hill.

DOOB, L. W. (1947). The behavior of attitudes. *Psychol. Rev.*, *54*, 135-56.

DORCUS, R. M. (1932). Habitual word associations to colors as a possible factor in advertising. *J. appl. Psychol.*, *16*, 277-87.

DUNLAP, J. W., AND A. KROLL. (1939). Observations on the methodology of attitude scales. *J. soc. Psychol.*, *10*, 475-87.

FINFGELD, T. E. (1953). An experimental study of the ability to select words to convey intended meaning. Unpublished doctor's dissertation, University of Illinois.

FISHER, R. A. (1941). *Statistical methods for research workers*. Edinburgh: Oliver and Boyd.

FOLEY, J. P., AND Z. L. MACMILLAN. (1943). Mediated generalization and the interpretation of verbal behavior: V. "Free association" as related to differences in professional training. *J. exp. Psychol.*, *33*, 299-310.

GLAZE, J. A. (1928). The association value of nonsense syllables. *J. genet. Psychol.*, *35*, 255-69.

GULLIKSEN, H. (1954). A least squares solution for successive intervals assuming unequal standard deviations. *Psychometrika*, *19*, 117-39.

HAAGEN, C. H. (1949). Synonymity, vividness, familiarity, and association value ratings of 400 pairs of common adjectives. *J. Psychol.*, *27*, 453-63.

HARRIS, Z. S. (1951). *Methods in structural linguistics*. Chicago: University of Chicago Press.

HEIDER, F. (1946). Attitudes and cognitive organization. *J. Psychol.*, *21*, 107-12.

HEVNER, KATE. (1936). Experimental studies of the elements of expression in music. *Amer. J. Psychol.*, *48*, 246-68.

HOVLAND, C. I., I. JANIS, AND H. H. KELLEY. (1953). *Communications and persuasion.* New Haven: Yale University Press.

——, A. A. LUMSDAINE, AND F. D. SHEFFIELD. (1949). *Experiments in mass communication.* Princeton: Princeton University Press.

HOWES, D., AND C. E. OSGOOD. (1954). On the combination of associative probabilities in linguistic contexts. *Amer. J. Psychol., 67,* 241-58.

HULL, C. L. (1933). The meaningfulness of 320 selected nonsense syllables. *Amer. J. Psychol., 45,* 730-34.

JACOBSON, E. (1932). Electrophysiology of mental activities. *Amer. J. Psychol., 44,* 677-94.

JOHNSON, W. (1946). *People in quandaries.* New York: Harpers.

JOOS, M. (1950). Description of language design. *J. acoust. Soc. Amer., 22,* 701-8.

KARWOSKI, T. F., F. W. GRAMLICH, AND P. ARNOTT. (1944). Psychological studies in semantics: I. Free association reactions to words, drawings, and objects. *J. soc. Psychol., 20,* 233-47.

——, AND H. S. ODBERT. (1938). Color-music. *Psychol. Monogr., 50,* No. 2 (Whole No. 222).

——, H. S. ODBERT, AND C. E. OSGOOD. (1942). Studies in synesthetic thinking: II. The roles of form in visual responses to music. *J. gen. Psychol., 26,* 199-222.

KATZ, D. (1944). The measurement of intensity. In H. Cantril (ed.), *Gauging public opinion.* Princeton: Princeton University Press, pp. 51-65.

KELLY, G. A. (1955). *The psychology of personal constructs.* New York: Norton.

KENT, GRACE H., AND A. J. ROSANOFF. (1910). A study of association in insanity. *Amer. J. Insanity, 67,* 37-96; 317-90.

KERRICK, JEAN S. (1954). The effects of intelligence and manifest anxiety on attitude change through communications. Unpublished doctor's dissertation, University of Illinois.

——. (1955). The influence of captions in picture interpretation. *Journ. Quart., 32,* 177-82.

KOFFKA, K. (1935). *Principles of gestalt psychology.* New York: Harcourt Brace.

KRECH, D., AND R. S. CRUTCHFIELD. (1948). *Theory and problems in social psychology.* New York: McGraw-Hill.

KUMATA, H., AND W. SCHRAMM. (1956). A pilot study of cross-cultural meaning. *Publ. Opin. Quart.,* in press.

LAZOWICK, L. M. (1955). On the nature of identification. *J. abnorm. soc. Psychol., 51,* 175-83.

MASON, M. (1941). Changes in the galvanic skin response accompanying reports of changes in meaning during oral repetition. *J. gen. Psychol., 25,* 353-401.

MAX, L. W. (1935). An experimental study of the motor theory of consciousness. III. Action-current responses in deaf-mutes during sleep, sensory stimulation, and dreams. *J. comp. Psychol., 19,* 469-86.

——. (1937). An experimental study of the motor theory of consciousness. IV. Action-current responses in the deaf during awakening, kinaesthetic imagery, and abstract thinking. *J. comp. Psychol.*, *24*, 301-44.

McClelland, D. C., and J. W. Atkinson. (1948). The projective expression of needs: I. The effect of different intensities of the hunger drive on perception. *J. Psychol.*, *25*, 205-22.

McNemar, Q. (1946). Opinion-attitude methodology. *Psychol. Bull.*, *43*, 289-374.

McQuitty, L. L. (1956). Agreement analysis: a method of classifying subjects according to their patterns of responses. *Brit. J. Psychol.*, in press.

Miller, N. E., and J. Dollard. (1941). *Social learning and imitation.* New Haven: Yale University Press.

Mindak, W. A. (1955). Measuring advertising effectiveness from a communications point of view. Unpublished doctor's dissertation, University of Illinois.

Morris, C. W. (1946). *Signs, language, and behavior.* New York: Prentice-Hall.

Mosier, C. I. (1941). A psychometric study of meaning. *J. soc. Psychol.*, *13*, 123-40.

Moss, C. S. (1953). An experimental investigation of symbolic dream processes. Unpublished doctor's dissertation, University of Illinois.

Mowrer, O. H. (1953). *Psychotherapy: theory and research.* New York: Ronald Press.

Neuhaus, J. O., and C. F. Wrigley. (1954). The quartimax method, an analytic approach to orthogonal simple structure. *Brit. J. Statist. Psychol.*, *7*, 81-91.

Newcomb, T. M. (1941). Attitude scales. In O. K. Buros (ed.), *The 1940 mental measurements yearbook.* Highland Park, N. J.: Gryphen Press, pp. 58-59.

———. (1953). An approach to the study of communicative acts. *Psychol. Rev.*, *60*, 393-404.

Noble, C. E. (1952). An analysis of meaning. *Psychol. Rev.*, *59*, 421-30.

Odbert, H. S., T. F. Karwoski, and A. B. Eckerson. (1942). Studies in synesthetic thinking: I. Musical and verbal associations of color and mood. *J. gen. Psychol.*, *26*, 153-73.

Ogden, C. K., and I. A. Richards. (1923). *The meaning of meaning.* New York: Harcourt, Brace.

Osgood, C. E. (1941). Ease of individual judgment-processes in relation to polarization of attitudes in the culture. *J. soc. Psychol.*, *49*, 403-18.

———. (1946). Meaningful similarity and interference in learning. *J. exp. Psychol.*, *36*, 277-301.

———. (1948). An investigation into the causes of retroactive interference. *J. exp. Psychol.*, *38*, 132-54.

———. (1952). The nature and measurement of meaning. *Psychol. Bull.*, *49*, 197-237.

———. (1953). *Method and theory in experimental psychology.* New York: Oxford University Press.

———. (1956). Fidelity and reliability. In H. Quastler (ed.), *Information theory in psychology.* Glencoe, Ill.: Free Press.

OSGOOD, C. E., AND ZELLA LURIA. (1954). A blind analysis of a case of multiple personality using the semantic differential. *J. abnorm. soc. Psychol., 49*, 579-91.

————, S. SAPORTA, AND J. C. NUNNALLY. (1956). *Evaluative assertion analysis.* Urbana: Inst. of Communications Research, University of Illinois. (Mimeographed.)

————, AND T. A. SEBEOK. (1954). Psycholinguistics: a survey of theory and research problems. *J. abnorm. soc. Psychol., 49* (Morton Prince Memorial Supplement).

————, AND G. J. SUCI. (1952). A measure of relation determined by both mean difference and profile information. *Psychol. Bull., 49*, 251-62.

————, AND P. H. TANNENBAUM. (1955). The principle of congruity in the prediction of attitude change. *Psychol. Rev., 62*, 42-55.

POSTMAN, L., AND J. S. BRUNER. (1948). Perception under stress. *Psychol. Rev., 55*, 314-24.

————, J. S. BRUNER, AND E. MCGINNIES. (1948). Personal values as selected factors in perception. *J. abnorm. soc. Psychol., 43*, 142-54.

RAO, C. R. (1948). The utilization of multiple measurements in problems of biological classification. *J. royal stat. Soc., Sec. B, 10*, 159-203.

RAZRAN, G. H. S. (1935-36). Salivating and thinking in different languages. *J. Psychol., 1*, 145-51.

————. (1939). A quantitative study of meaning by a conditioned salivary technique (semantic conditioning). *Science, 90*, 89-90.

REEVES, MARGARET P. (1954). An application of the semantic differential to thematic apperception test material. Unpublished doctor's dissertation, University of Illinois.

REMMERS, H. H. (1934). Studies in attitudes. *Bull. Purdue Univ. Stud. higher Educ., 35*, No. 4.

————. (1954). *Introduction to opinion and attitude measurement.* New York: Harpers.

————, AND ELLA B. SILANCE. (1934). Generalized attitude scales, *J. soc. Psychol., 5*, 298-312.

RIESS, B. F. (1940). Semantic conditioning involving the galvanic skin reflex. *J. exp. Psychol., 26*, 238-40.

————. (1946). Genetic changes in semantic conditioning. *J. exp. Psychol., 36*, 143-52.

ROWAN, T. C. (1954). Some developments in multidimensional scaling applied to semantic relationships. Unpublished doctor's dissertation, University of Illinois.

SAFFIR, M. (1937). A comparative study of scales constructed by three psychophysical methods. *Psychometrika, 2*, 179-98.

SHAW, D. R. (1955). Variation in inter-scale correlation on the semantic differential as a function of the concept judged. Unpublished master's thesis, University of Illinois.

SKINNER, B. F. (1936). The verbal summator and a method for the study of latent speech. *J. Psychol., 2*, 71-107.

SNEDECOR, G. W. (1946). *Statistical methods.* Ames, Iowa: Iowa State College Press.

SOLOMON, L. N. (1954). A factorial study of complex auditory stimuli (passive sonar sounds). Unpublished doctor's dissertation, University of Illinois.

STAGNER, R., AND C. E. OSGOOD. (1946). Impact of war on a nationalistic frame of reference: I. Changes in general approval and qualitative patterning of certain stereotypes. *J. soc. Psychol.*, *24*, 187-215.

SUCI, G. J. (1952). A multidimensional analysis of social attitudes with special reference to ethnocentrism. Unpublished doctor's dissertation, University of Illinois.

――――, AND P. H. TANNENBAUM. (1955). On the relationship between the generalized distance measure D^2 and the intraclass correlation coefficient. Urbana: Inst. of Communications Research, University of Illinois. (Mimeographed.)

TANNENBAUM, P. H. (1953). Attitudes toward source and concept as factors in attitude change through communications. Unpublished doctor's dissertation, University of Illinois.

――――. (1955). What effect when TV covers a congressional hearing? *Journ. Quart.*, *32*, 434-40.

――――. (1956). The effect of background music on interpretation of stage and television drama. *Audio-Visual Communications Rev.*, in press.

TAYLOR, JANET A., AND K. W. SPENCE. (1952). The relationship of anxiety level to performance in serial learning. *J. exp. Psychol.*, *44*, 61-64.

THIGPEN, C. H., AND H. CLECKLEY. (1954). A case of multiple personality. *J. abnorm. soc. Psychol.*, *49*, 135-51.

THORSON, A. M. (1925). The relation of tongue movements to internal speech. *J. exp. Psychol.*, *8*, 1-32.

THURSTONE, L. L. (1931). *Scales for the measurement of social attitudes.* Chicago: University of Chicago Press.

――――. (1947). *Multiple-factor analysis.* Chicago: University of Chicago Press.

TORGERSON, W. S. (1952). Multidimensional scaling: I. Theory and method. *Psychometrika*, *17*, 401-19.

TRAUGOTT, N. N., AND V. K. FADEYEVA. (1934). The effect of difficult extinction of food-procuring conditioned reflexes upon the general and speech behavior of children (trans. from Russian title). *Psychol. Abstracts*, *9*, No. 1167.

TUCKER, L. R. (1951). A method for synthesis of factor analysis studies. *Dept. Army, Personnel Res. Sec. Rep.*, No. 984, p. 43.

TUCKER, W. T. (1955). Experiments in aesthetic communications. Unpublished doctor's dissertation, University of Illinois.

WARREN, H. C. (1934). *Dictionary of psychology.* Boston: Houghton Mifflin.

WEBSTER, H. (1952). A note on profile similarity. *Psychol. Bull.*, *49*, 538-39.

WERNER, H., AND EDITH KAPLAN. (1950). Development of word meaning through verbal context: an experimental study. *J. Psychol.*, *29*, 251-57.

WHORF, B. J. (1949). *Four articles on metalinguistics*. Washington: Foreign Service Inst., Dept. of State.

WILSON, K. (1954). Multidimensional scaling of data obtained by method of triads. Urbana: Control Systems Lab., University of Illinois. (Mimeographed.)

WOLFINGER, R. E. (1955). Attitude change toward source and issue resulting from one-sided and two-sided communication. Unpublished master's thesis, University of Illinois.

WRIGLEY, C., AND L. L. McQUITTY. (1953). The square root method of factor analysis. Dept. of Psychology, University of Illinois. (Mimeographed.)